Composers of North America

Series Editors: Sam Dennison, William C. Loring, Margery Lowens, Ezra Schabas

Hard Trials :
the life and music of
Harry T. Burleigh

by
ANNE KEY SIMPSON

Composers of North America,
No. 8

The Scarecrow Press, Inc.
Metuchen, N.J., & London
1990

HOUSTON PUBLIC LIBRARY

The author gratefully acknowledges the following publishers for granting permission to reprint extracts from the songs of Harry T. Burleigh; all mentioned are protected by copyright.

G. Ricordi & C.,Milan, Italy, and Hendon Music, Inc., a Boosey & Hawkes Company, U.S. Agent for G. Ricordi, granted permission for these songs:
"Ethiopia Saluting the Colors," "Her Eyes Twin Pools," "Southland Sketches," "Worthwhile," and "He Met Her in the Meadow."
Belwin Mills Publishing Corp., a division of Columbia Pictures Publications, Miami, Florida, and International Music Publications, Essex, England, granted permission for these songs:
"Behold That Star," "Deep River," "Don't Be Weary Traveler," "Go Down, Moses," "Hard Trials," "I Don't Feel No-Ways Tired," "Oh Peter Go Ring-A Dem Bells," "Steal Away," "Weepin' Mary," and "Were You There?"
Talladega College of Talladega, Alabama, granted permission for:
"Fair Talladega."

British Library Cataloguing-in-Publication data available

Library of Congress Cataloging-in-Publication Data

Simpson, Anne K. (Anne Key), 1924-
    Hard trials : the life and music of Harry T. Burleigh / by Anne K. Simpson
        p.   cm. – (Composers of North America ; no. 8)
    Discography: p.
    Includes bibliographical references and index.
    ISBN 0-8108-2291-1 (acid-free paper)
    1. Burleigh, H. T. (Harry Thacker), 1866-1949. 2. Composers – United States – Biography. I. Title. II. Series.
ML410.B97S5   1990
780 .92 – dc20
[B]   90-38249

Hard Trials is dedicated to
Thetis and Christopher,
my daughter and grandson.

Contents

Illustrations

Musical Examples

Foreword

This biographical series is designed to focus attention on significant North American composers from colonial times until the present. Few had their works performed frequently during their lifetime; all have suffered from undeserved neglect.

Each volume consists of a substantial essay about the composer and a complete catalog of compositions. The essay deals with the composer's life and works in the context of the artistic thought and musical world of his or her time. Critical comments by contemporaries are included, as are illustrations and musical examples. Some works which merit performance today are singled out for analysis and discussion. The catalog of the composer's output has full publication details, locations of unpublished works and, where necessary, incipits.

We hope that this series will make its readers more conscious and appreciative of our North American musical heritage and serve as a guide to performing musicians seeking works of interest.

Sam Dennison
William C. Loring
Margery M. Lowens
Ezra Schabas
Series Editors

Preface

This book does not pretend to be the ultimate, definitive work on Harry Thacker Burleigh, but rather an honest and readable one about a gifted, intelligent man. Information in the body of the text, not cited in endnotes, has been taken from standard biographical material and extensive references already familiar to Afro-American scholars and from special library collections, microfilm, and contact either by correspondence or interviews with Burleigh's contemporaries.

Dr. Harry T. Burleigh II, Burleigh's grandson, has generously supplied corrections on a goodly amount of trivial errata concerning Burleigh. Dr. James Hall, Burleigh's godson, has contributed fascinating reminiscences from his youth concerning Burleigh. Drs. Burleigh and Hall each furnished materials impossible to locate elsewhere.

I am grateful to many other people, each of whom has helped in some way to form this volume. Dr. Eileen Southern said to me, "You should write a book on Harry Burleigh – there isn't one, you know." She also suggested that I contact Dr. William C. Loring, who subsequently became my editor. Every author of a first book, or any other, should be so fortunate. I cannot thank this gentleman enough. He is a kind, unselfish and thorough scholar, who has patiently guided each chapter.

Very special thanks go to the Inter-Library Loan, Reference, and Microform professionals in Dupré Library at the University of Southwestern Louisiana.

The following persons have aided also, by furnishing either information, photographs, or moral support: Helen Andrews, John Claridge, Fannie Moorhead, Virginia Moorhead, Dr. David Cantrell, Dr. Dominique René de Lerma, Josephine Harreld Love, Dr. Eva

Jessye, Rev. Edward O. Miller (Rector Emeritus of St. George's Church, New York), Dr. John F. Garst, Jean E. Snyder, Elizabeth White, Dr. John Seagle, Galen Lurwick, Mrs. Leslie Mims, Edward Wheeler, Dr. George Mead, L. C. Melchior, Dr. Joseph Skvorecky, Claire and Patrick Shelby, Gene Speyrer, Jim Przepasniac, Floyd C. Hardy, Dr. Edith Borroff, Thetis Simpson, Deborra A. Richardson, Christa Sammons, A. J. Goldwyn, Margaret C. Dusch, Dr. Caldwell Titcomb, Adelaide Cromwell, Grace and Willis Ducrest, Dr. Doris McGinty, J. Rigbie Turner, J. Roland Braithwaite, Barbara Stoner, Mary F. Yearwood, Maude M. Jones, Roland M. Carter, Margaret and Paul Colmorgan, Fritz J. Malval, Kenneth A. Lohf, Peter F. Dolan, The Dark Room of Lafayette, Louisiana, Talladega College, and the Pennsylvania Humanities Council.

My sincere appreciation goes to Martha LaFleur, The Wordpro, for her instruction and the use of her facilities in wordprocessing final drafts of the manuscript; for her unflagging aid in proofing, correcting, formatting, and indexing the manuscript; and for typesetting the final book. Joan Landry was my cheerful, efficient, and interested final co-proofreader/indexer, to whom I am very grateful.

Anne K. Simpson
Researcher in Musicology
Lafayette, LA

Introduction

Reluctant to consider himself a composer, Harry Thacker Burleigh nonetheless fared well. His own modest words were, "Composer, oh no, just a few songs I've done and practically no orchestration." His name, however, continues to hold a prominent place in the history of American music, for he was the first black composer to gain recognition both for his art songs and for the elevation of Negro spirituals through his arrangements of them.

Written over sixty years ago, Burleigh's highly successful "Deep River" remains his best known arrangement. Many scholars and musicians outside the Afro-American musicological field are still unaware of his prodigiousness in the art song realm.

To my knowledge, Burleigh's total musical output, except for some early piano pieces and a few short orchestral arrangements, was published by the most reputable houses of his day. Now, unfortunately, many of his art songs are out of print, though arrangements of most of the spirituals are still available for both solo voice and ensemble.

Burleigh was a superb singer, meticulous editor, and serious intellectual composer, highly respected for his accomplishments and ideals by his contemporaries, both black and white. He was a dignified, courtly gentleman, a stellar representative of his race, both socially and professionally.

PART ONE:
Life

CHAPTER I

The Beginning and the Ascent, 1866-1913

♪

Family Background and Early Life

Life for black families in Erie, Pennsylvania, was never luxurious. Jobs were menial and pay was low. In 1832 Hamilton Waters was freed from the plantation of James Tilghman in Somerset County, Maryland. At the time he was described as "five feet eight inches in height and of a bright mulatto complexion, partially blind, orderly and intelligent, about thirty two years of age, and a native of Somerset County."[1] He, his Michigan-born, Scottish-Indian wife, Lucinda, and their infant daughter, Elizabeth, had settled in Erie by 1838. Elizabeth had been born in a covered wagon near Lansing, Michigan, en route to Canada, a land they never reached. The Waters home and lot at 137 East Third between Holland and French Streets in Erie, acquired for $500 through Waters's skillful frugality, was to become the birthplace and residence of Harry Thacker Burleigh, Elizabeth's third child.

As a slave Hamilton Waters had been forbidden to study or to have books. His blindness was most probably the result of injuries to the optic nerve, for when he was discovered hiding a speller under his blouse, he received seventy lashes. Despite this handicap, native intelligence enabled him to procure work in Erie as the town crier and lamplighter, and as a presser of men's clothing. He financed Elizabeth's education through graduation from Avery College in Allegheny, Pennsylvania.

Teaching positions for blacks were scarce at best, so Elizabeth, proficient in French and Greek, became a janitress at Erie Public School No. 1 while also working as a private tutor. She was later asked to teach the largest white Bible class in Erie.

In her early twenties Elizabeth married Henry Thacker Burleigh, a mulatto, originally from Newburgh, New York, and at the time a bank messenger and servant in the employ of Mrs. Elizabeth Russell. Mrs. Burleigh, deeply and sincerely religious, strove successfully to impart her own spiritual attitudes to her children. After a son and daughter, Reginald and Adah (Adie), Harry Thacker Burleigh (actually named Henry for his father) was born on December 2, 1866. Thacker was a family name of Mr. Burleigh. Eva, a fourth child, followed, though she was not listed in Erie's 1870 census. Harry remembered his mother's singing at her chores, and how he, his father, and Reginald all harmonized while helping her.

As he and brother Reginald helped their grandfather Waters along the lamplighting route, he was taught many of the old plantation melodies, a repertoire which inevitably became a part of his unsophisticated but rich inheritance. Harry recalled:

> I was about twelve years old when my brother and I got the job of lighting the street lamps in the First Ward of Erie. They were oil lamps and we had to use matches. I found a lot of solace singing as I started out to extinguish the lamps at 4 o'clock in the morning. A few hours later would find me delivering the *Erie Dispatch* to subscribers and still singing.[2]

Sometimes he had only an apple for breakfast, but he earned enough money for school books.

Two years after Henry Burleigh's death in 1873, Elizabeth married John Elmendorf, an Erie stableman and carriage driver. A daughter, Bessie, was born of the union. The 1880 Erie census listed two Elmendorf children, three-year-old Elzie, a boy, and one-year-old Bessie. Financial ease was never enjoyed in the growing household, which for a time included Elizabeth's sister Louise Waters.

Left to right: H. T. Burleigh as a baby, Hamilton Waters, and Reginald Burleigh. Courtesy of Dr. David Cantrell.

Henry T. Burleigh, father of H. T. Burleigh. Courtesy of Dr. James Hall, Jr.

H. T. Burleigh, 1873, seven years old. Courtesy of Dr. James Hall, Jr.

Harry often helped at the Russell home, Erie's cultural mecca, where he once became ill standing in the snow listening to the music inside. His naturally beautiful voice and innate musicality prompted his Aunt Louise to pay for a few piano lessons in his early teens, furthering Mrs. Burleigh's earlier instruction. Mrs. Russell, having also discovered this talent, made him her doorman and thereafter he was invited inside to hear such guest performers as Teresa Carreño, Rafael Joseffy, and Italo Campanini. Often in attendance as a guest pianist was Mrs. Frances MacDowell, mother of Edward MacDowell. Burleigh's desire to hear and absorb music was insatiable.

> I shall never forget the time a company of singers headed by Campanini made their appearance at the Park Opera House. I was then running an elevator at the Reed House. Forgetting that the concert was to be presented in the evening, I managed to get by attaches of the theater and make my way to the peanut gallery where I hid all afternoon between the benches. I did not stir, so fearful was I of detection. But I heard Campanini and his fellow-artists and enjoyed the concert immensely.[3]

By the age of sixteen Burleigh, of Episcopalian faith, was singing in three Erie church choirs: the First Presbyterian, St. Paul's Episcopal, and the Reform Jewish Temple. The name Harry Burleigh first appeared in the 1882 City Directory of Erie as a "servant" living at 150 East Sixth Street. He likely assisted his stepfather as a carriage driver for the Carroll, Reitzell, and Starr families, and for a few summers worked as a deck steward on Great Lakes passenger boats.

In 1887 Burleigh, now twenty-one, graduated from Erie High School and was listed on the superintendent's report as Henry Thacker Burleigh. His activities the following year are not well documented. A news item in the *Erie Morning Gazette* for December 2, 1888, stated that Burleigh, a recent visitor and performer at the Erie YMCA, had been touring with singers from New Orleans University for the past eight months and was a favorite at their student concerts. Five New Orleans libraries, however, have been unable to confirm Burleigh's affiliation with such a group. For the following five or six years two businesses, the Brown Folding Machine Company and the

Burleigh (*back row, second from right*), c. 1880. Courtesy of Dr. David Cantrell.

Colby Piano Company, where he was allowed to practice piano, employed him as a stenographer. Mr. Charles C. Colby's piano company had moved from New York to Erie in 1888.

An abbreviated report of Burleigh's performance in the GAR Hall in the Hays Building on State Street in Erie, January 5, 1891, appeared in the Strong Vincent Post 67 GAR Ledger B, 1887-91: "Harry T. Burleigh in vocal solo elegantly rendered, being rapturously recalled. Gave 'Nicodemus' in a most happy manner."

From Erie to New York

In 1892 Burleigh learned of scholarships offered by the National Conservatory of Music in New York which had been established in the mid-1880s. Its founder and first registrar, Jeanette M. Thurber, the wife of a millionaire grocer, had previously managed a now defunct opera company which promoted opera in English. The scholarship application necessitated a trip to New York which Burleigh could ill afford. Nevertheless, he set out in shabby patched clothes, a timid young man of exceptional voice, with a little borrowed money and some donated by Erie citizens Isador Sobel and Charles Allis. Years later the *Erie Times* stated that Burleigh had $30, far less than would cover his own itemized expenses:

10 weeks' board	$ 52.50
Rented a piano	10.00
10 weeks' room	20.00
Pair pants	8.00
Shoes	3.75
Dress suit (rented 3 times)	15.00

Sadly, his grades on the entrance exam were unsuitably low: "I think I was given A, B, A for reading and B for voice . . . A, A was the required mark, below which I had fallen a little." Some of the jurors were Joseffy, Romualdo Sapio, and Adele Margulies. Discouragement tempted Burleigh to join a minstrel show, but his mother's dissuasion and Registrar Frances MacDowell's insistence on a second try bore fruit. Shortly he presented to Mrs. MacDowell a letter from

H. T. Burleigh, c. 1892. Courtesy of Dr. James Hall, Jr.

Mrs. Russell, reminding her that they had met when Mme Carreno played in Erie. He was told to come back within a few days, at which time he did receive a scholarship.

The Conservatory Years: The Dvorak Association

Once accepted, there was no tuition fee, but Burleigh still lived meagerly, sometimes sleeping in the Conservatory where he worked as a handyman and secretary to Mrs. MacDowell, who continued to champion his efforts in future years. There is slim evidence that her son Edward, an already successful composer, fully shared her sentiments. Burleigh's supplementary income came from private teaching, singing in the choir of St. Philip's Protestant Episcopal Church in Harlem, and training other choirs in the area. But he often did not have enough to eat, confirmed by his own words:

> I used to stand hungry in front of one of Dennett's downtown restaurants and watch the man in the window cook cakes. Then I would take a toothpick from my pocket, use it as if I had eaten, draw on my imagination and walk down the street singing to myself. That happened more than once or twice.[4]

At the Conservatory Burleigh studied voice, solfeggio, music history, stage deportment, and fencing. He was the orchestra librarian and played string bass and tympani in the orchestra under both Frank van der Stucken and Gustav Heinrichs. Some of his professors included Christian Fritsch, John White, Max Spicker, and Rubin Goldmark, a former student of the Conservatory, who taught there in 1893-94.

Of no small import during Burleigh's Conservatory years was the beginning of a long and profitable friendship with Victor Herbert, who may well have responsible for securing a summer job for him as a wine waiter at Saratoga's Grand Union Hotel in 1893. According to Burleigh's son, Alston, his father could never get the wine cold enough to suit the maestro! The following summer he returned to Saratoga as a baritone soloist at the Bethesda Episcopal Church and also sang with Herbert's hotel orchestra. Data on Herbert's faculty affiliation at the Conservatory is inconsistent, varying from 1884 to

1899, but it is not a farfetched idea that the two might have met elsewhere, considering that Herbert was already an established band and orchestra director in the New York area, and a great admirer of Negro spirituals, especially in the style in which Burleigh sang them.

Much has been written of the powerful influence of Dvorak and Burleigh upon each other. Mrs. Thurber hired Anton Dvorak as Director of the Conservatory at a yearly salary of $15,000, a position commencing in the fall of 1892. Given a heavy teaching load in composition and theory, he was also expected to conduct the orchestra and choir. Most biographical sketches of Burleigh say that he was a student of Dvorak, but Burleigh himself stated in an interview with A. Walter Kramer that he was not.[5]

Burleigh is rarely written of without mentioning his association with Dvorak, most particularly Dvorak's use of the "Goin' Home" and "Swing Low, Sweet Chariot" themes in his *From the New World*, Op.95. The theme is first stated by the flute in measure 149, taken then by the second violins in measure 157. (See Musical Example No. 1.) According to H. C. Colles, a biographer of Dvorak who had heard Burleigh sing spirituals, Dvorak used the *cor anglais* to announce the theme of the Largo movement of this work because it so closely resembled Burleigh's voice quality.[6] Dvorak's "American" Quartet, Op.96, and "Quintet in E-flat Major", Op.97, both written during his stay at the Conservatory, exude a similar flavor.

Fiction has it that Dvorak first heard Burleigh sing while he cleaned halls at the Conservatory and thereupon invited him to dinner in his home at 327 East Seventeenth Street. As a regular visitor there Burleigh loved listening to the caged thrushes that sang in the master's study, according to Louis Biancolli's short story, "The House on 17th Street." Burleigh himself explained:

> Dvorak used to get tired during the day and I would sing to him after supper. I had been hungry in my time, I had known how hard it was to overcome discrimination and I knew what a great man Dvorak was in music. It seemed impossible to me that he should be able to get anything from me, and wonderful that he should ask for it.
>
> I gave him what I knew of Negro songs – no one called them spirituals then – and he wrote some of my tunes (my

Musical Example No. 1, measures 148-56, *From the New World*. Flute entrance above in measure 149.

First and second violins repeat the above theme in measures 157-64. It is then restated by celli and bass, horn, piccolo, etc., throughout the first movement.

people's music) into the New World Symphony which was performed for the first time by the New York Philharmonic on December 15, 1893. I never forgot that first public performance. I suppose it was the first time in the history of music that a Negro's song had been a major theme in a great symphonic work.[7]

Under the baton of Anton Seidl, recent successor to Theodore Thomas as conductor of the New York Philharmonic, *From the New World*, completed the preceding May, was premiered on December 15, 1893. The work was published in early 1894 by N. Simrock in Berlin. (Burleigh's arrangement of "Swing Low, Sweet Chariot" was not published until 1917.) When the symphony was played by the Philharmonic Society of New York years later, in March of 1918, a letter from Burleigh was included in the program book. Of the use of fragments from "Swing Low, Sweet Chariot" Burleigh wrote:

> . . . part of this old "spiritual" will be found in the second theme of the first movement of the symphony, in G major, first given out by the flute. The similarity is so evident that it doesn't even need to be heard; the eye can see it. Dvorak saturated himself with the spirit of these old tunes and then invented his own themes. There is a subsidiary theme in G minor in the first movement with a flat seventh, and I feel sure the composer caught this peculiarity of most of the slave songs from some that I sang to him; for he used to stop me and ask if that was the way the slaves sang.[8]

Dvorak gradually turned over to Burleigh the task of copying his manuscripts as they were completed. The master would say to Burleigh, "Make the notes as big as my head, Harry, so I can see them."[9] Burleigh worked with the precision of an engraver, which meticulousness served him well. He was occasionally employed to copy scores for the Metropolitan Opera, usually remunerated with tickets to the performances. Once on quite short notice he copied a new harp part for *Die Meistersinger*, receiving standing room at the performance instead of cash.[10]

Seeking to develop a noble and nationalistic school of music while at the Conservatory, Dvorak felt strongly that the source lay in Afro-American and Native American themes. Burleigh undoubtedly served as a channel for Dvorak's theories, meanwhile absorbing ideas for later developments of his own. Dr. Dominique René de Lerma, prodigious bibliographer and writer on Afro-American music and musicians, provides further insight into Dvorak's aspirations for a true American music. He advances the idea that German influence, which dominated American composers past the turn of the century, plus racial prejudice, in large part accounted for our country's cultural inferiority complex.

Under Burleigh's direct stimulus this Czech tried to a-waken Whites to their Black potentials. The fact that the

New World Symphony is more Czech than Black is irrele-
vant.[11]

Periodically Dvorak brought black teachers and students to the
Conservatory, securing scholarships for them as needed. At this time
Burleigh and white students William Arms Fisher (1861-1948) and
Rubin Goldmark (1872-1936) had been among the very first to notate
songs and spirituals of southern blacks. Fisher is particularly remembered for his arrangement of "Goin' Home." Most of the trained
black composers knew how to compose in traditional European style
and did so in order to sell their music. Dr. Eileen Southern has neatly
summed up their position as naturalistic composers:

> The songwriters set the poems of black poets and made
> vocal and choral arrangements of spirituals and other folk-
> song types. The instrumental composers wrote program
> music, drawing heavily upon characteristic Negro melodic
> idioms and dance rhythms. All the composers placed special
> emphasis upon traditional Negro performance practices, and
> made efforts to reflect the individualities of these practices
> in their composed music. The composers who won recogni-
> tion in the field of concert music generally began to publish
> late, first pursuing careers as performers or teachers.[12]

On January 23, 1894, Dvorak presented a concert of black choral
music in Madison Square Concert Hall using an all-black chorus. Actually, the event was planned by Mrs. Thurber. St. Philip's Colored
Choir comprised a good part of the chorus. Soloists for Dvorak's arrangement of "Old Folks at Home" were Harry Burleigh and Sissieretta Jones.[13] The *New York Herald*, January 24, 1894, called the
undertaking a "noble deed," but enjoyable "largely from an anthropo-
logical standpoint." That fall after a summer visit to Czechoslovakia
Dvorak returned to the Conservatory, to remain only through the
1895 spring term. Nostalgia for his homeland and unsatisfactory
financial arrangements forced him to decline Mrs. Thurber's pleas to
stay on as the school's director.

Amidst academic and financial pursuits Burleigh's fine voice had
certainly not gone unnoticed. In 1893 the World's Columbian Exposition, a World's Fair held in Chicago honoring the four-hundredth

anniversary of the discovery of America, drew approximately twenty-five million visitors. In late August the Exposition's "Colored American Day" featured baritone soloist Harry Burleigh, as well as Paul Laurence Dunbar reading his own poetry, and violinist Joseph Douglass, grandson of Frederick Douglass. During the fair nationwide musical talent got exposure. Both black and white bands were employed in night clubs and dance halls. It was an early recognition and utilization of the mass of black entertainers and musicians waiting to express themselves.

Among Burleigh's student friends was violinist and budding composer Will Marion Cook, who spoke of his own "disconnection" with the Conservatory, due to unpleasant experiences there:

> I was barred anyhow from the classes . . . because I wouldn't play my fiddle in the orchestra under Dvorak. I couldn't play; my fingers had grown too stiff. Dvorak didn't like me anyway; Harry T. Burleigh was his pet.[14]

Their friendship spanned several years, in spite of Cook's reportedly abrasive personality. Abbie Mitchell (1884-1960), one of Burleigh's young protégées, became Cook's wife in 1899 and later the mother of their son, Mercer Cook. She toured both the United States and England as a soloist and with various groups, including Cook's Syncopated Orchestra, while studying voice with Mme Emilia Serrano and Jean de Reszke. After her last stage appearance in 1935 as Clara in *Porgy and Bess*, she joined the faculty at Tuskegee Institute.

St. George's Church; Other Professional Activities

In 1894 Burleigh's life underwent a veritable face lift. Out of sixty applicants who auditioned for a position as baritone soloist in the choir of fashionable and wealthy St. George's Episcopal Church on Stuyvesant Square, Burleigh was chosen. At a salary of $800 per year, he was the first black singer to be employed there. It is understandable that the church's all-white congregation was shocked, moreover, chagrined, at this decision. St. George's rector at the time was Dr. William S. Rainsford, who demanded musical perfection of his singers. Years later Burleigh described the incident:

I can easily recall my feeling of timidity when I applied for a position in the choir. An usher told me I might get a chance to see Dr. Rainsford if I would hang around after services. I remember my anxiety as I approached the man whose words, heard but a few moments before, had seemed so helpful and sincere.

I summoned courage and handed Dr. Rainsford my card. Reading it, he grasped my hand warmly and told me he would tell his organist of my application. Something in his tone and simple manner set me completely at ease. I left the church full of hope that a man who could be so big and yet so simple would not allow my color to prejudice him, but would give me a chance. I was the only Negro who applied and the position went to me.[15]

Reverend Rainsford, though outwardly serene, was not immediately at ease with the unprecedented situation, though he had recommended that Burleigh apply for the position after presentation of a letter on Burleigh's behalf from Mrs. Thurber. He wrote an account of this "revolutionary innovation:"

I broke the news to them [St. George's choir] that I was going to have for soloist a Negro, Harry Burleigh. Then division, consternation, confusion and protest reigned for a time. I never knew how the troubled waters settled down. Indeed, I carefully avoided knowing who was for and who against my revolutionary arrangement. Nothing like it had ever been known in the church's musical history. The thing was arranged and I gave no opportunity for its discussion.[16]

Remonstrations did rear among several temporarily outraged parishioners, however, one of whom told Rainsford that "if the church was to become a minstrel house," he would resign. "Yes, I have heard that you prefer burlesque," Rainsford replied, after which the matter was closed.[17]

In an interview with Henry Beckett of the *New York Post*, published in April 24, 1944, Burleigh spoke of his mother: "I couldn't have done much without that lady."

He took out a torn, patched letter that she wrote him in 1894 . . . his message to tell her that St. George's had engaged him. She wrote: "The household rejoiceth. Now you'll be able to live in New York and prosecute your studies."

The sea remained calm, allowing Burleigh to sing at St. George's for fifty-two consecutive years, during which time he gained tremendous respect from the entire church community. He missed only one performance, when he attended his mother's funeral in 1903. He not only sang the regular choir rehearsal, but often rehearsed again on Sundays to ready himself for both morning and afternoon services.

In the early 1900s St. George's, founded in 1749 as the first chapel of Trinity Parish, was one of the best-known and most productive churches in the East. Reverend Rainsford's tenure there spanned twenty-two years (1883-1905), though toward the end of his career he suffered an emotional breakdown precipitated by religious self-doubts. Other ministers at St. George's during Burleigh's time were Hugh Birckhead (1905-12); Karl Reiland (1912-36); Elmore M. McKee (1936-46); and Edward Miller, who officiated at Burleigh's funeral in 1949. The choir master and organist with whom Burleigh worked longest was George W. Kemmer, who went to St. George's in 1924. Kemmer and Burleigh had first met earlier, when Kemmer was a boy singer at Grace Church.[18]

Among Burleigh's staunch supporters and admirers at St. George's was J. Pierpont Morgan, Sr., a senior warden. So immediately and completely smitten was he with Burleigh's beautiful rich baritone voice that he arranged numerous extra performances for him outside the church. Burleigh sang in most of the wealthiest New York homes and often for visiting dignitaries.

Though black recitalists had not yet come into favor, through such exposure Burleigh rapidly became in constant demand for both private musicals, at $50 a performance, and public concerts. Sometime between 1898 and 1900, when Theodore Roosevelt was Governor of New York, Burleigh sang at a private musical in Albany, an engagement necessitating an overnight stay. Since housing for him presented a problem, Roosevelt took him to his own mansion where he occupied the guest chamber. Later, as President, Roosevelt's efforts in behalf of blacks were given wide coverage in the *New York*

Age. He lectured and spoke frequently at black colleges and universities throughout the United States.[19]

Despite his spreading fame Burleigh was no opportunist. Neither was he presumptuous on the hospitality of New York socialites, but rather discreetly aware of racial undertones. At social engagements he often accompanied himself. Due to his pianistic prowess it was not noticeable that the fourth finger of his right hand was no longer than his little finger, a congenital handicap which could have deterred a lesser musician.[20]

Burleigh had an annual standing engagement to sing Christmas carols at the Morgan mansion on Thirty-sixth Street. The Morgan family Christmas Eve routine included "a tree for the grandchildren, an expedition in a cab to leave presents at friends' houses, and a big Christmas dinner with the choir of St. George's to sing for the company with the famous Negro baritone Harry Burleigh as soloist."[21]

One highly publicized fact about Burleigh has been his singing of "The Palms" ("Les Rameaux"), by French operatic baritone and Conservatoire professor Jean-Baptiste Fauré, a ritual begun on Palm Sunday in April of 1895 and continued for the following fifty-one years. After Burleigh's fortieth performance of the work the *New York Herald* offered this comment:

> As "The Palms" has been translated from the French by several persons, Mr. Burleigh has used more than one version of the lyric during this span of solos. . . . Mr. Burleigh sings "The Palms" rather rapidly now, possibly because he fears his once vigorous barytone will not hold out through the last verse, although it has never shown signs of failing him. . . . The anthem was sung yesterday at 11 a.m. and at 4 p.m. before two overflow congregations. . . . The Negro barytone will sing the famous anthem with similar richness on his fiftieth anniversary at St. George's.

Entwined with Burleigh's church activities was the completion of his degree at the Conservatory. The following letter from Burleigh to Mrs. Thurber, dated July 8, 1895, indicates her high regard for his talents.

Dear Mrs. Thurber;

Your letter in reference to the colored chorus for the ensuing year is before me. Permit me to thank you for the confidence reposed in me by placing me as conductor for such a branch.

It shall be my duty to work diligently during the summer to get the assurance of as many as possible who will engage in the enterprise. I think it should be a success and by being a little more careful for quality rather than quantity I am sure I can meet your expectations and achieve a fair measure of success.

Thanking you again I remain
Very sincerely
H. T. Burleigh[22]

During his last year he was offered a teaching position at the Conservatory in solfeggio which he kept for two years after graduation in 1896.

By now Burleigh had become acquainted with many of New York's struggling black performers and composers. His friend Cook gave a touching account of Burleigh's generosity in the mid-1890s:

I was desperate. My feet, with soles worn through, were burnt black by walking on the hot cobblestones of New York streets. I was hungry almost all of the time, except when I could meet Harry Burleigh, who had recently become soloist in St. George's. He only made a small salary but always had enough to treat me to coffee and crullers at a little dairy called Cushman's . . . or to a twenty-five cent dinner.[23]

Cook had begun to compose for the black comedy team, Bert Williams and George Walker, who came to New York in 1896. In 1897 Burleigh was persuaded to join the Black Patti Company for a few weeks. It was the most respectable minstrel show of its day, traveling the United States each year to hundreds of towns and cities. Its director, Black Patti, was actually concert singer Sissieretta Jones.

Burleigh's other short stint in vaudeville came in 1898 as an orchestral player with the Senegambian Carnival, a short-lived black touring group whose cast included Williams and Walker. After their nightly shows, the performers thought it chic, as well as good for business, to be seen getting into a cab, getting out, and going into a restaurant. Burleigh joined them occasionally though such speciousness would hardly seem to suit his taste. He was requested to stay on as conductor at a good salary but declined, likely dissuaded by his mother who urged him to stick with his job at St. George's.

New Family, New Adventures

The year 1898 marked Burleigh's marriage to Louise Alston, poet and actress of Negro and Indian descent, whom he met and married in Washington, DC. One writer suggests that she was with the Williams and Walker troupe at this time.[24] Contrary to common belief, Louise Alston's Native American heritage is doubtful, according to Burleigh's grandson, Dr. Harry T. Burleigh II.

Louise, a dozen or so years younger than Burleigh, enjoyed some success in the New York area as a reader of her own dialect poetry. The manuscript of her collection of unpublished poems, "Echoes from the Southland," was in the possession of Mrs. Erma Burleigh, her daughter-in-law, a former first grade teacher who resided in Washington, DC, until her death on May 23, 1987. Harry Burleigh used a few of Louise's poems as song texts. Others, "A June Rose Bloomed" for female voices and piano, and two solos, "If I Could Love Thee" and "A Vision," were set by Samuel Coleridge-Taylor and published in 1906 by William Maxwell Company.

Professional events of 1898 were highlighted by the publication by G. Schirmer, Inc., of Burleigh's first three songs: "If You But Knew," "Life," and "A Birthday Song." On August 18, 1899, the birth of a son, Alston Waters Burleigh, added yet another dimension to the musician's busy life.

Louise entrusted most of Alston's care to her thrice-married mother, at that time Mrs. Farley of Washington, DC. Louise was the product of her mother's second marriage, to Philip Alston, a plantation owner. Louise's half-sister, Ray Farley, also residing in Washington, was killed in a skating accident in the early 1920s. By the time Alston was eleven Burleigh was financially able to send him to a private school in England for four years.

It would be an undocumented assumption to say that the Burleigh marriage was incompatible. For a time the Burleighs lived on Park Avenue in New York. A *Time* reviewer spoke of their estrangement after a twenty-five year marriage, but their problems arose earlier. Though the exact year that Louise Burleigh left her husband is not certain, she did join an act with a Native American partner, possibly around 1914, following him to Wisconsin and billing herself as "Princess Red Feather." When the genuine "Princess Red Feather" appeared on the show scene, Louise changed her stage name to "Nadonis Shawa." Despite her professional commitments, she raised several foster daughters.

Fundamentally opposed to divorce, Burleigh never obtained one and continued to support his wife financially. He told an interviewer in 1944 that she was doing Indian work in Wisconsin. She did not attend Burleigh's funeral, but was remembered in a bittersweet clause in his first will of 1942. She died from colon cancer in Dells, Wisconsin, in 1958, at the age of seventy-eight.[25]

Burleigh's family involvement around the turn of the century did not exclude association with old friends of similar profession. Black New York musicians were humming their own tunes. Things were happening that portended progress. The *New York Age*, a reputable and well-established black newspaper, eagerly reported the arts and entertainment scene. Public attention was drawn to the fact that blacks had something worthwhile to offer, evidenced by the impact of the Fisk Jubilee Singers, Burleigh's respectable status as a singer and composer, Dvorak's enthusiasm for Afro-American music, the increasing success of Williams and Walker, and favorable rumblings concerning the works of the English black composer Samuel Coleridge-Taylor, together with the devotion of crusading activists Booker T. Washington and W. E. B. DuBois.

A glimmer of hope was detectable, though in 1899 plenty of black New York talent, including Will Marion Cook, was still either hungry or broke. During that summer Cook's operetta *Clorindy, the Origin of the Cakewalk* was first performed at the Casino Theater Roof Garden. Among other evening clothes borrowed for the occasion Cook, as conductor, wore a vest belonging to Burleigh. He recounted, "Harry was very short; I quite tall." The show's success he took as a good omen for black performers.

At least two New York hotels, the Marshall and the Maceo, opened in 1897, were run by black proprietors. Both served good meals at reasonable prices and the Marshall boasted a four-piece orchestra. They offered a heretofore nonexistent civilized, comfortable atmosphere where the after-show crowd could congregate to dine, drink, smoke, and dance.

Burleigh occasionally visited Cook, Williams, and Walker, and their mutual circle, gathering either at the comedians' place on Fifty-third Street or at the nearby Marshall, created the perfect scenario for some unforgettable evenings and the making of lasting friendships. At one of these evenings, in 1899, Burleigh met James Weldon Johnson, a future collaborator and a man on the rise. Johnson lived at the Marshall with his brother, J. Rosamond, later the partner of talented Robert ("Bob") Cole, who lived two doors away.

The Johnsons' room was a place of ongoing discussion, mainly of the Afro-American's status as writer, composer, or musical performer. The bitterest clashes of opinion and personality were between Cole and Cook, who seemed to thrive on insulting each other. For these aspiring professionals time was precious and interruptions rarely permitted, but Harry Burleigh was one of the few outsiders always welcomed to their quarters, along with Theodore Drury, singer and director of the Drury Opera Company, poet Paul Laurence Dunbar, and Jack (John) Nail, aspiring realtor and business man. Burleigh often brought in a new song for their approval.

The hospitality was mutual. While writing *The Cannibal King*, Johnson and Cook borrowed Burleigh's apartment on Park Avenue, a few blocks from the Marshall. "We celebrated the end of the first day's work with a beefsteak dinner, deliciously cooked by Harry's brother Reginald," Johnson recalled.

Professional and biographical details of Burleigh's siblings Reginald and Adah are not known. Bessie Elmendorf, Burleigh's half-sister, was a teacher. Eva Burleigh, a trained musician who taught in the Erie Public Schools, was later known in both institutional and educational circles around the New York City area. Once established in New York himself, Burleigh was able to follow her career and stay abreast of her activities. She was not alive at the time of his death.

Burleigh, generous with his talents, sang for a Hampton Institute benefit at the Waldorf-Astoria in February of 1899. On the same program were Dunbar, the Hampton Quartet, and Charles Winter Wood, reader.

In 1900 Burleigh secured a second church position with the wealthy Temple Emanu-El, as its first Negro choir member. Already proficient in Hebrew, he made a substantial addition to the group, remaining there until 1925. Organists during Burleigh's time at Temple Emanu-El were Max Spicker and William MacFarlane. Johnson felt that Burleigh had, in a word, arrived:

> Among us it was as a master that he was held. On all questions in the theory and science of music he was the final authority. In this acceptance both Cook and my brother always joined. Some years later Kurt Schindler said to me that on a question in the theory of music he would accept Mr. Burleigh's decision as quickly as that of any other musician in New York.[26]

Schindler, who came to New York in 1904 from Germany, served as assistant chorus master at the Metropolitan Opera and later became an editor at Schirmer's. In 1909 he founded the MacDowell Chorus (which in 1910 was renamed the Schola Cantorum), a prestigious group whose repertoire was to include some of his friend Burleigh's arrangements of Negro spirituals.

Instances of more frivolous camaraderie in this milieu of the late 1890s were described by Bert Williams:

> The shabby apartment house on Fifty-third Street became a meeting place where vaudevillians like Harry Burleigh, Will Accooe, Cole and Johnson and Jesse Shipp could sit around in their shirt sleeves and talk, drink, and play endless hands of a poker game called "smut." We had a sooty plate that we smoked up over the lamp, and the loser of each hand had to smear a daub of the soot on his face as a penalty. Then we would sit around and howl at the grotesque appearance.[27]

Lyricist Jesse Shipp was later stage manager for the Primrose and West Minstrel Company, a mixed touring troupe. Will Accooe, a former tenor soloist, was a pianist with Puggsley's Tennessee Warblers, and director for Cole and Johnson's *A Trip to Coontown*, for which he also composed some songs. For two years before his death in 1904 he was musical director for Williams and Walker.

With all due respect to the professions of such jolly and worthy friends, Burleigh himself did not want to be categorized as a vaudevillian or as a minstrel composer, even a sophisticated one. Curiously, an item from an undated Philadelphia newspaper carried an almost incredible statement by Andreas Dippel, former director of the Philadelphia-Chicago Opera Company and enthusiastic advocate of American composers. Of Burleigh, whom he complimented highly as a "gifted composer and thorough musician," he stated: "For many years he has been compelled to earn his living by writing popular songs under the nom de plume of Rogers." Dippel was amazed when singer Grace La Rue first introduced him to Burleigh's more serious work.

The Recognized Composer and Acclaimed Singer

Burleigh, now holding two prestigious church jobs, had laid the ground work for his future as a composer and arranger. A gradual withdrawal from the popular show business environment undoubtedly affected the rest of his life. In later years, secure as a serious composer, he did not encourage the closeness of popular or jazz musicians, a choice in no way to be construed as a personal feeling of superiority or snobbery. Jazz was simply never one of Burleigh's interests.[28]

In 1901 G. Schirmer, Inc., published a collection of seven songs arranged by Burleigh, titled *Plantation Melodies Old and New*. The complete text of the last one, "An Ante-Bellum Sermon," a rhythmically repetitive but clever eleven-stanza poem by Paul Laurence Dunbar, was likely condensed. Burleigh's other compositions this year were a set of *Six Plantation Melodies for Violin and Piano*. No information confirms or denies their publication or content.[29]

The following year Schirmer (1902) issued Burleigh's vocal works "Thy Heart" and *Plantation Songs*, including "Ring, My Bawnjer, Ring" and "You'll Git Dar in de Mornin'." Other publications that year were "Sleep, Li'l Chile, Go Sleep!" (Harry von Tilzer Publishing Company, established that year) and "Love's Garden" (William Maxwell Company). The Maxwell Company, Burleigh's publisher for the next few years, loaned him an upright piano for his work.

By 1902 in Pittsburgh a Burleigh Choral Society had been formed with its own publication, *The Negro Music Journal*, published in Washington, DC. Of its members the society required "good moral character and willingness to work." Agnes Carroll, editor of the Club Department of the *Journal* commented: "This Society has at heart the real upbuilding of the race and believes that choral singing is one of the strongest means by which we may hope to do so."[30] Concerned with worthy black musicians and composers, plus the musical interest and education of the black community, the *Journal* unfortunately saw only fifteen issues, from September of 1902 through November of 1903. Burleigh's efforts as singer, composer, and educator were frequently mentioned in the publication.

"Jean" (1903), dedicated to Mrs. James Speyer, wife of a New York banker and philanthropist, was perhaps Burleigh's first song to receive considerable performance. It may be assumed that Burleigh performed at the two palatial homes owned by the Speyers. In the same year he enjoyed the success of "Mammy's Li'l Baby," to words by Louise Burleigh, "specially composed" for Mme Ernestine Schumann-Heink. The famous singer had been in the United States since 1898, performing opera in Chicago and at the Metropolitan. Though forty-two, she seemed at the peak of her amazingly long career. Burleigh could hardly have dreamed for more propitious timing.

Prior to 1900 German *lied* comprised a good part of the recitalist's art song repertoire. Most recitals often included two or three performers, typically a singer assisted by a solo violinist and a pianist. The time was ripe for American song composers. Some of the well-established ones around the turn of the century were Dudley Buck, Sidney Homer, Ethelbert Nevin, and Edward MacDowell. However, traditional emphasis at recitals on operatic arias and *lieder* made it difficult for American song composers to get a hearing, despite the need for fresh repertoire.

Improved travel facilities helped established performers attract decently paying audiences in the larger cities. Advertisements for concert management grew plentiful in the leading music journals. Similarly, American composers were eager to push their own compositions, a cue for music publishers to snap into action. If a song's cover carried an endorsement by a favorite artist, sales skyrocketed.

The phonograph and recording business was about to be born. It is a pity that Burleigh never recorded his own voice.

As time permitted Burleigh toured the East Coast, lecturing and performing at black colleges and universities. During the summers he assisted Booker T. Washington's efforts on behalf of black people, performing both spirituals and art songs. He often used the "Prologue" from *Pagliacci* on his programs.

Whether construed as another effort for "The Cause," or simply for personal gratification, Cook wrote to Washington on March 29, 1901, suggesting the organization of "Tuskegee's Real Negro Singers," a touring group of eight singers and an accompanist. His scheme called for an initial concert of twelve numbers at the Waldorf-Astoria with press critics in attendance. Cook's works and those by Burleigh, Coleridge-Taylor, and others, of "a rather ambitious character which would display the range of voice and musical cultivation of the singers," would be presented. Thereafter the group would be available for public and private concerts, half of their proceeds going to Tuskegee "to the glorious work" being done by Washington there. Cook's point for the venture was sound, but Tuskegee already had its own touring quartet. Further correspondence did not show that Washington acted upon the plan.[31]

Sharing the limelight with Washington, but from a different position, was Dr. W. E. B. DuBois. Burleigh's correspondence to Washington clearly revealed that his sympathies were not totally with DuBois, who in his book *The Souls of Black Folk* rather bitterly bared his pessimistic attitude, meanwhile offering very little solution to racial problems. Burleigh, the conservative, believed that Afro-Americans should advance themselves through individual effort rather than by political action. As a musician Burleigh was as forceful for the black cause as were Washington and DuBois in their ways. One timely rescue of a meeting which had grown into a near riot at the Zion A. M. E. Church in Boston on July 31, 1903, was reported by the *Boston Globe*: "Harry Burleigh, a New York singer of some repute, arose and opportunely sang 'King of Kings.' The song had a quieting effect."[32]

Early in January of 1904 Burleigh performed again in Boston, his first full concert there, in behalf of Fernside, the Working Girls' Vacation House at Princeton, Massachusetts. In anticipation of the event, Percy Lee Atherton wrote to the editor of the *Boston Transcript*:

> He gives something distinctively his own, a reading of the melodious folk songs of his own people in the light of their whole pathetic history. . . . Mr. Burleigh's accompaniments, characterized by invariable judgment and good taste, form an important feature of his work.

Thoughtfully, Burleigh included a group of American songs, chiefly by Boston composers.

A performance with Samuel Coleridge-Taylor was scheduled later in 1904, due to the sprouting of a seed planted by Burleigh in 1898 with Mr. and Mrs. Andrew W. Hilyer of Washington. Burleigh had sent Mrs. Hilyer a copy of Coleridge-Taylor's cantata *Scenes from the Song of Hiawatha*, a work whose appeal had by 1901 drawn a nucleus of black singers soon to be the Samuel Coleridge-Taylor Choral Society. After intensive rehearsals the group presented the work on April 23, 1903, in the Metropolitan A. M. E. Church in Washington, with approximately 1,500 in the mixed audience. Mr. John T. Layton, a church choir and public school choral director, conducted and the singers were accompanied by two pianists. Vocal soloists were Mrs. Skeene-Mitchell, Sidney Woodward, and Burleigh.

News of the concert's success so pleased Coleridge-Taylor that he accepted an invitation to conduct a concert of his own music during the 1904 season in the United States. He wrote to Mrs. Hilyer on May 2, 1903: "I have heard a great deal about Mr. Burleigh from people I have met here. . . . Everyone agrees that he is a splendid singer and also – more rare – a splendid musician."[33]

When Coleridge-Taylor wrote Booker T. Washington the following May, asking Tuskegee's assistance rather than that of an agent in publicizing his coming U.S. visit, Washington replied:

> I shall lay the whole matter before Mr. Harry T. Burleigh, with whom I think you are already acquainted. Mr. Burleigh's judgment is sound and he is a man on whose word you can depend.[34]

Coleridge-Taylor arrived in the United States early in November of 1904 to prepare for the first concert, given on November 16 at

Convention Hall in Washington. The entire *Hiawatha* was presented, with soloists Mme Estelle Clough, well-known operatic singer; Mr. J. Arthur Freeman, a foremost black tenor; and Mr. Burleigh. About one third of the audience was white. News coverage by both black and white papers was generous. The orchestra, described as "an enlarged U.S. Marine Band orchestra of fifty-two pieces," conducted by Lt. William H. Santelmann, accompanied the soloists and a 200-voice chorus.

A reviewer for *The Washington Post*, November 17, 1904, said:

> Burleigh was not a stranger, having sung the part on its first presentation in this city. He has a voice of beautiful quality, sings with fine dramatic effect, finish, and deep feeling. . . . The orchestra was at times inexcusably bad, playing out of tune, . . . very ragged and amateurish.

Coleridge-Taylor sincerely admired Burleigh's voice, his dramatic instinct, and the total interpretation of the work. The following evening a second all-Coleridge-Taylor concert, repeated later in Baltimore, consisted of smaller works, except for one large choral piece, *Choral Ballads*. Burleigh participated in the Washington concert by singing "A Corn Song." The *Post* again commented that the orchestra played "wretchedly" but praised Burleigh's fine vocal qualities and good method, admitting that he needed "no apologists."

At a concert in Chicago on December 13, 1904, shortly before Coleridge-Taylor left for England, Burleigh shared a program of shorter works with Mary Peck Thomson and the violinist Theodore Spiering. Having sung the powerful *Hiawatha*, Burleigh felt a tremendous challenge to spread music of the blacks, for Coleridge-Taylor's visit had galvanized those interested in it. Their friendship had blossomed. A letter to Mrs. Hilyer from the Englishman dated September 30, 1905, suggested that Burleigh help select the soloists for his projected U.S. concerts in 1906.[35]

The year 1904 proved fruitful for composer Burleigh. Maxwell published fourteen of his songs, the best known being "O Perfect Love." Sometime between or during 1904 and 1905 Burleigh and Mattie Allen McAdoo – a contralto, wife of Orpheus Myron McAdoo, singer and impressario – donated their talents in behalf of Atlanta University and the Calhoun Colored School. The recital was held in Cambridge at Potter Hall, which was "filled to overflowing and many persons had to stand." Burleigh accompanied himself in his own arrangements of "De Danville Chariot," "W'en de Angels Call," "Song of de Watcher," and "Joshua Fit de Battle of Jericho." Another group, art songs, included his own "Life," "One Day," and "Thy Heart," plus two songs by Coleridge-Taylor, accompanied by J.P. White. The review continued:

> Mr. Burleigh's voice is a rather high baritone of great power and pleasing quality and capable of the gentlest modulation. He was equally at home in elaborate modern compositions and in simple plantation ditties, though he met most favor in these latter. There are songs and songs, but we don't get plantation songs sung as Mr. Burleigh sings them every day. . . . At the close of the programme, while the audience, reluctant to depart, lingered in aisles and seats, Mr. Burleigh returned to sing the most delightful song of all, an apology for the universal father of the human race and an explanation of his troubles and ours in the fact that "Adam Never Had a Mammy."[36]

As the year 1905 rolled on James Weldon Johnson was soon to embark on his long and stellar career in government service. Of his friend Burleigh, whose works along with Coleridge-Taylor's he considered the least identifiably black in sound, he wrote: "If the twelve foremost classic song writers of America were named Mr. Burleigh would be included in the list."[37]

Burleigh with his varied repertoire continued to be in demand. He sang an *Elijah* at Knoxville College in Aurora in early July. The audience's expectations were "more than fulfilled." The laudatory review from the *New York Age*, July 6, 1905, went on:

> We all knew that we had been fortunate in securing Mr. Burleigh, but few of us realized how much was in store for us till we had been led captive by his really splendid interpretation of Mendelssohn's masterpiece . . . expression that kindled the imagination and stirred the heart.

Burleigh, the appreciative gentleman, was in turn highly complimentary of the work of the chorus and its director.

In mid-November he was asked to sing for Prince Louis of Battenberg at the residence of Colonel and Mrs. Robert M. Thompson. His selections were "Jean" and some plantation melodies, a program arranged especially for the Prince "who paid special attention to his singing."[38] Undoubtedly the soiree was a feather in Burleigh's cap, though more of a routine occurrence for the Thompsons, who two years later chartered a yacht to take other royal guests on a round-the-world cruise.

As to texts, romance, reverence, and religious fervor dominated the nine songs of Burleigh that William Maxwell Company published in 1905. Through association with this publisher he developed a close and professionally beneficial friendship with George Maxwell, William's brother, who was later employed as managing editor for G. Ricordi and Company when its American branch opened in 1911. Shortly after its opening, before Burleigh was officially added to Ricordi's staff, he was given occasional editorial work by George Maxwell, confirmed in a letter to Mrs. Thurber, December 10, 1911.

By 1906 the black cultural scene had begun to assume a new dimension. Cole and Johnson's *A Trip to Coontown* had long since triumphed in London; the Tuskegee Choir had made its mark; Theodore Drury's opera company was not only staging such ambitious productions as *Aïda* but giving sacred concerts as well; President Roosevelt was traveling over the country addressing such outstanding student bodies as Howard and Hampton, urging blacks to "help themselves"; and the *Age* was promoting the name "Afro-American" as the correct one for those of African origin in the United States. One editorialist regretted that men of such stature as DuBois and Washington had not seen fit to use the term in their writings and addresses.

Burleigh's activities, too, had definitely broadened. He and his gifted young accompanist, Melville Charlton, equally excellent at piano and organ, made an imposing team. Charlton was also to work with Mme Azalia Hackley and other worthy vocal artists. He became the first black associate of the American Guild of Organists and was assistant organist at St. George's until 1911, when he joined Temple Emanu-El's Religion School. He was trained at both New York University City College and the National Conservatory of Music. Charlton was a composer in his own right; the piano composition *Poem Ero-*

tique (1911) was his best-known work. He was awarded an honorary doctorate from Howard University in 1930.

On February 20, 1906, the *Erie Daily Times* announced a concert to be given by Burleigh on March 6. The item's quaintness bears quoting:

> The concert . . . under the auspices of the senior class of the Erie high school promises to be a great success. The seniors have taken a hold and are now distributing the tickets . . . placed at 25 cents for students and 50 cents for non-students.
>
> Harry Burleigh graduated from the Erie high school with the class of 1887. Since his graduation he has been engaged in musical work and now enjoys the position of soloist in one of New York's largest churches. Mr. Burleigh's compositions are published by the best of printing houses and are numbered among the finest creations of the day. Mr. Burleigh has probably achieved more musical fame than any other man Erie has ever produced.
>
> The members of the class of '87 will all probably turn out and give Mr. Burleigh a welcome.

The day of the concert another announcement appeared in the same newspaper, anticipating it to be "one of the finest concerts the musician has ever given." And going on:

> The program, upon request, has been made more popular than classic, thereby accommodating more people.
>
> Mr. Burleigh arrived in the city yesterday and spent a part of Monday and today greeting old friends. It is expected that all of his old classmates in the city and many of his schoolmates will turn out to greet him.
>
> All who have ever heard Mr. Burleigh's voice pronounce it as one of the most perfect sweetness and harmony.

A reviewer for the *Erie Daily Times*, March 7, 1906, called this concert by "the former Erie boy, of whom all have just cause to feel proud," a "great success" and "one of the best musical treats ever offered in Erie." Burleigh's accompanist was not Melville Charlton, but H. B. Vincent, whose compositions from *The Garden of Karna* were programmed, as well as some plantation songs which "took the audience by storm." Burleigh also sang his own art song "Dreamland" and his arrangement of "You'll Git Dar in de Mornin'," showing "his ability as a composer as well as a singer." The song, "To the Hills," which brought out the "great strength and power of his magnificent baritone voice," one also of "great range and sweetness," was repeated by demand.

In early June of 1906 Burleigh was soloist at the Majestic Theater in Brooklyn for the Garnet Club, a men's organization formed in 1895 for Afro-Americans from all parts of the United States and the islands of the West Indies. Though at the time Burleigh was suffering from a cold, he performed with fine style and authority to Charlton's well-played accompaniments. Within a few days he sang again in Newark for the Women's Mission Aid Society, a recital "not as well attended as the worthy cause and the really good artists demanded." Of the five songs programmed two, "A Corn Song" and "Beat, Beat, Drums" were by Coleridge-Taylor.

On July 4 Burleigh was a guest at Wigfall Cottage in Asbury Park, singing several times during the day to his own accompaniment, delighting Mrs. Wigfall and her guests.[39]

An announcement appeared in the November 1, 1906, *Age*, heralding a momentous occasion, "the greatest musical event among Afro-Americans in New York City," for "Mr. Burleigh is the most accomplished and talented of Afro-American singers and song writers."

Coleridge-Taylor was to return, conducting his own works. He was both soloist and accompanist for this initial concert, after which he and Burleigh made a brief tour, performing in several U.S. cities with other artists.

A larger white audience than was expected attended the Mendelssohn Hall concert. Impressive was Coleridge-Taylor's modesty. He was shy, hesitant to respond to encores. The music seemed almost a reflection of his own varying moods. A glowing and lengthy review of Burleigh's performance by Elsie Johnson appeared in the *Age*, November 22, 1906:

> All of us know Mr. Henry T. Burleigh and what to expect when his name occurs on a program, so there was a

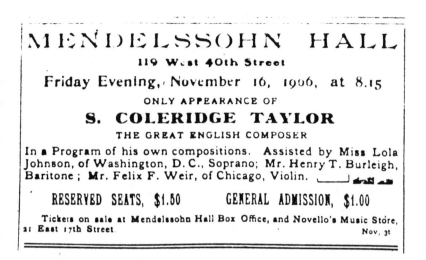

MENDELSSOHN HALL

119 West 40th Street

Friday Evening, November 16, 1906, at 8.15

ONLY APPEARANCE OF

S. COLERIDGE TAYLOR

THE GREAT ENGLISH COMPOSER

In a Program of his own compositions. Assisted by Miss Lola Johnson, of Washington, D.C., Soprano; Mr. Henry T. Burleigh, Baritone ; Mr. Felix F. Weir, of Chicago, Violin.

RESERVED SEATS, $1.50   GENERAL ADMISSION, $1.00

Tickets on sale at Mendelssohn Hall Box Office, and Novello's Music Store, 21 East 17th Street.   Nov, 3t

burst of applause when he appeared. He was in excellent form, and his voice was full, rich and ringing. His first number, "Substitution" from "In Memoriam," a composition of dignity, was rendered as Mr. Burleigh always sings songs of this character. "Love's Passing" . . . was thoroughly understood and sympathetically rendered. . . . Then the "Corn Song!" Mr. Burleigh's joy in interpreting it was manifest. Those near enough saw his bright face lighten and his head nod as he sang the droning slave chorus. This song . . . went straight to the heart of the audience. Mr. Burleigh's voice improved as he proceeded. "Only Once" rang with virility . . . especially striking and forceful.

Burleigh's final group included "She Rested by the Broken Brook" and "Beat, Beat, Drums" and an encore, "Unmindful of the Roses." In "Drums" Burleigh brought out "with force all the thrilling martial relentless spirit of the master's song. No wonder there were storms of applause." After the concert Burleigh and Melville Charlton received and introduced guests to Coleridge-Taylor.

Richard Aldrich's review in the *New York Times*, November 17, was highly complimentary. Speaking of the soloists he remarked:

Of these Mr. Burleigh, who is well known as a singer in
this city, was the only one of artistic capacities really sufficient for the demands made upon him. . . . He sang "Corn
Song" with sympathy and feeling and with uncommonly good
enunciation.

The *New York Herald* carried this interesting comment:

Many coloured persons were in the audience, but
probably through fear of making themselves conspicuous
they failed to give the composer an enthusiastic demonstra-
tion. There was, however, no lack of applause, because the
whites in the assembly did not hesitate to express their
approval heartily.[40]

Coleridge-Taylor's tour continued to Pittsburgh where a similar
program was given in Carnegie Music Hall on November 28. On
December 12 in Boston at New England Conservatory's Jordan Hall
Burleigh shared the program with Willy Hess, violinist, at that time
concert master of the Boston Symphony; Georges Grisez, clarinetist;
and the Boston Symphony Quartet. A critic for the *Boston Evening
Transcript*, December 13, was not overly impressed with Coleridge-
Taylor's compositions, but was complimentary to Burleigh's singing:

At times it is a conventional music, as it seemed in the
songs that Mr. Burleigh sang admirably. . . . The songs were
pleasant and no more. A ready and easy sentiment animated
them, a ready and easy gift of musical writing carried them
forward.

Within the week another concert was presented in the Charles
Street A. M. E. Church in Boston. Violinist Clarence Cameron
White, sopranos Marjorie Groves and Ada Gaskins, contralto Gene-
vieve Lee, and baritone Burleigh performed another program of
Coleridge-Taylor's works. Though no specific date is given, mention
is also made in 1906 of Burleigh's performance on two recitals in
Chicago at the Pekin Theater, the city's first to be owned and
managed by a black person, Robert T. Motts.

The few weeks of Coleridge-Taylor's tour were indeed lively. He
accepted an invitation from the Litchfield County Choral Union in

S. COLERIDGE-TAYLOR – BURLEIGH CONCERT
CARNEGIE MUSIC HALL, PITTSBURGH
November 28, 1906

Sponsored by the Warren Methodist Episcopal Church

Toccata in F Major	Bach
Melville Charlton, organist	
"Two Gipsy Movements"	S. Coleridge-Taylor
Clarence Cameron White, violinist	
"Spring Had Come" (Hiawatha's Departure)	S. Coleridge-Taylor
Madame K. Skeene-Mitchell, soprano	
"Love's Passing" (Louise Burleigh)	S. Coleridge-Taylor
"Beat, Beat, Drums" (Whitman)	S. Coleridge-Taylor
Henry T. Burleigh, baritone	
Oriental Waltz No. 2 for Piano	S. Coleridge-Taylor
"Sometimes I Feel Like a Motherless Child"	
(Five Negro Melodies)	S. Coleridge-Taylor
S. Coleridge-Taylor, pianist	
"Oneway, Away,, Awake, Beloved"	
(Hiawatha's Wedding Feast)	S. Coleridge-Taylor
J. W. Loguen, tenor	
Romance in E Flat	S. Coleridge-Taylor
Clarence Cameron White, violinist	
"The Young Indian Maid" (Moore)	S. Coleridge-Taylor
Madame K. Skeene-Mitchell, soprano	
"She Rested by the Broken Brook" (Stevenson)	S. Coleridge-Taylor
"A Corn Song" (Dunbar)	S. Coleridge-Taylor
Henry T. Burleigh, baritone	
Four African Dances	S. Coleridge-Taylor
Clarence Cameron White, violinist	
"Chromatic Fantasie"	Thiele
Melville Charlton, organist	

Program courtesy of Jean Snyder of Pittsburgh.

Norfolk, Connecticut, to give a complimentary recital in recognition of his election as honorary member of the Winsted Choral Union. Burleigh, with Reed Miller, tenor, and Felix Weir, violinist, gave a program similar to the earlier one in Mendelssohn Hall. The enthusiastic audience was comprised mainly of the Norfolk Glee Club, the Winsted Choral Union, and invited guests.[41]

Amid this flurry of engagements Burleigh executed faithfully his duties at both churches, while managing to compose and see published another nine songs by the end of 1906.

The *Age* for April 25, 1907, combining cultural and social happenings, wrote of a "grand musical entertainment" at the Women's Institute in Yonkers, sponsored by the Susan B. Anthony Association for the benefit of a Day Nursery. Miss Dora Cole, actress, reader, and entertainment agent, gave two readings; Burleigh sang the "Toreador Song" and "May Morning, if Thou Wert Blind." On the day of the concert the Burleighs were guests of Mr. and Mrs. Wallace N. Towns.

In early June the Choral Study Club of Chicago presented *Hiawatha*, directed by P. T. Tinsley. A florid review of the production, printed on June 13 in the *Age*, lavished almost as much praise on the appreciative audience as on the singers. Joining Burleigh as soloists were soprano Katherine Skeene-Mitchell and tenor George Holt, who had

> already earned the reputation of being the greatest Cole-ridge-Taylor soloists in the United States. . . . New York's prize baritone, Mr. Harry T. Burleigh, made a profound impression. His splendid art and superb voice fairly overwhelmed the audience with emotions of joy.

Accompaniment was provided by orchestra, piano, and organ.

In the summer of 1907 the *Age* added to its staff as music and drama editor Lester A. Walton. His columns carried full accounts of musical happenings, related colorfully and accurately. There was no lack of entertainment for concert- and show-goers. There was something for everyone, no matter his taste. Women entertainers such as Abbie Mitchell Cook, Aida Overton Walker, and Lottie Williams had become quite popular. Walton was a devoted friend of actor Ernest Hogan, from whom he learned the intricacies of theater while playing a few minor roles in his shows. Poems of black writers appeared almost weekly on his page. Burleigh's efforts, along with those of Cook and White, were periodically praised in the news as being of "incalculable value in dissipating preconceived notions" about their abilities as black artists.

Another of Burleigh's charity benefit performances took place in late October, sponsored by Christ Hospital at Hasbrouck Hall in Jersey City. He was assisted by Charlton as accompanist and Mrs. Walter Craig, violinist in her husband's orchestra. Craig's society dance orchestra, established around 1900, was much in demand by both black and white groups. Dr. Craig was also the organizer of the Pre-Lenten Concerts, a series for the special purpose of honoring black performers. Burleigh participated in some of these between 1905 and 1915.

Also in 1907 *Two Plantation Songs* and four art songs, of which "You Ask Me If I Love You" is the best known, were added to Burleigh's growing list of publications.

Events of 1908 further solidified Burleigh's prominence as a musician, not only in the New York area but throughout America. Following the splendid example set earlier by the Fisk Jubilee Singers, various quartets, traveling glee clubs, and community choirs had by now become extremely popular along the Eastern seaboard. Many of them – such as the sixteen-voice Williams and Walker Glee Club and later the Amphion Club of Melrose, Massachusetts, the Orpheus Club of Philadelphia, the International Singers of New York, and the Lotus Quartette of Boston – used Burleigh's arrangements of spirituals, love songs, and folk songs. Large choirs with 200 to 300 or more voices were in vogue. The Amphion, a first-class male musical organization established in the early 1890s, was especially in demand now for posh social functions.

In February of 1908 Burleigh was able to combine business with pleasure at the home of Melville Charlton, when the latter entertained Monsieur Leon Cazauran, tenor soloist of the Manhattan Opera Company. At this gathering Burleigh sang a Schubert selection, though his repertoire of American composers such as Edward Boatner, Amy Beach, and Ethelbert Nevin was ample.

A folklore concert was given at Mendelssohn Hall on March 13 by the black and Native American students of Hampton Institute, with Burleigh's assistance, under the auspices of the Armstrong Association of New York, a white group which devoted their finances and energies toward the betterment of blacks and black institutions. A gala social occasion in dress and manner, the concert drew surprisingly few blacks to the filled hall, a pattern typical of benefits given by whites for blacks. Blacks may have avoided attending the function due to cost or simply because they preferred the more informal up-tempo comedy shows.

Critic Walton suggested that the musical program was overly lengthy, due to too many "long winded" stories, and that a few people were seen falling asleep. However, he was enthusiastic about Burleigh's participation:

> The appearance of Henry T. Burleigh in Negro dialect songs was the treat of the evening. The pleasing manner in which he rendered the lullaby "Hush-a-Bye" deserves special mention and at the end of his number he was heartily applauded.

Besides this selection Burleigh performed four more Negro dialect spirituals and songs.[42] On April 20 Burleigh shared a concert with three other artists for the benefit of the centennial committee at the Charles Street A. M. E. Church in Boston.

Burleigh was an avid opera-goer. A report from Boston in the *Age*, April 30, 1908, read:

> Mr. Harry T. Burleigh, while in town had apartments at the Parker House as the guest of Dr. S. E. Courtney, and attended the Handel and Haydn Society's rendition of Samson and Delila.

It is almost certain, however, that *Tristan und Isolde* was his favorite. He confessed to having seen it sixty-six times during his life.[43]

Neither did Mrs. Burleigh lack for activity, a situation evidenced by Walton's rather comic comment in the same issue of the *Age* following an amateur minstrel show. After praising John Nail's superb imitation of Bert Williams, he continued:

> The writer knows that Harry Burleigh never bothers about coon songs, but Mrs. Louise Burleigh tried herself as

a coon shouter when she sang "I've Got Good Common Sense." Her rendition was above the ordinary. However, someone near me remarked when she was dancing that her feet hurt her. Of course we won't touch that – it's a live wire.

In early May a volunteer group including Burleigh, Charlton, Elizabeth Howard, J. William Loguen, Helen E. Smith, and Walter Craig performed at the opening of the St. Cyprian Parish House. "Those present were without a doubt treated to one of the best recitals ever given in New York by colored talent," reported the *Age*. Burleigh's selections were the *Pagliacci* "Prologue," "May Morning," and "O for a Day of Spring." More than one hundred white persons were in the audience.

The summer of 1908 was one of the most significant periods in Burleigh's life. On June 1, the *Age* carried an elegant and distinguished portrait of him with an article titled "Mr. Burleigh Sails for Europe." Both Mr. and Mrs. Burleigh sailed on the White Star Steamship *Cedric* in late May. The article gave some details:

> Mr. Burleigh has a number of letters of introduction to the best people of London for whom he hopes to sing. Some of them are: Ambassador and Mrs. Reid at Dorchester House; the Duchess of Marborough; Mrs. Ronalds; Madame Melba; Mrs. Lewis Harcourt, wife of Commissioner of Works, from Mrs. Hamilton, daughter of J. Pierpont Morgan; Lady Evans of Hempstead, England; Lady Cromer, Mrs. Edward Jaffrey; Arthur Shipley, M.A., Cambridge University; and Mrs. Bradley Martin.
>
> Mr. Burleigh hopes to return in time to assume his positions in the fall at St. George's Church and Temple Emanuel.

The trip had been arranged by J. P. Morgan with the help and permission of the Mayor of New York and Ambassador Whitelaw Reid, who was to introduce Burleigh to King Edward VII. From Liverpool some days later, Burleigh's report to the *Age* was: "All well. Had a fine trip over. Fooled the fish after all."

On July 16 the *Age* received word that Burleigh, "the New York baritone [had] sung himself into the hearts of European royalty":

H. T. Burleigh, c. 1908. Courtesy of Dr. David Cantrell.

Since his arrival here – a little over a month ago – he has appeared before many of the crowned heads of Europe. To sing before a Duke or a Duchess is an everyday happening with him. Even the King and Queen of England have heard his folk lore songs. They agree with the rest of the nobility that the New Yorker is a singer of no little merit.

So successful has he been in private recitals that arrangements have been completed whereby he is to return to England next summer and will appear in a big public recital. As royalty has put its stamp of approval on his singing there is little doubt that the public recital will be a flattering success.

The most important event in the baritone's stay abroad was July 3, when he appeared before the King and Queen of England at the home of the Earl of Lonsdale. On the same evening he sang at Stafford House for the Duke and Duchess of Sutherland.

So proud was Ambassador Whitelaw Reid of Harry Burleigh's success in England that the singer was asked to give a recital at Dorchester House for the American Ambassador and Mrs. Reid at which many distinguished persons were present. After the recital Ambassador Reid highly complimented his fellow countryman on his singing.

About the second event of importance to the appearance before the King took place July 7. Harry Burleigh sang for the Crown Princess of Sweden, who is visiting her parents the Duke and Duchess of Connaught, the former a brother of the King.

Lord and Lady Algernon Gordon-Lennox had the singer at Broughton Castle . . . and after the recital Lord Algernon presented him with pictures of the castle.

Royalty has also seen fit to treat Mr. Burleigh and his wife with some social recognition. While singing at Dorchester House Mrs. Burleigh attended a tea given by the Persian Embassy. The couple also took tea at the home of Lady Maude Warrender, who is a big social favorite, at which

Signor Tosti and many prominent musicians were present.
They expect to return to America by August 1.

Burleigh's comment on this scene of pomp and circumstance was: "I
think the King liked my voice."[44]

Other notables for whom Burleigh sang either on his trips abroad
or at private homes in the United States were Anton Seidel, the Duke
and Duchess of Manchester, the Dowager Countess of Dudley, the
Earl and Countess of Dudley, and the Archbishop of Canterbury.
The list also included Ignace Paderewski (who accompanied him on
one of his own Polish songs), Darius Milhaud, and Enrique Caruso
during their stays in the United States.

In 1902 when Prince Henry of Prussia had visited the United
States Burleigh "stood on the floor of the hall in front of the Prince
and sang in his inimitable and artistic manner the melodies of the
Southern Negro, including some numbers of his own composition."
The Prince, quite taken with his singing, personally invited him to
visit the German Court; acceptance is unconfirmed.[45]

Clarence Cameron White, who studied composition with Coleridge-Taylor during the summers of 1908-10, wrote to the *Age* the
following December:

> Mr. Burleigh's remarkable success during the past
> summer in singing before the King and Queen of England
> and many other members of the nobility only goes to show
> that it is here more a question of fitness than of color.

Burleigh visited Coleridge-Taylor several times during the period
1908-11. He was housed with Dr. John Alcindor, a medical doctor
and friend of Coleridge-Taylor, as evidenced by postcards from
Coleridge-Taylor to Burleigh at Alcindor's address, 31 Talbot Road,
Bayswater. Photos of Burleigh taken with Coleridge-Taylor's young
daughter at their home indicate at least one later visit.[46]

While Burleigh was abroad in the summer of 1908 Melville
Charlton received a due honor. Cited as "one of the few colored
musicians who has mastered harmony and counterpoint and who had
written a double fugue," he was the only black recitalist chosen to
perform at the New York State Music Teachers' Convention.[47]

By now Burleigh's old pals Williams and Walker had reached a salary of $2,300 per week. Walker, incurably ill with syphilis, gave his last performance with Williams in 1909 and died in 1911. Williams continued in show business until his death in 1922 from pneumonia and poor circulation.[48]

In November of 1908 Burleigh was asked to sing at the Washington Conservatory of Music by its director, Mrs. Harriet Gibbs Marshall.[49] Burleigh's grand but sincere style as the consummate gentleman is evident in his reply dated December 20, 1908, on stationery from the St. George's Men's Club:

> Dear Mrs. Marshall;
>
> Your letter of Nov. 23d would have been answered much sooner, but we've been so upset by our boy's serious illness that many important matters had to be neglected.
>
> I see no prospect now of being in Washington in March, but I should like to give a recital, if possible, in your course. It will have to be arranged with my manager whose address you will find on my new circular which I enclose. He will give you figures and most available dates.
>
> Trusting you will be successful in your work, I am glad to remain
>
> > Very truly yours
> > H. T. Burleigh
>
> P. S. Miss Childers wrote me some time ago to ask me to sing in Samson & Delilah in the Spring, but I don't know the date.

A letter to Mrs. Marshall dated January 26, 1909, from a Mr. Buton, representing Brooks and Denton, New York agents of "Music and Amusements for Social Functions of Every Description," stated:

> Dear Madam:
>
> I regret to state Mr. Burleigh is already engaged in N. Y. for the 5th of March. His terms however in case you should wish his services another date will be $50. & expenses.

Throughout 1909 Burleigh continued to sing, teach, and be publicized. Said to be a "favorite with the music lovers of Richmond Hill," New York, he assisted in a recital by piano pupils of Miss Nellie Moore at the Temple Forum Auditorium in that city on March 19, singing several of his own "characteristic melodies," plus encores. Another concert reported in the *Age* occurred on April 22, when the Gerald Tyler Choral Society of Kansas City, Missouri, presented Massenet's "Mary Magdalene" at New York's Central High School auditorium, with Burleigh as soloist.

Despite his busy schedule in New York Burleigh had not forgotten Erie and its people. Every two or three years he went back for a visit, particularly to see his Jewish friend Isador Sobel, Dr. Earle Lawrence and family, and Mr. John C. Diehl, a principal at Academy High School and later Superintendent of Schools, who shared Burleigh's love for fishing. Diehl, who cherished him and his accomplishments, continued to resent the inhumanities inflicted on the black race through racial discrimination.

The Lawrence home was usually headquarters for Burleigh when he was in Erie. As a young girl, Ada, Dr. Lawrence's daughter, received an autographed photo and a book about opera from Burleigh. Proudly she showed the book at school, but her teacher, far from enthusiastic, berated it as distastefully risqué. Ada recalled of Burleigh that his own relaxed quality made others feel at ease when he was with them. "Surprisingly enough," she said, "he liked the things that normal, ordinary people liked. He wasn't looking for fancy fixings when he came to Erie because he had all that in the big cities."

Mrs. Belle Lawrence, Ada's mother, said of Burleigh:

> He was the warmest person you ever did see. When he came to Erie the Presbyterian Church considered him a very special friend. He always wanted to stay with our family. Harry never forgot the people he knew as a child. He liked all kinds of food, just so it was good![50]

Though the specific year is omitted from a program of a performance given in Erie by Burleigh, ECHS librarians believe it to

PROGRAM *Song Recital*

By HARRY T. BURLEIGH, (Baritone)
of New York City

AT ST. PAUL'S PARISH HOUSE, ERIE, PA., MAY FOURTEENTH.

UNDER AUSPICES OF BROTHERHOOD OF ST.
ANDREW OF TRINITY EPISCOPAL CHURCH.

GROUP No. 1.

"The Wanderer" . . . . ⎫
      (Schmidt)   ⎬ . Schubert
"Serenade" . . . . . ⎭

"Ich Grolle Nicht" . . . . . Schumann
      (Heine)

"Verrath" . . . . . . Brahms
      (Lemcke)

"Du Bist Wie Eine Blume" . . . Rubenstein
      (Heine)

"Ich Liebe Dich" . . . . . Greig

"Don Juan's Serenade" . . . Tschaikowsky
      Tolstoi)

GROUP No. 2.

"De Danville Chariot" . . ⎫
"Josua Fit the Battle ob Jericho" ⎬ Plantation Songs
"Moanin' Dove" . . . ⎬
"I Don't Feel No Ways Tired" . ⎭

GROUP No. 3.

"All the World Awakes To-Day." . . Ed. G......
      (Boulton)

"O, For a Day of Spring" . . . Andrews
      (Blunt)

"May Morning" . . . . . Denza
      (Weatherly)

"The Years at the Spring" . . . Beach
      (Browning)

GROUP No. 4.

"Mighty Lak a Rose" . . . . Nevin
      (Stanton)

"Li'l Gal" . . . . . Johnson
      (Dunbar)

"A-Singinan' A-Singin" . . . Neidlinger
      (Stanton)

"Dreamland" . . . . ⎫
      (Louise Burleigh) ⎬ . . Burleigh
"Keep a Good Grip on the Hoe" . ⎬
      (Howard Weedon)

GROUP No. 5.

"A Corn Song" . . . . ⎫
      (Dunbar) ⎬ . Coleridge-Taylor
"Beat, Beat Drums" . . . ⎬
      (Whitman)

"The Deserted Plantation" . ⎫
      (Dunbar) ⎬ . . . Damrosch
"Mandalay" . . . . . ⎬
      (Kipling)

HUMBLE PRINT, 631 WEST 11TH ST.

have been in 1909 or 1910, considering the period that Humble Printers operated at 631 West Eleventh Street. Since no accompanist is listed, Burleigh may have accompanied himself.[51]

Burleigh's second summer in Europe was probably subsidized. An item in the Hampton *School Journal* for April 1909 gave his combined annual salary from St. George's and Temple Emanu-El as $2,400. This income, of course, was supplemented from his private voice teaching and frequent appearances as guest soloist.

Specific performances during this period abroad are not documented, but according to an announcement in the *Philadelphia*

Tribune, January 8, 1910, he was soon to share some of them with the American audiences. It is almost certain that Burleigh spent a part of his summer in Europe studying languages.

Toward the end of 1909 an ad appeared in the *Age* which ran through the following May. No explanation for its discontinuance was given.

Burleigh's compositions for 1908-09 were substantial, consisting of seven songs published separately and *Negro Minstrel Melodies,* a collection of twenty-one songs with piano accompaniment, which he edited. *Melodies* contained tunes by Stephen Foster, James A. Bland, and others, but none of his own. Neither was Burleigh's name actually mentioned in the collection's lengthy preface by W. J. Henderson.[52]

Group efforts for recognition of black musicians were on the up-
swing. In 1910 the Clef Club was organized, an orchestra based in
New York City and in essence the first black musician's union. Also
during that summer the Colored Music Association was organized in
New York under First Congregational Church auspices for the purpose of "bringing annually to the city the best musical talent of the
race." On August 5, in celebration of its founding, Burleigh and
violinist Joseph Douglass gave a concert in Atlanta, Georgia, a new
area for Burleigh. A review was sent to the *Age*, August 11:

> Harry T. Burleigh of New York sang well, though one
> could not help regretting that simpler songs had not been
> chosen. His own composition, "You Ask Me If I Love You,"
> was a very pretty little song. . . . One section of the house
> was reserved entirely for white people. . . . Some of the most
> enthusiastic applause was from the white people, but the
> occasion was essentially one of gratification for the colored
> people themselves. Nearly 2,000 were in the audience.

Another letter to Mrs. Marshall dated September 26, 1910, this
time on William Maxwell Music Company letterhead, indicates his
continued support and enthusiasm for her efforts:

> My dear Mrs. Marshall:
>   I have but recently returned from a two months vacation
> and find your letter among a huge pile.
>   I cannot answer you as I want to at this writing; I simply
> will acknowledge the receipt of your letter and beg you to
> wait a day or so longer for its proper answer.
>   I fear I cannot send you a competent teacher of voice.
> Would a lady do? I know two or three men who are good,
> but unsteady and unreliable.
>   I wish so much I could be with you in your work; I really
> feel that the field is very fruitful and attractive, but unfortu-
> nately I must remain at my post and sing. If you could secure
> something in the shape of an endowment, it would allow you
> to extend the work so much.

Just think of the possibility of having in Washington something like the Boston Conservatory! Then you could expect students from all over the country.

I'll write you again as soon as possible. I'm "full up" with rehearsals for the coming Jewish holidays and also I've been engaged to sing in St. Patrick's Cathedral at the Consecration Service Oct. 5th and this demands a lot of rehearsing also, so you see how busy I am. Keep well and let me hear from you again.

Very truly yours
H. T. Burleigh

P. S. I like the idea of a select chorus for Commencement. Where would you get your voices?

A large audience gathered on October 19 at the American Academy of Music in Philadelphia for a recital under Mme Azalia Hackley's direction. Participating were Mme Hackley, soprano; Clarence Cameron White, violinist; and Louise Burleigh, who read her own Southern poems. Her recitation of "Marie Brown" caused "uproarious applause. . . . The occasion marked the most important musical event of the year."

Though he sang only minor parts, "An Ox" and "A Herdsman," in Gabriel Pierné's *The Children of Bethlehem*, "Mr. Burleigh was one of the few participants that got a real ovation." The work was presented in Carnegie Hall in late December under the direction of Walter Damrosch with the New York Symphony Orchestra.[53]

Evidence of Burleigh's magnetism is found in a letter from Charles William Anderson to his close friend and political ally Booker T. Washington in Washington's *Papers*, dated January 7, 1911. Anderson had been appointed in 1905 by President Roosevelt as Collector of Internal Revenue, a position he held for ten years. Contact with various organizations in his district, which included the Wall Street area, provided an analytical overview of events. Commenting on the small attendance at an NAACP meeting in New York, he wrote: "I am not so sure that as many of these were drawn thither because Mr. Burleigh was expected to sing as for any other reason."

Perhaps due to the relentless tempo of Burleigh's multifaceted professional life, only one of his compositions, a song titled "It Was Nothing but a Rose," was published in 1910.

Activities for the Burleighs began early in 1911. On January 25, Mrs. Burleigh was featured in more poetry readings on a recital with singer Arthur Smith under the direction of Theodore Drury at the Legion of Honor Building in Boston. A joint recital on March 7 by the Burleighs for the benefit of St. Monica's Home for Sick Colored Women drew "only a few colored people," though the large audience, mostly white, was very appreciative. The program included five "plantation spirituals"; readings of dialect poems; art songs by Edvard Grieg, Coleridge-Taylor, and Sidney Homer; three readings; and concluded with three American art songs, one of which was Burleigh's own "Dreamland," with words by Mrs. Burleigh.[54]

Further publicity was given Mrs. Burleigh in the *Age*, April 27, when she assisted on a program for a Willing Worker's Circle of the King's Daughters' twenty-first annual entertainment:

> Mrs. Burleigh in her readings gives promise of succeed-ing Paul Laurence Dunbar in carrying on the songs of the Negro. Her poems are true to nature and give evidence of much thought as well as genuine talent. Mrs. Burleigh's interpretation of her words are beyond criticism as she has set her own standard for them. Others rightfully should follow, and yet Mrs. Burleigh may not have been at her best, due to the large auditorium and the small crowd (which would have helped the performance greatly had they been ushered nearer to the footlights). Had Mrs. Burleigh been before an audience in a smaller music chamber many of her most artistic points which were lost in the echo of the large hall would have been more enthusiastically received.

Closing the recital, after selections from pianist Helen Hagan and others from the Dabney-Wilson-Tuck Trio, Mrs. Burleigh and R. Henri Savage staged a "creditable rendition" of a scene from *Ingomar*, an old play translated from German by Maria Lovell.

Arrangements of two of Burleigh's piano works, "A Jubilee" and "On Bended Knees," were performed by the Clef Club Symphony Orchestra at its third semi-annual concert in May 1911. "On Bended

Knees" was cited for special mention, both as a composition and for its rendition by the players. The Clef Club used these arrangements on several subsequent occasions. There is no evidence that they were ever published.

Burleigh offered to appear on one of the "Supper Club" concerts scheduled for May 30-31 at the Howard Theater in the Washington Conservatory, proceeds from which would be used to erect a monument over the late George Walker's grave. The concert materialized, but Burleigh was not mentioned as a performer.[55]

The summer of 1911 would be the logical time that Burleigh would have enrolled his son in a private English school where he spent the next four years, though these specific years are not confirmed by Burleigh's family.

A photo of Louise Burleigh appeared in the September 14, 1911, *Age*, accompanied by an article stating that her poems had been praised by literary critics, kudos resulting from a number of successful recitals given during the summer. At one in August at Green Acre in Eliot, Maine, she was highly complimented by professors from Harvard, Cornell, and Yale. On September 4 she and Burleigh gave a joint recital at Lake Mohony House, Lake Mohony, New York, before an exclusive audience, including a "titled lady" from Scotland who was "charmed with the poet and is planning to have her come to Scotland next year." Also mentioned were Mrs. Burleigh's spring bookings for European engagements and plans to publish her volume of poems "Echoes from the Southland" and to tour the South as a reader. "She has a magnetic and charming personality and deserves much credit for her splendid work."

The October 12 *Age* reported a joint recital by Burleigh and his "talented wife" given in New York's Mt. Olivet Baptist Church, for a YMCA benefit. At this "artistic success" Mrs. Burleigh's readings were

well received and delivered in characteristic style. . . . This was her first appearance before a large audience in New York. Mr. Burleigh sang in his usual fine voice and pleasing style and was greatly enjoyed.

Accompanied by Charlton, Burleigh's program of three groups contained the well-used "Prologue," spirituals, and art songs. This period may have marked Mrs. Burleigh's peak as a performer in the New York area, for further publicity on her was almost nonexistent during the following few years.

Apparently Mrs. Thurber periodically needed Burleigh's talents and expertise in various matters. On December 10, 1911, on stationery from St. George's Men's Club at 207 East Sixteenth Street, Burleigh wrote:

> My dear Mrs. Thurber:
> Thank you for your letter and the enclosure. I have not the time to attend to that kind of arranging, since I am doing editorial work for Ricordi & Co., but I will try to locate someone for them.
> Trusting you are enjoying continued good health and wishing you a successful year I am privileged to remain
> Very truly yours
> H. T. Burleigh

The much sought after Mr. Burleigh was not to be imposed upon. Another letter from Burleigh to Mrs. Marshall, dated January 4, 1912, is a friendly but firm declination.

> My dear Mrs. Marshall:
> So sorry I missed seeing you when you were here. Louise told me what a pleasant evening she had with you and her poems.
> About singing for your Artist's Course Recitals, I am in more of an uncertain state now than I was when you first spoke of the plan. You must not set your heart too much on my being able to come at all, for as I said long ago, before I knew you were going to advertise me, the fact of my coming is very doubtful.
> Even at this early date I've booked three dates in March and I have no doubt others will come in thicker and faster than I can attend to them.
> Now suppose I had taken a chance and had promised to sing for you March 21st for instance; and along comes the Choral Club of Toronto with an engagement for that same

date; you see what disturbance it would cause of efforts to switch the date or of disappointment and even if 'twas changed we still run the risk of conflicting with some other engagement.

I find it harder and harder to take dates out of the city. If you must be certain and sure of a definite date, I must advise you to substitute some one in my place. This will not be so hard as it may seem to be at first thought.

How is Williams doing in the Vocal Department? He ought to make a big success of it. Give him my best wishes.

Very truly yours

H. T. Burleigh

In April 1912, Burleigh joined the Board of Directors for the Music School Settlement for Colored People, Inc., whose aim was to purchase a building adequate for both teaching and social activities. Burleigh, never known as a "joiner," evidently felt strongly about this particular worthy cause. A concert under Settlement auspices was scheduled in Carnegie Hall for May 2, on which Burleigh was represented with his "Jean," sung by Elizabeth Payne.

On May 13, at Brattle Hall in Cambridge, Burleigh collaborated with violinist White. The recital was deemed by the *Age*'s critic another "artistic success, largely attended." Burleigh's two segments proffered songs by Coleridge-Taylor and Sidney Homer. The following August Burleigh assisted Cook with arrangements for a "Negro Life Festival," originally scheduled for October 16-20. Due to the project's elaborate scope, however, it was postponed until March of 1913.

Burleigh's only compositions published in 1911-12 were two religious songs. The first, "Tarry With Me, O My Savior!" was the last of his works issued by William Maxwell Company; and "Child Jesus Come from Heav'nly Height" was his first accepted by George Maxwell at G. Ricordi, Inc.

Friendship with and encouragement from George Maxwell were some of the strongest influences in Burleigh's life. The exact month in 1913 of Burleigh's joining G. Ricordi and Company is relatively unimportant. Of more consequence is the fact that George Maxwell, managing director of Ricordi since its American branch opened in

1911 at 14 East Forty-third Street, had continued to admire Burleigh's musical expertise and overall professionalism, a respect shared
by his co-editor and friend Clarence Laubscher. The situation has
been summed up properly by Burleigh's friend Charlotte Murray, a
singer at New York's Riverside Church:

> One of the most fortunate, significant and far-reaching
> periods in the life of Mr. Burleigh occurred as a result of
> having been engaged as one of the editors at Ricordi and
> Co., Inc., internationally known music publishers. This came
> about because of his capacity for critical analysis and
> synthesis. For over thirty years he was such an important
> member of the staff that no piece of music was submitted
> to them which did not pass through his hands and rest its
> fate on his judgment. While at Ricordi's he had a faithful ally
> in the person of Mr. George Maxwell who was managing
> director from 1911 to 1931 and the first president of ASCAP.
>
> A. Walter Kramer has this to say of him: "George Max-
> well's whole-hearted championing of Harry Burleigh was a
> fine thing for it was he who was responsible for publishing
> Burleigh's too-little known art-songs and for making his
> spirituals nationally known."[56]

Burleigh's chief regret as a composer was this very situation, the
"too-little known art-songs." In later life, he preferred to be remembered foremost as a composer in this genre, rather than as an arranger of spirituals alone. During his friendship with Mrs. Josephine
H. Love he showed her several drawers at Ricordi containing his
published songs.

Through George Maxwell Burleigh met Frank St. Leger, Nellie
Melba's accompanist for a time, who liked his nonextravagant arrangements of the spirituals. St. Leger felt that they resembled art
songs, with their exotic and romantic harmonies. Melba first used
Burleigh's spirituals as encores, then began to program them as a
group, a habit practiced by more and more concert singers toward
1920.

Though far from presumptuous in his new position, Burleigh did
recommend to Schirmer James Weldon Johnson, whose Spanish was
fluent, as a translator for Granados's opera *Goyescas*. This version

was performed at the Metropolitan in 1916. While working at Ricordi Burleigh was in contact with countless musicians who came there to purchase, chat, or ask advice, some of them being Eva Jessye, Jester Hairston, Dr. John Seagle, and Mrs. Josephine H. Love, all of whom remember him as a courteous gentleman.[57]

For Burleigh the 1913 musical fabric became an olio of color and excitement. Though he did not participate in as many pre-Lenten concerts at Palm Garden as is assumed, his music was performed at them by Roland Hayes and other artists of stature, often accompanied by Melville Charlton. Considered a first class social as well as musical event the concerts caused much to-do over the ladies' gowns and accessories. Current fads for this particular spring were split skirts and jeweled heels. On February 6 the *Age*'s reviewer named Miss Eva Burleigh as having been seen in a pair of these sassy shoes at the concert.

At this time seat prices in respectable halls such as the Lafayette Theater ranged from five cents in the balcony for a matinee to thirty-five in a box for an evening performance. A new dance, described as the "fascinating and strictly proper society tango," was waiting to be introduced by dance instructor Henry S. Creamer. By early October the Marshall Hotel announced its imminent closing, no longer viable as a rendezvous or late dining spot for theater-goers, due to a recently enforced 1:00 a.m. closure ordinance. Several black orchestras and dance bands were thriving. An orchestra called The Tempo Club, preferred by the famous dance team Vernon and Irene Castle, was now all the rage. The integrated audience, still a precarious and unpredictable phenomenon, had become more common. Lester Walton expressed his ongoing fear that the whites might imagine some intangible malaise and blame it on the blacks in adjoining seats, thereby causing a commotion.[58]

Sadness had tinged the music world the previous September due to Coleridge-Taylor's death. On January 13, 1913, the Coleridge-Taylor Choral Society held a memorial concert in Boston's Jordan Hall. Participating in the solemnity were Dr. W. E. B. DuBois, speaker; Harry Burleigh and William H. Richardson, baritones; Roland Hayes, tenor; Maud Cuney-Hare, pianist; Frederick P. White, organist; and two string players from the Boston Symphony. Charlton accompanied.[59]

In mid-April of 1913 Burleigh lost his friend and supporter J. P. Morgan, Sr., who died in Italy. The prominent financier's body was shipped to New York for his funeral held at St. George's Church. Burleigh, selected by the Morgan family as soloist, sang the requested "Calvary" by Paul Rodney. Some years later he repeated the piece with a choir at the funeral of Morgan's son. Whenever Anne, the elder Morgan's daughter, visited the family church, she made a point of renewing her old and warm friendship with Burleigh until he retired.[60] Miss Morgan, a philanthropist after her father, died in 1952 at the age of eighty-three.

For his part in the ceremony Burleigh received a beautiful tribute in the *New York Sun*, partially reprinted with editorial asides by *The Colored Virginian*, April 19, 1913. Speaking of Burleigh, "who for years has sung each Christmas Eve at Mr. Morgan's home," the eulogist continued:

> Conjure in your minds this magnificent scene. Picture this beautiful church; the service being lead by three bishops of the church, and the congregation being made up of the brains and wealth of this country, and then let your minds dwell on the fact that they are listening to the soul-stirring music that literally pours from this gifted Negro's throat! . . . Do we not have cause for rejoicing? . . . WORTH TELLS. No matter what might have been the friendly relations existing between the late Mr. Morgan and Mr. Burleigh, if at the crucial time he had not been able to deliver the goods he would not have been heard! His years of toil, of study, of frugality, of hope, of pertinacity, of perseverance, at last spelled SUCCESS.

Hiawatha was again performed on May 2 by the Mozart Society of Fisk University at its seventy-first concert in Nashville with Burleigh, "the distinguised baritone of New York," as soloist. The audience was integrated and fashionable. As the "star attraction, Mr. Burleigh never sang better, nor before a more critical audience of music lovers," reported the *Age*, May 8, 1913.

In late November the St. George's Club, mindful of Burleigh's professional progress, presented him with a solid gold Tiffany watch to mark his twenty years of faithful service. The inscription read:

The Brotherhood of Men to Harry T. Burleigh as a
Token of Esteem from His Fellow Members of St. George's
Club, November 29, 1913.

Reverend Karl Reiland, who presented the token to Burleigh, considered it a great privilege especially since the recipient was "still
alive." [61]

Two Negro spirituals, "Deep River" and "Dig My Grave," were
Burleigh's sole publications for the year, the first particularly
significant. This first choral setting of "Deep River" spawned the
stirring 1917 solo arrangement which was to cause such a sensation.
"Dig My Grave" was selected from Henry E. Krehbiel's large collection, *Afro-American Folksongs, a Study in Racial and National
Music*, published in 1914 by G. Schirmer, Inc. Burleigh set another
song from this collection in 1921. Krehbiel, doyen of musical criti-
cism, revered editor, and Beethoven scholar, was music critic for the
New York Tribune from 1880 until his death in 1923.

Now forty-seven, Burleigh had passed a little more than half of
his life. He was favorably and securely established professionally and
had long since settled comfortably into an apartment in the Bronx at
823 East 166th Street. As a composer and arranger his most productive years were just ahead. He was yet to meet and be recognized
musically by the foremost concert and opera singers of the day. Un-
told honors were in the offing.

Chapter II

Singer, Composer and Arranger (1914-1949)

♪

America's Musical Scene Preceding World War I

Europeans in the second decade of the 1900s saw the demise of the Golden Age of opera, a period lasting from approximately 1870 through 1913. Opera in America was holding its own. Audiences were treated to more than just the remnants of the past glorious aura, due to the appearance of competent native singers, several of whom were equally proficient in oratorio and art song as well. Moreover, European-born stars, such as Schumann-Heink, Pasquale Amato, Frieda Hempel, Lucrezia Bori, and John McCormack had come to America permanently. Solo recitals shared by two or three performers were in vogue. Musical activities were myriad. American singers, in particular George Hamlin, Christine Miller, and Oscar Seagle, had begun to fill seasonal schedules which required superhuman stamina.

Though vibrations of World War I were soon to be felt, 1914 still belonged to the age of romance. Opera stars, both male and female, were photographed emulating the "great profile" of John Barrymore. Many of them were pictured with their pets or children, others in frolicsome poses on shipboard, on horses, in boats, or beside their motor cars. Some were snapped playing at chess, and one operatic duo was honeymooning on camel-back in Africa. Caruso, the bon vivant, was often seen flaunting a cigarette. In a more contemplative mood, the ladies were captured languishing seductively on couches against floral backdrops. Their gowns and hats of exquisite fabrics – featuring jewels, feathers, furs, ribbon, lace, or other frou frou – were elaborately designed by exclusive modistes. Divas were typically temperamental and competitive. They got divorces, haggled with their agents, and some made life miserable for their accompanists.

Continuing Achievement

Harry Burleigh, on the periphery of this colorful world of poseurs, had attained a place of permanent prominence in New York's black community. He was constantly called for more singing engagements than he could fill. One which he declined in late January of 1914 was with James Reese Europe's newly formed Society Orchestra.

The following month, through Victor Herbert's invitation, Burleigh was one of the 170 composers who became charter members of the American Society of Composers, Authors, and Publishers (ASCAP). Five other black composers who joined at this time were Will Marion Cook, brothers James Weldon and John Rosamund Johnson, William Tyers (Europe's co-director), and Cecil Mack, the ragtime songwriter.

ASCAP's first president was George Maxwell, "owing to his knowledge of the inner workings of foreign organizations of composers."[1] Basically the organization's purpose was to give remuneration to the composer when his works were performed. Its structure was modeled after similar societies in Europe. Maxwell's statements on the subject were given in the *New York Times*, February 14, 1914, predicting that ASCAP would collect approximately $1,000,000 to distribute among New York City area members alone.

A concert for March 11 in Carnegie Hall benefitting the Music School Settlement for Colored People was announced in the *Age*. Prominent black performers were to take part; composers, namely Cook, Burleigh, and Nathaniel Dett, a young pianist newly appointed to the faculty at Hampton Institute, to present their works; and Burleigh to sing compositions by Coleridge-Taylor. On March 12 the *Times* reported it as "an interesting concert, and one calculated to stimulate the musical imagination," showing what black composers could do when trained in modern technique "as they are affected by their racial traits in music." The music that was

> . . . harmonized, arranged or developed demonstrated that they can form an art of their own on the basis of their own material. . . . The subject of Negro Music is receiving a good deal of attention nowadays. . . . The singing was well performed and forced serious consideration. The orchestral work was perhaps a step far outside the natural genius of the race . . . but it demonstrated that painstaking attention is being given to this branch of musical development.

Specific works by Burleigh were not mentioned.

Two of Burleigh's a cappella choral arrangements were used on a Schola Cantorum concert conducted by Kurt Schindler in Carnegie Hall on April 1, 1914. It was purposefully devoted to folksongs of several races. The chorus was assisted by the New York Symphony Orchestra and soloists Mary Jordan, contralto, and Royal Dadmun, baritone. Burleigh later dedicated works to both of these singers. He received favorable exposure in a *New York Times* review on April 2, 1914. His harmonic four-part writing was

> . . . truly in place because it exchanges the significance and spirit of the times and makes them beautiful choruses. There was an evident desire on the part of the audience to applaud Mr. Burleigh but he did not appear.

The following month Burleigh assisted Dett with his first choral concert at Hampton Institute, by the newly formed Hampton Choral Union. The prestigious occasion on May 14 drew the "largest crowd ever assembled on the school grounds up to that time." In pre-concert publicity from *The Hampton Student* Burleigh was called "one of the most gifted of all the living American barytones and easily the foremost singer of his race."

His selections were Massenet's "Legend of the Sage Brush," "Corn Song" by Coleridge-Taylor, Damrosch's "Danny Deever," and his own arrangements of Indian and Negro melodies. He was commended for an "unusually effective interpretation," especially of his own arrangements:

. . . the artist carried his audience on the top wave of enthusiasm. The spontaneous outbursts of applause, the frequent encores, and the many flowers were some of the ways in which the audience showed its high appreciation of the artist.[2]

In approximately a month, the first all-black composers' concert ever given in this area of Illinois was held in Chicago at Orchestra Hall. Though Burleigh could not attend the event due to a previous commitment, some of his works were performed, according to Karleton Hackett writing for the *Chicago Evening Post*, June 4, 1914. Burleigh was in New York at the Manhattan Casino, conducting the Clef Glee Club in his arrangement for four-part male voices of "O, Southland," a setting of James Weldon Johnson's poem.

Burleigh's works were beginning to be increasingly programmed. A song published this year, "The Hour Glass," was performed by Mr. Henri La Bonte at the Von Ende School of Music in New York on a faculty recital in late July. Both Burleigh's solo and choral arrangements of spirituals were favorites of the Hampton Institute Music School. He was not unaware of the activities of recitalists and operatic stars, many of whom were soon to introduce his works to larger concert audiences.

The Burleigh Champions

During the middle years of this decade several famous singers were linked with performances of Burleigh's works. The more influential ones were Oscar Seagle, George Hamlin, Herbert J. Witherspoon, Christine Miller, Mary Jordan, and John McCormack. Though Burleigh dedicated at least one spiritual or art song to most of these, early scripting proscribed his taking social advantage of this. For instance, he never visited baritone Seagle's colony at Schroon Lake, New York, where Seagle taught almost every summer beginning in 1917. Seagle's son wrote:

. . . nor can I recall Burleigh ever attending one of my father's concerts. If he had tried to attend all the concerts

Oscar Seagle, c. late 1920s or early 1930s. Courtesy of Willis Ducrest.

on which his compositions were performed he would not have had much time for his own work.[3]

Seagle, never a member of an operatic company, was an indefatigable performer and teacher.

George Hamlin, versatile American-born tenor, was already deep into his career by 1914, having debuted in Herbert's *Natoma* in 1911. He was as well known in Berlin as in New York or Chicago, where he was with the Chicago Opera from 1911 to 1915. As early as 1910 he, Witherspoon, and Miller had shared oratorio recitals. Though the *lied*, particularly Strauss, was Hamlin's forte, he strongly encouraged performance of opera and song recitals in English and made a great point of seeking out works by Burleigh and other American composers. He spoke of Burleigh as the "beloved soloist of St. George's Church . . . a wonderful black composer and singer who arranged Negro spirituals for concert use, which was quite an innovation at that time."[4]

By the end of 1914 Hamlin's recitals had encompassed the works of over thirty American composers. He had a great sense of humor, evidenced by his articles in *Musical Courier*, one of which was on the delicacy of garlic.

Operatic basso Herbert Witherspoon, after retiring from the Metropolitan in 1914, made yearly concert tours and with his second wife, singer Florence Hinkle, ran a large voice studio in New York, which by the end of 1917 boasted 150 students. He had debuted at the Metropolitan in 1908 as Titurel in *Parsifal*, a role which begot a marathon of Wagnerian performances. After his presidency of the Chicago Musical College (1925-30), he became artistic director of the Chicago Civic Opera for one year. For four years (1931-35) he was president of the Cincinnati Conservatory and in 1935 succeeded Giulio Gatti-Casazza as general manager of the Metropolitan Opera, a position cut short by his sudden death that year.

Christine Miller, like Seagle, was never affiliated with an opera company, though she performed in *Aïda* in Utica under nonprofessional auspices. In 1914 she was fairly new to New York concert audiences, but through her superb voice, personal charm, and warmth she rapidly got almost more bookings as an oratorio and concert

Christine Miller, c. 1917. Courtesy of Carnegie Library of Pittsburgh.

soloist than were possible to fill. This shrewd Scottish-born, Pittsburgh-reared business woman acted as her own impressario. Her rich contralto was considered a perfect one for recording. Critics spoke of her in superlatives and could not praise her enough. Rave reviews followed her beautiful performances and no one was lovelier to look upon, as she "charmed, swayed, soothed, and electrified her hearers."[5]

Equally personable and in great demand was contralto Mary Jordan, to whom Burleigh later dedicated "Deep River." Repeated announcements by Jordan's managers, Foster and David, appeared in the *Courier* in the spring of 1914, making her available for a "limited number of appearances in concert, recital and oratorio." At this time she was soloist at Temple Emanu-El and a member of New York's Century Opera Company, a struggling group promoting "opera in English" at reduced prices. Despite the best long-range plans, the Century, bankrupt, closed its doors in May of 1915. Previously Jordan had toured with the revived Savage Opera Company.

John McCormack, the Irish tenor, had taken U.S. audiences by storm. He was the biggest drawing card of the entire musical scene. By 1914 nearly every house, even the Hippodrome which seated over 5,000, was sold out in a matter of hours after his concerts were announced. Hundreds of seats were often placed on the stage, and extras in the orchestra pit, to accommodate the crowds. With his able accompanists Vincent O'Brien and later Edwin Schneider, McCormack shared many an exciting evening on stage with violinist Donald McBeath.

McCormack never suffered from a jaded press. Contrarily, music journals and the newspapers were *au courant* concerning his every move, including the fact that he smoked cigarettes. One flattering ad appearing in April 1914 issues of the *Courier* read:

Why are the McCormack concerts like Christmas?
CHRISTMAS is a matter of PRESENTS and
MCCORMACK CONCERTS are a matter of PRESENCE

His return engagements in the larger cities continued to be sellouts. Often his ten to a dozen encores included a Burleigh song or two, in this year particularly "Mother O' Mine," which he performed on April 14, 1914, in Newark, New Jersey, for "McCormack Night."[6]

John McCormack, c. 1917. Courtesy of the John McCormack Society of America in New York.

Offsetting the neglect by *Courier* editor Leonard Liebling of Burleigh's efforts and personage at this time was the accord given him by Lester Walton and Lucien White, critics for the *Age*. Between them the essence of black musicians and their activities was well captured.

Just as Mme Azalia Hackley and pianist Hazel Harrison were prompted by the war to return from Europe at this time, it is logical to assume that Burleigh was in England during the summer of 1914 only for the purpose of bringing his son home. By early October Alston, now fifteen, expecting to enter Yale University within the next two years, had been enrolled in the Hopkins School in New Haven.

This same month saw the opening of the new building for the Music School Settlement on West 131st Street, soon to be directed by J. Rosamond Johnson. For the happy occasion on October 8, 1914, Burleigh sang two spirituals. An appreciative review from the *Age* followed on October 15:

> The audience was with Mr. Burleigh from the beginning, because the general personality of this rare genius is wont to impress itself favorably from the first. His resonant baritone gave satisfaction in each of his numbers, . . . in which his wonderful lingual facility and breath control was marked.

Some Significant Art Songs and Three Cycles (1914-15)

In 1914 Ricordi published separately seven of Burleigh's art songs; six piano pieces under the title *From the Southland*; and *Saracen Songs*, the first of his three cycles, set to poems of Frederick G. Bowles. The seven songs of the *Saracen* cycle are rather like an operatic scene, alternating between male and female voice.

As a first song cycle the ambitious scope of *Saracen Songs* was significant, though evidence does not show that it was frequently performed in toto. Roland Hayes, the young black tenor whose career Burleigh furthered, performed two of them for a New York Pre-Lenten recital early in January of 1915. Other parts were programmed by students of Mrs. F. H. Snyder in St. Paul and by Marian Veryl in Aeolian Hall in New York later that year.[7]

Burleigh's longer compositions of 1915 were among his best known, due to their performances by leading artists. "The Young Warrior," with its martial motif, received wide publicity and became a marching song for the Italian army. Its stirring text by James Weldon Johnson is filled with the thoughts of a mother and her soldier son. Though not publicly launched until February of 1916 by operatic baritone Pasquale Amato at an Italian war benefit concert in the Biltmore Hotel, it was an immediate hit. The affair was under the auspices of the Italian Ambassador and Countess Delores de Allere, through patronage of the Queen of Italy. "Warrior" was translated into Italian by Eduardo Petri. The fiery Italian Richard Zandonai orchestrated "Warrior" and dedicated his score to Burleigh. This splendidly martial song

> . . . swept Italy like a flash. Italian soldiers sang it on the battlefield and their people sang it at home. One musical critic has said that it was "one of the few really admirable songs America has produced in recent years."[8]

Many newspapers and journals, such as the *Boston Evening Transcript*, the *Baltimore Afro-American*, and the *New York Tribune*, carried favorable critiques. Belated others bear quoting in part:

> This is a high honor for a Negro boy from Erie, Pa. The Young Warrior is not to be classed with Tipperary, which is of a pretty cheap order. Burleigh's song is the product of a fine musicianly imagination, a talent not of mushroom growth, but of thorough artistic development. When Amato sang the song at the Biltmore for an Allied Benefit it proved to be the sensation of the evening.[9]

Other kudos came from the *Philadelphia Tribune*, October 7, 1916:

> It is of general interest to the Afro-American people that one of their number had achieved such a high distinction in the land of music and of song, for such Italy is. What Italy stamps as poetry and music the world usually accepts. . . . An important point in the success achieved by Mr. Bur-

leigh is stated when it is said that his growth has been gradual in the mastery and development of his art. We remember very well twenty years ago when he was regarded only as a splendid vocalist with a local reputation, and we have watched his development year by year.

In connection with Burleigh's recent success and professional involvement, Lucien White wrote, in a tribute also including Coleridge-Taylor and James Weldon Johnson:

> He has had as pupils members of the most prominent families of the city, but increased demands of his new work has necessitated a curtailment of teaching duties. Few colored pupils have been able to pay the price of lessons from Mr. Burleigh and this is unfortunate.[10]

By Burleigh's "new work" White specified his contract with Ricordi.

Two song cycles, *Five Songs on Poems by Laurence Hope*, claimed to be Burleigh's finest, and *Passionale*, in collaboration with James Weldon Johnson, were both published in 1915. Each of the four songs in *Passionale* was separately dedicated. McCormack concluded with the *Hope* cycle at his Carnegie Hall concert on March 19, 1915, the first time it had been sung publicly. On the following day a review appeared in the *New York Times*:

> The songs of Mr. Burleigh constituting a whole division on the program attracted interest as novelties. They are well-made songs which contain some rich and appropriate coloring and generally find fitting expression for the words of the texts, which are oriental. Mr. Burleigh does not remain consistently oriental in his musical style. Most of the middle sections of the songs, especially, employ harmonization and melodic line, and the devices of form in sequence and "working over" that are not suggestive of oriental music. Very likely this is done deliberately, with the idea of furnishing contrast, but it is an element which, in the way it is handled, is strong in supplying the feeling that although the music is the work of a practiced hand and a taste that is above mediocrity, it is still not a strongly individual product that goes into the highest class.

Though there is no dedication in the printed score, Burleigh, according to a reviewer in the *Courier*, wrote "Kashmiri Song," the third of the cycle, for McCormack. The reviewer stated that 600 were seated on the stage and, speaking of the cycle, the song titled "Till I Wake"

> . . . had to be repeated, and the others likewise pleased the audience both by their novelty and by reason of the delicacy of phrasing and consummate artistry which Mr. McCormack brought to the interpretation.[11]

Almost a month later McCormack performed three of the *Hope* songs in Boston's Symphony Hall, their first hearing in that city. H. T. Parker's review in the *Boston Transcript* was reprinted in the *Courier*, April 13, 1916.

> Three more novel numbers were songs by Mr. Burleigh the negro composer, scarcely known to Mr. McCormack's manifold public and too little known to any outside a few close followers of American music as it comes from press and concert hall. Mr. Burleigh has a vein of fresh melody that is individually fragrant and without a hint of the commonness and triteness that beset most songs from American pens. He uses no cheap or hackneyed devices to catch the expectant ear; he has sensibility, humor and even imagination; and he shuns our molasses-like sentimentality as though it were the plague upon our songs that it really is.

McCormack was commended in the review for choosing Burleigh's pieces, setting them "before a public that he persuades to better taste and finer appreciation each time that it hears him."

In an entirely different compositional vein were "Ethiopia Saluting the Colors," a narrative, and "The Grey Wolf," a strikingly dramatic piece. Mary Jordan, to whom the latter was dedicated, repeatedly gave its "grim tragedy" a uniquely artistic reading, which "fascinated the audience."[12]

"Just You," a bit of fluff by further contrast, was one of Burleigh's better-known songs issued this year. It was often used as an encore by Metropolitan Opera stars Lucrezia Bori (still concertizing though on sick leave from the Metropolitan[13]) and Paul Althouse.

Four other songs were published this year, among them "The Prayer," used by Roland Hayes along with "The Young Warrior" on his concert tours the following year. J. Rosamond Johnson, Fannie Wise, Sidney Woodward, Percy Hemus, Craig Campbell, Reinald Werrenrath, W. Henry Hackney, Joseph Matthieu, Arthur Herschmann, and Anne Arkadij programmed at least one Burleigh song on most of their concerts during 1915.

Werrenrath, director of the University Heights Choral Society at this time, used many of Burleigh's solo and choral arrangements of spirituals. Hamlin, rarely equalled as a program builder, was doing his best to support Burleigh, not only by singing his works, but by lauding him as a talented composer. Mme Hackley organized 160 volunteer singers for a concert in Chicago on August 24, 1915, on which two of Burleigh's arrangements were programmed. Afterwards she sold copies of them to the chorus members. These arrangements immediately became popular with church choirs throughout the United States. On a May concert of this year the Clef Club Orchestra used Burleigh's arrangement of "The Frolic," one of the piano pieces in *From the Southland.*

Other performers making news in 1915 were Metropolitan conductor Richard Hagemann, composer, pianist and accompanist, who was equally touted as a brilliant social host; Mrs. Edward MacDowell, sedulous fund-raiser in memory of her late husband; Mme Schumann-Heink, suffering temporarily from emotional exhaustion; Paul Robeson, a talented black high school orator who had just won a scholarship to Rutgers; and another black teenager making her piano debut, Carlette Thomas, who later studied theory with Burleigh. The American musical world marvelled that Camille Saint-Saëns, now eighty, was spry enough to make a visit to the United States.

Percy Grainger, Rudolph Ganz, Alexander Bloch, young Fritz Kreisler, the Flonzaley Quartet, and the Cherniavsky brothers' trio were travelling the concert circuit. The voice studios of Dudley Buck, Paul Draper, and Charles Bowes appeared to be thriving. Diplomat James Weldon Johnson was now a contributing editor of the *Age.* Seagle's accompanist Frank Bibb, and Frank La Forge, the accompanist's accompanist who would rather play from memory than a score, were almost as in demand as the singers whom they assisted. One of La Forge's unbelievable feats was to play 120 songs from memory at four recitals within five days.[14]

Summers

By the end of 1915 Burleigh, like other fashionable Boston and New York blacks, had arranged to spend his summer vacations in Oak Bluffs, Massachusetts, a resort area on Martha's Vineyard. But the ambience of idle elegance was, for Burleigh, mixed with the work that he loved – composition, singing, and the directing of a church choir. Forever a staunch Episcopalian, he arranged and composed each day on the piano in a quiet room of the Grace Episcopal Parish House. Here he prepared much of the music to be used for Christmas services in New York, first testing it with the Grace choir.

At this time Oak Bluffs had a larger number of vacationing blacks than any other section of the country, necessitating about a dozen rental cottages. For some years the black Bostonians had the idyllic panorama to themselves, one of family beach play, leisurely games of whist, evening band concerts, boats bringing newcomers, and much socializing in general. As a group they were quieter than the New Yorkers, who took longer to unwind from the city's frenetic pace.

A *Vineyard Gazette* journalist, reviewing the scene as late as 1938, did not lump Burleigh with the brassy, obnoxious New Yorkers who disturbed the former tranquility with their loud talk, expensive liquor, and flashy diamonds. As a special "summer person" Burleigh

> was the first to bring back glad tidings of the Island's fair land to his New York friends who had always thought of Massachusetts as a nice place to come from, but not go to unless bound and gagged. He was very good to the children of his friends. . . . He gave us money every time he saw us. . . . He rented cars and took us on tours of the Island. He told us about his trips abroad. To be with him was a learning experience.[15]

For approximately thirty summers Burleigh was housed at Shearer Cottage in the Highland section of Oak Bluffs, where he was fondly referred to as "H. T." by resident Elizabeth White, who said, "He loved it!"[16] His studio-bedroom overlooked the lush green countryside. The cottage was a family-operated guest house opened around 1900 by Charles H. Shearer, a graduate and former faculty member of the Hampton Institute. Prominent blacks in all professions, including Reverend Adam Clayton Powell, were among the island's summer residents.[17]

More Art Songs

The year 1916 was another which produced some of Burleigh's best-known works: four art songs, arrangements of three spirituals, and the four-part *Southland Sketches* for violin and piano. The nostalgic "By the Pool at the Third Rosses," dedicated to John McCormack, enjoyed wide performance. On the tenor's recital in Carnegie Hall, January 16, "Rosses" was still in manuscript, one of two songs on his program marked "first time." Later that month in Chicago "he seemed to render it more feelingly than any other number on the program."[18]

Burleigh's less serious "Three Shadows" is a love song. "One Year 1914-1915" and "The Soldier" explore the feelings of family and lovers caused by the war. Of "One Year," which McCormack premiered in Carnegie Hall, April 9, 1916, A. Walter Kramer wrote:

> The intensity of this "One Year" is colossal. Singers will grip their audiences mightily with it. . . . It is one of those cases of true simplicity of style wherein greatness is to be found; vital in every sense in this war essay!

At the time he was interviewing Burleigh, there was only an unfinished sketch of "The Soldier," which Kramer predicted would be

> among the important art products of the Great War . . . vital because it is not a contribution to a cause, but a spontaneous musical reflection of Rupert Brooke's sublime sentiment.

Kramer was on *Musical America*'s staff from 1910 to 1922, and in 1919 he became its Editor-in-Chief. Though bordering on verbosity, his journalistic volubility shows total knowledge and sincerity. More excerpts from his interview with Burleigh testify to his wholehearted support:

> Merit and merit alone has lifted him from obscurity to his present position. . . . He is winning the praise from musicians who withheld it, until he showed that he had in him not the average attainment of a composer of singable songs, but the extraordinary gifts to which his present output in the department of the art-song testifies. . . . He conceals nothing in his career, is ashamed of no past performance.[19]

Still reluctant to consider himself a composer, Burleigh reasoned that he *sang* for a living and had not written an opera nor a long symphonic or choral work. In the same interview he spoke to Kramer of his friend Kitty (Catherine Smiley) Cheatham, reiterating appreciation of their enjoyable professional association during some "delightful afternoons when she brought him out to assist her in the presentation of Negro spirituals." Kitty Cheatham (1865-1946), diseuse, author, lecturer, and pacifist, was the first artist to introduce old Negro songs to European audiences and a pioneer in organizing orchestral concerts for children. Her huge repertoire of over 1,000 songs in nine languages contained numerous works in manuscript by American composers.[20]

Continuing to perform Burleigh's songs and spirituals were black and white singers alike, among them tenor Paul Althouse. Black singers, less famous, were particularly anxious to promote his works in recitals and at benefits and festivals in 1916. Daisy Tapley, a protégée of Mme Hackley, presented some of them at a May festival in Hampton, Massachusetts, and in Dallas, Texas, at a Southern Negro Folk Songs Festival in late July. She gave numerous performances of "The Grey Wolf." As teaching pieces Burleigh's songs had made a valuable contribution to vocal repertoire, and were often presented on studio recitals.

In Demand

In early September of 1916 Burleigh was invited by Joel E. Sping-arn to "Troutbeck," his country home, for the Amenia Conference, whose purpose was to discuss race relations and promotion of worthy blacks. No specific reason was given in Burleigh's declination letter for not attending.[21]

On September 19 Burleigh was soloist at businessman Seth Low's funeral, held at St. George's Church. Low had been Mayor of Brooklyn, elected in 1900 for two terms. He had also served as President of Columbia University and as Chairman of the Board of Directors at Tuskegee Institute.[22]

That same month *Crisis* magazine, the official organ of the NAACP edited by W. E. B. DuBois, chose Burleigh as one of five "Men of the Month." The others were picked from education, architecture, and the ministry.

Not only was Burleigh's wisdom in demand, but as a singer he was as popular as ever. On October 5 he shared a concert with tenor Charles Waters and reader Fannie Belle De Knight at the Fleet Street Memorial A. M. E. Zion Church. In announcing the concert Lucien White of the *Age* praised Burleigh and expressed a personal desire to hear him sing his own compositions.

> For one thing, his songs, especially the recent ones are all of an unusual character. Their degree of difficulty places them out of the scope of most of the amateur singers of the race, consequently, as these . . . are the only ones heard by the majority . . . of the race, it is seldom that the people have an opportunity to hear the compositions of this man who in the realm of music is no longer a mediocrity. Person-ally, I'd be glad . . . to hear Mr. Burleigh interpret a number of his more recent songs.

Speaking of Melville Charlton, Burleigh's able accompanist, White said, "his work attracts the most critical favor wherever he is heard. It deserves it, too, for Charlton's art has a solid foundation." To a packed house Burleigh sang two programmed songs and two encores, not his own, "with consummate art and gave great pleasure to the audience."[23]

Melville Charlton, Burleigh's accompanist, c. 1918. Used by permission of the American Guild of Organists.

Though he was unable to fill an engagement offered by the St. Cecilia Society in Grand Rapids on October 21, the *Grand Rapids Press* of the following day reported that Burleigh and the American dancer Lada had been discussed at the meeting. At the time Lada, composer-pianist Charles Wakefield Cadman, and Princess Tsianina, a Native American singer discovered by Cadman, were receiving goodly recognition by the *Courier*.

Cadman and the Princess toured the United States, once performing to an audience of 7,000 in Kansas City. Their act usually consisted of Cadman's playing his own piano pieces, followed by a talk on Indian music, customs and instruments, while Tsianina, "Red Feather of the Oklahoma Creek tribe, in white doeskin attire, beads, and a red feather in her hair, sang in a dramatic manner Mr. Cadman's songs." The Princess designed and sewed all of her costumes. Actually, her presumed Creek or Cherokee heritage was not fully determined, nor did it seem to matter.[24]

On October 27 Burleigh did present a program at the First Baptist Church in Minneapolis. The review from a Minneapolis critic which reached the *Courier* said:

> The Afro-American song writer and lecturer . . . played his own accompaniments on the piano and the whole program was an artistic success. The large audience was grateful to this singer for bringing a touch of the old time Negro song and the real pathos of the race.

In one early November recital in the Harris Theater in New York tenor Charles Harrison was accompanied by both Burleigh and Cadman in their songs. No review followed the concert, though both the *Age* and the *Courier* carried announcements on November 2 and 9, 1916, respectively.

1916-17: Busy and Productive Years

"On Inishmaan: Isles of Aran," composed by Burleigh in 1916 but not published until the following year, was dedicated to Christine Miller, who premiered it in early October 1916. Besides this "cleverly written" piece, Miller also performed "The Grey Wolf" at the Ziegfeld Theater in Chicago for the first of a series of artist recitals

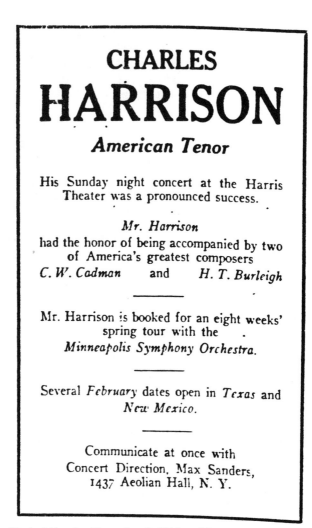

CHARLES
HARRISON
American Tenor

His Sunday night concert at the Harris
Theater was a pronounced success.

Mr. Harrison
had the honor of being accompanied by two
of America's greatest composers
C. W. Cadman   and   *H. T. Burleigh*

———

Mr. Harrison is booked for an eight weeks'
spring tour with the
Minneapolis Symphony Orchestra.

———

Several *February* dates open in *Texas* and
New Mexico.

———

Communicate at once with
Concert Direction, Max Sanders,
1437 Aeolian Hall, N. Y.

From *Musical Courier*, November 9, 1916, p. 26.

inaugurated by Carl Kinsey. In late October Miller repeated these
songs for the Tuesday Musical Club of Pittsburgh and in her Aeolian
Hall recital when "she sang as she always sings. Let that suffice."[25]

Another Burleigh enthusiast during 1916 was tenor William Wheeler, a professional church singer and an avid folksong hobbyist, collector, and lecturer. Wishing to popularize some of Burleigh's seldom-heard arrangements he sang two of them on his first public concert at Aeolian Hall on November 2. Emma Roberts, a sound interpreter of Burleigh's works, was mentioned in a *Times* review for "Deep River" after her Aeolian Hall recital on November 23. "Folk songs were represented on her program as they are on the programs of most intelligent singers."[26]

In December 1916, the *Courier* noted several performances of Burleigh's works, including those by Percy Hemus, Edgar Schofield, and Mary Jordan. Jordan featured the composer in Newark and Philadelphia with, among other of his works, "In the Wood of Finvara," dedicated to her, but not published until 1917. Even the Metropolitan's contentious Frances Alda was singing Burleigh. Nelda Hewitt Stevens's recital at the 39th Street Theater in New York, which included Burleigh's spirituals, was given in authentic costume enhanced by an antebellum parlor setting.

The year 1917 began happily for Burleigh. He was an important part of the dedication of Paul L. Dunbar High School in Washington, DC, during its week of programs, January 13-20, 1917. On January 17 he and Professor Roy W. Tibbs, organist from Howard University, gave the entire evening's program. One of Burleigh's selections was "A Corn Song" to a text by the late poet Dunbar.[27]

Earlier, on January 7, Burleigh's "Three Shadows" was amply exposed when McCormack sang it at the Hippodrome before an audience of 7,000. It never, however, gained the popularity of Burleigh's "Little Mother of Mine," one of McCormack's standards after its publication in 1917. Several accounts have been given of one spectacular evening when he performed "Little Mother of Mine" at the Hippodrome. Approximately 1,000 people were seated on the stage behind the singer. "At the close of the song the audience rose in an ovation and Mr. McCormack insisted that Burleigh, who sat near him, should go forward with him to acknowledge the applause." Other accounts agree that Burleigh, smiling modestly, declined the honor. "You went, of course?" he was asked. He shook his head. "I couldn't. I couldn't. But he sang it wonderfully."[28]

McCormack not only supported Burleigh professionally but also as a concerned human being. Appalled at racial injustices inflicted on blacks, he on at least one occasion acted in Burleigh's behalf, according to an incident related in the *Erie Morning News*, October 19, 1970, by Mili Roberts. The tenor was so outraged that Burleigh was asked to use the freight elevator in a New York hotel that he immediately intervened with the manager.

McCormack's gargantuan schedule required a repertoire of the same proportions, though most of his adoring audiences would have been content to hear the same songs repeatedly. In early March of 1917 the tenor gave four recitals in Boston within eight days at a "One Man Festival of Song." For this marathon he programmed a total of fifty-eight songs with no duplications. The entire programs, excluding his forty-one encores, were printed in the *Courier*, March 15, 1917 (p.26). The last one, all in English, included three compositions by Burleigh:

IV.

One Year (1914-15)	H.T. Burleigh
Your Eyes	Edwin Schneider
Cradle Song	Hamilton Heard
Her Portrait	John Melvin
When I Awake	H. T. Burleigh
Unmindful of the Roses	Edwin Schneider
The Day is Done	Margaret R. Lang
The Trumpeter	Arlie Dix
The Bitterness of Love	James Dunn
One Gave Me a Rose	Edwin Schneider
Deep River (Old Negro Melody) Arranged by	H. T. Burleigh
Exaltation	Mrs. H. H. A. Beach
O Moon Upon the Waters	Charles W. Cadman
A California Troubadour	Henry Hadley
Go Lovely Rose	John A. Carpenter
The Sea Hath Its Pearls	Rudolph Ganz

Of Burleigh's dozen spiritual arrangements published in 1917, the revision of "Deep River" remained his most outstanding and the work for which he would be best remembered. Though dedicated to and frequently sung by Mary Jordan, it was also performed by nearly every other concert artist in subsequent years. Its appeal and pathos were irresistible. Issued in three keys, its uniqueness was significant partially for its fitting accompaniment, an element previously undeveloped in the arrangement of Negro spirituals. Commended for rich harmonic treatment and superb balance of vocal line with accompaniment, it took the musical world by storm.

Kramer suggested that the spirituals issued in 1917 were arranged especially for Oscar Seagle, though there is no dedication on the published scores to this effect. In any case, Seagle put them on the musical map, so to speak, with his total endorsement of them. He was the "first artist to include an entire group of Burleigh spirituals in a vocal recital of significance. Seagle complained, however, that some white singers dropped Burleigh's music when they learned that the composer was black."[29]

The word had spread. Burleigh had actually been brought to the attention of *Courier*'s readers, not as an oddity, but as a composer. Curiosity about his work was addressed by Albert J. Weber who answered a *New York Sun* reader's questions on the subject. Speaking of Burleigh, "the American Negro composer," Weber described his work as

> . . . a development of an idea which has had as its main inception and essential character the bringing out of the peculiar and individual negroid qualities, so far as the theme and rhythm are concerned – of course seriously harmonically treated, but nevertheless with the idea of establishing a splendid and delightful color in his work and the existence of a characteristic that he attributes solely to the Southern plantation negro.[30]

The *Courier* began to report several performances of Burleigh's works each month during 1917, not only in the New York area but throughout the country, by both soloists and choral societies. Additionally, the students of the Witherspoon studio used them. Frieda Hempel, Alice Nielson, and Arthur Hackett were among the better advertised soloists popularizing them.

This year Burleigh's "In the Wood of Finvara" was performed for the first time in New York at Aeolian Hall on February 8 by Mary Jordan. A part of the *Courier*'s review for February 15, 1917, read:

> While "In the Wood of Finvara" was being sung one felt
> throughout the audience the tenseness with which they
> received a thing of great and fleeting beauty. The pianissimo
> climax of the song melted away in a hush of profound
> stillness broken by tremendous applause. . . . Miss Jordan
> was fairly overwhelmed with flowers, which overflowed the
> piano and made a bower of the stage.

Christine Miller was swamped with up to fifteen engagements per
month. McCormack plunged unselfishly into the war effort by giving
benefit performances, raising phenomenal amounts for worthy organizations, such as the Red Cross, various liberty bond campaigns, and
relief funds. He became treasurer of the Red Cross Musician's Unit
in the United States.

In both April and May Burleigh's works were heard in Erie. On
April 29 McCormack sang to an audience of 4,000 there in Exposition Hall. The *Erie Dispatch*, April 30, 1917, reported:

> Two songs of marked interest in the last group were
> Burleigh's "Deep River" and "Your Eyes" by the accompa-
> nist, Edwin Schneider. The singer's interpretation of "Deep
> River" accorded well with the merit of the song and Erie's
> esteem of the writer, a native of this city.

On May 7 Erie's Apollo Club, a men's chorus, sang Burleigh's
"Mother O' Mine" at its third annual music festival.[31]

On May 17, Burleigh received the Spingarn Medal, an award
given by Dr. Joel E. Spingarn, author and former professor of
literature at Columbia University, at that time in the U.S. Army
awaiting his commission as Major. Interestingly, the Jewish
Dr. Spingarn had been president of the New York branch of the
National Association for the Advancement of Colored People
(NAACP) and was presently chairman of its National Board of
Directors. The medal had been presented annually since 1915

> . . . to the man or woman of African descent and
> American citizenship who shall have made the highest
> achievement during the preceding year or years in any field
> of elevated or honorable human endeavor.[32]

Under the auspices of the NAACP, at the First Congregational Church in Washington, DC, the medal, donated by Spingarn, was presented to Burleigh by the Honorable Wesley L. Jones, U.S. Senator from Washington. Mr. Moorfield Story of Boston, the national president of NAACP, presided at the gathering of 700 people. Burleigh was chosen by a committee composed of Bishop John Hurst of Baltimore; Honorable William Howard Taft; Dr. John Hope, president of Morehouse College, Atlanta; Dr. James H. Dilliard, director of the Slater and Jeannes Funds; and Mr. Oswald Garrison Villard of the *New York Evening Post.*

Not limited to any particular field, the committee chose from a wide range, encompassing the intellectual, spiritual, commercial, physical, scientific, and educational. Winning the Spingarn Medal, valued at $100, "has come to be the greatest honor which can be conferred on an American Negro," a writer for the *Cincinnati Union* reported. Speaking of Burleigh's output to date the article continued:

> Mr. Burleigh's compositions include about 100 songs, a few festival anthems for church chorus and a volume of plantation melodies which he compiled in an effort to save them from falling into oblivion. . . . The winner is a composer whose songs have for two or three seasons past been sung by a list of prominent singers which would make any composer's mouth water, from John McCormack to Kitty Cheatham. . . . These creative achievements have necessarily been snatched from a life of routine musical toil, by which Mr. Burleigh has earned his daily bread. . . . The achievements last year which won Mr. Burleigh the Spingarn Medal are but the mature fruitage of a long life of consecrated labor.[33]

Other news of the award was carried that year in the *Washington Bee*, May 26, and the *Crisis* for July. The *Courier*, June 14, at least mentioned the event in its "I See That – " column: "Harry T. Burleigh was awarded the Spingarn Medal." The *Age*, May 17, carried a front page article with Burleigh's photograph.

Spingarn became national president of the NAACP in 1936, a position held until his death in 1939. His brother Arthur B. Spingarn, a Manhattan lawyer, succeeded him in the presidency in 1940, and in 1948 donated his books, newspapers, manuscripts, and other relics of Afro-American lore collected over a thirty-five year period to the Moorland-Spingarn Research Center, a vital part of the Howard University Archives. He died in 1971 at the age of ninety-three.[34]

Burleigh's energy was enviable. In June 1917, under the *Baltimore Afro-American*'s tall headline "Big Crowd Hears Burleigh Sing," was a thrilling concert review about the "Premiere Baritone of the Race." At the Bethel A. M. E. Church in Baltimore Burleigh shared an evening of song with the Cosmopolitan Choral Society and the Amphion Glee Club. Once again Melville Charlton accompanied on both piano and organ. For the packed audience of between twelve and fourteen hundred persons,

> The centre of attraction was Mr. Burleigh, who recently was awarded the Spingarn Medal for excellence as a singer and composer. Mr. Burleigh sang the Prologue of Pagliacci, "The Trumpeter" by Arlie Dix, Coleridge-Taylor's "Corn Song" and "Danny Deever" by Damrosch. Into this last number the singer put the full volume of his baritone voice, rich and melodious despite his fifty-one years, until the house was taken by storm. The applause did not cease until Mr. Burleigh appeared again and sang an encore. Most of the audience called for "The Young Warrior," . . . and were rather disappointed that he did not bring the music with him.[35]

Burleigh accompanied himself in a last group of four spirituals which he had arranged: "Swing Low, Sweet Chariot," "Dig My Grave Long and Narrow," "Sinner Don't Let Dis Harves' Pass," and "I Don't Feel No Ways Tired."

Documentation of separate performances of Burleigh's works during 1917 would comprise a catalog of its own. As a composer and arranger Burleigh remained well in the spotlight. Most singers, including Burleigh, were doing more singing than ever, a goodly part of which aided the war effort. McCormack made many American homes familiar with "Little Mother of Mine" via talking machines. Pasquale Amato, whose veins coursed with native Italian blood, was now a member of the Advisory Council of the Italian Ambulance in Italy, a group supplying ambulances to the front.

The *Erie Dispatch*, April 30 and May 1, 1917, announced and reviewed a concert by Paul Althouse and Zabetta Brenska in that city's Masonic Hall. Burleigh's "The Young Warrior" was spoken of as "one of the best productions of this Erie composer, and one which has won approval abroad as well at home." The review's headline read: "Burleigh Numbers Feature [of] Althouse – Brenska Recital." The hall overflowed. Chairs were placed in the foyer and people stood at the entrance. Brenska sang "Deep River" as an encore after her first group. American art songs comprised most of Althouse's program. "Warrior" was "best liked in its group for the sake of his [Burleigh's] nativity." Althouse sang "Just You" as an encore, and his last group included "The Glory of the Day Was in Her Face" from *Passionale.*

Most biographical material on Burleigh states that he was awarded an honorary Master of Arts degree from Atlanta University in 1918. Perhaps this was not the correct year, since the *Age* of June 7, 1917, gave the award date as May 30, 1917. Both Burleigh and J. Rosamond Johnson, now director of the New York Music School Settlement, were honored similarly. The degrees were presented by former president Reverend Horace Bumstead, who described Burleigh as

> a composer and interpreter of music, a broad-minded, congenial man, welcome in the homes of wealth and in the humblest cottages, attacking the fastnesses of prejudice by the winsome power of song and good will.

Burleigh responded at a reception that evening, "giving a characteristic impromptu song recital."

In early October of 1917 Burleigh's works were performed at two festivals. At the second annual American Musical Convention in Lockport, New York, originated and coordinated by Albert A. van de Mark, Burleigh's name was listed as a composer whose works would be performed in the course of the five days of programs. More specifically, at the third concert of the Maine Music Festival on October 2, "One Year 1914-1915" was sung by Vernon Stiles, and perhaps of even more significance fabulous Christine Miller premiered "The Sailor's Wife," written for and dedicated to her. It was soon to become an audience favorite.

Early in November Eva Burleigh collapsed on the street from a heart attack. Mentioned in the *Age*, November 7, 1917, as the sister of Elzie Elmendorf and Harry T. Burleigh, she had most recently been associated with the Urban League and the Sojourner of Truth House. After a funeral in New York Miss Burleigh was to be buried in Erie.

Mary Jordan helped to popularize the dozen or so spirituals arranged by Burleigh in 1917, which remained some of his very finest. Of these she performed "Weepin' Mary," "My Way's Cloudy," "Nobody Knows de Trouble I've Seen," and "I Want to be Ready" in an Aeolian Hall concert on November 15. The *Musical Courier* printed opposing reviews of her performance, while seeing fit to mention that Burleigh was in the audience. Of Jordan's spiritual offerings the next day's *New York Evening Mail* reported: "The singer was at her best in Burleigh's arrangements of Negro spirituals, in which her ecclesiastical experience helped out her natural dramatic sense." The *New York World* was less impressed, remarking, "Something of the essence of the spirituals was lacking."[36]

Burleigh's rewardingly productive year of 1917 closed with some memorable performances of his works. On November 15, as Mary Jordan captivated her audience in Aeolian Hall, Roland Hayes drew the largest crowd ever assembled in Boston's Symphony Hall, excepting that attending a recent McCormack concert. Accompanied by Burleigh, "the most notable of colored composers," Hayes sang "Swing Low, Sweet Chariot," "By and By," and "Go Down Moses." "There were many recalls and the tenor added H. T. Burleigh's 'Mother O' Mine' and the 'Deep River' arrangement."[37] Accompanist William Lawrence, who played the other songs, was to remain with Hayes, "the leading Negro tenor," for several years, as they concertized throughout the United States and Europe. A Baltimore concert on November 26 by the Germania Maennerchor featured Anna M. Diener as soloist in three Burleigh spirituals.[38]

On December 13 Florence Hinkle (Mrs. Herbert Witherspoon), soloing with the Junger Maennerchor's concert in Scranton, Pennsylvania, sang "Nobody Knows de Trouble I've Seen." Three days later the Madison Avenue A. M. E. choir participated in a multi-choir concert in New York, performing "Deep River," "Father Abraham," and "So Sad." Later in December Margaret Woodrow Wilson, daughter of the U.S. president, gave a benefit recital in Charleston, South Carolina, for the American War Relief Fund. The critics felt that she was her best in "Deep River," catching its real spirit.

Burleigh was called the "hero of the hour" at the twenty-fifth anniversary concert of the Musical Art Society in Carnegie Hall on December 18. Conducted by Frank Damrosch, the orchestra played three of Burleigh's arrangements, after which the composer rose and acknowledged tribute from the audience for the spirituals, which were every bit as impressive as the program's other segments.[39]

The War Years (1918-19)

Many of the musical events in 1918 were firmly in support of the war effort. Quite a number of concert artists had enlisted in the service. As a singer Burleigh did his patriotic share for morale, performing generously when called. At least one black group travelled overseas to entertain and cheer troops of their own race.[40]

By fall of 1918 the massive flu epidemic had victimized so many artists that concerts were routinely cancelled. Due to the increasing popularity of patriotic songs, such as "There's a Long Long Trail" and "Keep the Home Fires Burning," American composers felt a new challenge. Music publishing companies advertised more than ever before. G. Schirmer sponsored recitals featuring its own publications, and much of the latest sheet music could be had for ten cents a copy.

The programming of American composers had become a matter of the artist's good taste. Burleigh's works were suffering no lack of performance, with "Deep River" leading in popularity. Additionally, lecturers cited him and his works frequently. Even the formerly begrudging and ambivalent *Courier* was relenting a bit, as evidenced in a complimentary review of Alma Gluck's concert in St. Louis on January 15, stating that "she could not avoid singing two of the negro spirituals by Harry Burleigh, applause bringers which are eagerly sung by nine out of ten this winter."[41] Earlier that month Liebling gave adequate biographies of both Burleigh and Coleridge-Taylor in answer to a reader's query on the two, Burleigh's actually receiving over twice the space of the Englishman's.

H. T. Burleigh, c. 1918-1920. Courtesy of Dr. David Cantrell.

Contralto Emma Parenteau and the Apollo Club shared a concert in Erie on February 1. The *Erie Dispatch* reviewer mentioned her pleasing interpretation of a group of Burleigh's spirituals which merited an encore. This same month the *Courier* announced that after a brief rest by doctor's orders, Christine Miller had married wealthy and prominent Pittsburgh steel manufacturer Daniel M. Clemson, who evidently took a dim view of his new wife's frantic schedule as a recitalist. After several months' absence from professional circulation, Christine Miller Clemson began to donate her services for war benefits and philanthropic causes.

At Jordan Hall in Boston on February 14 Burleigh accompanied violinist Clarence Cameron White and singer Lillian Evans. Burleigh's own works heard that evening were *Southland Sketches* performed by White and three spirituals and two art songs by Evans.

Tenor Theo Karle's March 3 recital in San Francisco prompted at least three reviews, parts of which are pertinent:

> Burleigh's "Little Mother of Mine" was rendered in a manner that brought distinction to both composer and artist – indeed, it proved one of the songs in which the artist was at his best.

Another, in speaking of his group of English "songs of tenderness," commented:

> Certainly from the group "Little Mother of Mine" by Burleigh will not be forgotten soon, and its very simplicity was the charm that the singer himself expressed his approval of with its choice on the list, and its repetition when the audience clamored for it.[42]

In April the *Courier*, remarking on the "plethora of negro spirituals these days," reported that Burleigh assisted in arrangements of such pieces for another Schola Cantorum concert at Carnegie Hall on April 9. In the same issue he was complimented on a later concert:

> H. T. Burleigh, the well known composer, known as "Harry" Burleigh by his friends, and also as "Burley Harry" by older friends, sang as soloist in "The Crucifixion" in Brooklyn during Holy Week. Burleigh's voice is heard too little in solos. He sings his own negro spirituals especially well.

A few weeks earlier the *Evening Star* of Lynn, Massachusetts, had reported somewhat floridly on a concert in that city given March 4 by John Finnegan, celebrated tenor soloist from St. Patrick's Cathedral in New York City.

> The Cathedral tenor thrilled the concert crowd at the Strand. One little song was worth it all – it was a rare gem

– the heart-appealing "Little Mother of Mine" by Burleigh
was easily the distinctive number at the concert. Finnegan
. . . superbly interpreted the song, a song that brought back
memories of childhood days, or the halcyon past when we
bent at mother's knee. He sang it with a tenderness that
gripped all; the lovely tones accentuated the lovely story told.
In that one song Mr. Finnegan showed his sterling worth as
an artist . . . the master number of his program in the
writer's opinion, "Little Mother of Mine."

Though Burleigh's vocal works were more popular than his
instrumental ones, a combination program was presented with
violinist Cyril Towbin's performance of *Southland Sketches* on
April 23 at a meeting of the Musical Art Club in New York. Burleigh
accompanied Dorothy Edwards, who sang "In the Wood of Finvara"
and three of his spirituals. Of the affair the *Courier*, May 2, 1918,
reported that Burleigh also made "some interesting remarks." They
repeated the performance on May 26 for the American Music
Optimists in the New York Hotel Marseilles.

Henry Burleigh, the composer who has done so much
for the music of the negro, was present, and played the
accompaniment for three of his songs. . . . Mr. Burleigh
preceded these numbers by a short interesting talk on the
negro spiritual which is not to be confused with minstrel
singing.[43]

According to the *Age* Burleigh gave two performances in May, at
the YWCA in Brooklyn and at the Lexington Opera House in New
York City for the 369th Infantry. At the latter concert he was
accompanied by Charlton and afterwards given a big reception.
Among his selections were "Danny Deever" and two other patriotic
songs. Earlier, on May 3, Burleigh had "added to the excellence of
the well selected program" of the University Glee Club in Providence, Rhode Island, his first performance in that city. The *Courier*
for June 6, 1918 stated that the "large audience was greatly pleased
with his work," and also gave news of five singers who had performed
Burleigh's works during May.

Burleigh was one of the featured composers at the 1918 Ohio Music Teachers' Association, June 25-28 in Cincinnati. He accompanied Mary Jordan, who sang "In the Wood of Finvara," plus five spirituals. "Mr. Burleigh . . . explained in clear language the 'spirituals,' adding greatly to the interest of their delivery." Others of his songs were given at a reception during the convention by Mrs. F. A. Seiberling of Akron.[44]

A listing of 160 composers represented on twenty-one programs at the Lockport, New York, National American Music Festival held September 2-8, 1918, included Burleigh. That same month American baritone Francis Rogers, contributing journalist to the *Courier*, Juilliard professor, and author of *Some Famous Singers of the Nineteenth Century*, compiled a special list published in the *Courier*, October 3, 1918, titled "Songs the Soldiers Like." First position went to "Negro Spirituals," and "Little Mother of Mine" was on another roster of approximately fifty favorites.

But Burleigh's name never appeared in the *Courier*'s running column "Concert Record of Best American Composers." Though this list included many of the leading art song composers of the time, Editor Liebling apparently would not acknowledge, at least in print, the high quality of Burleigh's works in this genre. In the November 7, 1918, issue he compared the merits of Burleigh and Coleridge-Taylor:

> He [Burleigh] is principally known as a composer of songs and has by no means the musical standing of Coleridge-Taylor, whose compositions in larger form are among the best modern works of the kind. . . . Curiously enough neither of these negro composers were born either in negro countries or in any parts of countries where negroes predominate.

The *Courier*'s lack of recognition must have been easy enough for Burleigh to ignore when he was so well represented in sellout concerts by Althouse, McCormack, Hayes, and others of their stature. *Musical America* carried numerous notices of concerts on which Burleigh's works were to be heard. Baritone Royal Dadmun, to whom Burleigh later dedicated "De Gospel Train," sang four of his spirituals as guest soloist for the Singers Club in Cleveland on December 12.

The years 1917 and 1918 marked the first publication of Burleigh's arrangements for ensemble, the beginning of an expansion based on their increasing popularity. As an arranger his works increased the repertoires of many choral clubs in the United States.

Throughout 1919 Roland Hayes's performances kept Burleigh before the musical public. At his formal debut in New York's Aeolian Hall on January 30, he sang four of the spirituals and two of Burleigh's art songs, accompanied by the composer. The *New York Times* reviewer spoke of the spirituals as "racy, of the flavor of the old soil," and of Hayes's use of the "unctious [sic] humor and pathos of his race." " 'Peter, Go Ringa dem Bells' . . . set one's feet unconsciously stepping to ragtime." Hayes "earned an uproarious recall" for "Didn't It Rain." The *Courier*'s comments were favorable:

> Starting with two songs by Burleigh (the composer at the piano) he showed his expressive lyric quality of tone in "By the Pool," and his contrasting verve in "Ahmed's Farewell." A high B flat, dainty mezza voce and pathos came to the fore in these songs, making effect. . . . Of course Mr. Burleigh's accompaniments to his own songs were beautiful.[45]

Hayes's beautiful singing of the spirituals that year continued with recitals in Louisville, February 16; San Diego in May; Wilmington, North Carolina, in late June; New Bedford, Connecticut, in October; and Boston's Symphony Hall on December 4. For the latter he purposefully chose four groups by black composers to show the steady development of Afro-American music. Another recital in June was shared with Ethel Smith in a Boston church, where he again presented the spirituals.

A second October recital in New Bedford must have added to Burleigh's prestige there according to a review sent to the *Courier* a few weeks later:

> The current musical season opened here on the evening of October 31 with a recital devoted largely to spirituals of H. T. Burleigh, given by a colored woman, Lyllian J. Gwynn. Mrs. Gwynn rendered these favorite songs with a remarkable

degree of life, vitality and keen understanding of their musical content. . . . She had the advantage of . . . Burleigh's supervision last summer, when he spent a few days with her and her husband at Martha's Vineyard.

During 1919 the *Courier* made mention of approximately forty singers who had programmed Burleigh's songs that year. Tenor Charles Harrison, on seasonal tour with the Columbia Stellar Quartet, received a dedication from Burleigh of "A Song of Rest." This and Burleigh's "Under a Blazing Star" became staples in Harrison's repertoire and were used on nearly every concert that he gave during the year. Mary Jordan often programmed a group of spirituals and another of Burleigh's art songs, and was able to express them well due to her personal delight with their uniqueness. Jordan, who sold $25,000 worth of war bonds in two hours at a performance in May, was once referred to as "Lady John McCormack."

Reviews of a few isolated concerts during the year are of interest. Emma Roberts, in an Aeolian Hall recital on January 7, sang "darky tunes" and a spiritual arranged by Burleigh that "stirred the lachrymal ducts." After a New York performance by Greta Torpadie, Burleigh was praised: "Harry Burleigh, who, if you are in search of a representative American composer, will serve better than some more celebrated names, was on the program." And at the Hippodrome an audience of 6,000 heard McCormack sing "Were I a Star" for the first time: "New songs such as H. T. Burleigh's 'Were I a Star' shared attention with McCormack's favorite Irish songs."[46]

Dr. Clarence Dickinson, organist, presented a lecture recital at the Union Theological Seminary on February 25 on "Music in America," having invited Burleigh as his soloist. Still an active accompanist, Burleigh assisted tenor George Dale in some of his compositions at the Pouch Gallery in Brooklyn on May 14. Dale was then soloist at New York's Little Church Around the Corner.

Peripheral events during the first half of 1919 bear mention. The *Age* dwelt oppressively but necessarily on the war in retrospect, giving the utmost praise to the black soldiers. Mounting race atrocities and lynchings were reported at length. Former President Theodore Roosevelt died in his sleep and James Reese Europe was fatally stabbed by a crazed drummer in his band.

Madame Ernestine Schumann-Heink, 1906.

But all the news was not dismal. St. George's Church presented Burleigh with a valuable watch, marking his twenty-fifth year as soloist with the choir. Pianist Artur Rubinstein debuted in Carnegie Hall, and Mme Schumann-Heink was heard by 10,000 at a concert on the eve of her fifty-ninth birthday in July. Though this courageous woman had lost her eldest son the previous February, she continued concert tours for the war fund and was an unrivalled favorite with the soldiers. Mary Jordan was wed to Lt. Col. Charles Clement Cresson, though she did not leave her career or augment her professional name.

In July of 1919 the efforts of three years materialized with the organization of the National Association of Negro Musicians (NANM) in Chicago. Notable among the thirteen charter members were music critic Nora Holt (NANM's first president), Nathaniel Dett, and Carl Diton. Burleigh apparently did not join, though he served as chairman of the advisory committee for the 1920 annual convention. Years later he was asked to attend their 1934 convention held in Pittsburgh, an invitation which he declined, according to a society columnist: "That was nice of the great Charles Wakefield Cadman and the talented Harry Burleigh to send greetings from New York!" Though Burleigh did not attend, he was represented by Lillian (Evans) Evanti's performance of "Lord, I Want to Be," arranged especially for her. In the 1920s Evanti was the first American black to sing operatic roles in Europe.[47]

Nine of Burleigh's art songs were published in 1919 by Ricordi. "The Victor," of patriotic flavor, was the only one bearing a dedication: "to all those who gave their lives for the Right." "A Song of Rest," dedicated to Charles Harrison, is still in manuscript. Arrangements of seven spirituals were published, four for both solo voice and ensemble.

The Early 1920s

The decade of the twenties afforded Burleigh no slackening pace or decrease in prestige. Roland Hayes, ever faithful to Burleigh's talents, sang five of his spirituals in Buckingham Palace for King George V in April. Another of his concerts in London, at Wigmore Hall in September was reviewed by the *Musical News and Herald:*

We have to thank Mr. Roland Hayes for making us familiar with the true spirit and inner meaning of Afro-American folk-song "spirituals," and his interpretations of several of these were the distinctive feature of his recital. . . . He was in splendid form . . . in his rendering of a new song – at least, new to many, "Ahmed's Farewell."[48]

On June 11, 1920, an honorary Doctor of Music degree was conferred upon Burleigh at Howard University in Washington, DC, by its president, Dr. Stanley J. Durkee.[49]

Sidney Woodward, William Richardson, Wilson Lamb, Marian Anderson, and Cleota Collins, all black singers, frequently programmed Burleigh's works on their 1920-21 concerts. Burleigh accompanied Judson House's performance of his art songs at the Casino Theater for a Fisk University benefit in late September, 1920.

In March or April of 1921, Burleigh received a form letter signed by Natalie Curtis, Mrs. Harriet Marshall, Wm. Jay Schieffelin (President, Hampton Association), David Mannes (Director of the Mannes School of Music), and George Foster Peabody, asking his patronage in sponsoring a joint effort to present black actors and musicians in a Town Hall performance on April 24. The proceeds would go equally to the Washington Conservatory, Hampton Institute, and Tuskegee Institute.

From the tone of Mrs. Marshall's letter following the concert, one gathers that Burleigh refused to be listed as a patron, an attitude which hurt, insulted, and disappointed her. He was never one to ostentatiously promote Afro-American causes. He did, however, attend the performance, evidently assisting in some way. If he performed, he may have expected to be paid. Too, he may have questioned the Conservatory's financial records. Mrs. Marshall's protesting letter reads in part:

My Dear Mr. Burleigh:
    I was unable to reach you after your phone call, asking if Miss Hughes had an accompanist. I wished to send you complimentary tickets and so many things were on my mind that night, I neglected to mention it.

Please find inclosed check for $1.50 to cover same and accept our cordial thanks for your assistance on the program.

Mr. Burleigh, with most friendly feeling toward you and with greatest admiration for your attainments in our beloved art, I regret sincerely for you and the cause that you see fit to talk as you do concerning our humble effort to contribute to race advancement.

. . . Your remarks at the hall were all overheard and other remarks you have made have been brought to me since, which I am sorry to say are being discussed much to your discredit.

As we are so proud of your position and attainments we grieve over this mistake you are making. The history, status and ideals of the Washington Conservatory are broadly known throughout the country and many prominent people whose integrity is unquestioned can give information concerning its management.

Though an incorporated body, never has its president allowed a just debt go unpaid. Do not think that people will not investigate these things.

It pains me to say that you are the first musician to disparage our efforts. . . . Teachers of Howard Conservatory contributed without cost to the program.

The Locals of the National Association of Colored Musicians in several cities are doing special work for this broad cause. One has already sent a contribution with promise of more.

The work is progressing with great rapidity and I would consider the time wasted in thus writing at length if I did not feel that your ignorance of the actual facts places you in an undesirable position. I will send you our financial statement from 1903 and will let Dean Cook of Howard U and others give you any further information you desire.

Very sincerely
(this draft unsigned)

P. S. Did Mrs. Thurber ask you about the Conservatory some years ago before my long illness about 1910 or 1911?

she said she would and I often wondered if she did as I never heard from her again.

Burleigh's May 12 reply was uncharacteristically brief:

> My dear Mrs. Marshall:
>   Pardon me for returning the check for $1.50, but I cannot accept it.
>   I got more than that amount of pleasure in the unique entertainment and wish I could have contributed more.
>   Very truly yours
>   H. T. Burleigh

No further correspondence between the heretofore friendly associates has been located.

The Howard University Glee Club, conducted by Roy W. Tibbs, sang a new arrangement of "Just You," dedicated to the group by Burleigh, plus two of his spirituals, "Go Down Moses" and "Deep River," on a May 7 concert in 1921. On May 12 Burleigh sang at a post-Lenten concert at St. Philip's Episcopal Church in New York, for which a fifty cents admission fee was charged. Some of his compositions were performed at the NANM convention that August in Nashville, Tennessee, as well as in London. While in the English city that summer Burleigh heard a concert in Wigmore Hall on July 8 by the Royal Southern Singers, who performed his "Adoration" and several spirituals.[50]

The year 1922 marked the passing of two of Burleigh's friends, Bert Williams and Azalia Hackley. Burleigh was honorary pallbearer at Williams's funeral. Mme Hackley's generous efforts through choral activities and her protégées in behalf of black composers, especially Burleigh, were beyond reproach.

On October 14, 1922, Burleigh was guest soloist and speaker for "Cheyney Day" at the Cheyney Training School for Teachers in Pennsylvania.

> Before singing, Mr. Burleigh gave a stimulating talk on Negro folk songs, explaining the circumstances under which they were written, their melodic peculiarities, their Biblical content, and their spiritual values.

Following his inspiring discourse, Mr. Burleigh proved himself an artist not only in his chosen field but as his own accompanist. In his very generous program he preceded each number by a brief analysis, giving to his audience an appreciation and understanding of the treasures he was revealing to them. His skill as an interpreter was at its best in such songs as "Let My People Go," "Steal Away," and "I Don't Feel Noways Tired."

The enthusiastic applause following every number was evidence of the depths to which Mr. Burleigh had stirred his audience.[51]

Philadelphia artist Julia Gilbert sang three of Burleigh's spirituals on a morning program for "Cheyney Day."

Also this year Burleigh funded a scholarship for baritone Frank G. Harrison to both Columbia University Teacher's College and the Institute of Musical Art, Juilliard's predecessor. Harrison later became a college voice professor.[52]

On June 24, 1923, Burleigh gave a concert of spirituals at Ocean Parkway M. E. Church, one of New York's very wealthy and influential white churches. The following September he was on a committee for the New York Music Week Association to structure a forty-five category competition for nonprofessional musicians. Winners of the contests were announced in the *Age* for several months following.

A highly successful concert by Abbie Mitchell in October 1923 moved Burleigh to write Melville Charlton, Mitchell's accompanist for the occasion. The lengthy letter was published in the *Age*, October 20, 1923. After praising the versatile Mitchell's progress "from musical comedy, through the exacting demands of spoken drama on to the dizzy heights of opera," Burleigh commented on her excellent programming of eighteen art songs, and her "special tone color for every emotion." Attributing her sensitive interpretations largely to having studied drama, Burleigh could not seem to say enough of the musicality of his former protégée. Moreover, he was eloquent in speaking of Charlton's impeccable accompaniments.

The following month John Payne, baritone, performed sixteen works by black composers in London's Wigmore Hall. Payne was an American singer and actor who had chosen to make his home in

England. His concert marked the first time an all black-composers program had been presented at the hall; seven of the twelve spirituals listed were by Burleigh. A letter concerning the concert from Englishwoman Lady May Cook was printed in the *Age*, November 10, 1923. In part it read: "Of course, Mr. Harry Burleigh's songs and arrangements are well known and loved in London." Earlier Lady Cook had proved to be a Roland Hayes enthusiast.

By 1924 Marian Anderson was concertizing in some of the major American cities. In January of that year Burleigh was scheduled to appear with her in Philadelphia's Stratton Hotel, but a cold limited his participation to speaking about spirituals and accompanying Webster Blix, who sang in his place.

Between 1920 and 1930 many concerts that included Burleigh's compositions were presented under Hampton Institute auspices, either by the Hampton Institute Choir or by notable visiting artists. On April 2, 1921, the Howard University Glee Club, assisted by young Marian Anderson, programmed Burleigh's "Deep River." That same year Alston Burleigh of Washington was listed in *The Hampton Student* as having been a "reader with the Glee Club." Alston was at this time a student at Howard University.

At Hampton's annual spring concert in May 1924, the choral half, conducted by Nathaniel Dett, was presented as a tribute to Burleigh. On the program were ensemble arrangements of four spirituals, two art songs, *Southland Sketches*, and a processional hymn, all written or arranged by Burleigh.[53] Programs from Hampton Institute spanning two dozen years indicate that Dett was eager to use Burleigh's arrangements for his choir, whether on the home campus or on tour. Dett, however, arranged quite a few of the spirituals himself. Though reviews lauding Dett's expertise as a choir director were exciting, separate performances are too numerous to list.

Anderson sang four of Burleigh's spirituals on a recital at Hampton on December 13, 1929. The previous spring a four-choir National Negro Music Festival had been held in Philadelphia where at least two of the participating groups, the Howard University Glee Club and the Hampton Institute Choir, performed Burleigh's arrangements.

In 1924 plans begun the previous year at St. George's, for the inauguration of a service of Negro spirituals using arrangements and harmonizations by Burleigh, became a reality which continued through 1955. The first tribute concert, a vesper service on March 30, 1924, marked Burleigh's thirtieth anniversary with the choir. An announcement in the *Times* on the preceding day stated that there would be singing of spirituals by the choir and that parts II and III from *Southland Sketches* for violin would be performed. George Kemmer, organist, mailed out hundreds of post cards listing the program, and prepared a special brochure featuring Burleigh, with photos from 1894 and 1924 and a biographical sketch.

The occasion was much publicized. The *Age*, April 5, 1924, carried Burleigh's picture on the front page, proudly stating that his honor was "well deserved." The *New York Times* headline on March 31 read: "Crowds at Church Honor Negro Singer," and "Hundreds Unable to Enter St. George's for Harry T. Burleigh Anniversary Service." A descriptive article followed:

> So dense were the throngs outside that police were called to keep the streets open for traffic. The church was filled and the doors were ordered closed half an hour before the services opened. . . . The program was devoted chiefly to singing by the choir, but Reverend Dr. Karl Reiland, the rector, made a short address in which he referred to Mr. Burleigh as the leading singer of the church and to his long and notable service there.

Maud Cuney-Hare quoted pertinent parts of Reiland's address:

> Mr. Burleigh carries his thirty years' membership in this choir remarkably well indeed. With the years he has changed, but he has not grown old. There has been an ever deepening regard for him with the passage of time. He is a great composer, singer, and musician and a faithful servant in the Chancel of this church. May this day bring him a moiety of that great satisfaction he has given to thousands and cheer his generous and devoted heart.[54]

H. T. Burleigh, c. 1924. Courtesy of Dr. James Hall, Jr.

Before he concluded Dr. Reiland called Burleigh to the pulpit. The *Times* continued:

> There was no applause, of course, but an audible murmur swept through the crowded auditorium as the white-haired Negro, garbed in snowy vestments, stood beside the rector and bowed several times.

Burleigh responded:

> It has indeed been a rare privilege to have been allowed to serve the good people of St. George's Church for so long a time. I am profoundly touched by the honor they are conferring upon me.[55]

As he left the pulpit, the choir sang "I Couldn't Hear Nobody Pray." Burleigh shook hands with many of the visitors afterwards and said: "I hope to make my greatest reputation as an arranger of Negro spirituals. In them my race has pure gold and they should be taken as the Negro's contribution to art." Especially for the service Burleigh arranged "I Hope my Mother Will be There," a simple four-part vesper hymn based largely on Christmas themes.[56]

1924-1928

From 1924 to 1928 Burleigh was an active soloist in a series of broadcasts sponsored by St. George's, among other endeavors. In the summer of 1924 when Roland Hayes was awarded the Spingarn Medal, Burleigh, acting as surrogate, accepted it for him. Hayes was filling engagements abroad and could not be present, according to his biographer, MacKinley Helm.

On April 19 and May 3 of 1925, actor-singer Paul Robeson, now twenty-seven, with no previous vocal training, gave concerts in New York's Greenwich Village Theater. With the aid of family and friends both of them were sold out.

> Carl van Vechten nailed up posters, passed out handbills, and encouraged his friends to attend. Heywood Broun drummed up interest through his column and Walter White ballyhooed the concert through the Associated Negro Press.

A nervous Robeson opened with Burleigh's "Go Down Moses," then
went on with four more spirituals, and accompanist Lawrence Brown
joined spontaneously singing with Robeson a fifth. The entire concert
was a tremendous success, and the first solo concert made up totally
of Negro music to receive such attention.[57]

Speaking of Robeson's interpretation of Negro spirituals the *New
York Times* reviewer on April 20 described them as a

> . . . cry from the depths, this universal humanism that
> touches the heart. The spirituals, arranged by H. T. Burleigh
> . . . were all well known but it was Mr. Robeson's gift to
> make them tell in every line . . . by an overwhelming inward
> conviction . . . they voiced the hopes and sorrows of a
> people.

For the second concert, also reviewed by the *New York Times*, two of
Robeson's encores were Burleigh's spirituals.

In May of 1925 two entire recitals of Burleigh's works, both
mentioned by the *Age*, were given at the Siloam Presbyterian Church
in Brooklyn. One was by the choir on May 10, and the other, two
weeks later, was presented by G. Warren Tarrant.

Also in this month Burleigh retired from the Temple Emanu-
El choir. The Emanu-El Congregation of the City of New York, as
it was now named, acknowledged his twenty-five years of service with
a testimonial inscribed on parchment. It was bound in gold-tooled
Moroccan leather and read:

> You have contributed much to the maintenance of the
> high standard of excellence for which we have striven in the
> musical portion of our services. Your melodious voice and
> your artistic compositions have added greatly to the devo-
> tional attitude of the worshippers within our sanctuary.[58]

Perhaps in order to celebrate the event in his own fashion,
Burleigh vacationed for three months in Europe with his son, Alston,
and, returning in mid or late August, spent the rest of the summer in
Oak Bluffs. On various trips abroad Burleigh spent some time in the
Ricordi office in Milan.[59]

In this year James Weldon Johnson received the Spingarn Medal, Dr. John W. Work passed away, and Melville Charlton dedicated a new organ at Mother A. M. E. Zion Church in Brooklyn in October. His program included Burleigh's "In de Col' Moonlight," possibly arranged especially for the occasion. There is no evidence that the piece, one of the six in *From the Southland* for piano, was published for organ. Burleigh shared a December recital with pianist Lydia Mason in Englewood, New Jersey, singing two groups of spirituals.[60]

In 1926 a young black woman, Eva Jessye, met Burleigh for the first time as she was buying music at Ricordi's. Jessye, then a struggling singer, arranger, and aspiring choral director, had come to New York from Kansas in 1922. She did not see Burleigh often, but they kept in touch and in 1931 collaborated on an arrangement of "Who's Dat Yondah?" for voice and organ. In correspondence in the summer of 1986, Dr. Jessye wrote of him:

> He was cordial to me, though considered cool and almost a snob. He was a fine baritone. . . . He was very critical and impatient, but explained that he found most people ungrateful, but supposed one should assist anyone who aspired.

In conversation she said that "people kept their distance; some were in awe of him, some thought he wanted to disclaim his heritage."[61] Dr. Jessye is remembered as the choral director for the premiere and subsequent performances of *Porgy and Bess*, and as the first black woman to win international distinction for directing a professional choral group.

The *Age*, February 13, 1926, reported that on February 3 of that year Burleigh sang a whole program of spirituals in Rochester, New York, at the YMCA for the Men's Club of St. Paul's Episcopal Church. It was his first visit to that city in twenty years. The next month the vesper service at St. George's was broadcast, prompting letters and poems to Burleigh which were printed in the *Age*, congratulating him and reiterating respect.

In late April the *Age* reported that members of St. George's choir, Reverend Reiland, George Kemmer, and Burleigh were honored at Mother A. M. E. Zion Church in New York. "Harry found himself so overcome with emotion that tears filled his eyes, and his voice failed him for a while." Dr. Reiland was greeted cordially and appreciatively by the large audience, whom he reminded that because of Burleigh's work at St. George's it was the first northern church to use spirituals in its services. Zion pastor Dr. James W. Brown also spoke at the occasion. Burleigh sang solos and was encored. A reception was given by the ladies of the church.

On May 23, 1926, Burleigh was guest soloist with the Trinity Choir Alumni Association in St. Paul's Parish House. Dr. George Mead, choir director at Trinity, recalled Burleigh's polite declination to have dinner with the group, saying that "it might not be right." At the event Burleigh was offered congratulations on his thirty-first year at St. George's and for his broadcasts over WEAF's Edison Hour, on which show he usually sang fifteen minutes of spirituals.

Perhaps in appreciation for its supportive coverage, Burleigh wrote in commemoration of the *Age*'s fortieth year in business. It was the first black newspaper to devote a whole page to music and theater, and provide space for in-depth, unbiased reviews.[62]

Burleigh's activities in 1927 were closely followed by the *Age*. Nearly every weekly issue mentioned a performance of his works by choral groups and solo artists. Occasionally Burleigh was mentioned as one of the audience.

1927 marked Burleigh's thirty-third anniversary at St. George's. At the service of spirituals on May 22, all but three arrangements were by Burleigh. He sang four of them himself, including "I've Been in the Storm So Long," not published at the time. A week later the *Age* reported:

> The large congregation gave Dr. Burleigh an ovation and many of the most distinguished members of the wealthy and aristocratic church were present and added their personal congratulations to Dr. Burleigh.

Burleigh was asked to conduct the Howard University Glee Club at Town Hall on May 31, an engagement not met, though Alston Burleigh was a reader on the concert. On June 15 Burleigh was soloist and delivered the commencement address at Cheyney Normal School.

In the news this year were Charles Lindbergh; Ethel Waters, a new star reprimanded for her impersonation of Josephine Baker; and

"Fats" Waller, organist at the Lafayette Theater. Popular dancer and comedy star Florence Mills died, the stage play *Porgy* had its premiere, and James Weldon Johnson was a second place winner of the Harmon Award.

In the fall of 1927 Burleigh enjoyed participating in and receiving honors at two events. At the first, an informal lecture recital on November 10 at Larchmont Avenue Church in Larchmont, New York, he sang ten of his own spiritual arrangements, accompanying himself. The program, reviewed in the November 13 *Age* and titled "From Bach to Burleigh," also featured soprano Ella Belle Davis and her sister Marie, pianist. It was presented to a mixed audience who

> braved the exceedingly inclement weather. . . . The reception accorded Dr. Burleigh . . . was a distinctive tribute to his musical attainment and well-deserved personal popularity.

Burleigh, judged as good an orator as a musician,

> spoke briefly of the wonderful quality contained in the Negro folksong and declared that its belated recognition as a musical quantity was really a reflection upon the boasted cultural perception of our Nordic neighbors.

The review further mentioned Burleigh's running commentary on efforts to correlate harmonic arrangements with the spirit of the original melodies, accentuating the "marvelous imagery and descriptive beauty of the race conception." Burleigh recollected a previously unpublicized association with Edward MacDowell, who influenced his arrangements of spirituals, in particular "Swing Low, Sweet Chariot," somewhat clarifying the sophistication of his settings of melodies of primitive origin as noted by many critics.[63]

Back in June Burleigh had been selected as one of five judges of the Wanamaker Negro Composer Awards recognizing the best compositions by Afro-American composers. He had lectured and sung on several occasions for the Robert C. Ogden Association, formed by an associate of the Wanamaker stores. Wanamaker's employed blacks in many of their departments, a policy copied for a while by their competitors.

On November 23 he was "surprised by the presentation of an exquisite gold watch of French make, bearing on its back the simple inscription 'H. B'." Inside it read:

> Presented to Harry Burleigh by the Robert C. Ogden Association of the John Wanamaker Store, Philadelphia, Wednesday evening, Nov. 23, 1927 in recognition of his constant desire to bring joy with beautiful music to all mankind.

The watch remained one of Burleigh's most cherished possessions.

On November 29 Burleigh was an honored guest of ASCAP in Central Park for the unveiling of a statue of Victor Herbert, Burleigh's longtime friend, who had died in 1924.[64]

By 1928 Burleigh was scheduling fewer concerts outside St. George's, though he continued to be in demand and apparently his energy was unflagging. Duties at Ricordi pretty well occupied his time, however. This year James Weldon Johnson was first place winner in literature of the Harmon Award. Lester Walton, former music critic for the *Age*, directed *Meek Mose*, a play about blacks effectively interpolating several spirituals. Alston Burleigh, a member of the cast, was also musical director.

The Hall Johnson Choir, Bill "Bojangles" Robinson, singer-teacher Wilson Lamb, and Noble Sissle were receiving ample publicity. Spirituals and new arrangements of them were definitely in vogue. Paul Robeson had just dazzled London audiences with *Showboat*. Marian Anderson was preparing an American tour under Judson Management. Hoover was the new U.S. president. W. E. Harmon died in July. John W. Work, Jr., had recently succeeded his deceased father as head of the Fisk University Music Conservatory. Dr. Melville Charlton was now organist and choir director at New York's St. James Presbyterian Church.

Burleigh's close friend, Carlette Thomas, had carved a niche for herself. Thomas, still a young lady, studied piano with an assistant of Ernest Hutchinson at Juilliard and in June of 1928, via strenuous examination, became an Associate of the American Guild of Organists.

Lucien White reviewed a gala broadcast from NBC in the *Age*, February 28, 1928. Sponsored by General Motors, the Frigidaire

Hour featured Burleigh in one group of spirituals with the Hall Johnson Jubilee Singers and another with chorus and organ. "Deep River," also with chorus, was accompanied by a concert band directed by Edwin Franko Goldman. Roderic Graham conducted an orchestra in part of Dvorak's *From the New World*. On another broadcast on April 27 over Station WGBS Burleigh shared a lecture recital of spirituals with singer Roberta Bosley. She was later a popularity contest winner over station WEVD, having used his spirituals in the competition.

Burleigh served as Chairman of the Harlem Music Committee, under YMCA auspices, for Music Week programs, May 7-12, 1928, helping select and supervise six programs for a general theme, "The Story of Music." On May 14 he was soloist in Erie at Academy High School in a concert by the Girls' Chorus, directed by Morton J. Luvaas. He sang eight of his spirituals in two groups, and the chorus performed some of his arrangements.[65]

The annual vesper service at St. George's took place on May 27. This was Burleigh's thirty-fourth year there. He sang four spirituals, the choir two. Edwin Ideler played Burleigh's arrangements for solo violin. The program was announced in St. George's *Bulletin* for May 20, 1928.

Burleigh spent August of 1928 in Oak Bluffs. Herbert S. Sammon, visiting organist, was in charge of a church service late that month at the Union Chapel. As anthems the choir offered "Were You There" and "Deep River" by Burleigh, who was in the congregation at the time.

Cheyney Day, 1928

This was also the year that Burleigh Hall, a men's dormitory, was named for him on "Cheyney Day" at Cheyney Training School for Teachers. Apparently the construction of Burleigh Hall had been long aborning and its actual dedication delayed, evidenced by the following letters provided by Dr. James Hall, Jr., Burleigh's godson. Burleigh's reply to Mr. Leslie P. Hill, President of Cheyney, dated May 21, 1928, from his apartment in New York read:

CONCERT

BY

Girls' Chorus of Academy High School, Erie, Pa.

MR. MORTON J. LUVAAS, Director

assisted by

Mr. Harry T. Burleigh, Baritone New York, N. Y.

MARCH 6, 1928

* * * * *

P R O G R A M
-1-

a.	Where e'er you Walk	Handel
b.	O Bone Jesu	Palestrina
c.	Merrily, Merri.y	Richardson

Girls' Chorus

-2-

Brief remarks on the Spirituals

a.	I've Been in de Storm so Long	
b.	Don't You Weep When I'm Gone	Arranged
c.	Heav'n, Heav'n	by
d.	I don't Feel no-ways Tired	Burleigh

Mr. Burleigh

-3-

(The following two songs are dedicated to the Academy Girls' Chorus by the composer)

a.	Were You There	Burleigh
b.	Ezekiel Saw de Wheel	Burleigh

Girls' Chorus

-4-

a.	My Lord What a Mornin'	
b.	De Blin' Man Stood on de Road an' Cried	Arranged
c	Didn't my Lord Deliver Daniel	by
d.	Let us Cheer de Weary Traveler	Burleigh

Mr. Burleigh

a.	God of all Nature	Tschaikowski
b.	Go Ask of the High Stars	Mexican Folk Song
c.	Still as the Night	Bohm
d.	Cradle Song	Brahms

Girls' Chorus

My dear Mr. Hill:

Just a hurried line before I leave for Detroit, Mich. I note what you say concerning the new dormitory and am sorry you are so delayed with the culmination of your original plans.

It will be a pleasure to await your advice about the dedication in October.

With every wish for a glorious commencement I am as ever

Yours sincerely
H. T. Burleigh

A letter from Hill is missing, but must have prompted Burleigh's next one dated October 16, 1928, the overall tone of which suggests the composer's reluctance to interrupt his habitual schedule. The half-brother mentioned is Elzie Elmendorf. The letter reads:

My dear Mr. Hill:

Your letter, with the program for Cheyney Day Exercises enclosed, came this morning. I note what you say and what the printed program calls for.

I wish I had been consulted prior to the printing of your programs. Of course it is impossible for me to come *Friday* on account of my regular choir rehearsals which I cannot neglect.

I have two important engagements Saturday, but I think I can finish one of them in time to arrive for the exercises at the new building where you wish me to respond to Mr. Biddle's remarks.

Can I leave N. Y. at 11 a.m. and reach you by 2 p.m.? My engagement is at 10 a.m. in St. George's but it will only take 20 minutes. (Short funeral service.)

May have to disappoint you re the "address and singing for a half-hour." Will talk it over when I see you.

Sorry I cannot avail myself of the quiet hospitality at "Melrose" but thank you sincerely for remembering and inviting Alston who is in Kansas City with the road company of "In Abraham's Bosom." He will be glad to know you thought of him.

I shall have my half-brother and Miss Carlette Thomas with me for the short time I can stay. Miss Thomas is the first colored woman to qualify as an Associate also one of our most talented pianistes.

Just drop a note stating the latest hour I can leave N. Y. to arrive in time for the Dedicatory Exercises.

With every good wish I am

Faithfully yours
H. T. Burleigh

Mr. Hill's letter of concern to Burleigh follows:

My dear Dr. Burleigh:

We shall be exceedingly sorry if there is anything in our arrangements for Saturday that may not be pleasing to you. All our effort and intention lie the other way. Of course we greatly regret your inability to come Friday and remain over the weekend, but we are quite aware of your inescapable engagements and of the numerous demands upon your time.

You can leave Broad Street Station, Philadelphia, no later than 12:59 p.m. That train will arrive here at 1:47, and you will then have thirteen minutes before the exercises. It would be far better if you could leave Broad Street Station not later than 12:02 p.m. In either case the 11:00 a.m. train from New York will be quite out of the question for a 2:00 p.m. engagement.

Now if this is wholly impossible for you *please wire me immediately*, and I will do my very best to make such shifts, even at this hour, as may be possible.

We are looking forward with the greatest pleasure to Saturday. I hope you will be happy here.

Cordially yours,
Leslie Pinckney Hill,
Principal
October 18, 1928

News of the well-planned ceremony was carried in at least one Pittsburgh paper and in *The Cheyney Record*, a quarterly published by the school. The *Record* article included a picture of Burleigh speaking on the steps of Burleigh Hall, and was reprinted in the *Washington Post*'s description of the event.

> This is another one of the group of grey stone buildings, crowning the hills which form the circle of the campus. Built of the lovely Pennsylvania "Foxcroft" stone, it dominates a part of the campus, which needed just a touch to relieve it of possible bleakness. It is a splendid building, within and without, two stories and a basement high, furnished within with a fine taste that is educative. It cost $65,000, and looks as if it cost more.
>
> Principal Leslie Pinckney Hill and the Board of Trustees had a happy idea of naming it "Burleigh Hall," after Harry T. Burleigh. He is the foremost Negro whom Pennsylvania has produced. . . . Therefore was Burleigh Hall well named. And on the gracious porch in the autumnal sunshine, he voiced his appreciation of the honor conferred upon him while yet living, and afterwards in the chapel, sang just enough to whet the appetite for more.
>
> In the evening there was a recital by Charlotte Wallace Murray. Her lovely rich voice was never better . . . in "Deep River."[66]

A detailed morning and afternoon program included not only the participants and names of committee members, but train schedules to and from Cheyney as well. An October 28 *Pittsburgh Courier* article on "Cheyney Day" lauded both Burleigh and the fine building, giving its measurements as ninety-four feet, eleven inches by thirty-six feet, with gum floors, adequate to house twenty-one students.

> It has 11 single rooms, five double rooms, two guest rooms, an apartment of three rooms on the first floor for the dean, an apartment of two rooms on the second floor for a professor, a billiard room, pressing shop, trunk room, athletic room, a living room on the first and second floor, a bath on the first and second floor.

At the 2:00 p.m. ceremony Principal Hill introduced speaker James Biddle, president of the board of trustees, to approximately 600 mixed attendees. Burleigh's response to his honor was: "It is a great distinction and also a great encouragement. I accept it with profound humility on my part and also with an humble spirit."

The article mentioned Burleigh's work at the two New York churches and some of his better known compositions. A photo of Burleigh captioned "Namesake" accompanied it.

In a thank-you letter to Burleigh written October 23, 1928, Hill promised to send him photos of the event and said in appreciation:

> I need not try to tell you again how much we valued your presence here, especially in view of the difficulties you had to overcome in making the trip. This was the finest of the eight Cheyney Days we have had, and we are all most happy that you were at the heart and center of it.

In 1964 Burleigh Hall was converted into a classroom building for the humanities, and in part of 1986 was empty, "awaiting extensive restoration."[67]

The popularity of Burleigh's music was not suffering. Marian Anderson had to repeat his "De Gospel Train" on her Carnegie Hall recital, December 30, 1928.

The events of 1929 were again fully covered by the *Age*. In January Burleigh was soloist in a program honoring Paul C. Bolin's thirty years as organist at St. Philip's Episcopal Church. Melville Charlton and Carlette Thomas also performed. Thomas accompanied Burleigh in a Christmas song and a setting of the 124th Psalm, which showed the singer's clear diction and dramatic power.

In mid-April Burleigh was Master of Ceremonies at a testimonial for Charlton, held at St. James Presbyterian Church. He introduced the performers and also presided at the banquet, saying of Charlton: "With sincere pride I embrace the privilege of saying that I consider Melville Charlton the greatest organist that we have produced." The choir honored Burleigh by singing "Were You There."[68]

Burleigh was mentioned three times in the *Age*, May 4, 1929. A cablegram to him from Lillian Evanti in Italy, telling of her successful opera performances there in March, was reprinted. At a performance in Atlantic City sponsored by the Board of Education, Burleigh sang sixteen spirituals accompanied by a talk about them. Critic George R. Weintraub remarked:

> Hearing Mr. Burleigh, the listener marvels afresh at how the Negro has achieved such powerful self-expression with a fairly simple use of existing mediums. The sufferings and aspirations of a whole race expressed themselves in profoundly moving fashion.

Burleigh, Charlton, and critic Lucien White were to be musical advisors to the H. T. Burleigh Music Study Club, a group composed initially of a dozen women, among whom was Mrs. William Pickens. Dr. Pickens had been a recent collaborator of Burleigh's. The Study Club's purpose was to improve its own musical appreciation, and to present and aid worthy black talent. Burleigh and Charlton performed for them in May of the next year.

In collaboration with Dorothy G. Bolton, a white Georgian woman, Burleigh set 187 Negro songs, useful in church, home, and school and which preserved the black heritage, under the title *Old Songs Hymnal*. Most of the Afro-American hymns were from Bolton's own area. The volume was "closely related to the goals of the Harry T. Burleigh Association organized in Terre Haute, Indiana, with the purpose to perform and preserve Negro music." It strove also to present talent in musical and dramatic performances.[69]

The *Hymnal* was published by the Century Publishing Company, Inc., in 1929, perhaps at the instigation of Bolton, as Ricordi did not ordinarily deal with material of this type. No further information on Bolton or the Harry Burleigh Association is contained in the volume's Foreword nor has any been located elsewhere, despite queries to Ashley Dealers, Century's successor, and churches and libraries in Indiana, Ohio, and Georgia.

Burleigh's publications from 1920 to 1929 numbered approximately eighty-five, including art songs, arrangements of spirituals for both solo and ensemble, and sacred texts and responses. Two of his spirituals, "Ezekiel Saw de Wheel" (1927) and "Don't Be Weary Traveler" (1928), were composed respectively for Academy High School, and for Old Central High School's a cappella choir.[70] Publishers other than Ricordi and Century were Oliver Ditson Company,

Theodore Presser Company, Talladega College, and St. George's
Church.

The 1930s

Another honor was bestowed upon Burleigh on February 9, 1930.
He was one of seven New Yorkers to receive the Harmon Award
from the W. E. Harmon Foundation for his arrangements and compositions. William Elmer Harmon, a realtor and developer of city
suburbs, was also a philanthropist with interests of wide span. He
was a generous endower of playgrounds, charities, and a religious
motion picture company. The seven fields of selection considered by
the foundation's five judges were music, literature, education,
religious service, fine arts, business, and race relations. Not confined
to persons of a particular race or color, the award, established in
1927, was given for distinguished achievement. Other musicians receiving the Harmon Award were Harry L. Freeman, operatic composer, and Carl R. Diton, composer and pianist. The presentation to
Burleigh, $400 and a gold medal, was made by Dr. John H. Finley
at Mount Olivet Baptist Church in New York.[71]

On February 20 Burleigh and Ella Belle Davis gave a joint recital
in Larchmont, New York, with 500 people present. Burleigh spoke on
spirituals and sang four of them. A similar address was given for the
NANM's local group in New York in early March, when Burleigh
traced the spiritual's beginnings up to its use by the Fisk Jubilee
Singers:

> Dr. Burleigh lamented the fact that America was the last
> cultural society to accept the Spirituals as serious music,
> having treated them up until about 15 years ago primarily as
> minstrel songs. . . . It was foreign criticism and foreign music
> lovers who first recognized them after hearing the Fisk
> Singers abroad.[72]

At this time Abbie Mitchell and Charlotte Murray were frequently programming Burleigh's spirituals; movies were a favorite pastime;
Robeson's *Otello* in London got rave reviews, and a large-scale
sculpture of him by Antonio Salemme was now housed in the
Brooklyn Museum.

Violinist Edwin Ideler and actor Richard Harrison, of *Green Pastures* fame, participated in Burleigh's thirty-sixth anniversary service at St. George's. Both Burleigh and the choir sang. In complimenting Burleigh and Harrison, Reverend Reiland said: "It has been our privilege to hear the most illustrious composer of his race. . . . Let us all honor these two men, for whose gifts and kindness we give thanks to God."[73]

Opening 1931's activities was a prestigious concert by Burleigh, Charlton, Ella Belle, and Marie Davis on January 29, given at the new one million dollar Westchester Center in White Plains, New York. Charlton played two of Burleigh's arrangements on the $75,000 organ and also accompanied Burleigh at the piano before 2,000 listeners.

The *Erie Times*, April 23, 1931, gave news of a concert given by Burleigh at Academy High:

> One of the finest song recitals ever rendered in this city occurred Tuesday at the Academy, when Harry T. Burleigh made a special appearance here. The same songs which made Mr. Burleigh internationally famous, many of them of his own composition, scored with the audience here. After the recital a reception was given in his honor by his host and hostess, Mr. and Mrs. Earle E. Lawrence, in their beautiful home.

Hall Johnson was a Harmon Award winner this year. Richard Harrison received the Spingarn Medal and James Weldon Johnson, given a testimonial dinner on his retirement as secretary of the NAACP, was soon to take a teaching position in creative literature at Fisk University. Burleigh was on the committee which arranged the festivities in New York's Pennsylvania Hotel on May 14. The next month Charlotte Murray, now president of the H. T. Burleigh Music Study Club, was honored by friends at a large gathering as a graduate of Juilliard and for having received an alumni study fellowship.

For the next two years or so Burleigh's activities either diminished or got less coverage by the *Age* critic. Lucien White's column appeared infrequently, taken over irregularly by aspiring violinist Richard Durant. Making the news was the younger set, including Cab Calloway, Duke Ellington, the Mills Brothers, Louis Armstrong,

Eubie Blake, and Earl Hines. Courageous Eleanor Roosevelt was an advocate for the black community. Paul Robeson was given an honorary Master's degree by Rutgers. Charlie Chan movies, hugely intriguing and later a near addiction to Burleigh, were just beginning. Clarence Cameron White was to succeed Dett as Head of Hampton's Music School.

This overview does not mean that Burleigh was idle, but that he had more freedom to pick and choose his engagements and benefit performances. On January 21, 1932, he was the first guest on Howard University's recital series. On February 13 the *Age* carried Charlton's gratuitous tribute to Burleigh. Characterizing his compositions, Charlton said that they contained "harmonic richness, emotional profundity, and poetic suggestion." He rated Burleigh as "one of the most remarkable musicians in the annals of music in America."

The *Sentinel* of Washington, DC, June 4, 1932, carried an article on Burleigh's thirty-eighth year with St. George's choir at which he conducted all the music. The item also mentioned George Kemmer's interest in and support of Burleigh's musicianship. An Oak Bluffs journalist, continually mindful of Burleigh's recognition, mentioned the occasion in the *Vineyard Gazette*, May 30, 1932, and the following August spoke of him as "one of the greatest living Negro singers, one of the foremost musicians in America," "a composer of genius," and as a knowledgeable historian of the island. Burleigh was asked to present an address at the First Baptist Church of Vineyard Haven that month.

Solo artists of repute continued to perform his works, namely Charlotte Murray, who was now broadcasting fairly regularly, having starred the summer of 1932 in an all-black opera, *Tom-Tom*, with Jules Bledsoe. Jackson Norris, a black baritone from Brooklyn, sang in Stockholm at a musical soiree on October 6. The *Age*, December 10, 1932, reported that he sang four Burleigh spirituals for the King of Sweden and English dignitaries there.

Burleigh's thirty-ninth anniversary at St. George's was celebrated on May 19, 1933, also marking the tenth consecutive year of the Negro spiritual vesper services. All but three of the spirituals on the program had been arranged by Burleigh, who sang four of them himself. His friend Hall Johnson sang another, and an unnamed violinist played the Largo of Dvorak's symphony *From the New World*.

H. T. Burleigh at Oak Bluffs, 1930. Courtesy of Elizabeth White.

Alston Burleigh, having just played in *Run Little Chillun*, was present and helped greet the audience after the service, chatting about his father's contribution to spiritual repertoire, while slipping in a few humorous stories about him. Mrs. Walter Rosen had prepared a reception for Burleigh following the ceremony. As Alston finished his anecdotes,

> Mr. Burleigh emerged from the locker room, where he had been dressing, smart in a cutaway, piped vest, and pearl gray necktie. He gathered in the crowd with one broad smile, told them it was time to go to the party, and led them off to it happily but hurriedly, for he had to sing again at the evening service and he wanted every minute of enjoyment.[74]

Burleigh's concern for aspiring black students continued. His former student Carlette Thomas was hearing some of her own newly published works played in 1932. In 1933 he first met Juilliard student Josephine Harreld, later to become Mrs. Josephine Love, at the home of hospitable friend Charlotte Murray, now a singer at Riverside Church.

A letter from Burleigh in Oak Bluffs to Marian Anderson dated July 25, 1933, indicated his continuing interest in her growing career. Maestro Alfredo Salmaggi, referred to in the letter, was then director of the Chicago Opera Company. Caterina Jarboro, a successful Broadway singer until the mid-1920s, studied seriously in Europe, and debuted in Milan in 1930, singing the title role in *Aïda*. In subsequent years she toured the United States and Europe as an operatic singer.

> My dear Marian:
>   Did you attend the premiere debut of Jarboro in "Aida"? I looked for your attractively alluring face but in all that immense audience I fear it was not possible to recognize many individual ones.
>   However, I regretted not meeting you for I had hoped to get an opportunity of introducing you to Maestro Salmaggi who has displayed such unusual and encouraging broadmindedness in hearing and employing our singers.
>   Possibly Mr. LaForge can arrange an audition for you. There is no telling where this all may lead to. I have visions

of a Negro Grand Opera Company under Maestro Salmaggi's direction. Wouldn't that be a novelty and an achievement!

May I not hear from you soon? I thought the press comments on "Aida" very just and liberal. Didn't you?

With every good wish and with confident expectation of receiving a letter from you shortly, I am

Faithfully yours
H. T. Burleigh[75]

That Anderson followed Burleigh's suggestion at this time is doubtful, though by her own admission she had studied about a year with LaForge in the late twenties at the urgence of her agent, Arthur Judson. Of the association she later recalled:

Working with Mr. LaForge was pleasant. He was always kind and thoughtful, conscious of what I wanted to achieve and eager to help. He was always willing to give me a few more minutes of work.

At the time, however, she thought the lessons were too expensive for her.[76]

Despite Burleigh's long friendship with Marian Anderson, described by her accompanist Kosti Vehanen in *Marian Anderson, a Portrait*,[77] Anderson did not appear to be as taken with Burleigh as he with her. However, Vehanen felt that she considered him one of the finest musicians of the black race. Burleigh often met her and Vehanen when they returned to the United States after tours abroad. He was fascinated by the fact that she owned a sunken bathtub, the first one he had ever seen. Forever in awe of the stunning contralto, Burleigh said:

Her voice – she has a great voice – but it's something more, something within herself. Whenever I shake hands with her I just stand still, for a moment I can't speak, I look into her face. It's so true. I'm emotional and impressionable. It comes from my mother, but it's never led me astray.[78]

Journalist R. J. Douglass, noting Burleigh's fortieth anniversary as soloist at St. George's in late March of 1934, referred to him as "Dr. Harry T. Burleigh . . . one of America's greatest composers."

> An immense audience crowded the church in apprecia-
> tion of the life of this splendid leader in the musical world.
> . . . A much sought out figure in the race's musical activities,
> he was always ready to show a helping hand to some
> struggling artist. . . . Dr. Burleigh has written several
> hundred songs concerning every phase of life. They embody
> the highest calibre of musicianship and many are standard
> classics. . . . In knowing Dr. Burleigh we know ourselves as
> a race. He is a true leader in the musical world. Not taught,
> but caught. Not gained, but earned.[79]

A Juilliard Student Club program titled "The Negro in Music" was presented on May 10, 1934, and reported in the *Age*, May 19. As the main speaker Burleigh focused on the distinction made between music by Afro-American composers and Negro music itself. He cited examples and explained unfamiliar harmonic and thematic construc-tions, as well as the music's origin and preservation. After Charlotte Murray's presentation of two Coleridge-Taylor songs Burleigh pointed out that "while much of this composer's work was based on pure African themes, a considerable amount bore no relation at all to the music of his paternal ancestors." Burleigh's "Lovely Dark and Lonely One," still in manuscript, was added to the program, sung by Ruby Elzy.

Lucien White's review in the *Age* continued: "Several of the solo numbers and the trio had to be repeated in response to insistent demands from the students." After the program an informal sympo-sium for the students was held, guided by Burleigh, Diton, White, Mrs. Murray, and Miss Harreld's mother, Mrs. Kemper Harreld. Violinist Richard Durant, who participated in the program was at the time a contributing music critic to the *Age*.

Burleigh was still a sought after lecturer, and frequently gave lecture recitals. One was mentioned by the *Boston Chronicle*, Septem-ber 8, 1934, in connection with his composing the yet unpublished

H. T. Burleigh, 1934. Courtesy of Dr. James Hall, Jr.

JULLIARD STUDENT CLUB

The Negro in Music

Thursday, May 10, 1934, at 7:45 o'clock

HARRY T. BURLEIGH, Presiding

PROGRAM

Organ.	Keep Me from Sinking Down (Spiritual)........ arranged by Carl Diton
	Carlette THomas, A.A.G.O.
Soprano.	You Ask Me if I Love You ....Burleigh
	Tide ....Burleigh
	Anne Wiggins Brown
Piano	Juba Dance ....R. Nathaniel Dett. ("In the Bottoms" Suite)
	Loretta Anthony
Mezzo-soprano.	Two Songs ....Coleridge-Taylor
	Charlotte Wallace Murray
Violin	African Dance II ....Coleridge-Taylor
	Richard Durant
Soprano.	Cabin Boy (Mississippi Boat Song) .... arranged by Willis Lawrence James
	City Called Heaven ..arranged by Hall Johnson
	Ruby Elzy
Contralto.	Scandalize My Name ......arranged by Burleigh
	Carmen Shepperd
Trio.	Were you There? ....arranged by Burleigh
	Sinner, Please Doan Let This Harvest Pass ... arranged by Burleigh

Ruby Elzy, Anne Wiggins Brown, Carmen Shepperd

Accompanists: Carol Blanton, Maurice Graham
Josephine Harreld

Program courtesy of Mrs. Josephine H. Love.

"Hymn to St. Matthew" for a nun: "Boston would do well to capture this versatile artist who speaks extemporaneously and well for a lecture recital."

More public tributes were heaped on the sixty-eight-year-old Burleigh in 1935. April marked his forty-first annual performance of "The Palms" since 1895. And at another service of spirituals on May 1 honoring the same anniversary 2,000 people squeezed into St. George's, a crowd exceeding the 1,200 expected. With robust voice Burleigh sang three spirituals in his inimitable fashion. Arrangers feted on the program besides Burleigh were St. George's organist George Kemmer and Alston Burleigh, at the time director of the black section of the Westchester Choral Society. Alston had arranged "Great Day! de Righteous Marchin' " for the choir. Violinist Edwin Ideler played the "Adagio" from *Southland Sketches* and additional selections were offered by the choir. Dr. Reiland praised Burleigh, Kemmer, and the choir in his address.

That same day an announcement was made over NBC that Burleigh's works, conducted by Alston Burleigh, would be broadcast later in the month. On May 10 at Temple Emanu-El congregation's evening service the choir sang Burleigh's response to silent prayer, titled "May the Words," based on "Deep River." Burleigh and Charlotte Murray shared a recital preceding a benefit bridge and whist tournament at the YWCA in New York on June 18, 1935.[80]

Eva Jessye and Todd Duncan made news in 1935 as choral director and star at the premiere of George Gershwin's *Porgy and Bess* in Boston, September 30. Earlier in the year Duncan had included three of Burleigh's spirituals on a private concert at the home of Mr. and Mrs. Henry Morgenthau. One of Burleigh's most beautiful art songs, "Lovely Dark and Lonely One," with text by Langston Hughes, was published this year.

The spirituals on Marian Anderson's Town Hall recital in New York on January 20, 1936, were Burleigh's arrangements, according to the *Age*, though the *New York Times* reviewer, more concerned by the cast on the singer's leg necessitated by a shipboard accident, did not mention Burleigh. This was probably the first time that Kosti Vehanen had publicly accompanied Anderson in the United States. She sang "Deep River," "I Don't Feel Noways Tired," "Swing Low, Sweet Chariot," and "Heav'n, Heav'n." Lucien White wrote:

All of these have been heard many times, but never have they been sung with such thrilling simplicity. There was no attempt at embellishment or ornate decoration. Simply and unaffectedly were they sung, but the singer brought to them all the devotion and faith which attended their conception.

Due to the leg cast, Anderson could not walk off the stage between groups. Rather, the curtain was drawn and she rested on a chair.[81]

This same year, 1936, Anderson and Vehanen recorded Burleigh's arrangements of "Heav'n, Heav'n" and "Deep River" along with some operatic arias. Years later in her autobiography she spoke disinterestedly of the recording:

> I have no idea whether RCA Victor has a copy of the first recording I made. . . . There is no reason why the company should still have the master; it was made when I was unknown, I did not hear the completed record after it was issued. In fact I was hardly aware that it was available publicly and had forgotten it completely.[82]

The *Age*, February 29, 1936, mentioned that Burleigh composed "Greeting" especially for the Burleigh Glee Club, directed by Ella Belle and Marie Davis. The performance on February 20 was at the Bethesda Baptist Church in New Rochelle, New York. Burleigh wrote his regrets for not attending, due to illness. The Glee Club was composed of about two dozen high school girls.

Burleigh was soloist with the Samuel Coleridge-Taylor Choral Club of Hartford in early May at Avery Memorial Hall, confirmed by an announcement in the *Courant* of that city, May 10, 1936. The annual vesper service at St. George's in May highlighted Burleigh's forty-second year there. His arrangements, as well as those by organist George Kemmer, musicologist Natalie Curtis Burlin, and Alston Burleigh were used.

> . . . midway in the service Mr. Burleigh stepped down from his high seat in the choir stalls, descended to near the center of the chancel, and in his own inimitable artistic manner sang two spirituals.[83]

For a singer of seventy years his voice, which "rang out in joyous strains," was spoken of as "robust and clear" by the *International Negro Press*, June 1936.

In a month or so he was off to Italy for the summer, and returned "refreshed in mind, body and spirit." This may have been one of the summers that Ricordi sent him there to review procedures at the Milan branch. However, vacationing abroad was the thing to do for those who could afford it.

In a letter to Josephine Harreld dated November 11, 1936, Burleigh expressed some of his pleasure during the trip.

> My dear Josephine:
>
> Thank you so much for your letter. I was beginning to feel that with the many things you must do now as Head of the Music at Bennett you will have little time left to keep in touch with your friends in remote places.
>
> However, I am hoping that you will always find time to keep in touch with me. (I hope that does not seem selfish or unreasonable.)
>
> Regarding someone to teach voice and perhaps Solfeggio I cannot think of anyone, at the moment, whom I consider competent. May I suggest that you get in touch with the Music Department at Howard University. Miss Childers or Miss Nickerson may have one of their advanced pupils who would "fill the bill" and who may be looking for just such an opening.
>
> When you get the time, do write me about your work and yourself. I will never be too busy to listen.
>
> Had a wonderfully revealing summer in Italy – Naples – (Capri, Sorrento, etc.) – Rome, Florence – best beloved city in Italy – Milan, Venice etc., etc. Came back in September refreshed in mind, body and spirit.
>
> With really intense wishes for your success and assurances of my personal regard, I beg to remain, as ever
>
> > Faithfully yours
> > H. T. Burleigh

Burleigh was not present at "An Evening with Harry T. Burleigh" on November 17 at Grace Congregational Church in New York. Soloists and chorus, directed by the Thomas Negro Composers Study Group, participated and a biography of the composer was given by Carlette Thomas. On December 9 Burleigh gave a lecture recital on spirituals for the benefit of the St. Andrew mission in Passaic, New Jersey. He "explained the keen imagination possessed by the Negro slave," demonstrating with "I Stood on der Ribber of Jordan" and "De Gospel Train." He kept in dialect while singing, but pointed out that all spirituals were not meant to be in dialect, e.g., "Were You There" and "Go Down Moses." Commenting on his recent seventieth birthday, he recalled that Booker T. Washington often whistled "I Don't Feel Noways Tired" to rest himself after a strenuous day.[84]

The exact year that Burleigh joined the Erie Club of New York is not known, though it was likely around 1936. Norman Sobel, a former Erieite whose father helped fund Burleigh's scholarship to the Conservatory, became president of this prestigious businessmen's group in 1933 and was largely responsible for promoting Burleigh's acceptance for membership.[85] Often a hired singer at Erie Club gatherings, Burleigh had never been asked to eat at the table with the guests, a fact confirmed by Mrs. Virginia Moorhead in a letter to the author dated January 26, 1986.

> In 1935 the Erie Club of New York City gave a Testimonial Dinner for my father at a Hotel in N. Y.C. Harry Burleigh was invited to attend. He called my father at the Hotel and said that he would not be able to attend. He was sorry not to attend but that the policy of the Hotel was he could attend as a performer at the Dinner but, of course, would not be present for the meal. Also he would have to use the freight elevator to get to the Banquet Room and could not stay as a guest for the rest of the Banquet. I was about 22 yrs old and I remember really being hurt that such things happened in the "north."

In the mid-thirties Burleigh often took Miss Josephine Harreld to the opera and also for supper to an oyster bar in Grand Central

Station. He still enjoyed talking with the red caps there and be-
moaned the fact that these blacks of native intelligence had had no
chance to follow another profession. He helped Miss Harreld (the
future Mrs. Love) select her trousseau. She described him as about
five feet six or seven inches in height, weighing approximately 180
pounds, and of very distinguished personage. She remembered that
he kept a daily journal, but did not know what became of it after his
death. As a gentleman of the old school, Mr. Burleigh customarily
offered his concert or opera seat to others. Well over twice
Miss Harreld's age, he remained her dear and respected friend. She
heard his fiftieth performance of "The Palms" in 1944, about the
time that his advancing senility was vaguely detectable. She sadly
recalled having seen him once in front of Carnegie Hall, when he did
not recognize her.[86]

In April of 1937 Burleigh was soloist for the Federation of Musicians at Howard University's Sojourner of Truth Hall. The event was
his first solo recital in that city, according to the *Washington Times*,
April 14, 1937.

Special new arrangements and harmonizations by Harry and
Alston Burleigh were featured at the fourteenth annual service of
Negro spirituals in St. George's on May 23, 1937. The next day's
Herald Tribune mentioned Alston's "Great Day! de Righteous
Marchin'." Burleigh sang two of his own solo arrangements.

The *Age* carried almost no news of Burleigh's activities in 1937-
38. Too, there is slim evidence of publication of any Burleigh works
for these particular years.

For his forty-third Palm Sunday performance at St. George's in
1937 Burleigh used his own arrangement of "The Palms," according
to an undated issue of the *Baltimore Afro-American*, which pictured
him in a choir vestment. "Literally hundreds" were turned away from
this anticipated service. Added arrangements and compositions by
Kemmer, A. Walter Kramer, Hall Johnson, and Carl Diton were
used. The concert was indeed livened up not only by antiphonal
singing and varied ensembles, but also by a solo on the theremin, an
electronic instrument resembling a radio receiving set, played by
moving the hands near but not upon it. Its tone quality is somewhat
imitative of the human voice.

H. T. Burleigh, 1938. Courtesy of Dr. James Hall, Jr.

Marian Anderson was now with the Sol Hurok agency. The spiritual "Were You There?" was programmed in the last of a five-group concert which she presented at Hampton Institute, March 23, 1938.

Enjoying the summer of 1938 in Vineyard Haven, Burleigh was far from idle. An interviewer gave a colorful description of the composer at work:

> A piano thrumming fitfully in a cool Sunday School room, a table littered with papers, outside the heat and insect-hum of a summer morning – and a small figure in shirt sleeves at the piano.

Burleigh was composing Christmas music for the 120-voice choir who would sing it there. He was reticent to talk of his career and past life, preferring to chat of his friendship with Dvorak. He told the interviewer:

> I sometimes think that those who simply love music for the enjoyment, the pleasant experience it gives them in hearing, have more than we who create it. We are constantly listening for effects, noting construction as we hear a composition – we seldom just sit back and enjoy.

Burleigh loved talking with his vacationing friends along the beach, in restaurants, and on the streets, and aimed for a twenty-fifth summer there.[87]

Burleigh was featured in August of 1938 in a column titled "Personalities in Music" which found its way to newspapers in several states. A collage of three excellent photos accompanied the biographical article.[88] Within the next few months an eight-frame cartoon summarizing Burleigh's life appeared in the *Age* (October 29, 1938) and other syndicated papers.

Though not usually in the Oak Bluffs area in the winter, Burleigh did go back to the Edgartown Methodist Church in late December to speak and accompany singers of his spirituals in a benefit concert.

> The event proved a rewarding one, with the soloists winning favor, and the spirituals, directed by the noted Harry T. Burleigh, climaxing the program. . . . Mr. Burleigh . . .

showed how the spirituals are truly folksongs since they sprang from the people themselves. . . . There is no malice, bitterness or resentment, although they came from people in slavery, . . . an expression of what was in the hearts of the people.[89]

As early as February, 1939, two black newspapers, the *Washington Tribune* and the *St. Louis Argus*, carried articles with photos of Burleigh, anticipating his forty-fifth presentation of "The Palms." On April 7 the Palm Sunday service was mentioned in the *Vineyard Gazette*.

At the St. George annual service of Negro spirituals on May 21 that year an eloquent address was made by Reverend Elmore McKee in honor of Burleigh. After a rather lengthy generalization on the nature of the Negro spiritual he spoke more personally of Burleigh.

Today we celebrate with enthusiasm and deep gratitude forty-five years of Harry T. Burleigh's membership in St. George's choir. We are here, not to bury or retire Burleigh, but to praise him, to give opportunity for the spontaneous appreciation of multitudes to express itself and to venture the hope that he will sing with us for many more years to come. Did we not a few moments ago hear him sing "I don't feel noways tired"?

We salute a man who has sung for most of his life in one chancel, in one parish. Wisdom, friendliness, and the lifting power of religion – these have consecrated the genius of the musician – have enriched the parish, community and nation.

Multitudes of white people would gladly and quickly testify that Harry Burleigh has given to them . . . a cultural and spiritual life along the highroad of life. . . . We would like to express our congratulations, our appreciation and our affection.[90]

Though no locatable news reports followed the tribute planned to Burleigh by the NANM at its August 20-25, 1939, convention, he

St. George's Church

in the City of New York

Vol. 27.   **Sunday, May 21st, 1939**   **No. 34.**

The Spirituals--- and Mr. Burleigh

The sixteenth annual service of Negro Spirituals brings us to the eternal drama of man's relations to his fellowman and to God. The peculiar genius of the "spiritual" quickly and in simplicity makes us face the issues of sin, suffering, God, Jesus, Eternal Life. If one enters deeply into this afternoon's experience one will realize that the colored race is sublimating its suffering through the creativeness of great music and transcending today's injustices by the leap of great Christian faith. Rarely does art become so richly laden with meaning for contemporary living. The Choir of St. George's has rendered significant service to American music and religion by bringing the "spiritual" significantly into the worship of the Church.

Forty-five years ago last February, Harry T. Burleigh was invited by Dr. Rainsford, Rector, and William S. Chester, organist, to become a soloist in St. George's Choir. A year before, coming from Erie, Pennsylvania, on borrowed money to compete for a scholarship at the National Conservatory of Music on East 17th Street, of which Miss Jeannette M. Thurber was founder, he was successful and began his musical career in New York. He has sung in Church, Synagogue, university and on the public platform. He has traveled considerably and in 1908-1909 sang before King Edward VII. He is a composer of distinction, and assisted Dvorak in the composition of the first movement of the New World Symphony.

St. George's has enjoyed a share of Mr. Burleigh's time. Only a man with greatness in his soul could maintain the unqualified admiration and affection of colleagues and fellow-parishioners through all the hard work and changes of forty-five years. How many of us could pass that kind of test? Mr. Burleigh has passed it not only because he is a musician of distinction but because he is also a man of religion. He is in Church Sunday mornings long before most of us, getting the "feel" of it. Underneath his song and his composition are the wings of triumphant faith. Before I came to St. George's a friend in Buffalo said, "Are you going to Mr. Burleigh's Church?" An affirmative answer brought approval. His ministry here has helped to give character and depth to this great Parish for nearly half a century. The spontaneity of today's tribute to him establishes this fact beyond doubt. My words are simply the inevitable expression of the gratitude of thousands here and Beyond. We hope Mr. Burleigh's ministry may enrich our life for many years to come.

E. M. M.

H. T. Burleigh, c. 1939. Courtesy of Dr. David Cantrell.

was one of its honorees. At the time Dr. Kemper Harreld was the organization's president.[91]

In his dissertation Roland Lewis Allison mentions that Burleigh gave a program of Negro spirituals during the New York World's Fair in 1939 at the Temple of Religion (completed in mid-March), though neither he nor the *New York Times* gives a specific date. Several black choirs of the area performed there that year, one directed by Mrs. Blanche K. Thomas, organizer of the Burleigh Study Club. Several of the Fair's concerts were heard over a huge speaker system and some were broadcast.[92]

Burleigh, along with W. C. Handy and J. Rosamond Johnson, was in charge of arranging an all-Negro program "from symphony to swing," for October 2, 1939, as a part of ASCAP's Silver Jubilee Week in Chicago. Burleigh was present to hear some of his spirituals that evening, among them "Deep River," sung by Jules Bledsoe of "concert stage and *Showboat* fame." ASCAP was asked to repeat the festival in New York on October 24, 1940, in the Music Hall at the World's Fair, a performance which Burleigh missed. American musicians representing all fields of music participated. New York's Mayor Fiorello La Guardia, co-organizer of the affair, led a band composed of firemen, police, and the Sanitation Department. During the week there were nine programs which an estimated 30,000 attended.[93]

During the 1930s Burleigh's compositional output totalled approximately two dozen art songs and arrangements of spirituals. By 1940 his accomplishments had long since come to the attention of Alexander Alland, writer and photographer, who planned a volume covering seventy-five years of Afro-American history. A suggestion from W. E. B. DuBois to include Burleigh among the outstanding musicians in the book was revealed through correspondence. The proposed photographic text, a collaborative effort by Alland and DuBois, unfortunately never materialized.[94]

The Last Decade

Marian Anderson, in a five-segment concert at Hampton on April 30, 1940, included Burleigh's "Steal Away" and "Oh Peter Go Ring-a Dem Bells." The month before, Burleigh sang his forty-sixth

Palm Sunday Service, afterwards remarking to a parishioner "I'm seventy-three. Isn't that awful? Isn't that terrible? You should have been here forty years ago. Then you would have heard a voice." At the event the 120 singers, children and adults wearing blue, purple, and scarlet cassocks, banked both sides of the chancel. Burleigh, in a scarlet robe, accompanied himself at the piano.[95]

That same year *Cue* magazine described Burleigh, "the chunky, voluble little man," as "incredibly nimble. Neatly groomed, he carries a cane and wears spats." As sprightly as he appeared, he nevertheless expressed weariness and thoughts of retirement. Withal, the mellowness and vibrancy of his voice was still exciting. This interview marked the first time he had spoken publicly of retiring, an idea considered absurd by the rector and choirmaster at St. George's. Burleigh had begun to suspect that people came to hear him sing out of curiosity for his continuing ability. What he really desired was time to arrange more spirituals and to compose, in particular a service for the church.

On March 17, 1941, assisted by organist Grace Lisenden, Burleigh gave a lecture on the Negro spiritual at Immanuel Union Church, Westerleigh, Staten Island. His illustrative material was from Dvorak's *From the New World* and from his own spirituals.

The 1941 occasion of Burleigh's forty-seventh Palm Service in April and the eighteenth annual service of Negro spirituals on May 11 were well publicized. Still able to "put it over" to the misty-eyed audience, his "resonant voice sounded over all the others." After the latter program he was polite, but in a rush to a photography engagement. "He ascended the ramp from the choir room to the chantry at a pace that a reporter almost half a century his junior found brisk."[96]

In early August of 1941 Burleigh was one of eight nominees for three vacancies on the Board of Directors of ASCAP. Other composers nominated were Deems Taylor and Oley Speaks, already members, plus Clara Edwards, Horace Johnson, Geoffrey O'Hara, John Tasker Howard, and Harvey Endress. Burleigh was selected, the first black to hold such a position.[97] This same month Alston Burleigh was promoted to the rank of Major in the U.S. Army.

December 13, 1941, occasioned Dvorak's 100th anniversary, marked at 327 Seventeenth Street in New York, his former residence. Speakers at the ceremony were Jan Masaryk, Czech Minister of

H. T. Burleigh in his home, c. late 1930s or early 1940s. Courtesy of
Dr. James Hall, Jr.

H. T. Burleigh in typical dress with umbrella and spats, c. early 1940s. Courtesy of Dr. James Hall, Jr.

Foreign Affairs, who unveiled the commemorative plaque on the residence; J. G. Kovarík, Dvorak's former secretary; New York's Mayor Fiorello La Guardia; and Harry T. Burleigh. Also present were such eminent musicians as Bruno Walter, Fritz Kreisler, and impresario Arthur Judson.[98]

In the empty rooms of the house a small exhibition of memorabilia (playbills, photographs, and manuscripts) was installed by the initiative of Kovarík, Burleigh, and Milos Safranek, a Czech whom Burleigh met in the United States during World War II. Safranek wrote of the commemoration:

> It was a moving ceremony – it was raining heavily – Kovarík was so deeply moved that he was unable to speak. Burleigh took over, with emotion and sensitivity. . . . Oh, how Burleigh did speak! . . . Everybody was deeply moved. . . . The house was so crowded that some feared it would collapse. Burleigh paid tribute to the greatness, simplicity and humane charm of Master Dvorak and thanked him not only for having made the black folk melodies capable of artistic rendition, but for making them into spokesmen of the black people, that stand firmly against oppression and humiliation.

In 1954 Safranek spoke of Burleigh's genuine enthusiasm for Dvorak in an article titled "The Story Dvorak's Black Friend Told Me."[99]

The following delightful letter from Burleigh[100] dated January 5, 1942, indicates that Carl Van Vechten, the famous photographer, had wanted to include Burleigh in his portraits collection. Evidently Burleigh was frankly aware of his own image.

Dear Mr. Van Vechten:

> The photographs were received with great pleasure and solely the many extra services in a choir-singers life at Christmas time prevented me from thanking you sooner.

> They are excellent likenesses – almost too true in their revelation of every wrinkle and skin texture. Those without my habitual eye-glasses are less realistic.

> You were kind to take so much interest and I wish it were in my power to reciprocate in some way.

With every good wish, I am
                    Sincerely
                    H. T. Burleigh

Other portraits of Burleigh, now in the possession of the Harmon Foundation in Roslyn, NY, were done by painters Betsy Graves Rayneau and Laura Wheeler Waring (1887-1948). With a preference for Afro-American subjects, both artists exhibited widely in the United States during the 1940s. Waring depicted Burleigh standing at his piano. In 1927 she was a Harmon Gold Award winner for an earlier painting of Anne Washington Derry, a Negro woman.

In 1942 Burleigh's beautiful singing of "The Palms" brought tears of emotion to the eyes of the congregation, according to a review in the *Vineyard Gazette*, April 4, 1942, which quoted Burleigh's own remarks after this presentation:

> I want to retire, but the church won't let me.
> You see, I think a man ought to quit while he can
> still sing instead of waiting until people tell him he
> is too old or his voice is no good.

S. Lewis Elmer, registrar of the American Guild of Organists who heard this performance, according to the same account said that Burleigh "was putting his whole soul into his music. . . . I have never heard him sing better."

Perhaps one of the first things that occupied Burleigh in 1943 was the writing of a letter to Eva Jessye, dated January 1, which included a photo of himself at the piano. The following is from Jessye's typed copy of the letter:

Dearly Beloved Eva Jessye!
        Sincerely do I thank you for your letter of December 31st. While you were writing that letter in the waning hours of 1942, I was in our Watch-night service in St.George's singing:

> "A few more years shall roll,
> A few more seasons come,
> And we shall be with those that rest
> Asleep within the tomb."

H. T. Burleigh, photographed in his home in the 1940s. Courtesy of
Dr. James Hall, Jr.

H. T. Burleigh at the fiftieth anniversary at St. George's Church, 1944.
Courtesy of Dr. James Hall, Jr.

And then, as the church bells rang at twelve, we arose and sang:
> "Awake, my soul, stretch every nerve,
> And press with vigor on."

'Twas inspiring!

It is nice to know your whereabouts and what you are doing. These photographs are the only ones I have. They were taken years ago and must suffice. But there is one postcard size which looks like me now. I've autographed it and I want you to keep it in your warm, sweet, capacious heart.

> Sincerely, H.B.
> (Harry T. Burleigh)

With organist Carlette Thomas, a former theory student, Burleigh presented a recital at Ebenezer Baptist Church in New York, on April 28, 1943.[101]

On February 4, 1944, Burleigh's "golden anniversary" was celebrated in St. George's Parish Memorial House, receiving ample news coverage. At a reception in his honor he received $1,500 from St. George's parishioners and a scroll, presented by Bishop William T. Manning. Bishop Manning and Reverend Elmore McKee were speakers for the occasion. Also, Mr. J. M. Fassett, president of the Erie Club, gave Burleigh a silver-banded cane in behalf of the club, saying: "Harry Burleigh's accomplishments have for many years reflected great credit on the city of Erie and distinction on the entire nation as well." Burleigh responded with an address thanking those who had helped him.[102] He said facetiously, "That's right, I'm getting old. I'll need one of these pretty soon."

Among the 700 people at the celebration were a goodly number from Erie, an attendance arranged through reservation. Burleigh sang "I Don't Feel Noways Tired" and "Go Down Moses" at the reception, following the choir's offering of his contrapuntal choral ode, "Ethiopia's Paean of Exultation."

Burleigh is quoted in Nora Holt's account of the occasion as saying:

> I have done nothing. It was my mother. All through the
> years she has been my guiding light. She was a remarkable

woman, intelligent and lofty, with a fixity of purpose from which she never deviated. I feel humble and proud if I have reflected a small degree of her nobility.[103]

Time magazine's biographical article with photo gave a vivid report of the festivities:

White-haired Henry Thacker Burleigh put on a white tie and tails and stood affably in St. George's parish house while admirers thronged around in celebration of his 50th anniversary.

The following April Burleigh sang "The Palms" at St. George's for the fiftieth time, after which George Kemmer mused, "the remarkable thing about Mr. Burleigh is he's kept so young." Between morning and afternoon services Burleigh broadcast the work by special invitation of Mayor La Guardia over WNYC. A piano was brought in and placed near the mayor's desk and a special police car was sent to fetch Burleigh to City Hall. La Guardia, long a supportive music lover, asked, "Wasn't that beautiful?"[104]

On June 9, 1944, Burleigh arrived in Erie, two days before a scheduled concert, and was met at the train by Earle Lawrence, Mr. and Mrs. A. S. Way, and Dr. and Mrs. Federal Lee Whittlesey. He told the press: "It is a wonderful thrill to be back in Erie, but it is a little sad too, because all my people here are dead and gone."[105] On the day of the concert, June 11, 1944, Burleigh gave the address and sang the solos at "A Service of Negro Spirituals" at the Church of the Covenant in Erie. It was his first performance in the city since 1931, and his last documented one. Both the Covenant Choir, directed by Dr. Whittlesey, and the Uthmann Choir, directed by James Cross, performed on the program. Six hundred people filled the church and 1,400 more crowded into nearby Knox Hall to hear the concert through speakers.

During this visit to Erie Burleigh was also guest soloist on other concerts. He was honored by the Erie Chapter of the American Guild of Organists and spoke at the Women's Club, Kiwanis Club, and at a music teachers' festival, saying he wished he knew more about "this boogie-woogie."[106] At this time his music was on display at the Erie County Public Library.

H. T. Burleigh at Martha's Vineyard. Courtesy of Dr. James Hall, Jr.

H. T. Burleigh (*left*) and Henry Robbins at Oak Bluffs, 1945. Courtesy of Elizabeth White.

Henry Beckett, interviewing Burleigh two months earlier, was intrigued with the memorabilia in the composer's apartment. Besides desk drawers stuffed with manuscripts and reminders of his former personal associations, there were photos of John McCormack signed with a tribute; Coleridge-Taylor, inscribed "My true friend and greatest singer of my songs"; Marian Anderson; St. George's Choir; Louise Burleigh; a colored print of Giovanni Bellini's "Portrait of a Youth"; and one of Alston Burleigh, inscribed "To dad, the noblest Roman of them all."[107] According to Dr. Harry T. Burleigh II, most of his grandfather's treasures were lost or destroyed through the carelessness of Santini and Sons, a large moving and storage company hired by the executor of Burleigh's estate.

H. T. Burleigh, c. 1945. Courtesy of Dr. David Cantrell.

Between 1940 and 1944 Burleigh's publications numbered only seven. Then there were no more until his last one in 1949, "Lawd, Whatcha Gonna Do Wid Me?", perhaps an earlier collaboration with J. C. Johnson, published by Record Music Publishing Company.

Programs by several area choral groups were presented during Inter-American Music Week, May 6-12, 1945, at Hampton Institute. An arrangement of "Just You" was sung by the Harry Burleigh Glee Club, conducted by Wallace Campbell. Campbell's group was a community choir, composed of Baptist churchmen. It later became the Harry Burleigh Chorale, conducted for a few years by Margaret Davis, now a retired music education teacher in Hampton. Mrs. Davis doubted that Burleigh was aware of the groups' names, chosen out of respect for his merits as a composer and arranger.[108]

When Paul Robeson received the Spingarn Medal on November 3, 1945, at the Biltmore Hotel in New York, Burleigh and Marian Anderson were seated at the speakers' table at dinner. Robeson paid tribute to them, saying, "I am proud to be a part of the work they represent."[109]

In 1946 Burleigh sang at St. George's for the last time. Fatigue and evidences of senility had crept up on him. His most famous remark concerning the situation was, "Do you want me to go till I drop?" St. George's was reluctant to relinquish its most precious legend. Between his two fifty-second "Palms" services that year Burleigh said to the churchmen: "This morning I really do think I sang fairly well for a man my age, but I'll do it even better this afternoon. Well, excuse me, everybody, but I've got to run."[110]

Reported at length by leading newspapers, including the *Age* with a front page portrait, Burleigh's resignation was accepted in November of 1946, with St. George's deep regrets. He attended church for the next few months, joining in the hymns from a regular pew. Reverend Edward Miller, pastor at the time, saw that a pension was provided for Burleigh.

Within the next few months, while Burleigh still occupied his Bronx apartment, Henry Lee of *Coronet* magazine interviewed him.

> As he talked to me of his age, he walked briskly through
> the 5 o'clock rush hour in mid Manhattan. In his right hand
> he jauntily swung an umbrella. He was dressed youthfully in

light-blue tweeds, blue and white striped tie, spats, and a somewhat battered gray felt hat. During the day he reads, composes, practices. Usually he goes down town to see his publishers.[111]

Within a few months Burleigh's son and daughter-in-law had moved him to The Oakes, a convalescent home in Amityville, Long Island. There, on his eighty-first birthday, December 2, 1947, Carlette Thomas, her mother, and two other friends gave Burleigh a surprise party. They brought a portable organ on which Burleigh accompanied himself, singing his three favorite spirituals, "Go Down Moses," "Were You There," and "I Know the Lord Laid His Hand on Me." Fred Waring's Glee Club had paid tribute by a broadcast earlier that day, singing "Were You There." Though in his last years Burleigh was said to have fretted over failing eyesight and ill-fitting glasses, at this time he was reported to be in excellent health and voice. He sent his thanks to those who had remembered him with telegrams and letters.[112]

Despite this cheerful report on Burleigh's health, Alston Burleigh suspected the overly heavy administering of sedatives to his father by the Oakes staff. Three months later, on the recommendation of friends, Burleigh was moved to Stamford Hall, a private nursing home in Stamford, Connecticut. Here, on March 24, 1948, the touring Howard University Choir performed in Burleigh's honor. The professionally dressed singers presented a full-length concert to 300 guests who were allowed to attend through the courtesy of Dr. Clifford Moore, supervisor of the home. Nonambulatory and bed patients heard the concert through a speaker system.

The musical selections, directed by William Lawson, included two of Burleigh's arrangements, "Were You There" and "My Lord, What a Morning." Burleigh made an appreciative, rather nostalgic speech. Major and Mrs. Alston Burleigh were there and subsequently spent Easter Sunday with Burleigh.[113]

Approximately eighteen months later, on September 12, 1949, at 6:15 a.m., Burleigh died of cardiac failure. He was eighty-two. Other factors contributing to his demise were general arteriosclerosis and senile psychosis. In earlier years Burleigh had expressed a wish to be buried by his mother in Erie, but "before senility took its toll, Harry decided to be buried in New York where he had spent most of his adult life."[114]

Two thousand attended Burleigh's funeral at St. George's on September 14, 1949, at 8:30 p.m., after the body had lain in state in St. George's Chapel of Peace the previous day.

> The slowly-winding line of mourners included persons to whom the name Harry T. Burleigh represented the apex of Negro musical attainment, for Mr. Burleigh was the undisputed "dean" of composers and arrangers of Negro spirituals and chorales.[115]

Writers of the many obituaries could not seem to say enough in praise of Burleigh. A man of dignity and poise, he had helped bridge the gap between the people of two races. Ministers were in awe of the spirituality which this outstanding American imparted as he sang. His death was a loss to rich and poor, black and white. Obituaries were found in the *New York Times*, *Age*, *Herald Tribune*, *Atlanta Daily World*, *Memphis World*, *Washington Evening Star*, *Pittsburgh Courier*, *Time*, *Newsweek*, and *Norfolk Journal and Guide* during September 1949. *Musical America* for October and *The Etude* of November 1949 also carried them.

The funeral music was chosen especially to honor the deceased. One hundred voices in two choirs sang his arrangements of spirituals. Soloists were Carol Brice and Helen Phillips, whose careers Burleigh had furthered, and Ernest McChesney. Each sang a spiritual, "Swing Low, Sweet Chariot," "I Know the Lord Laid His Hands on Me," and "I Hope My Mother Will Be There," all in arrangements by Burleigh. The ceremony closed with the combined choirs' "Deep River."

Carol Brice's Town Hall recital in 1946 was probably one of the last that Burleigh had attended. She was a soloist at St. George's during the 1940s and after a successful career on Broadway and as a recitalist she taught at the University of Oklahoma until her death from cancer in 1985. Helen Phillips, not as well known at the time, debuted in Town Hall in 1954. Tenor McChesney turned from light opera to more serious music, assisting Schumann-Heink on her last U.S. tour.

Among the honorary pall bearers were musicians Hall Johnson, Noble Sissle, Eubie Blake, W. C. Handy, Clarence Cameron White, and members of the vestry. Alston Burleigh, at the time on the Morgan State College faculty, was present at the ceremony, though other members of the Burleigh family were not mentioned as attending. Louise Burleigh is said to have been living in Wisconsin at the time. Donations to a Harry T. Burleigh Memorial Fund, rather than flowers, had been requested.[116]

Reverend Karl Reiland, rector emeritus, gave the funeral eulogy, paying high tribute to Burleigh, not only for his service to St. George's, but for his respectful attitude toward his race and for his worth as an individual. He spoke of him as displaying "peculiar genius . . . a great man, a great artist and a great friend who has gone out from among us." Reverend Edward Miller gave a closing prayer.

The "dapper little man with the white mustache" had indeed laid down his burden. He was buried in Mount Hope Cemetery, Hastings-on-Hudson in White Plains, New York. The A. P. Burton and Sons Funeral Home was in charge of burial arrangements. A few weeks later another tribute was paid Burleigh in the St. George's *Bulletin*, October 2, which read in part: "He seemed aware of deeper tones of brotherhood and throbbing harmonies of humanity which others did not hear."

Burleigh did not die intestate. The *New York Times* revealed details of his estate without tact. A first will signed by Burleigh on September 10, 1942, made no provision for his estranged wife, Louise, "for the reason that she deserted and abandoned me without cause." A second one made on June 28, 1946, however, left her $2,500. The remainder of the estate was to be divided among Burleigh's grandson, Harry T. Burleigh II; Elsie Elmendorf, a niece; and Mrs. Thelma Teasdale Hall, a teacher and also Burleigh's housekeeper from the mid-thirties until 1947. Burleigh had referred to Mrs. Hall as "my devoted friend, whose friendship has contributed greatly to my happiness."

The Burleigh family, dissatisfied, filed a claim on the estate, saying that Burleigh had been adjudged mentally incompetent in a court hearing a few years before his death. After much ado in court, the settlement's denouement resulted in a division among five parties:

Louise Burleigh received one-ninth; Thelma Hall's heirs, Elsie Elmendorf's heirs, Harry T. Burleigh II, and Alston Burleigh each received two-ninths. Particulars vary as to the amount of Burleigh's total estate. It was reported to be anywhere from $10,000 to $250,000.[117]

Chapter III

In Retrospect

♪

Burleigh was well-deserving of the many posthumous honors and tributes paid him, both in Erie and elsewhere in the United States. Two years before he died Burleigh was quoted as saying, "It is a wonderful thing to feel that you amount to something in music."[1] Burleigh definitely amounted to something. Forty years after his death his spirituals are still in print, indicating that they have remained in concert repertoire, despite the wealth and popularity of arrangements made by others.

Legacy

Composer and pianist Margaret Bonds (1913-1972), perhaps more than anyone else, is generally considered to have been influenced by Burleigh's style. She was a student of both Roy Harris and Robert Starer at Juilliard and also studied with Florence Price and William L. Dawson. Her degrees were from Northwestern University.

Bonds's professional activities included solo recitals (a Town Hall debut in 1952), accompanying, editing, radio performances, musical theater directing, composition and arranging. Her compositions encompassed a variety of idioms: symphony, musical comedy, ballet, cantata, piano music, and numerous songs. Some of her best-known piano arrangements are "Five Spirituals" and "Spiritual Suite for the Piano." She also set "The Negro Speaks of Rivers" and "Three

Dream Portraits" for voice, with texts by Langston Hughes, plus several of the better-known spirituals.

Some of Bonds's honors were a Rosenwald Fellowship, and special awards from the National Council of Negro Women (1962) and the Northwestern University Alumni Association (1967). She joined ASCAP in 1952.

Bonds organized the Margaret Bonds Chamber Music Society, "a group dedicated to the perpetuation and promotion of the contribution of Negro composers and poets."[2] The Society's sponsoring committee listed such luminaries as Leontyne Price, Roland Hayes, John Work, Lester Walton, Clarence Cameron White, Abbie Mitchell, Langston Hughes, Carol Brice, and Edward Boatner.

One memorial concert of significance presented by the Bonds Society was held in the Carnegie Recital Hall in New York on November 3, 1956, in Norman J. Seaman's Twilight Concerts series. A copy of the program was sent to the writer by Mrs. Josephine Love of Detroit. A review of the concert appeared in the *New York Times*, November 4, 1956.

> With the exception of the perennial favorite "Deep River" the Burleigh songs are little heard today. Hearing them, the listener is reminded afresh that . . . they are a part of the nineteenth century tradition. Nevertheless, they have charm, and it was agreeable to hear them.

The same review stated that in an intermission speech at the concert Dr. Clarence Cameron White paid tribute "to Mr. Burleigh's well-rounded musicianship" and "fluent" pianism, and recalled his generous aid to younger artists.

Events in Erie Honoring Burleigh Since His Death

Burleigh's home town has been well aware of its native son as an outstanding musician. Just a week after Burleigh's death a half-hour dramatization of his early life was planned for Erie Station WIKK. James Justice, a well-known Erie singer, was scheduled to participate.[3] However, in a phone conversation with the writer in early December of 1985, Paul Brown, Erie Channel 54 official, revealed that this documentary did not materialize.

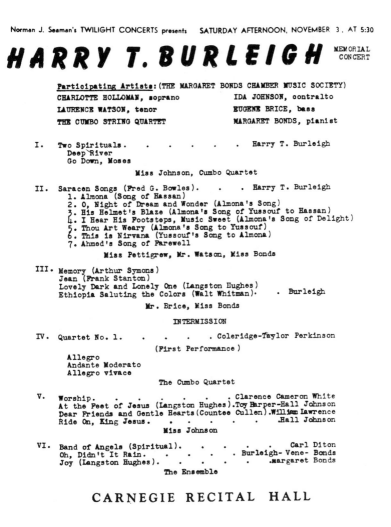

Norman J. Seaman's TWILIGHT CONCERTS presents   SATURDAY AFTERNOON, NOVEMBER 3 , AT 5:30

HARRY T. BURLEIGH MEMORIAL CONCERT

Participating Artists: (THE MARGARET BONDS CHAMBER MUSIC SOCIETY)

CHARLOTTE HOLLOMAN, soprano   IDA JOHNSON, contralto

LAURENCE WATSON, tenor   EUGENE BRICE, bass

THE CUMBO STRING QUARTET   MARGARET BONDS, pianist

I.   Two Spirituals. .   .   .   .   . Harry T. Burleigh
     Deep River
     Go Down, Moses
                    Miss Johnson, Cumbo Quartet

II. Saracen Songs (Fred G. Bowles). .   . Harry T. Burleigh
     1. Almona (Song of Hassan)
     2. O, Night of Dream and Wonder (Almona's Song)
     3. His Helmet's Blaze (Almona's Song of Yussouf to Hassan)
     4. I Hear His Footsteps, Music Sweet (Almona's Song of Delight)
     5. Thou Art Weary (Almona's Song to Yussouf)
     6. This is Nirvana (Yussouf's Song to Almona)
     7. Ahmed's Song of Farewell
                    Miss Pettigrew, Mr. Watson, Miss Bonds

III. Memory (Arthur Symons)
     Jean (Frank Stanton)
     Lovely Dark and Lonely One (Langston Hughes)
     Ethiopia Saluting the Colors (Walt Whitman).   . Burleigh
                    Mr. Brice, Miss Bonds

                    INTERMISSION

IV. Quartet No. 1.   .   .   .   . Coleridge-Taylor Perkinson
                    (First Performance)
     Allegro
     Andante Moderato
     Allegro vivace
                    The Cumbo Quartet

V.   Worship.   .   .   .   .   .   . Clarence Cameron White
     At the Feet of Jesus (Langston Hughes).Toy Harper-Hall Johnson
     Dear Friends and Gentle Hearts(Countee Cullen).William Lawrence
     Ride On, King Jesus. .   .   .   .   .Hall Johnson
                    Miss Johnson

VI. Band of Angels (Spiritual). .   .   .   . Carl Diton
     Oh, Didn't It Rain. .   .   .   . Burleigh- Vene- Bonds
     Joy (Langston Hughes). .   .   .   . Margaret Bonds
                    The Ensemble

CARNEGIE RECITAL HALL

But on December 2, 1952, Erie Mayor Thomas Flatley proclaimed "Harry T. Burleigh Memorial Day," a date also marking the
establishment of a Harry T. Burleigh Memorial Scholarship Fund,

sponsored by the Erie chapter of the NAACP. Among the honors in memory of Burleigh on this occasion was a special exhibit of his sheet music, press releases, and photos in the Erie County Library.

Burleigh's friend Dr. Earle Lawrence, at the time instructor at the Erie Conservatory of Music, and his daughter, Ada, were on committees for the events. Mrs. Robert Hagans was chairperson of the Scholarship Fund, a drive which began the following May 5 with an open house program in Dorn Auditorium. An announcement stated that students from Erie or Erie County, as well as first- or second-year college students in an accredited college, would be eligible to apply, regardless of race. The college applicants were to be recommended by their department heads; the high schoolers were to be capable of doing college work in the fields of arts and sciences. Qualified needy students were given first consideration.

In 1954 the scholarship was discontinued, a termination not satisfactorily explained in the *Erie Dispatch* of April 25, 1954: "Other activities make it undesirable to continue fund raising." The fund's balance of $1,628.45 was to be divided among the three college student recipients: Jane Anne Enis, Raymond Frith, and Henry Dunn.[4]

That year, however, the Pennsylvania Historical and Museum Commission authorized a marker, erected by the Booker T. Washington Center on East Sixth between Holland and French Streets.

One significant musical event honoring Burleigh posthumously was a Memorial Concert presented by the Erie Symphonic Choir. Under the direction of Obed L. Grender, the program included three spirituals arranged by Burleigh.

Some years later, on November 11, 1969, the Erie County Historical Society sponsored "The Life and Music of Harry T. Burleigh" at the Church of the Covenant. It was over a decade before a similar program was scheduled in Erie, co-sponsored by the Martin Luther King Center, Edinboro State College, and Mercyhurst College on November 9, 1982.

Concerned Erie educators had honored Burleigh on May 2, 1980 by dedicating Pfeiffer-Burleigh Elementary School, located at 235 East Eleventh Street, a plant designed to consolidate several older small schools in downtown Erie. It was co-named for Burleigh and Elizabeth C. Pfeiffer (1889-1984), a favorite and inspirational teacher

HARRY T. BURLEIGH

Eminent American baritone, composer, and arranger, was born 3 blocks north in 1866. He arranged "Deep River" and other spirituals, and set to music poems by Walt Whitman. Was a student and associate of Dvorak. He died in 1949.

PENNSYLVANIA HISTORICAL AND MUSEUM COMMISSION

Soon, this won't be the only plaque dedicated to Henry T. Burleigh, famous singer-composer from Erie. The National Music Council is sponsoring a bronze plaque for Burleigh as part of bicentennial celebrations. The plaque above was set up by the state government about three blocks from Burleigh's birthplace. It stands near the Erie Insurance Exchange.

Photo from the *Erie Morning News*, April 21, 1976, courtesy of the Erie County Historical Society Library.

$\mathcal{P}_{rogram}$

ORGAN PRELUDES .... Helen K. Flanigan

WELCOME .... Richard Wright

DIRECTOR OF PROGRAM .... David S. Gifford

THE LIFE OF HARRY BURLEIGH .... James Wade, Executive Director

Urban Coalition

THREE BURLEIGH SPIRITUALS .... Junior Choir, Shiloh Baptist Church

Mrs. Irma James, Director

No Hiding Place

Let Us Cheer The Weary Traveler

In That Great Getting Up Morning

SOLO .... Go Down Moses – Burleigh .... Henry Jones

BURLEIGH'S CONTRIBUTION TO AMERICAN MUSIC .... Carl Peterson

The Knabe Piano "The Official Piano of the Metropolitan Opera"

COURTESY OF

FROESS PIANO & ORGAN CO.

ERIE'S LARGEST DEALERS

8th and Cherry Streets

Program of *The Life and Music of Harry T. Burleigh*, presented by the Erie
County Historical Society, at Church of the Covenant, November 11, 1969,
8:00 p.m. Courtesy of the Erie County Historical Society Library.

Audience Participation

Hymn .... In Christ There is No East or West .... Harry Burleigh

In Christ there is no East or West
In Him no South or North
But one great fellowship of love
Throughout the whole wide earth

In Him shall true hearts ev'rywhere
Their high communion find
His service is the golden chord
Close binding all mankind

Join hands then, brothers of the faith
Whate'er your race may be
Who serves my Father as a son
Is surely kin to me

In Christ now meet both East and West
In Him meet South and North
All Christly souls are one in Him
Throughout the whole wide earth. Amen

REMINISCENCES .... Ada Lawrence Teacher, Wayne School

THREE BURLEIGH SPIRITUALS .... Strong Vincent Concert Choir

Mrs. Brenda Humphries, Director

My Lord What a Morning

Were You There

Deep River

BENEDICTION .... Reverend Alan B. Darling

Prelude:

Improvizations on Burleigh spirituals

Mr. Roger Knepshield

A Life In Music:

Dr. John Marsh

Burleigh's spirituals climaxed an already successful career as a composer of songs. Equally to the point, his skills as a song writer were in no small measure responsible for the artistic excellence of his spirituals.

The Composer Of Songs:

Mr. Robert Waterstripe
Mrs. Dianne Cordell

The most characteristic of Burleigh's songs were favorites at salon musicals and seem of a piece with compositions approved by teachers at the National Conservatory of Music. Burleigh, a student at the Conservatory from 1892 to 1896, fell under the influence of faculty members like Victor Herbert.

Group One   Mrs. Cordell

Morning, by Oley Speaks
Just You, by Harry Burleigh

Group Two   Mr. Waterstripe

Thine Alone, by Victor Herbert
Jean, by Burleigh

Group Three   Mr. Waterstripe/Mrs. Cordell

Almona, fr. Saracen Songs by Burleigh
I Hear His Footsteps, fr. Saracen Songs

Group Four   Mr. Waterstripe/Mrs. Cordell

Isle of Our Dreams from the **Red Mill,** by
Victor Herbert, 1906

Program of *The Life and Music of Harry Thacker Burleigh*, Recital Hall, Mercyhurst College, Erie, Pa., November 9, 1982, at 8:15 p.m. Courtesy of the Erie County Historical Society Library.

-- to Harry Thacker Burleigh --

The Preserver and Promoter Of Spirituals

Mr. Charles Kennedy, Jr.

Though Burleigh's reputation rests on his pioneering the genre. That distinction belongs to the Fisk Jubilee Singers, who, as early as 1871, began concertizing to raise funds for Fisk Institute. And there has been a collegiate continuity of interest in spirituals almost ever since -- certainly since Burleigh's arrangements.

Edinboro State College's Concert Chorale   Dr. Gordon Flood

Swing Low, Sweet Chariot
Steal Away
Nobody Knows The Trouble I've Seen
Little David
Wade in de Water
Were You There?

arranged by Burleigh

Burleigh's Contribution

Dr. Marsh

To the point that Burleigh became an active promoter of spirituals, there had been no arrangements of them for solo voice with independent piano accompaniment. Beginning with "Deep River" (1916), Harry Burleigh produced a succession of authoritative solo arrangements that not only enhanced the popularity but the respectability of the genre. As evidence of the latter, leading concert artists of the day began including them in their recital programs -- a tribute to the artistic integrity of Harry Burleigh, one of the most learned and technically able of our black musicians.

Spirituals for solo voice

Mr. Waterstripe

Deep River
Hard Trials
Stan' Still Jordan

Burleigh's Spirituals Today

Mr. Bruce Morton Wright

Burleigh's profoundly moving arrangements challenge performers far removed from the world in which the spirituals originated. Challenge choir directors unaware of Burleigh's belief that spirituals have "a plaintive, tender quality but they are not sad -- rather they are inspirational in character . . . They stand today a permanent evidence of the race's spiritual ascendency over oppression and humiliation." -- 1934 --

Junior Choir, Shiloh Baptist Church

Mrs. Sarah Wright, director

Little David Play on Your Harp
Oh Lord Deliver Us

Senior Choir, Shiloh Baptist Church

Mrs. Irma James, director

Couldn't Hear Nobody Pray
Keep Your Lamps Trimmed and Burning

Guest Soloist

Viola Williams

Sometimes I Feel Like A Motherless Child
Steal Away

Credits

The sponsors of the program are the Martin Luther King Center, Edinboro State College and Mercyhurst College. Those interested in discovering more about Burleigh's life and art should consult the extensive collection of materials in the Erie Co. Historical Society. Working with the collection, Dr. John Marsh authored "Harry Thacker Burleigh: Hard Knocks and Triumphant Days," **Journal of Erie Studies,** Fall, 1980, pp. 18-28.

in Erie for fifty-two years. Aspiring early to become a gym teacher, Miss Pfeiffer remained athletic as a horseback rider and ice skater, as borne out by charming photos in Erie newspapers. The very active "Sisty," as she was called, suffered multiple ailments, among them failing eye-sight, in the last few years of her long and productive life.[5] Photos of both Miss Pfeiffer and Burleigh hang in one of the halls at the school. Burleigh's had been a gift from him to Ada Lawrence, who donated it to the school.

During Black History Week held in Erie on May 8-9, 1986, Dr. Doris McGinty of Howard University read a paper titled "The Music of Harry T. Burleigh." A recital of Burleigh's art songs was given by baritone Patrick Shelby and pianist Anne Simpson of the University of Southwestern Louisiana. The well-conceived convention poster, featuring a drawing of Burleigh which is also on the program cover, was designed by Laurie Marks.

Other Posthumous Remembrances Outside Erie

It is neither practical nor necessary to cite all of the performances of Burleigh's works or all of the occasional news articles printed about him since his death. Suffice it to say that though his art songs seldom appear on a recital program today, his arrangements of spirituals continue to be used by many solo singers and choirs.

The annual service of spirituals begun at St. George's church in 1924 continued through the mid-1950s. A program of the service on May 21, 1955, listed soloists Carol Brice, Mary Robbs, Barbara Terry, and Gayla Glenn, assisted by the St. George's Choral Society, St. George's Choir, and the Junior and Children's Choir. Burleigh's arrangements of the Processional Hymn, "O Brothers Lift Your Voices" and "What a Friend We Have in Jesus," plus nine of his spirituals were presented with other spirituals arranged by organist George W. Kemmer, Edward Boatner, Hall Johnson and John W. Work.[6]

Perpetuating the Burleigh aura at St. George's were comments in a letter to Mrs. Mary Benedict of Erie from Charles Henderson, a former organist at that church.

By the time we arrived at St. George's in 1955 Burleigh
was long gone to his reward and he was a very important
legend in the parish. Many people spoke of him, his singing,
his courtly manner, his cultural distinction.

The rector Miller (he came to St. George's in 1946) had
known him and often mentioned him in sermons. In the 1964
history of St. George's, which was authored by Elizabeth
Moulton, a parishioner, Burleigh is mentioned several times.

While we were at St. George's the archives were assembled, including many photos and facts about Burleigh.
However, the archivist is long gone, and I fear the collection
has disappeared over the years. I know that she (Irene
Golden) was most helpful to any number of students and
scholars who were doing research on Burleigh.[7]

In an article from the *New York Amsterdam News* (June 9, 1966)
by ASCAP member Jack Yellen, Burleigh was included among a
select dozen black composers who had achieved success.[8]

During "Black Music in College and University Curricula," a
four-day seminar at Indiana University, June 18-21, 1969, Burleigh's
works again proved themselves worthy of attention. "Deep River" and
Southland Sketches were performed on one of three programs given
at the seminar. At a session on "Black Composers and the Avant-
Garde" the question, "What IS Black Music?" arose. One speaker
replied:

> Quite a heavy emphasis on rhythm appears on the west
> coast, but as you go farther east there is less. I'm not so sure
> I could tell the difference between Burleigh's *Southland
> Sketches* and a work by John Powell, who was a White
> racist.[9]

Speaking on teaching and curricula at the same conference
Dominique René de Lerma said:

> I feel . . . that the student should learn not only history,
> but repertoire. Cannot Burleigh's "Deep River" teach the
> Black violinist how to treat certain problems as well as Raff's
> "Cavatina?"[10]

Burleigh was featured in a series by Washington *Evening Star* journalists George Reasons and Sam Patrick, titled "They Had a Dream." The particular article, "Burleigh Saved Negro Spirituals," which appeared in that paper on August 1, 1970, though not entirely accurate in fact, did present an impressive picture of Burleigh's professional life. The authors attributed the popularity of "Little Mother of Mine" to Enrico Caruso with no mention of John McCormack's success with the song. A drawing of Burleigh by Patrick accompanied the article.

Benjamin Matthews, concert singer and opera director, though admitting to unfamiliarity with Burleigh's art songs, remarked after a concert at the University of Southwestern Louisiana in Lafayette, February 5, 1986: "Oh, I do a lot of Burleigh!" Though no Burleigh spirituals were programmed that particular evening, Matthews fully demonstrated his superb sensitivity for the spiritual in arrangements by Bonds and Work.

From October 31 through November 2 of 1986 Burleigh was highlighted as a part of the NAACP's forty-eighth New England Regional Conference held at Edgartown, Massachusetts. One of the biographical news items preceding the conference stated that Burleigh coached Enrico Caruso, whom he met on a business trip to Milan.[11]

Ample publicity heralded the conference's culmination, a program on Burleigh's life and works, staged at the Old Whaling Church by singers Georgia Franklin of Queens, New York, and Vineyard Haven, and Helen Jennings of Springfield and Oak Bluffs, with narrator Isaac Patterson, who brought to life a script written by William Anderson. An audience more knowledgeable of Burleigh's serious side, especially with regard to his music and his personal privacy, might look askance at the authenticity of this production. Parts of a review by Shirley Adams bear out the inaccuracies compounded in Anderson's script:

> It was a clever, interesting, beautiful and excellently performed production. The narrator, Isaac Patterson, began by impersonating H. T. Burleigh by walking through the audience, greeting old-time friends from the Vineyard: Dorothy West, Barbara Townes, Elizabeth White and

Dr. John Moseley, whom he knew from the forty summers he spent vacationing at the Shearer Cottage in East Chop.

The music began with the duet, "John's Gone Down on De Island," composed in 1917 at the Shearer Cottage, sung by the two sopranos in beautiful ensemble. Taking turns, each sang two songs: "Swing Low, Sweet Chariot" and "I've Been in the Storm So Long," followed by "Give Me Jesus" and "De Gospel Train." In between each song, the narrator gave a short resume of Burleigh's life. His mother was a Creole with four children (he was the youngest) and a blind father, who had been a slave, to support.

. . . She taught him every song she knew, how to play the piano and also French, as that was her language, he was singing at an early age at St. Paul's Cathedral and also at parties in wealthy homes. A great friend of his mother's, a Mrs. Russell, knew a woman who married a MacDowell in New York City whose son was on the board of the Juilliard School of Music and, therefore, H. T. got a voice scholarship there. . . . While at Juilliard, H.T. had become fascinated by the great composer, Anton Dvorak.

. . . Nellie Melba had the idea of ending every concert by singing a spiritual. He wrote accompaniments for her and then wrote "Deep River." There was a great demand for his spirituals and he became so absorbed in his writing that Louise left him for another man, taking their son with her and leaving him devastated. This was embodied in the song, "The Grey Wolf."

Victor Herbert and Burleigh formed ASCAP and he became an editor for Riccardi [sic] Publishing Company, which meant he had to travel to Italy every year. . . .

The spoken part of the program ended with the thought – the next time you go to the shore, think of the water as a bridge leading everywhere.

Helen Jennings has a lovely, sweet voice and an engaging personality. She wore a stunning blue short evening dress with a pattern of brilliants on it. Georgia Franklin has a well-trained, beautiful, full-bodied, commanding voice. Their duets were beautifully done, with perfect ensemble.

The piano accompanist, Carleton Inniss, was tremendous. The piano parts were as difficult and demanding as a solo would have been, and he followed the singers like their own shadows, never covering them over. I talked with him afterward, and he said it had taken a year to put on this program.

The narrator, Isaac Patterson, was an excellent actor, and I understand, learned this part in three weeks as it was first planned as a concert and then it was decided more or less at the last moment to make it a play.

Congratulations to all involved. It was a marvelous performance. It was a privilege to hear all the beautiful music of Harry Thacker Burleigh.[12]

Another account of the show was given by Randall Pease. Not without humor, he captured some of Burleigh's charm with more accurate data. He called the singing in this Freedom Concert "joyous and wonderful."

A full house rode The Gospel Train into the Life, Time and Music of Harry T. Burleigh Saturday night at the Old Whaling Church. . . .

We can thank H. T. that we remember gospel music at all. He helped to make the oral tradition literate, and in the process preserved gospel music for the jazz and classical artists who drew inspiration from it, like water from a deep well.

. . . At the National Conservatory of Music he met Anton Dvorak, and the rest, as they say, is history.

And after the opening vocal duet Pease continued:

Then Mr. Burleigh himself came down the aisle from the back of the church. On his way he recognized a longtime Island resident whom he had known when she was a teenager. "Elizabeth White? It is you. You are still beautiful," he said to her. And she answered, "Yes I am." That set H. T. back on his heels for a moment.

He asked her if she remembered the first time he took her to the opera: "Listen to the singer, I told you. Listen to that glorious voice. But all you were saying, Elizabeth, was that she will never fit into that chair!" And to that Elizabeth shot back, "And you scolded me, 'We are not interested in fannies tonight.' "

He moved on, greeting all of us, until he noticed another familiar face in the audience: "Those beautiful blue eyes. They could only belong to Dorothy West." But H. T. did not visit us, in the final analysis, to reminisce, either about his life or his music.

About the spirituals the review went on to say:

As H. T. Burleigh – or his spokesman William Anderson – tells it: "Those spirituals built a bridge that came to rest on undreamed of shores. I was the first to cross it, but it wasn't long before others followed – Marian Anderson, Paul Robeson and so many others. But that bridge was not just for artists. The love I gave and got guided so many Vineyard children, and my own boy, and his children on to that spiritual bridge that led them to all kinds of places and positions in the world. And the thousands of children I don't know, and who don't know me. For it's their bridge, too. And I don't mean just our children. All children."

Spirituals – or to put it a more universal way, spirit or faith – are what he calls his bridge. It's an old story, that faith can move mountains, or build bridges in this case. Saturday night in the Old Whaling Church it was renewed. We could see, and hear it working in H. T.'s life.

. . . Isaac Patterson moves backstage, and Helen Jennings moves forward and sings "Deep River." Similarly, H. T. Burleigh's music was centerstage in the man's life, not vice versa. For this reason Helen Jennings and Georgia Franklin – who was especially powerful in "The Gray Wolf" – made the program work.

. . . As Harry T. Burleigh told the audience, "Now it's time for me to be goin' home. Next time you walk down to the shore, and look out across the water, you remember – you're not at land's end; you're where a bridge begins! And it leads anywhere! Even from this world to the next." The show ended with another superb duet – "I Stood on the River of Jordan" – which left NAACP delegates and Islanders at least wanting to believe.[13]

As recently as April 4, 1987, Jean E. Snyder, a graduate student at the University of Pittsburgh, presented a detailed paper, "The Music of Harry T. Burleigh in Pittsburgh," to the International Association for the Study of Popular Music.

Performances of Burleigh's works in Pittsburgh were meticulously documented by Snyder from 1903 until early 1960. Her thorough research proves that Burleigh's music was alive and well for many years in Pittsburgh. In Snyder's interview with Dr. Ralph T. Hill, founder of the Sounds of Heritage, a choir which sings only unaccompanied spirituals, he remarked: "I never let a performance of spirituals go by without some Burleigh."[14]

Pittsburgh conductor and composer Harvey Gaul's description of Burleigh indicated that they were personally acquainted:

> He was born singing. . . . He is a scholar, a composer, and a splendid arranger. Being a Negro, he was entirely at home in the "spirichel" idiom, and so a quarter of a century ago be began where another distinguished Negro composer left off – Coleridge-Taylor. Mr. Burleigh has done more for – and with – Negro spirituals than any other composer-arranger. He has some one hundred arrangements; and whether it is "Were You There When They Crucified My Lord," or the noble "Deep River," he never ruins them with his own idiosyncracies – and that is more than can be said for many of our arrangers. Harry Burleigh is a credit to his race – or any race – and an inspiration to other editors.[15]

It is enigmatic that Burleigh is not mentioned in the entry on Spirituals in *The New Grove Dictionary of American Music* (1986). Research for *Hard Trials* has yet to reveal a single unkind, cutting, or derogatory remark about Harry T. Burleigh. One priceless statement was made by Paul Robeson's biographer, Marie Seton, who spoke of Dvorak as "a friend of Harry T. Burleigh, the distinguished Negro composer."[16]

In Praise of Burleigh:
Opinions of Contemporaries

Approximately three weeks after Burleigh's death *St. George's Bulletin* for October 2, 1949, devoted a page in memory of him, with a photo and an encomium by Reverend Edward O. Miller. In part it read:

> Few men have had so long and rich an influence on the life of a parish as our beloved friend Harry T. Burleigh. Brought to St. George's by Dr. Rainsford in 1894, he sang in the Choir for 52 years. All who came in contact with him felt his unusual power, not only as a musician and composer, but as a Christian gentleman and a devoted friend. Long before the hour of Sunday morning choir rehearsal, he could be found sitting quietly in the Church "just getting the feel of it." He seemed aware of deeper tones of brotherhood and throbbing harmonies of humanity which others did not hear.
>
> Those who filled the Church for his funeral on September 15 felt something of this power. A long life of Christian influence had found its response among us and had ended in a service of triumph. Dr. Reiland spoke of his happy years with Mr. Burleigh. . . .
>
> Long will we remember the loyal presence of Harry Burleigh. Long will we continue to feel the strength and joy which flowed from his life to others through the beauty of song. St. George's is a better place because of the many years of faithful service which he gave. We shall pause often to thank God for all that he came to mean to each one of us and to our Church.[17]

Reverend Miller, now retired and living in Castine, Maine, generously shared the following personal remembrances of Burleigh in a letter to the author, March 15, 1988.

> Before me, as I write, is the silver nameplate from Harry Burleigh's choir locker at St. George's Church, New York. He was choir soloist for fifty-two years, retiring after the Easter service in 1946. I arrived in November of that year,

and remained as rector for thirty years. From 1938 to 1941, however, I had served on the staff of St. George's as assistant to the rector; during this period I came to know Mr. Burleigh quite well. He seemed to enjoy taking me, as a very young man, under his tutelage.

I remember this dignified gentleman, with balding white hair and finely-trimmed mustache, sitting alone in the church every Sunday at least a half hour before choir rehearsal. As he said to me: "I have to get the feel of the place before I sing."

When, in 1946, my wife and I arrived in Pennsylvania Station to take up our new church duties, I told the cab driver to take us to St. George's Church. "Where's that?" "On Stuyvesant Square, on the East Side." "Oh, you mean Mr. Burleigh's church."

Though the parish worshipped Mr. Burleigh, he remained aloof. Mr. Morgan might invite him to his home, but always as a performer. The Rectory was located between the church and the parish house; Mr. Burleigh had to walk past it twice a week for fifty-two years, yet never would he accept the most cordial invitation to come inisde.

He was a very private person. Long before his retirement his voice began to falter, embarrassingly so at the end, yet he would not retire. Estranged from his son, he bottled up his personal life, especially toward the end, when his mind was not sharp. I knew that his mother, a college graduate, had been forced to work as a janitress in a Pennsylvania public school, where, because of race prejudice, a teaching post had been denied her. And that she was the daughter of a blind slave who was discarded by his Maryland owners when his usefulness had ceased. But only once, for a brief moment, did he refer to them. He was fond of his grandson, who became a doctor and corresponded with me for some years.

I often think of Harry Burleigh when I repeat my conviction that the Lord has a sense of humor. When I arrived at St. George's the Vestry consisted of twelve aristocratic gentlemen who met once a month in dinner jackets. They

were leaders in the fields of law and finance. At my first
meeting, the entire session was taken to discuss what kind of
pension the church should pay Mr. Burleigh, who had recently retired. All that he had meant to the parish was enu-
merated, and he should receive a generous pension for the
rest of his life. It was a condescending manner in which they
spoke of the financial needs of an elderly muscian who was
also black. Finally they voted the munificent sum of $60 per
month. After his death it was found that his estate was estimated at $300,000 and that royalties from his 300 songs
amounted to $15,000 annually!

Mr. Burleigh's death produced turmoil. I have a tele-
gram from an Erie funeral director demanding that he be
buried next to his mother there. His widow in Wisconsin, his
housekeeper in New York, and his son all had strong ideas.
Finally I worked it out so that he would be buried in New
York, whereupon I discovered that none of the well-known
cemeteries in the New York area would bury a black man.
I was disgusted and angry. A man good enough to sing twice
before King Edward VII, and every Christmas in Mr. Morgan's home! I protested by calling prominent members of the
boards of the cemeteries, but to no avail.

In the end I persuaded Mt. Hope Cemetery in Hastings-
on-Hudson to sell us a lot. The service at St. George's was
overwhelming, the church packed, and the congregational
singing rasied the roof. A large number drove in the cortege
to the cemetery. As I was conducting the sevice, suddenly it
came over me that I was hallucinating, for louder and louder
came the strains of "Swing Low, Sweet Chariot." Someone
had placed a loud speaker beneath the blanket of flowers
that covered his grave, and the music of Harry Burleigh was
engulfing us, even beyond his death.

Composer William Grant Still, after completing his opera
Troubled Island (c. 1940), telephoned Burleigh asking his help in
getting the attention of someone influential at the Metropolitan
Opera. "Burleigh was very kind but he told the young man [Still] that
the manuscript should be submitted directly to the Met." Still, at the

time, took this as a rebuff, but later understood the wisdom of Burleigh's advice: that the Met went its own way and listened to no one. In later years Burleigh was more friendly and encouraging to Still. After hearing the New York Philharmonic under Pierre Monteux play Still's *Old California*, Burleigh wrote on the program "'Twas a triumph!"[18]

Still wrote: "I did know Harry Burleigh. He was such a gentleman; he had beautiful manners, courtly."[19] In Still's opinion Burleigh, with White and Dett, was one of the "pioneers in the field of serious music who showed the way" to him and other black composers.[20]

Concurrence with Still's comment was expressed by a writer for the *Vineyard Gazette*, September 16, 1949:

> Music helped to design for Mr. Burleigh personally an existence that knew a full share of fulfillment. But the music that he made as a composer and singer was even more important in what it did for others.

He continued, quoting another *Gazette* reporter who had interviewed Burleigh in 1927:

> The only difficult thing about interviewing this singer and composer with the worldwide reputation is that he is constantly veering away from the subject of his own work to praise that of others.

Singer John Seagle, son of Oscar Seagle, often used Burleigh's "Jean" and several of his spirituals in concert. As one of a vocal quartet for NBC which performed many of the arrangements, Seagle was quite often telephoned by Burleigh, who thanked him for "using his tunes."[21]

Jester Hairston, prominent singer, choir director, and arranger, who knew Burleigh and was a friend of Alston Burleigh's college roommate in the early to mid-1920s, remembered falling heir to a pair of $18 shoes that Burleigh had bought for Alston. "Best pair of shoes I ever had," Hairston said.[22] Too, Hairston told Jean E. Snyder of Pittsburgh that

> he and other young black musicians would take their arrangements to him in the music store at Ricordi for criticism

and suggestions. Burleigh was never too busy to stop and help. Hairston believes that Burleigh was a great asset to Ricordi working behind the counter, as his arrangements were so popular and he brought them a lot of business.[23]

One writer on talented blacks says:

> If only someone had had the vision, in Burleigh's youth, to set him free from that long struggle for mere existence and make it possible for him to spend his strength in the work he was made for, he would rank with MacDowell himself. . . . America, and the whole world of art, is the poorer because Burleigh had to fight for his daily bread so long.[24]

Maud Cuney-Hare lauds Burleigh as "the most famous of Negro musicians," saying that

> His career as a singer, untainted by sensationalism, differed somewhat from that of an earlier group of talented vocalists of the race in that he had the advantage of an educated mind as well as a trained voice. His generosity to struggling musicians and to all worthy causes is a well-known trait of his character. The mental attainment which this composer has reached is unquestionably one of the principal causes of his being one of the foremost writers of music to the English text.[25]

In an almost spiritualistic, certainly eulogistic, vein Reverend Elmore M. McKee of St. George's (1936-46) wrote of Burleigh:

> A man of grace, gentleness, courtesy, humor and loyalty.
> A musician who, as composer, singer and interpreter has given to multitudes a lift along life's steep ascent.
> A representative of a race which, having suffered much at the hands of its brothers, has chosen to express its suffering not in retaliation, but in song.
> A man of faith who took his religion seriously and counted it a high privilege to pray much, to serve humbly and to sing for half a century to the glory of God in St. George's, New York.[26]

Norman Tyler Sobel's Unfinished Dream

Around the turn of the century all facets of America's cultural, industrial, and spiritual life invited growth and offered a wealth of hitherto untapped ideas, ripe for expansion and improvement. Erie, as a developing city, was fortunate to have had Isador Sobel, lawyer and philanthropist, in residency from 1889 until his death in 1939. A near replica of the Renaissance Man, he possessed the added virtue of altruism.

A born organizer, Sobel's concerns and interests were unlimited, especially as a fund raiser for worthy ventures in the Erie area. Largely responsible for the creation of Presque Isle State Park, he was also active as a supporter and leader in Erie's Jewish community. Additionally, he extended his talents for the benefit of Pennsylvania as a whole. Honors for his good works were myriad.[27]

One of Isador Sobel's smaller charitable acts was in behalf of Harry Thacker Burleigh in 1892, when he raised a purse among his friends and associates, enabling Burleigh to apply for a scholarship at the National Conservatory in New York. Burleigh respectfully kept in touch over the years with his friend Sobel by visits to Erie, on which occasions he usually sang for him.[28]

Emma and Isador Sobel, wed in 1891, had four sons. Norman, born in 1899, evidently inherited his father's philanthropic drive, though his civic involvements were not as magnanimous as his father's had been. After graduation from Erie High School in 1918 Norman attended the University of Pennsylvania in Philadelphia, but he did not finish a degree there.

During the early 1920s, as a real estate agent, Norman Sobel made a map of Erie, which is now in the ECHS Library. By the mid-1920s he had established his own firm in Flushing, New York, the Norman T. Sobel Company, of which he was real estate/insurance agent and broker. It was not until the late 1970s, having been asked by the Erie County Historical Society to collect all available material on Harry Burleigh, that he began earnest research. Mrs. Helen Andrews, ECHS librarian and a personal friend of Sobel, commented:

Mr. Sobel was not a scholarly researcher, but he was very active in his methods of research. . . . The Sobels had a life long interest in Burleigh. Norman was rather elderly when he did his research, his last years. It seemed to be his last great effort! . . . Some of the records are disjointed but there are many sources given.[29]

A letter to the Library of Congress written when Sobel was eighty, dated November 5, 1980, shows his continued sincerity in pursuing the project, one intended to culminate in a biography of Burleigh. In part the letter reads:

Gentlemen:

I desire to obtain a list of ALL of the titles, of the musical compositions and arrangement[s] of Harry Thacker Burleigh and bound volumes, etc. of his musical compositions and arrangements. I am of the opinion, that he, Harry Thacker Burleigh and/or each and every one, of the publishers of Harry Thacker Burleigh's musical compositions and arrangements, – copyrighted through your office, each and every one of Harry Thacker Burleigh's musical compositions and arrangements, and bound volumes, etc. thereof, and that, therefore, your office can supply me with a complete list of those musical compositions, arrangements and bound volumes thereof, and give me besides their titles, other pertinent information about them.

The Erie County Historical Society, situated in Erie, Pa., has asked me to try to collect from every source, all the material I can regarding the life and music of Harry Thacker Burleigh, for its archives. . . .

. . . I had met Harry Thacker Burleigh in my father's office, in the year 1922, and after he became a member of the Erie Club of New York, I got to know him well. . . . I wish to thank you in advance for your assistance in this matter.

Sincerely,
Norman T. Sobel

Coming from a prominent, well-off, and non-prejudiced Jewish family in Erie, it is possible that the traumas of racial injustice had not been felt with great impact by Norman Sobel. As a hired entertainer Burleigh had often sung at the Erie Club of New York, a prestigious business and professional men's group, of which Sobel was a member and later president. Sobel wrote to Martin Winkler, president of Belwin-Mills music publishers: "He [Burleigh] played and sang many of his arrangements and compositions at the meetings."[30]

However, it was obvious that the hotel management which hosted the Erie Club was free to include blacks only as entertainers, not as guests. A letter, dated January 26, 1986, confirming this situation was sent to the writer by Mrs. Virginia D. Moorhead of Erie. Mrs. Moorhead's father, John C. Diehl, was a member of the Erie Club.

But as Sobel stated in his letter of November 5, 1980, Burleigh was later allowed to join the club, and as a member was treated with mounting respect, in no little part due to Sobel's friendship and concern. In 1944 during a reception at St. George's honoring Burleigh for his fiftieth year with that church, the Erie Club presented him with a silver-banded cane.

An examination of Sobel's collection in the ECHS Library reveals some insight into the large scope of his plans. He was a sedulous correspondent and querist, for there are numerous copies of letters asking for information and permissions. He did not give up easily, a fact evidenced by repeated efforts from 1976 to 1979 towards obtaining musical scores of Burleigh's work from Belwin-Mills. Belwin-Mills finally donated the music, which had not been selling well for several years, for distribution through Sobel.

Other Sobel correspondence requested information on recordings of Burleigh's works from the Copyright Office in the Library of Congress with the answer: "The copyright office has no information on sound recordings produced before 1972."[31] Supposedly this dead end sparked the idea of Sobel's backing such recordings himself, though he felt that the project would not be commercially remunerative. He had hoped to record through church auspices, using church choirs and the best available recording equipment.[32] On his list of contacts were contralto Marian Anderson and two church groups.

Sobel also wanted to make a biographical movie of Burleigh, re-sembling *Roots*, which would reach large audiences. For these two ideas, the recordings and the movie, he envisioned draft advisory boards and committees comprised of such personages as Avery Fisher, Ralph Bunche, Peter Mennin, and John D. Rockefeller III. Shortly before his death he had planned to contact Leon Thompson, Director of Educational Activities with the New York Philharmonic, who was a friend of Burleigh's grandson, Dr. Harry T. Burleigh II.

During July to September of 1980 Sobel wrote for material to the Beinecke Rare Books and Manuscripts Library at Yale University, where the James Weldon Johnson Collection is housed. Johnson, the poet, author, and diplomat, had collaborated with Burleigh on *Passionale*, a cycle of four songs published in 1915. Sobel also received material from the American Society of Composers, Authors and Publishers (ASCAP).

Another of Sobel's letters to the Library of Congress requested its tracking down registration of approximately 800 copyrights on Burleigh's works. The reply stated that for a fee of $3,000 it would be possible. According to Mrs. Helen Andrews, Sobel did not pursue the matter further.[33]

Sobel was a determined and tenacious genealogical researcher. Throughout his correspondence he seemed particularly obsessed with data, or rather the lack thereof, on Lucinda Waters, Burleigh's maternal grandmother, wife of Hamilton Waters. The intrigue focused on the fact that Lucinda was of Scottish-Indian ancestry. Concerning her, Sobel issued many letters whose answers never actually satisfied him. One, in particular, from the Department of General Services in Annapolis, Maryland, indicated that Somerset County Marriage Records (1815-41), the Census Index (1830), various years of Church Baptism and Marriage Records, and Tilghman wills for the early nineteenth century had all been checked. No references concerning Hamilton Waters or Lucinda Waters were found.

His sketches of the projected biography run the gamut of hand-written fragmented phrases on one-inch strips of yellow paper to detailed accounts. Many of the same notes are jotted or typed repeatedly. One gem buried among the small strips stated that Burleigh was pleased to know that Sobel loved to sing and was particularly fond of "Deep River." A good part of Sobel's firsthand material was gained through interviews with Burleigh himself, Alston Burleigh, and Dr. Harry T. Burleigh II, as well as with Erieites who knew Burleigh, especially the Earle Lawrence family.

Clues to Sobel's persistency are further revealed in personal letters from 1976 to 1980 to Mrs. Andrews, his dear friend. He was both adamant and critical when she occasionally failed to answer promptly concerning some matter of involved research. Often, however, his impatience with her was momentary, as he signed almost every request, "Fondly, Norman."

Duplicates of nearly the entire collection on Burleigh at the ECHS Library were given by Sobel to the Schomburg Library and the Performing Arts Research Center, Music Division, both at the New York Public Library. Within the ECHS collection are four autographed copies to Isador and Norman Sobel of Burleigh's songs, copies of biographical material on Burleigh, approximately sixty copies of Burleigh's art songs and arrangements of spirituals, numerous recital programs, a copy of a manuscript of "Deep River," dated 1926, and Sobel's voluminous correspondence. A detailed list of holdings, i.e., exact titles of songs and arrangements, specific articles, etc., may be obtained from the ECHS Library.

The growing importance of Norman Sobel's contribution is inestimable. Several scholars from various universities over the United States have visited the collection to prepare articles, addresses, and lectures. Perhaps more information on Norman Sobel himself will be made available one day, when final details of his estate are settled.

As yet, his personal papers, promised to the ECHS Library, have not been received. Awaiting them, Director John Claridge wrote: "The buckram boxes into which they were supposed to go stand empty."[34] These twenty-four lettered boxes were made to order, but not without some unpleasantries between Sobel and the Heckman Bindery in North Manchester, Indiana. A delay in their completion and shipment to Erie piqued Sobel almost beyond endurance, causing him, in his own words, to spend "many hundreds of dollars" to spray the 100-year-old papers with a special preservative.

Norman Sobel died suddenly on August 26, 1981, during a visit to Erie for a class reunion. Unmarried, he left no heirs who might have been interested in carrying on his project.

In Retrospect: A Young
Man's Impressions

Burleigh was unquestionably a role model for his godson, James Hall (b. August 10, 1932), the son of Mrs. Thelma Teasdale Hall (d. 1981), Burleigh's housekeeper for almost ten years.

Presently, Dr. James C. Hall, Jr., is Dean of Adult and Continuing Education at York College, City University of New York. Prior to this position Dr. Hall served as Dean of Students at New York City Community College. He has been active as a teacher, a curriculum coordinator, and an educational advisor and consultant in a number of New York colleges and public schools. In 1968-69 he was an education specialist for the Peace Corps, a post preceded by an assistant professorship in teacher education at the College of the Virgin Islands in St. Thomas.

Dr. Hall has contributed articles to several education journals and travelled extensively, not only in the United States, but in Latin and Central America, Europe, Africa, the Middle East, and the Far East. He serves on numerous civic and educational committees in the New York area. From his first marriage Dr. Hall has one daughter, Marie-Elena. He enjoys sailing, cooking, films, art, and travel.

Having learned of this biography of Burleigh through a Cheyney librarian, Dr. Hall has willingly shared his memories of Mr. Burleigh. The following reminiscences, presented in first person, were taken from tapes made by Hall in December of 1986 and January of 1987.

Some details of Hall's early schooling seem necessary, for in large degree they shed light, if indirectly, on Burleigh's standards and expectations. For his own son, Alston, Burleigh wanted the best, as indicated by the fact that Alston attended private school in England for four years. Burleigh's sense of responsibility and guidance evidently did not change a great deal. Hall related on a tape,

> As a teenager my mother, Thelma Teasdale, worked at summer homes in northern New Jersey with my grandmother, who was a cook. My mother helped her with light housekeeping, watching children, and so on.

Mrs. Thelma Teasdale Hall and son James on Prospect Avenue in the Bronx, 1933. Courtesy of Dr. James Hall, Jr.

Mrs. Thelma Hall, c. 1931. Courtesy of Dr. James Hall, Jr.

Mrs. Thelma Hall and H. T. Burleigh in the early 1940s. Courtesy of
Dr. James Hall, Jr.

Minnie, my mother's life-long friend from childhood who went to the same high school with her, cannot recollect when or how my mother met Mr. Burleigh. She knows that while my father was with her, during the early years, they knew Mr. Burleigh, but no one that is alive that I can reach knows exactly how my mother and Mr. Burleigh became acquainted.

One possible scenario is that Mr. Burleigh lived in an apartment house next door to a family called the Joneses, a mother and several daughters who were close to the age of my mother. I knew that my grandmother and probably my mother knew the Joneses. Mr. Burleigh may have asked, seeing that there were a number of girls in the family, if anybody was interested in some light housework and they may have recommended my mother. This seems more likely than his advertising for a housekeeper.

My mother must have first met Mr. Burleigh in the late 1920s or early 1930s, certainly prior to my birth in 1932. I had an older sister who died while my mother was carrying me and the doctor that delivered me, a Dr. Dunne, a Scotch doctor and surgeon, was a friend of Mr. Burleigh's at the time.

While working for Mr. Burleigh my mother, an uncertified elementary teacher, was also working at a small private black school run by the wife and daughter (Mildred) of James Weldon Johnson. Called the Modern School, it was located in upper Harlem in some brownstone houses. It catered to the children of middle class black families, anywhere from fifteen to fifty of them in a given year. It also became a sort of mini minority prep school for preparing children to go on to some of the better private white schools of adult ethical culture where I attended, such as Dalton, Walden, Horace Mann, and a number of the others which are still in existence.

As early as the late 30s and early 40s these schools were actively seeking to integrate – I chuckle because what they meant by "integrate" was that out of a student population of

100 they wanted to have maybe one black, or one oriental, and a few Christians on each grade level. So when I was going to the Ethical Culture System, I believe there were two or three black youngsters, some of them with prominent names.

People representative of these schools would periodically come to visit the Modern School and take a look at the youngsters. It was almost like a farm in the sense that they were selected to go on to the white schools. The curriculum was a very liberal, wide-based one. They did a lot of music, dance and cultural kinds of things. We put on our own plays – once we did "The Nutcracker Suite." We were encouraged to attend the Saturday morning concerts at Carnegie Hall – a phenomena beyond belief. That was when Dean Dixon was the conductor, the first black one.

There were about eight youngsters that I went through the class with, and one, Donald Johnson, younger than I, had been adopted by Mrs. Johnson and Mildred – I'm not sure whether there was an actual adoption. As I understood, his mother was a black entertainer, his father was a white businessman, and Donnie was a fair, blonde, blue-eyed youngster who was raised by the Johnsons. He and I were fairly close, along with a number of other youngsters. The point is that out of the group of eight two committed suicide, one is incurably insane, one who was the brightest ended up at Oxford and one of the loveliest ones became a drug addict and a prostitute. This mortality rate indicates the tremendous pressure that this group of youngsters was under to perform and to transcend their culture and their circumstances. Out of the eight, there are two of us still walking around, standing up straight.

By the fifth or sixth grade we were off and running to the private schools, and in the middle of the fourth grade I got into Ethical Culture, a society, quasi religious or philosophical society, that had several elementary schools and a junior high and high school with exquisite grounds in the Bronx called Fieldstone. I graduated from Fieldstone in a lot of difficulty. I was bright, but a prankster. They got me a

scholarship to Brown, but I was under probation by the time
I left Brown at the end of my first year. Again, bright, well-
liked, just wasn't doing any work, and pulling all sorts of
pranks that are still famous today in Providence.

I ran away, joined the Marine Corps, then went to New
York University, graduated as an elementary school teacher,
went back to get a Master's in Curriculum, and got my Doctorate in Administration, then took a few courses at Columbia.

But getting back to Mildred Johnson and her mother,
"Old Lady Johnson," as we used to call her, my mother
worked for them at least ten years at the Modern School.
During this time she obviously was in contact with Mr. Burleigh, since he knew the Johnsons and about the school. But
I never got any impression that there was much close social
or even professional collaboration between the Johnsons and
Mr. Burleigh. I know Mr. Burleigh was influential in encouraging my attendance at Ethical Culture, and he was very
happy about that and the fact that I went on to graduate
from Fieldstone, where I was known as Jimmie Teasdale.
Now remember, Teasdale was my mother's maiden name
and through the records she will not appear as Thelma Hall,
but possibly as Thelma Hall Teasdale. My name through
school was James Hall Teasdale, but my mother retained to
her death her original maiden name, though she married
again in later life.

I lived with the Johnsons for a year or more, probably
when I was between the ages of two and three. I guess this
was after my father was put in jail and my mother was out
on her own, trying to finish at New York University and get
her teaching certificate. She never talked very much about
those years.

I remember Donnie Johnson and I slept in the same bed
in this apartment. I remember James Weldon Johnson
vaguely. Mrs. Johnson used to berate and hen-peck him, and
I remember him sitting rather stoically and quietly, often in
the dark in a chair in the corner. We would tiptoe through
the room, Donnie and I, to go play in the kitchen or the

bedroom, but we never bothered him. Unlike with Mr. Burleigh, I don't ever remember having conversations with
Mr. Johnson.

In all the years that I knew Mr. Burleigh I don't ever
recall him having a guest at his apartment, which was like a
museum with artifacts, books and little knickknacks – it was
fascinating to me. You went into the front door of it – to the
right there was a small bathroom with the old tub with feet,
a sink and commode and a stand-up shower. To the left was
a small library in which he had shelves and shelves and
shelves of mystery books, Sherlock Holmes and Charlie
Chan, and the books had a great smell. They went from floor
to ceiling, plus many, many other books.

If you went down the hall just a step further on the left
there was a tiny bedroom, literally it was almost like a cell,
in the sense that there was a single bed against the wall, a
window at the end, a chest of drawers, and on the wall two
pictures. The one I was always fascinated with was Maxfield
Parrish's "Dinkey Bird," the nude youth swinging in the
swing, one of his famous ones.[35]

Then if you moved down the hall a few more feet and
turned right, you went into the kitchen which had a modest
breakfast table. To the right beyond the kitchen was his
study, again books, a lovely desk where he wrote music and
things, and to the left was a room with an old gas fire place
and the mantel piece, a couple of chairs, and his piano. That
was his apartment, and it was always dark, like a sanctuary.
Drapes on the windows, great brocades, but closed, because
the only windows looked onto shaftways. I remember the
metal gates on the fire escape and the low green glass
shaded lamps. It was always very quiet. It was a very homey,
comfortable, cave-like, womb-like abode.

It was warm, cozy, Spartan to an extent. Mr. Burleigh
did not spend money on artifacts in the sense of expensive
furniture or things, but there were delightful objects – some
of the oriental mode; the umbrella stand, canes, umbrellas,

James Hall, Jr., at age 6 or 7. Courtesy of Dr. James Hall, Jr.

James Hall, Jr., at age 10 or 11. Courtesy of Dr. James Hall, Jr.

a lot of books, small things here and there, a lot of photographs on the mantle, great lamps as I recall.

It seems to me that he often was writing letters. I don't know to whom, what was stated, but I do recall standing by his desk, and questions about getting the letters mailed, stamps. I do think he corresponded with people, more related to the music world and his professional life than to a personal life, but that is, again, pure speculation.

He did work on music at home. I remember him holding the pen at his desk very much like he did in the photo. I was always fascinated by his missing knuckle and how he held the pen, and also by the fact that he used green ink. He would work at his desk, but whether he was arranging, making notations, or composing anew, I don't know. Occasionally, not often, he would work at the piano, or play or sing something to try out a compositional idea. But he never entertained my mother and me in this sense. The times I was around at his home I do not remember him working heavily at the piano, but I do remember being told to be quiet and not disturb him, but it was fine to come and stand by his desk.

I know that Mr. Burleigh did have some music in the house by other composers, but I don't recall just what. He didn't own a record player as I remember. Listening to music at home, no – he would do that more going to concerts. He quite often read in bed, his Conan Doyle mysteries and so on.

He encouraged me to play the piano but would have nothing to do with teaching me. I'm not saying that he was asked to do so, but you'd have to know Mr. Burleigh. For him to teach a six-year old kid piano! I can't think of a proper analogy. It wasn't beneath him, it was just something that he would not do. It would be like expecting him to put on a jogging suit and go jog along Prospect Avenue. Or for him to put on a pair of levi jeans and go hang out on the corner – that was not Mr. Burleigh. But later I did have lessons on piano and flute with other teachers.

I didn't come to Mr. Burleigh's apartment after school.
He was never at home then. But when I did go there I went
on the street car or subway. I travelled all over the city by
myself. I often accompanied Mr. Burleigh to St. George's
and we would eat supper or dinner at Papa's, a Greek
restaurant across the street from the church. Biscuit Titani
was something that I learned to eat there. I used to wander
around the basement caverns of the "Little Cathedral," as I
thought of St. George's, while Mr. Burleigh was rehearsing.
But we went other places together. He was a gentleman and
had the appearance of wealth, confidence, control, and of
"being in charge."

Mr. Burleigh knew passages under the central part of
mid-town New York, like from Grand Central Station
through some of the Commodore Hotel across the street up
through Rockefeller Center and over to Ricordi. We literally
would go into a building on Forty-second Street and come
out on Forty-sixth Avenue, four or five blocks away without
ever going outside. And he walked at a rapid pace, swinging
his cane, and he would move through the subterranean
tunnels (they were well lighted), not subway tunnels, but
corridors. And there would be security rooms and maintenance people for these buildings, and they would all greet
him and tip their hats to him as if he were royalty. There
would be almost humorous adventures; while he wouldn't
say, "Hey, let's go do this or that," you would sense that we
were off and running, as if he were showing off in a sense.

That often occurred with just Mr. Burleigh and me, and
there were some times when there were the three of us together up at Martha's Vineyard. Sometimes my mother's sister, Dessie, went with us, maybe to Atlantic City, Asbury
Park, or the seashore. Sometimes Mr. Sumner would use his
taxi and we would go on a day's outing, but that was not
frequent.

I don't recall Mr. Burleigh ever owning a car in the
years that I knew him, or whether he even drove. However,
Mr. Sumner was one of the major characters in Mr. Burleigh's and our lives. He was a Jewish taxi driver who lived

in the Bronx. Mr. Sumner drove a regular yellow taxicab, but he was as close to a private chauffeur as one could have without really having one. Mr. Sumner would pick up Mr. Burleigh in the morning and deliver him to certain parts of the city. Often I would ride along and be dropped off at the school, or at other times Mr. Sumner would pick me up at school. He became a driver in the most positive sense for Mr. Burleigh, and to a degree for me, but not so much for my mother who travelled on her own.

I remember several emergencies: once when just my mother and I were at home, she became very ill. My father had been put into prison. Mr. Sumner came by for my mother, who was so weak and sick that he picked her up in his arms, put her in the cab and took her to the hospital. Another time Mr. Sumner came into the city to get me. I had one nickel and made a phone call and he came. He was tremendous in catering to Mr. Burleigh's needs, and was the driver for years and years. One summer, while I was at Mildred Johnson's camp, I had an attack of appendicitis. My mother called Mr. Sumner, who drove with her up to Greenwood Lake, New Jersey, probably seventy miles from New York, and took me to Dr. Dunne, who hospitalized me for an emergency appendectomy. That was the kind of person that Mr. Sumner was.

I think that for my twelfth birthday I was given children's books about opera by Mr. Burleigh, so that I would read about Siegfried and the "Ring of the Nibelungen." I must have been ten or so when my mother and Mr. Burleigh sent me to the Ring operas. I sat in a box by myself. Mr. Sumner or somebody dropped me off and then picked me up afterwards. It was part of my cultural indoctrination that they fostered.

Regarding Mr. Burleigh's smiling, yes there were laughs, but I can't tell you what we laughed about. There wasn't a lot of laughter about the normal things I laughed about with my own daughter, but I do remember extreme pleasure and great, great happiness in the joint solitude that we shared over the years.

We would go to the movies at a theater on Forty-second Street and Times Square, actually on Seventh Avenue and Forty-second, that always showed horror movies. It sounds incredible. Here is a great picture: there is this older very distinguished person. Whenever he went up to the window, they would know him and nod and he would deign to nod and say something to them. Then we would go into the cool blackness and sit about a third of the way down. During the day the theater would be practically empty, and we would watch these great B-rated movies, about zombies coming out of the Old South swamps or a tropical island – not violent horror movies in the sense of today's chain massacre, but ones with zombies and vampires and such.

I don't remember talking to Mr. Burleigh about what happened at school during the day, or any small talk or gossip. We lived several blocks from Mr. Burleigh, and once when I was eight or nine, I had a little canary. I remember taking the cover off "Beepie's" cage and finding him dead. I was so distressed that I walked to Mr. Burleigh's in my pajamas and robe. My mother was there fixing breakfast. The report of Beepie's death was just matter of fact, but I did have that feeling of being able to go to the house, and of the freedom, though it wasn't a spontaneous kind of thing.

There would be probably two or three shopping excursions a year when my mother went along. Mr. Burleigh always knew I needed clothes for the school year. "Junior needs clothes to go away to camp," or "We have to take Junior shopping for his school clothes," he would say. In his presence I listened, I followed. We'd go to Macy's, Best and Company, or Wanamaker's. Best and Company it usually was because it was often empty and the tailors were there, so there was greater attention paid. There was deference to the little Eton cap and the tweed coat, the short pants, while Mr. Burleigh said "This isn't right" or "I want this cut," and the tailors would run out and surround me and Mr. Burleigh would sit there by my mother with his hands on his cane.

It was like something out of *Little Lord Fauntleroy*. I didn't know how great it was at the time, and I look back and can't help but smile. And he pulled it off. John Wanamaker was another store that we shopped at, but Best, across from St. Patrick's Cathedral, was one of the major shops and everybody knew Mr. Burleigh in the store so we got service beyond belief. There would be lunch at a nice restaurant and I would have to reach into the grab bag and get a prize.

I never looked at Mr. Burleigh as a father or an uncle, but there was a closeness. We didn't go out somewhere together regularly, but there were times, maybe during the Easter vacation, when I would spend more time with him. It was always a privilege, and though I didn't exactly look forward to "going out with Mr. Burleigh," it was enjoyable. I don't ever recall saying that I didn't want to see him or to go there.

Once in a while my mother would fix things in the morning, such as a poached egg and toast. Mr. Burleigh liked his toast well done, so he could scrape off the black and he was a great marmalade eater. (To this day I eat marmalade and I love white toast.) With the toast he had juice and tea. Sometimes she would leave things in the oven for him to heat up, but so infrequently that Mr. Burleigh would eat out. Some of his favorite places down town were the Oyster Bar at Grand Central Station, and another one there also. I mentioned Papa's. We would occasionally go with him. But he did not eat at home except on very rare occasions. He may have had his heaviest meal at noon. l don't recall him cooking for himself.

Josef Skvorecky's fictional biography of Anton Dvorak, based largely on fact but partly on imagination, pictures Burleigh as the type who sometimes took younger ladies to the opera, and out for breakfast or supper at this same Oyster Bar. (This harmless generosity has been confirmed in an interview with Mrs. Josephine Love of Detroit, who as a young student met Burleigh in New York in the mid 1930s.)

Wine with breakfast, then a cigar and family reminiscences usually followed.

Skvorecky gives a delightful description of Burleigh's personage and style:

> In the glare of the lights in the foyer of the Met stood a gentleman, perhaps in his seventies, with gold-rimmed glasses and a white, natty moustache that contrasted elegantly with his smooth brown face. A felt homburg sat aslant his head, his suit was a dark blue pinstripe, and the polished tips of two shiny black shoes peered out from under a pair of old-fashioned, spotless white spats.[36]

He mentioned a thick gold ring, a gold watch chain, "elegantly garlanding his stomach," "a raffish walking stick with a knob in the shape of a woman's head, carved in deep yellow ivory," as some of Burleigh's personal effects.[37]

Hall said that he knew nothing of the wine that Burleigh supposedly drank when he breakfasted out. He remembered the watch chain and the gold ring, but knew nothing of their origin. Hall also recalled his smoking "a rare cigar once in a while with a grand manner of distinguished enjoyment." Concerning the cane Hall recalled that Mr. Burleigh had several of them, all fascinating to him as a boy. And

> he had an umbrella-walking stick stand by the door out of which he would select one of several before going out. It was a small ritual I sometimes witnessed. Mr. Burleigh's style was to divide the process of daily existence into routines often highlighted by precise but delightful "ritualettes," small, fun rituals. It would seem logical that his music might reflect his living style.
>
> His rituals had a subtle twinkle and yet grandness to them which enhanced his style, and while he may have seemed aloof, there was an enjoyment-of-life aspect to them which may have been a bridge to others, despite class and caste, who were drawn to him – those astute enough to sense the humanness and good humor of them.[38]

As examples of his rituals Hall mentioned the well done-burnt scraped toast and marmalade in the mornings; the single glass of cold water, drunk at night, which sat in an otherwise often starkly empty icebox; his selection of canes and umbrellas; and other of his daily dressing habits. About these personal habits and Burleigh's personality, Hall continued on the tape:

> I remember that he was extremely tidy and neat. In the bathroom the shaving mug, the razors, where they were, he wanted things left in a very precise manner. He wore those stiff collars that used little gold or brass collar buttons, and cuffs, not cuff links, but cuffs on his shirts. If I ever heard him raise his voice it was because he couldn't find things that he thought to be in a certain place. My mother would chuckle and say "Here they are, right where you left them," or "They're just where they should be."
>
> He wasn't grouchy, but he wasn't a humorous person. Could he laugh? Yes, by God, he could laugh, and there was an inward joy in it – an enjoyment of life – not trivial or shallow laughter. He wasn't necessarily moody, but going back to tidy – he wanted his shirts done in a certain way, his underwear folded a certain way, and the apartment very tidy. Knowing other creative people I would say that Mr. Burleigh was a disciplined, meticulously routined kind of person. If an assassin wanted to kill him, it would be easy, because he could predict where he'd be at what time, what paths he followed, and so on. He was a creature of habit, like a bear, following the same paths over and over again.
>
> He had little patience with stupid people, or people who messed up, or store clerks or waiters that couldn't follow directions. There appeared to be a great reservoir of patience, almost indifference, and then there would come a point where he would, not in a loud, overt manner, but in a sharp pointed and focused manner, indicate his displeasure. He did it in such a royal way, that though he was quiet, it could be devastating. I did not see much of that at all.
>
> I guess that Mr. Burleigh had a certain charm and distinguishment about him that could have been very

attractive to women. He would put a flower in his lapel, he had a cane, wore spats, and his hat would be on at a jaunty angle, not in the Cab Calloway style, but more like David Niven. Mr. Burleigh was a black David Niven in his distinguished approach to life. He would walk down the street and there would be a "presence." Though he was not a big man, when I was with him there was almost a protective cloak. As he got older, even if his eyes didn't twinkle, there was a persevering charm to him. I wouldn't be at all unhappy if I had that presence as the years slip by. There was a timelessness about him. His style and what he wore, he could probably wear today, and while it would be totally out of vogue, he could carry it off.

He was aloof. I had no idea why – maybe because what other people were talking about didn't interest him. He had little or no interest in jazz in the popular style, only in jazz relative to Dvorak, and some of the connection between the spirituals and jazz. But that was very tenuous in the sense of the real delight of Ellington, Calloway and the other great bands. He didn't have overt contempt for that music – it was simply something outside his realm of experience, and he was not a person to delve into new areas just to try something different.

He was a person that had certain reference points. Martha's Vineyard, certain kinds of music, stores, restaurants, people, habits, and going to Ricordi's every day were routines not to divert from. To open up and explore wasn't his pattern. Why? I look at how much he acquired this confidence, presence and style of life which served him so well and gave him maximum control. For who he was and what he had, he probably stayed within that protected area much as a defense and a security. He risked nothing and was protected. Whereas if he ventured out into an unknown area, where people were addressing him as a peer, or he exposed himself, letting people know what he didn't know, his confidence may not have handled the situation. That may be an explanation.

If you wanted to talk about music he could be quite open and enthusiastic, but things that he didn't have high values for or care for just almost didn't exist. He was not a pompous or superior person, or patronizing in the negative sense of looking down his nose at people. He was just aloof and didn't bother with you if there was no reason to, if there was nothing in common.

I often think of Mr. Burleigh as a patron of people, such as my mother and me, and a few other people in his life. It wasn't so much the Pygmalion syndrome of taking an uncut diamond and honing it to something that is perfect. He wouldn't have had the tolerance for uncut diamonds. But he certainly would take a person that had demonstrated certain talents, and would become an emotional, and to a modest degree, physical supporter. He encouraged my mother to finish her degree. She had run away from home right after high school, married my father who was a taxi driver, a delightful human being, according to everybody. He was gregarious and charming, constantly borrowing money, and always on the borderline of fiscal disaster. During an unpleasant incident involving a loan agency debt, my father went to the agency and literally tore up the place, threatening the non-minority employees. As a result, he served a four- or five-year prison term, during which my parents got a divorce.

Mr. Burleigh became more prominent in that period. He gave support and counsel, such as "Junior must go away – he must have the best, and he's going to have it." He was very autocratic and decisive in that sense. There was little debate about maybe this or maybe that. He was a tough, but not a nasty, person, both professional and friendly, though not in a hail-fellow-well-met way. If people crossed him he let them know, and it didn't matter whether they were black, white, green or yellow – when he walked into a situation or a room, he took control. Too, he could be extremely pleasant.

The few times that I saw him singing or in rehearsal at St. George's I was wonderfully impressed. The choir master directed him, and while that didn't upset me, it was noteworthy, observing the fact that Mr. Burleigh was being told what to do and being handled by somebody else. But he never acted in a subservient manner. He was not treated like the colored boy that had a good voice. There was respect for him. But I suspect that his long association with St. George's was not a fifty-fifty proposition. It may have been forty-nine Mr. Burleigh and fifty-one St. George's as he worked for them, in the figurative sense.

And he handled that very well – he didn't lose his dignity at all. Mr. Burleigh had humility, not humbleness, but he had no distorted impression of his own contribution. He did not think he was God's gift to the musical world. He was very quick to recognize the greatness in other composers that he respected, but he had no humility relative to people he didn't respect or for musicians in fields other than his own.

Mr. Burleigh had a great influence on my life and values, and I knew where I came from and how I had to develop over the years. There was a neutrality in him as far as the ethnic identity goes, in the militant hard core sense of the more indigenous southern black, or the sleeping car Cole Porter syndrome. Throughout my life I've never thought of Mr. Burleigh as a black man. He just did not conduct himself subserviently, or sensitively to the fact that he lived in a white world. He handled the world as royalty would – in a royal, benevolent manner. I was always delighted when he was considered by others according to his rank and style, though as a youngster I had no idea what this was. But he had it, and people respected him for it.

I don't ever recall Mr. Burleigh talking about racial injustice – he didn't seem that socially oriented. I really feel that he was so devoted to his music and to people, that he was universal, and a strongly non-ethnic person.

I don't think that he viewed himself as a black man, even in his approach to the spirituals. I suspect that he thought of them as a very valid form of music, one having a certain important creativity for the world. He was in no way militant about the black or Negro thing. There may have been a con-

Dr. James Hall, Jr., 1986. Credit: Larry Brown.

servative streak in him based on his own life, that you can be
what you want to be, that your fate is in your own hands.

I have no idea how Ricordi felt about letting Mr. Burleigh go. I myself did not notice the senility, because as he
reached this stage, I was at school, isolated from him. There
were some years toward the end when my mother was distressed about what was happening to Mr. Burleigh. She
would lay out his clothes for the next day, only to notice that
he hadn't changed to them. His career ended in a rather
non-climactic way, I guess.

Mr. Burleigh lived in the Bronx, about a four or five
blocks' walk from the subway along Prospect Avenue to his
apartment. As the neighborhood changed in those days from
a predominantly Jewish white neighborhood to a minority
neighborhood, there were a number of bars with player
pianos and the like which opened along Prospect. My mother
was very concerned that Mr. Burleigh would stop in one of
them on the way home for a drink. I don't know what he
drank, but something mild probably. She worried that the
women who hung out there would "coo" and "ah" over this
good-natured, rather grand gentleman, and then take his
money.

The afternoon tippling was an aspect only of his declin-
ing years. I remember no degree of drinking earlier in his
life. My mother would have despaired, for my father at one
time was a severe alcoholic. Mr. Burleigh may have had a
drink at times but he was in no way a drinker.

My mother worried about shutting up the apartment
when he moved to the convalescent home. That wasn't really
the worry at that time, but there was a lot of unrest about
getting him into the home, notifying other people, and so on.
This must have been when the overt resentment and friction
began between Mr. Burleigh's family and my mother, about
who was to do what. There were fights about demanding
keys to his apartment, and worry that at night people would
get into the place and cart off things. A lot of items were not
located. We had very, very few things. For years I had a blue
silk robe of Mr. Burleigh's and some pictures of him. My

mother grieved over the loss of the artifacts, which may have
been misplaced by Santini and Sons, a moving and storage
company.

I was not made aware of Mr. Burleigh's death at the
time that it happened. My mother handled it matter-of-
factly. "You know, Mr. Burleigh died." I remember not
being particularly distressed or overwhelmed. I hadn't known
people who had died. I doubt that my mother attended the
funeral, because the inferences in publicity were that she had
greedily taken advantage of Mr. Burleigh's finances. However, I think she did attend some of the later commemorative
services at St. George's.

Though Hall feels that there still exist some resentment and mis-
understanding towards his mother from the Burleigh family, he does
not sense that it applies directly to him. As he reasoningly points out,
the Burleigh family felt no particular need or desire for a closeness
to him. He has never met any one of Burleigh's family, yet corre-
sponds occasionally with Burleigh's grandson, Dr. Harry T. Burleigh
II, concerning matters of ASCAP royalties, monies to charities, and
the like, a situation necessitated by the fact that Mrs. Thelma Hall
Teasdale and he were among the legal heirs mentioned in Burleigh's
will.

Hall recalls feeling that Mr. Burleigh had strong, positive
emotions for his wife and son, and an even warmer affection for his
grandson, though he was rarely verbal about it.

The Burleigh Family

If Harry Thacker Burleigh were alive today he would surely be
proud not only of Dr. Hall, but of his own immediate family of
professionals and their productivity. Their accomplishments are
worthy of another book. Dr. Harry T. Burleigh II, Burleigh's grandson, has shared most of the following information. As a youngster he
remembered visiting with his grandfather, Harry, at least twice a year,
and recalls a trip to Oak Bluffs when he was five years old. He
recalled only two short visits with his grandmother, Louise.

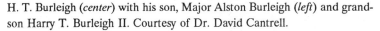

H. T. Burleigh (*center*) with his son, Major Alston Burleigh (*left*) and grandson Harry T. Burleigh II. Courtesy of Dr. David Cantrell.

Dr. Burleigh's father, Alston (son of Harry and Louise), was born August 18, 1899, in New York City. As a youngster he was cared for in large part by his maternal grandmother, Mrs. Farley, of Washington, DC. From ages eleven to fourteen he attended a private school in England, chosen especially for him "because his father was a musician. Class schools existed in England at that time."[39] After graduation from Dunbar High School in Washington, Alston volunteered for World War I, served briefly in the U.S. Army, and after discharge enrolled at Howard University. A Bachelor's degree in Music was conferred upon him there in 1922.

Mr. and Mrs. Alston Burleigh, c. early 1970s. Courtesy of Dr. David Cantrell.

His marriage to Erma Jones took place at about this time, though no definite date has been given by the Burleigh family. A son, Harry T. Burleigh II, was born on April 3, 1923.

Alston's teaching experiences began as a substitute at Dunbar High, followed by teaching in numerous elementary schools until 1927, when he turned to a career on the acting stage, one pursued until 1940. These years were interspersed with professorial positions in music and drama at Howard (1926-28) and at Virginia State College (1930-33) in Petersburg, where he headed the Department of Music and Drama. Other teaching posts were held at Wilberforce University and Morgan State College.

In a first stage experience with the Howard Dramatic Club, Alston supported Charles Gilpin in Eugene O'Neill's *Emperor Jones*, a play later taken on tour. Under the auspices of Abbie Mitchell's Lafayette Players, he acted in Paul Green's *In Abraham's Bosom*, a Pulitzer-prize winner, at the Provincetown Playhouse. After performing a leading role in *Harlem*, he later supervised the music in *Rope*, and acted in *Blackbirds*, *Show Girl*, and *Hot Chocolates*.[40]

Alston Burleigh's obituary in the *Washington Post* of November 30, 1977, stated that he had also worked with a stock company in Canada and made some Broadway appearances. Having remained in the reserves, he was called back to active military duty in March of 1940, at which time he was on the Wilberforce University faculty. In August of 1941 he was promoted from the rank of Captain to Major in the 366th Infantry, at the time stationed at Fort Devens, Massachusetts. For this regiment he had organized a sixty-voice choir which had appeared on radio and before many New England audiences. With the promotion Major Burleigh was transferred to the Anacosta Recreation Camp in Washington, DC.[41]

After release from active duty in 1946 Alston returned to teach in Washington. At the time of his father's death he was on the Morgan State College faculty. In 1958 he joined Washington's Roosevelt High School faculty, where he taught drama and music, and organized the Thespian Drama Group. After retirement in 1969 he continued to live in Washington. At the time of his death he was survived by his wife, Erma J. Burleigh, a former first grade teacher in the Washington public schools; a son, Dr. Harry T. Burleigh II; and three grandchildren. Mrs. Erma Burleigh lived in the family home in Washington

Alston Burleigh receives a record from two unidentified gentlemen as his wife and son look on, c. late 1950s. Courtesy of Dr. David Cantrell.

until her death in May of 1987.

Dr. Harry T. Burleigh II, a veterinarian in Clarksburg, West Virginia, kindly supplied information on his family and himself. Dr. Burleigh also had a military career, first with the 372nd Infantry Regiment from 1943-46, during which period he rose from Private to Master Sergeant, and then to Second Lieutenant in 1950 through the ROTC program at Virginia State College. He was later reassigned. Dr. Burleigh was not married at the time of his grandfather's death. He wrote in 1986:

> I am a veterinarian in small animal practice. I finished Tuskegee in 1956, where I stayed and taught clinical medicine for two years and then went into private practice. My

wife is Mary Footes Burleigh, who has an MS in Library Science from Simmons 1950. We have three children, Anne Elizabeth, Marie Louise and Harry T. III.

Anne is an accountant with Consolidated Gas Transmission Corporation. She has a degree in accounting from Salem College, Salem, W. V. Marie was a TV reporter and acting News Director for a local TV station for 4 years. She has a degree in broadcast journalism from West Va. University. She is now a TV production specialist for West Va. University Educational Telecommunications.

Harry T. III has a degree in graphic design from West Va. University. He worked as a graphic designer for a local TV station for a year and then took a job as a TV production specialist with West Va. University in Medical Television.

My wife worked as a librarian in New York City and Washington, DC, and she set up a library for the School of Nursing at Tuskegee Institute. She has been a housewife since I have been in practice.[42]

Someone of Dr. Burleigh's family still plans a biography of Harry T. Burleigh. Alston had begun one but never finished it. It is hoped that Mr. Burleigh's diary, a treasure mentioned by Mrs. Josephine Love but which Dr. Hall knew nothing of, has been preserved.

PART TWO:
Musical Works

CHAPTER IV

Art Songs And Instrumental Works

♪

Stylistic Characteristics

Compared to today's musical innovation, Burleigh's compositional style, devoid of contrivance, appears overly simplified, tame, and definitely "dated." In the early 1900s, however, this romantic sincerity befitted particularly well the ambience of waning Victorianism. That Burleigh composed from the heart is obvious. A. Walter Kramer's comment on Burleigh in 1916 bears repetition:

> This man is a composer by divine right, and what is more, he is a thinker, a man who writes music not because he enjoys seeing his name on the program of some singer, but because he feels deeply, profoundly, in the language of tone. . . . [He] is contributing to American art-song examples of creative music that deserve world-wide attention and respect.[1]

Burleigh did not inject his own personality into his compositions. The *noir* sound often identifiable with other black composers is not detectable as a conscious ingredient of Burleigh's art songs, but perhaps manifests itself through the syncopation and more complex rhythms employed in his three instrumental works: *Six Plantation Melodies for Violin and Piano* (1901); *From the Southland*, for piano

213

(1910); and *Southland Sketches*, for violin and piano (1916). These pieces will be discussed following the section on art songs.

Of his own non-diversity Burleigh remarked:

> I started a string quartet. I would like to do work in different fields but . . . you see, I have a mission. I must make my music known, and songs are the only things it pays publishers to issue. A chamber piece may be played once and forgotten. You can't get it published. You get a little discouraged and you go back to writing songs.[2]

Eileen Southern, in her *Biographical Dictionary of Afro-American and African Musicians*, terms Burleigh's style neoromantic. His sustaining accompaniments are mood setters, not moving on an equal plane with the lyrical melodies. In his dissertation Roland Lewis Allison characterizes Burleigh's style as including chromaticism; dramatic elements; reuse of themes from other works, e.g., the Dresden Amen in "The Hour Glass" (1914); syncopation; and well-written accompaniments of varying difficulty which usually grow to a climax of emotion, having contrasted the counter melody of the vocal line with non-detracting accents. Without specifying certain ones, Allison suggests that only twenty-five of Burleigh's works are not derived from religious folk music. Wide intervallic skips are frequently found in the songs written between 1914 and 1917, and many of these have a consistently high tessitura. Without naming them, Allison maintains that a few of Burleigh's songs hint at obscure tonal centers.

One writer described Burleigh's early efforts as "more than the trial of unused wings," lauding the composer's gift of poetic imagination and expert command of harmonic principles. Many of them might be called singable sentimental ballads, a form in vogue around the turn of the century.[3] English professor John L. Marsh of Erie, Pennsylvania, called Burleigh's approach to the ballad and art song "pragmatic," but admitted that he made an "indelible contribution to America's cultural heritage."[4]

Ellsworth Janifer commented on Burleigh's "pleasing melodic lines and stereotyped accompaniment, cast in massive blocks of chords," noting resemblances to Victor Herbert, Reginald de Koven, and Samuel Coleridge-Taylor, though "the poems that he set were often doggerel with words poorly wedded to the music." However,

Janifer did approve of "Jean," "The Prayer," "The Young Warrior," "Ethiopia Saluting the Colors," and "Lovely Dark and Lonely One," saying that Burleigh had the supreme ability to sustain the emotional mood, making each setting a "miniature masterpiece." [5]

A lengthy and more favorable article by Burleigh's friend, Charlotte Murray, quoted critic F. J. McIsaac as naming the composer a "worthy contemporary of Cadman, Carpenter, and MacDowell" and continued:

> In a period when a Negro was seldom taken seriously in the artistic field, this was a signal honor for Burleigh. It is erroneous to assume that he rose to fame because of his spiritual arrangements since those songs only climaxed a career already eminently successful. The art songs are set to fine poems whose essence he understood, and he was able to blend text and music into an aesthetically satisfying whole.[6]

When asked by Murray how he felt toward the modern art song, Burleigh replied:

> The text determines the character of the song. The kind of music one writes is governed by this solely, I believe. If the American composer will only remember that he is to look for poems in which the spiritual forces of mercy, justice, and truth play a part, he will be adding to the literature those things that have a big meaning. For me a poem must have more than just sentimental reference before I can set it. I read hundreds of perfectly good poems that I would never think of setting to music. There has been a neglect, on the part of our composers, of poems which in my estimation call out musical thought of real fibre.[7]

Early Art Songs

Although Burleigh's choice of song texts was occasionally fanciful, he always showed refined taste. Burleigh's friend Mrs. Josephine Love was positive that Burleigh did not necessarily know all of his contemporary collaborators, believing that he sometimes became smitten with a poem by an unfamiliar author in a newspaper or magazine. But, on the other hand, his friends at St. George's, as well as acquaintances through Ricordi, likely submitted poems of interest from time to time.

Obviously Burleigh did not know Walt Whitman, Christina Rossetti, Robert Burns, Alfred Tennyson, nor Laurence Hope. And, due to geographical location, it is unlikely that he came in contact with Rudyard Kipling, Arthur Symons, or William Ernest Henley, all well-known contemporary British poets whose texts he set.

Material has been found on Burleigh's better-known collaborators, but knowledge of those who might have been personal friends, not public figures, is scarce or nonexistent. One such curious example is Madge Marie Miller, poet of the famous "Just You" (1915) and later "Love's Likeness" (1929). Walter H. Brown, poet of the sensational "Little Mother of Mine" (1917), is equally obscure, as is Margaret M. Harlan, poet of "One Year, 1914-1915" (1916).

The poet of "Life," one of three songs published in 1898, was John Boyle O'Reilly (1844-90), a colorful Irishman interested in all causes pertaining to his native land. After escaping from an Australian penal colony where he was a life convict for treason against the British government, he came to the United States, settled in Boston, and established a name for himself in American literature. O'Reilly died of an overdose of insomnia medication at Nantucket Beach.[8]

English poet Christina Rossetti might be described as a romantic scholar, a product of both environment and family heritage. As a successful though enigmatic writer, she has been compared to the best in her genre. Supposedly deeply in love at least three times she never chose a suitor for marriage.

Rossetti's poem, "A Birthday," was first published in 1862. It was set by Burleigh as "A Birthday Song," another of his publications of 1898. Richard D. Lynde, writing on Rossetti in the 1970s, found in the poem associations with the Bible, world trade in Victorian England, and some reflections of Dante G. Rossetti's paintings – an interesting but heavy analysis of a seemingly simple piece. It reads:

> My heart is like a singing bird
> Whose nest is in a watered shoot;
> My heart is like an apple-tree
> Whose boughs are bent with thickset fruit;

My heart is like a rainbow shell
That paddles in a halcyon sea;
My heart is gladder than all these
Because my love is come to me.

Raise me a dais of silk and down;
Hang it with vair and purple dyes;
Carve it in doves, and pomegranates,
And peacocks with a hundred eyes;
Work it in gold and silver grapes,
In leaves, and silver fleurs-de-lys;
Because the birthday of my life
Is come, my love is come to me.[9]

Undoubtedly Burleigh knew George V. Hobart (1867-1926), his cohort for "Sleep, Li'l Chile, Go Sleep," as Hobart was a charter member of ASCAP. Born in Nova Scotia the versatile Hobart was an author, librettist, journalist, and playwright, who also assisted composers Reginald de Koven and Victor Herbert.

"Sleep, Li'l Chile" was one of two *Plantation Songs*, along with Frank L. Stanton's "You'll Git Dar in de Mornin'," published in 1902. Five other songs by Burleigh and Stanton followed: "Jean" (1903), "If Life be a Dream" and "The Way of the World" (both in 1904), "Just A-Wearying for You" (1906), and "Since Molly Went Away" (1907). Stanton (1857-1927) was a reporter and feature writer for several newspapers in Georgia. He was that state's first poet laureate and published five volumes of verse. Several of his poems have been set to music.[10]

"Jean," actually the first song to bring Burleigh recognition, was dedicated to Mrs. James Speyer, "one of the few New York society women who spend much time and thought as well as money in philanthropic work." Previous to her marriage in 1897 to Mr. Speyer, banker and philanthropist, she operated a tea room on Fifth Avenue in New York. At this time she was also president of the Working Girl's Club and active in settlement work on the lower Eastside, "going to and fro along the dark streets . . . often entirely alone." It is quite possible that Burleigh was a guest performer at one of the two Speyer mansions, where as members of the upper echelon of

New York's wealthy they hosted important and prestigious social events. The *New York Times* of July 23, 1905, gave a flatteringly frank picture of Mrs. Speyer:

> Mrs. Speyer's wit, cheerfulness, and cordial manners and sincerity have made her extremely popular with everyone. She is petite, with a slender, girlish figure, brown hair, with one great bunch in the front near the centre a pure gray. . . . She is several years older than her husband, but in everything but years seems younger.[11]

"Jean" is a typically sentimental song of lovers longing for each other. The accompaniment is repetitively chordal and scant in the opening, picking up in interest with an arpeggio figure after the first stanza. Neither vocally nor interpretatively difficult, its appealing message made it a favorite in thousands of homes and many vocal studios. Lucien White of the *Age* referred to "Jean" as "one of the most popular songs ever heard from the concert stage" whose beauty "age has not withered, nor custom staled."[12]

Burleigh's wife, Louise, a poet and reader, furnished five song texts between 1903 and 1906.

The first, "Mammy's Li'l Baby," was dedicated to the unrivalled Madame Ernestine Schumann-Heink, a stellar and tireless performer, outstanding in boosting the morale of World War I troops with her many performances. A mother of eight, her concern for humanity knew no limits.

"Mammy's Li'l Baby," originally a dialect poem by Louise, was not set in dialect by Burleigh, a thoughtful and tasteful move on his part, considering to whom it was dedicated. Ending "g's" on such words as *crying, weeping,* and *sleeping* were retained in the song as well as the complete word *your,* rather than *yo'. Li'l* became little, and *nevah,* never. The active vocal line, sustained by chordal accompaniment, is open to personal interpretation. The song's two short verses make it an ideal encore.

"Just My Love and I," subtitled "Boat Song" (1904); "Dreamland" (1905); and "Perhaps" (1907) were undedicated. Opening the score of "Just My Love and I" is an arpeggiated passage of sixths, to be played "quickly," which settles into a long-short, long-short pattern of 6/8 meter, suggesting the rocking motion of a boat. The vocal line of the second section hovers around top-line F, sustaining this note *fortissimo*, while the accompaniment repeats the opening figure, resolving in four *forte* chords. The words "just my love and I" are used seven times within the song, a joyous piece, but not necessarily an easy one for the singer. "Perhaps" was republished in *The Etude*, December 1919. A slightly longer, two-verse work, its range has an optional high A flat. Some of its sentiment reads:

> Perhaps you may remember! perhaps you may forget,
> My heart is ever constant, and says I love you yet;
> The years can never change me, Nor take from me your
>   kiss:
> Perhaps you may remember! perhaps you may forget.

"Love's Dawning" (1907), another of Louise's texts, was dedicated to Miss Annie M. Roth, about whom information is missing. Less taxing vocally, it is an ideal teaching piece, another love song with uncomplicated vocal line, rhythm and accompaniment, again in 6/8 meter, with the range of a tenth (from D up to F). Dynamic markings reach *fortissimo* near the close, then suddenly drop to *pianissimo*.

Though the publication date of Burleigh's "I Lo'e My Jean" was given by different sources as 1904, 1908, and 1914, the sheet music, published by William Maxwell Company (in the holdings of the Moorland-Spingarn Collection at Howard University), confirms the date as 1904. The life story of poet Robert Burns is familiar. Far from to the manor born, his lot was one of a talented peasant who took pleasure where and with whom he pleased. It is a pity that he died before the age of forty for he had much more to offer in Scottish dialect poetry. "I Lo'e my Jean," included in various editions of Burns's collected works, was reputedly written to Jean Armour, the mother of his child and later his wife.

"O, Perfect Love" (1904), one of Burleigh's better known songs, was his only collaboration with D. F. Blomfield. No information has emerged either on Blomfield or on Miss Dora J. Cole of Philadelphia, to whom the song was dedicated. Miss Cole may have been a sister of Burleigh's friend Robert Cole, or Dora Cole of New York who was a reader and theatrical agent. The latter became Mrs. Dora Cole Norman, a teacher of dancing at the Music School Settlement in New York.[13]

"O, Perfect Love" proved most popular for weddings. Simply structured and within a comfortable range, it presents no problems to either singer or accompanist. The organ-like, sustained accompaniment affords ample expression for the soloist. Interludes between verses restate the vocal theme effectively. Three forceful "Amens" at the end build scalewise to a fitting close.

Two poems by Laurence Hope, "Request" (1905) and "Malay Boat Song" (1906), had been set by Burleigh before he published the more publicized cycle *Five Songs on Poems by Laurence Hope* in 1915. More will be said of Hope, who was actually Adela Florence Cory, in connection with the cycle.

Burleigh furnished the words for at least three of his own songs: "Just Because" (1906), "The Last Good-Bye" (1908) and "He Met Her in the Meadow" (1921). Bordering on vaudeville, the naïveté of "Just Because" would suggest that Burleigh was his own worst lyricist. This tune is filled with so many clichés, both in vocal line and accompaniment, that a blind-folded audience could not fail to imagine its performer as a not-so-bright chanteuse with blond curls, beauty spot, and tiny laced waist, twirling a pretty ruffled parasol and probably singing off-key. The accompaniment, precisely duplicating the vocal line, could almost pass as a solo backing the love scene in a silent movie. One would hope that Burleigh did not take this piece seriously. A few of the words are:

> Just a dimple touched by Cupid,
> Just a tiny little frown,
> Just a blushing cheek so modest
> Just a ringlet curling down.

Also among Burleigh's more prestigious poets was Charles C. Stoddard (1876-1961), historian and reporter for the *New York Sun*, who lived on Staten Island for over sixty years. As librarian at the Staten Island Historical Museum, Stoddard edited its journal, *The Historian.* He also was editor for various publishing firms; wrote for *Century, Harper's,* and *Saturday Evening Post*; lectured on natural history; and gave public readings of his poetry. Burleigh set his poem "Through Love's Eternity" in 1906.

Burleigh also set "Hail to the King" by E. H. Sears in 1906. Sears (1852-1942), a Harvard graduate, was the son of Unitarian minister

Edmund Hamilton Sears (1810-1876), who wrote "Calm on the Listening Ear of Night" (1839) and "It Came Upon the Midnight Clear" (1849), Christmas hymns set to music by Richard Storrs Willis in 1850. Before becoming head of Mary Institute at Washington University in St. Louis in 1895, E. H. Sears established a girls' school in Boston. He later taught at Hampton Institute and the University of California. It is likely that Burleigh knew Sears through association with Hampton.[14]

"You Ask Me If I Love You" was one of Burleigh's more popular songs of 1907 and years following. Lillian Bennett Thompson, who wrote the words, could not be traced. The score reveals another typical salon ballad whose vocal line begins on the upbeat, not a usual Burleigh procedure. Burleigh suitably melded a 3/4 meter with Thompson's provocative words. Relieved by appropriate short interludes from the piano, the two-stanza poem makes a pleasant, tasty drawing room ditty and a worthy early effort.

It is reasonable to assume that Burleigh might have known Lawrence Perry (1876-1954), who became sports and stage columnist for the North American Newspaper Alliance in 1934. Perry was later *Yachting Magazine*'s first editor and writer of its "New York Skylines" column; a reporter on New York's *Journal, Morning Sun, Evening Sun*, and *Evening Post*; and author of ten books and a play, *Beyond the Terrace*. His poem "Pilgrim," set by Burleigh in 1908, is not available today.

Burleigh's private life sheds little light on with which of his collaborators he was intimate or even acquainted. One can draw conclusions only from dates, locale, and activities.

Alfred Tennyson's keen musical ear enabled him to project various moods for song literature. His beauteous "Now Sleeps the Crimson Petal," written between 1847 and 1850, veritably ached to be set to music and Burleigh responded to the call in 1908. Gossamer images fill the four stanzas with an ethereal loveliness. No rhyme scheme is detectable. A few of the lines are:

> Now droops the milkwhite peacock like a ghost
> And a ghost glimmers on to me.
> Now folds the lily all her sweetness up,
> And slips into the bosom of the lake.

>So fold thyself, my dearest, thou, and slip
>Into my bosom and be lost in me.

Lyric poet Tennyson (1809-92) was poet laureate of England for forty-two years.

Burleigh set two texts by Edward Oxenford, "Two Words" in 1908 and "Yours Alone" in 1909. Oxenford's expertise had previously been shared by composer Alexander Campbell in "Three Vocal Trios with Flute and Percussion" (1881) and another part song, "Three Merry Dwarfs" (1887). Also he wrote the English libretto, later translated into German, for Henry Hadley's opera *Safié*, which premiered in 1909.

In conception "Yours Alone" resembles the German art song. The accompaniment uses a right-hand counter melody over a left-hand after-beat figure, independent of the vocal line. The middle and ending sections give way to typically Schubertian triplets, an accompanimental figure rarely used by Burleigh. Key changes are predictable. It is not an earth-shaking piece, but its appeal could easily bring the house down if performed by a singer skillful at "taking the stage."

In 1909 and 1910, other than "Yours Alone," Burleigh set some anonymous poems, "Carry Me Back to the Pine Wood," "Myrra," and "It Was Nothing But a Rose."

ASCAP songwriter and author Clay Smith (1877-1920) may have been the C. L. Smith whose "Tarry With Me, O My Savior!" was set by Burleigh, his only song published in 1911. The following two years also yielded only one publication each, "Child Jesus Comes from Heav'nly Height" (anonymous, 1912) and "Deep River," *a cappella*, SATB (1913). This unaccountably sparse output seems almost a withdrawal preparatory to Burleigh's next few years of excessive activity.

As mentioned in Chapter I, there were no news items of Louise Burleigh or of the Burleighs together after 1912. This may have been the time that she left him, causing a temporary emotional readjustment or depression which affected his productivity.

Art Songs of 1914

Burleigh set six separate art songs in 1914. His "Mother O' Mine," using Rudyard Kipling's fervent poem, though popular enough, did not meet with quite the wild success of the 1917 "Little Mother of Mine." Kipling's message is heartfelt: if one were hanged on the highest hill, drowned in the deepest sea, or damned of body and soul, it is certain that a mother's tears, prayers, and love would come to the rescue. The phrase "Mother O' Mine" is repeated six times in the poem's three stanzas.

Kipling (1865-1936), a Bombay-born Englishman familiar to readers young and old, had a boundless imagination, evidenced in the varied subjects of his books and poems. Some are whimsical, some serious, all written with wisdom gleaned from his wide travels and personal experiences. In 1907 Kipling received the Nobel Prize for Literature.

The chorale-like "Hour Glass" by Alexander Groves, a lesser-known poet, encompasses "incidental use of a theme from the liturgy of the Dresden Church," according to a note on the first page of the song. Groves's three stanzas, basically in "aabb" rhyme scheme, form a love poem which in essence compares one's life to the sands of time. Burleigh's treatment of the martial opening theme is backed by chordal accompaniment in quarter notes, giving way to a repeated eighth note pattern which accelerates, crescendoes, and ascends to a high F in the vocal line. The piano postlude almost duplicates the introduction. Somehow, the music and words of this song seem ill-suited to each other.

Two Poems included "Bring Her Again to Me" and "The Spring, My Dear, Is No Longer Spring" by another famous Briton, William Ernest Henley (1849-1903). These short songs, though worthy and useful when programmed together, were not particularly in demand at the time of their publication.

Within the two-page "Bring Her Again to Me" Burleigh's four meter changes hardly seem necessary, though they do suggest a freedom found in the wind and sea. The range of this brief song is encompassed in the interval of a sixth. The second verse is in the natural minor key for contrast. Later Burleigh reset "Bring Her Again to Me" as "Bring Her Again, O Western Wind," likely published as an arrangement for ensemble by Galaxy in 1932.

The rhyme scheme of the sixteen brief lines of "The Spring, My Dear, Is No Longer Spring" is an "abba" pattern. The two verses vary not so much in the vocal line as in accompanimental changes. Toward a coda-like ending the meter is shifted from 3/4 to a brief three measures in 4/4 which culminate in *fortissimo*, at which point the singer is on a sustained high A flat. As many of Burleigh's other songs, this one ends softly. The harmonies, progressing chromatically, are unexpected. On the line "To be out of tune" he effectively uses a measure of urgent sixteenth notes and a discordant minor second.

Henley, editor and poet, was born in Gloucester, England. Tuberculosis of the bone necessitated amputation of his left leg in 1865. His most famous volume of poems is *Invictus*, an expression of personal courage. A close friendship with Robert Louis Stevenson resulted in their collaboration on four plays. Henley was editor of the *Scots Observer* and later the *National Observer*. He edited a volume of Robert Burns's poetry, in which his frank account of Burns's character outraged many Scottish readers.

In "Elysium" (words by James Weldon Johnson), Burleigh's flexible phrase markings are evidence of his expertise as a singer. The left hand of the piano has a viola-like melody of its own, with choral accompaniment provided by the right hand. Curiously enough Johnson's words are almost identical to those of "Your Lips Are Wine," the second of the *Passionale* cycle (1915), though Burleigh's music is not similar. The ending word, "still," is written to be held by the singer for four bars. The accompaniment ends fittingly at *ppp*.

"Elysium," a rather passionate love song, was dedicated to actor-singer Frank V. Pollock "with sincere admiration." One of Pollock's roles was that of Guido, Duke of Ventroso, in *The Bride Elect*, an opera by John Philip Sousa. A portrait of Pollock wearing an elaborate costume and hat with feathers appeared in the *New York Times*, April 17, 1898. No review of the play was given, nor the performance theater named. Sousa's *Bride*, produced first in New Haven, Connecticut, on December 28, 1897, opened at the Knickerbocker Theater on April 11, 1898, and also played eight times at the Harlem Opera House beginning in October of that year. On tour in 1900 it played to packed houses.[15]

"O Southland" was set for male ensemble. This longer poem by Johnson has been described as "essentially a plea for racial reconciliation, communicating its ideas strongly enough to secure a place in future anthologies."[16] The four stanzas of Johnson's stirring words urge both black and white races to cast off the "idle age and musty page" of former oppressive tradition. The strong must help the weak and "man shall be saved by man," with the help of God's love and guidance.[17]

"His Word Is Love" marked the beginning of occasional collaboration with Englishman Fred G. Bowles, whose poetry was obviously as attractive to Burleigh as to various other composers. Over 100 songs to his texts were published in both England and the United States. His birth date is not certain. Bowles's work was published continuously from 1899 until his death on June 25, 1925, both in London magazines and as volumes of poetry. Some of his better-known collections of verse include *In the Wake of the Sun* (1899), *Northern Lyrics, a Book of Verse* (1903), *The Tent by the Lake* (1906), *Saracen Songs* (1912), and *White Wings of Song* (1919).

Bowles was the English representative for *Talia* (Teatro Libero) in Milan. He also translated some poems by the Queen of Roumania. Richard le Gallienne, literary critic and poet, wrote of Bowles's *In the Wake of the Sun*: "Mr. Bowles's poetry has haunted me, sung itself to me again in omnibuses, hummed like a friend at my side in crowded thoroughfares."[18] Said to be kindhearted and entertaining, Bowles had the gift of easy social repartee, endearing him to many. It is likely that Burleigh knew Bowles personally through his visits to America, though no references to their friendship have been pinpointed.

Saracen Songs (1914)

The year 1914 also marked the composition and publication of Burleigh's first song cycle, *Saracen Songs*, to text by Bowles. The seven songs have a definite Eastern fiavor. Of the cycle W. J. Henderson, musical editor of the *New York Sun* wrote:

> The rich Orientalism of the text has warmed the composer's imagination so that it has found eloquent and captivating musical setting for the thoughts. . . . Poetic conceptions are paired with his masterly musicianship.[19]

An examination of the piano-vocal score confirms Henderson's views, stated in the prefatory note to the work. He comments on the cycle's "opulence of idea." Due to the high tessitura of the songs, they are suitable for either one adequate high voice or two alternating ones.

At the time of its publication *Saracen Songs* was acclaimed as Burleigh's "most ambitious and successful achievement."

Conceived almost in the manner of an operatic scene the four characters, Yussouf, Almona, Hassan, and Ahmed sing to each other of love, courage, and ultimate farewell. The seven songs are charmingly short, the last and longest only four pages. No. 1, "Almona," (Song of Hassan) employs throughout the same left-hand accompanimental figure as that of the "Habanera" in *Carmen*. The eight-bar introduction beckoning the singer to begin is repeated as an interlude between verses. A short quasi coda supporting the words "Almona, awake, awake, awake!" ends the song with a dynamic marking of *pianissimo*.

"O, Night of Dream and Wonder" is full of surprising but pleasant harmonic progressions. "His Helmet's Blaze," marked *allegro agitato*, is built almost entirely on augmented chords which support a descending chromatic vocal line. Prosody, used by French composers who placed unaccented words or syllables on main beats, is hinted at in this dramatic third song, which Henderson calls "a fiery utterance."

Back to an *allegretto* pace in 3/4 meter, the fourth *Saracen Song*, "I Hear his Footsteps, Music Sweet" sung by Almona, begins with a rhythmically seductive two-bar introduction:

$$\frac{3}{4}\ \, \text{♫.}\ \text{♩}\ \text{♫}\ |\ \text{♫.}\ \text{♩}\ \text{♫}\ |$$

It invites a descending vocal sigh on the word "Ah!" Passion, suggested by the words *sun, fire, torch,* and *flame*, accelerates to this love song's climax. The last word, *name*, is sustained in a retrograde ascending passage. Accompanied by the original rhythmic opening in E minor, the song ends on an unexpected E major chord. Burleigh's score is marked with a few broken chords, suggestive of a tambourine or plucked instrument.

In the key of G flat, one seldom used by Burleigh, the beautiful "Thou Art Weary" unfolds. The lush chordal accompaniment is well written in this two-page segment of the cycle. The sixth part, "This Is Nirvana," has a busy vocal line, spelled by three short piano interludes. One feels, indeed, that Nirvana has been attained in the joyous last few bars of heavy chords and arpeggios in the accompaniment, which subsides to *ppp*.

Pianist and arranger of spirituals Margaret Bonds, whose style shows Burleigh's influence, maintained that in "Ahmed's Song of Farewell," which concludes *Saracen Songs*, Burleigh used the theme from "Somebody's Knocking at Your Door." She felt that some blacks may have protested the use of this spiritual for a love song.[20]

In a few spots the words slurred on duplets seem a little awkward for the singer. There are a few meter changes within the piece, but not disruptive ones. After an accompanied recitative in B minor, marked *Andante doloroso*, the key changes to B major and the syncopated pattern of the accompaniment with its chromatic ballad-like interludes and fat chords builds to *fortissimo* under the singer's high A. A short piano tremolo, a device employed sparingly by Burleigh up to now, is used with tasteful dramatic effect. Fittingly he ended this last song of the cycle with two crashingly loud chords.

A critic for the London *Musical Opinion and Music Trade Review* remarked on the cycle's consistently good quality:

> We know not which to admire the most – the captivating rhythm or the rich luscious harmony. . . . A word of acknowledgement must be offered to Fred G. Bowles, whose beautiful lyrics have no doubt greatly inspired the composer in his work.[21]

A critic for the London *Musical Standard* commented:

> The music generally is of a haunting nature and is rich in expressive harmonies, whilst its Eastern character is well maintained throughout. There are seven numbers, and there is not one that does not disclose poetical imagination and true musicianly emotional feeling. It is volumes such as these that make the reviewer's task a pleasure. So uniform are the songs in quality that one hesitates whether to particularly commend the romantic love raptures of "Almona," "O Night of Dream and Wonder," and "I Hear His Footstep[s], Music Sweet," the tenderness of "Thou Art Weary," or the almost painful pathos of "Ahmed's Song of Farewell."

Oddly, neither the 1914 *Saracen Songs* nor the first of Burleigh's two cycles written in 1915, *Five Songs of Laurence Hope*, bears a dedication.

Five Songs of Laurence Hope (1915)

The songs of the *Hope* cycle are said to be Burleigh's very finest work. Henry Edward Krehbiel, dean of American critics and musical editor of the *New York Tribune* (1880-1923), called them "artists' songs . . . in which singer and pianist are paired in a lovely union and engaged in a mission calculated to warm the feelings of those who contemplate it." Throughout the five songs, which range from three to five pages each, the "pianoforte and voice are beautifully and truthfully consorted in the utterance of the poetic sentiment." Their melodic phrases are not commonplace. The cycle was immediately orchestrated by Alfredo Brüggemann and issued by Ricordi.[22]

The enigmatic poet, Laurence Hope, a pseudonym of Adela Florence Cory (1865-1904), was the daughter of a British military officer serving in India. After an education in England she went to India in 1889 and married M. H. Nicholson, Queen Victoria's aide-de-camp. As a military wife she had ample free time to write. Settings of her poems soon became the vogue for drawing room, concert, and radio vocalists. Her "torrid, Swinburnian verse" illustrated "a lover's aim for destruction of self-consciousness in union with the object of his desires and insisted on the right of woman to share this ecstacy."[23]

The pseudo-Oriental style of Hope's impassioned lyrics, influenced by Persian and Islamic poets, evidently had great appeal for Burleigh, who was still enjoying the exotic taste of the recently successful *Saracen Songs*. Of her four volumes of verse published just after the turn of the century, *Songs from the Garden of Karma*, generally considered to be the work of a man, was reissued in 1908. Hope's husband, Nicholson, who called her "Violet," died in 1904. Acute depression following his demise prompted her suicide within a few months by perchloride of mercury.

Burleigh's skillful combination of words and music make the *Hope* cycle even more sensuous than *Saracen Songs*. One critic, H. K. M. (further unidentified) of the *Boston Evening Transcript*, went into some detail on the pieces. His analytical comments are worthy:

> The "Five Songs of Laurence Hope" probably represent
> Mr. Burleigh's best work. Here are haunting melodies, ac-

companiments rich in detail, yet not overwritten, striking bits of delineation, and much skill in the wedding of music to words. In sheer emotional effectiveness these songs must receive high rank. Once more the composer shows much cleverness in the weaving of brief thematic snatches into the harmonic framework. The second song of the group, "The Jungle Flower," gains distinction from the exotic pulsating syncopation that throbs beneath. The third, "Pale Hands I Lov'd," ["Kashmiri"] is perhaps the best achieved of the five. Here the moody sentiment of the words is heightened into something approaching tragic pathos.

In the fourth song, "Among the Fuchsias," Mr. Burleigh has caught admirably that "oriental" exoticism which is none the less charming because it happens to be fashionable in present-day song literature. The final song, "Till I Wake," is a lyric of real distinction. The impressive opening theme is intoned as though by the brass choir, giving way to its statement by the voice above an accompaniment of wide arpeggii. Later this theme reaches a passionate climax introducing the words, "If there be an awakening," and the song ends in an emotional lyric strain. Though Mr. Burleigh has taken pains in these pieces, as in all his songs, to give the text its full value, he writes in a melodic rather than a declamatory idiom. The chief characteristic of the accompaniments, beyond their clever use of themes, is their easy chromatic flow.[24]

In the same article the author considered the cycle's "popular qualities" immediately evident:

One can easily understand that the melting tones of John McCormack's voice have made thousands applaud them. But it is not so evident, until one comes to study them, how much musicianship and taste have gone into their construction.[25]

Krehbiel, in his preface to the score, describes the overall structure of the five songs as "motival," saying that "the instrumental voice has an independent development which frequently carries along the emotion passion as on a flood. . . . The idiom of the East" was at Burleigh's command.

These poems were also set by Amy Woodford-Finden under the title of *Kashmiri Love Songs*, of which "Pale Hands I Lov'd" is the most familiar. But a writer for the *Musical Standard*, December 25, 1915, stated that "Burleigh's settings need fear nothing in comparison" with Finden's. In general, he was ecstatic about the cycle, praising Burleigh's "fine sense of harmonic coloring," and saying that some of the songs "arise to heights of passion that is [*sic*] as eloquent as it is rare."

Written for tenor voice, these are not easy pieces, ranging from middle D to high B flat, with unexpected, tricky intervallic skips. So, how did Burleigh put them together? Obviously drawn to the passionate nature of the poems, he treated them expressively and with much abandon, befitting their words. Throughout the cycle he used more terms of expression than heretofore, such as *affetuoso, teneramente, appassionata, rubato, con abbandono, a piacere, languido.* Frequent tempo changes indicated by such markings as *rallentando, ritard,* and *accelerando* show greater flexibility than in earlier songs.

The delightfully playable accompaniments are embellished by such subtleties as grace notes. Some of Burleigh's ninth chord progressions, whether he would have admitted it or not, would be classified as improvisatory by today's ears. Chromaticism, as well as diminished and augmented chords, definitely add to the torturous rapture of the lover's uncertainties.

Drama is evident in the first song, "Worth While." The words "swiftly thrown" are accented and sung loudly in an octave's jump up to "thrown" on a high A. (See Musical Example No. 2.) Beginning supposedly in B minor the song's tonal center is not readily established, though about half way through it emerges as D major.

"The Jungle Flower" (M.M. quarter = 80) uses a longer, more beautiful piano interlude between sections than has been found in any previous songs. The soft opening with slightly dissonant grace notes suggests the spicy intrigue of a Persian market. A fermata separates the accompaniment from the singer's entrance, after which the piano reinforces the vocal line. Most effective is the line "Lie back and frame thy face in the gloom of thy loosened hair," marked *con abbandono.* Burleigh wrote a measure of rest in both parts, as if to

Musical Example No. 2, "Worth While" from *Five Songs on Poems by Laurence Hope*, measures 20-28.

declare a grand pause, before a last phrase marked *largo* – "When Fate was gentle to me for a too-brief hour."

Third in the cycle, "Kashmiri Song," beginning "Pale hands I lov'd, beside the Shalimar," has a key change about mid-way, at which point this percussive-like rhythm in the left hand of the accompaniment adds excitement to the words "How the hot blood rush'd wildly through the veins:"

Unexpected plaintive chordal progressions enhance this song. Quite a dramatic piece, it goes into a high tessitura when, speaking of the pale hands, the words cry "I would have rather felt you round my throat, crushing out life than waving me farewell!"

"Among the Fuchsias" deals with a lover's temptation and the evils thereof. Its tessitura is also demandingly high. Burleigh's accompanimental figures are rhythmically varied and appropriately busy for the text. Somewhat fraught with accents, the accompaniment again closely follows the vocal line.

In the last of the *Hope* cycle, "Till I Wake," (M.M. quarter = 92) Burleigh's accompaniment departs in the first section from his usual chordal technique, using instead a broken-chord, harp-like figure. The returning chordal procedure builds excitement, leads up to high B flat for the singer, and accelerates to an interlude marked "maestoso," which ends with the voluptuous words:

> So I may when I wake keep what lull'd me to sleep – the
> touch of your lips, the touch of your lips, the touch of your
> lips on my mouth – the touch of your lips on my mouth.

Burleigh's own ability as a pianist and as a composer for the piano assumes a new dimension in the construction of both *Saracen Songs* and the *Hope* cycle. Is it any wonder that sensitive artists – John McCormack and Roland Hayes, in particular – interpreted these songs to their fullest?

Passionale (1915)

In the same year of the *Hope* cycle, Burleigh and personal friend James Weldon Johnson collaborated on a cycle of four songs, *Passionale*, and the timely and successful "The Young Warrior."

Unlike the other two cycles, each of the love songs in *Passionale* was dedicated to a different tenor.

The first two songs, "Her Eyes Twin Pools" and "Your Lips Are Wine," bear inscriptions "To Mr. John McCormack" and "To Mr. Evan Williams." Enough has been said of McCormack and his association with Burleigh.[26] Of Welsh parentage, Evan Williams was a coal miner in Ohio before embarking on a singing career. He then taught and sang for twenty-seven years, distinguishing himself with both U.S. and English oratorio societies. He died unexpectedly in late May 1918 of infection from a huge carbuncle on his neck. "He had appeared in a concert at the Akron Armory, May 14, but at that time was suffering from great pain."[27]

The other two songs in the cycle, "Your Eyes So Deep" and "The Glory of the Day Was in Her Face," are dedicated to Ben Davies and George Hamlin, respectively. Davies (1859-1943), another Welsh singer, was known as the "last of the white-gloved tenors." During his forty years in opera, light opera, and on the concert stage, he sang for Queen Victoria at least nine times and was featured at Chicago's Columbian World's Fair in 1893-94, where Burleigh also sang. Davies was best known for his interpretation of "Ivanhoe" and for roles in Italian opera at Covent Garden. He was the third singer to record Brahms.[28]

Hamlin shared a recital with Christine Miller in New York City on February 16, 1915, reviewed in the next day's *Times*. Hamlin "offered some American songs by H. T. Burleigh of this city, in manuscript," which pieces may well have been from the newly written *Passionale*.

All four songs exude high physical passion, poetically speaking, but not in an offensive way. Overall this cycle is just as beautiful and provocative as the two preceding it.

In "Her Eyes Twin Pools" (Musical Example No. 3), introduced by two measures of rolled chords, the singer's very first phrase might present a problem to a novice but not to an experienced vocalist. Enunciation is of prime importance. Should the singer try an elision, Her-r-eyes, or an articulated separation? The second time this phrase occurs the words are "Her eyes, twin pools so dark and deep." Between "pools" and "so" the listener is puzzled unless the singer enunciates both "esses." Burleigh ends the song with a rather showy, bravura passage, diminishing in volume, while the singer repeats "Her eyes, her eyes," ending on a high G marked *pianissimo*, supported by an arpeggiated glissando-like G major seventh chord in the piano.

The vocal line of "Your Lips Are Wine" is underlaid only by harmonic chordal structure from the piano, with syncopated off beats suggestive of a Latin element. Again, enunciation is of the utmost importance. Toward the end, perhaps for dramatic effect, Burleigh

116171

Musical Example No. 3, "Her Eyes Twin Pools" from *Passionale*, measures 1-10.

uses fermatas and hesitations to highlight the text. A few nondistract-
ing meter changes are effective, as is the accompanimental contrapuntal melody against the vocal line.

Burleigh treats the theme of "Your Eyes So Deep" sequentially,
weaving an echo effect into the accompaniment. A low G, reiterated
by the piano, fully confirms G minor as the key. In the second section, the piano's two independent chromatic themes descend steadily
for ten measures as the vocal line repeats the first theme. Four descending minor-seventh chords in the left hand, underlying one last
statement of the theme, resolve in a final G major chord with flatted
sixths.

Critic H. K. M. called "The Glory of the Day," the last song of
the cycle, "at once suave and impassioned." Burleigh retains a gen-
tleness in the accompanimental treatment, evident in the moving
lines, a joy to the pianist. Not immediately apparent is the difficulty
of the vocal line's high range and treacherous skips, both reminiscent
of certain vocal works by Charles Tomlinson Griffes (1884-1920).

Art Songs (1915-1940)

Another James Weldon Johnson text set by Burleigh, "The
Young Warrior," with an underlying beat announced in its opening
fanfare, (M.M. quarter = 88) has a strong message. The gist of the
poem is a soldier son's plea to his mother for her moral and spiritual
support in his military efforts. Adopted by the Italian army as a
marching song, "Warrior" actually becomes rather aria-like, with a
later passage marked *deciso ben declamando* and backed by dimin-
ished-chord tremolos. The fanfare ends the piece thrillingly, punctuated by three loud F major chords which in the orchestration would
be scored heavily for percussion. The fanfare rhythm is:

An optional high A flat undoubtedly taken by Pasquale Amato
in his performance of "Warrior" at the Biltmore Hotel in New York,
February 1916, could not have detracted from the song's sensational
impact. Despite the publicity crediting Amato with the first public
performance of "Warrior," soprano, writer, and lecturer Mabel Garri-

son named Reinald Werrenrath as first introducing the song at an
Aeolian Hall recital in January, 1917.[29]

This popular piece was composed shortly after the outbreak of
World War II, though not published until 1915. At the time Johnson
was Minister to Nicaragua and contributing editor to the *New York
Age*. H. K. M. commented:

> Mr. Burleigh has given the words one of those melodies
> that sings themselves [*sic*] – not exalted in style, but ruddy
> with the enthusiasm of the mob in its patriotic frenzy. . . .
> Probably Mr. Burleigh himself would not claim high artistic
> excellence for this song but it has that quality of mob
> enthusiasm which few of the highly trained composers can
> manage.[30]

The success of "Warrior" prompted a lengthy article in *Current
Opinion*, August 1916 (pp. 100-1) titled "An American Negro Whose
Music Stirs the Blood of Warring Italy." Though the author was un-
named, he obviously had great respect for Burleigh's ability:

> According to advices from Italy, that traditional land of
> song is throbbing to the accents of a song by an American
> Negro who has probably never set foot on Italian soil.

The article was largely biographical, with generous mention of Burleigh's best known works up to 1916.

Burleigh set eight works of English poet and critic Arthur
Symons (1865-1945) between 1915 and 1921. The four that achieved
widest performance and recognition are "The Grey Wolf," "By the
Pool at the Third Rosses," "In the Wood of Finvara," and "On
Inishmaan: Isles of Aran." Symons, influenced by Baudelaire and the
French Symbolists, became a chief exponent of the Symbolist school
in England. He was trilingual, having been educated in private schools
in Italy and France. Not an emotionally stable person, he suffered
bouts of amnesia, sometimes wandering aimlessly, and was once held
by the Italian police, put in a "dungeon, beaten, and starved," later
to be rescued by the British Ambassador to Italy. In spite of these
aberrations, he was a staff writer and translator for several journals,
editor of many poetry anthologies, and he wrote an aesthetic critique

of Debussy. Symons's face has been described as "a triangular wedge, . . . a terrible face, ravaged like a battlefield."[31]

Two 1915 Burleigh songs set to texts by Symons are "The Prayer" and "Memory." In the article previously cited from *Current Opinion* these two delicately-textured songs were called "deeply felt musical tone-paintings." "The Prayer" is usually mentioned when Burleigh's chief works are listed. H. K. M. called it a "simple melody set over a hymn-like accompaniment, well constructed and modulated."[32] The words actually constitute a love song, asking permission to love to the fullest, even if the love cannot be returned. The highest notes of the chordal accompaniment are written almost throughout a third below or above the vocal line. An organist would have no problems with Burleigh's piano score. The poem "Memory," which describes the loved one as a "haunting perfumed essence," was later the text for Norman Dello Joio's "All Things Leave Me" (1950).

Also published in 1915 and much better known than "The Prayer" and "Memory, "The Grey Wolf" is one of the few Burleigh songs in which the vocal line begins with a pick-up note. The introduction, an ominous, lower string-like foreboding motif, gives way to Burleigh's familiar syncopated chordal pattern. Though the accompaniment is amply supportive, it does not follow the vocal line completely but presents some rich counter melodies of its own, heightening the drama of the piece. Diminished and augmented chords lend agitation and suspense. The narrative of Symons's poem, perfect for dramatic interpretation, depicts the wolf as a predator, perhaps Death, relentlessly demanding the impossible. An orchestral accompaniment was made for the song, according to the title page of the vocal score, though the arranger was not specified.

H. K. M., in his previously cited article, described "The Grey Wolf" as a long declamatory scena, for robust voice and in heroic mood, showing Burleigh's feeling for structural effect. George Hamlin, as well as Jordan, had his way with the song, as indicated by a *Courier* review of a Hamlin concert in Omaha, January 30, 1916: "The last number, 'The Grey Wolf' by H. T. Burleigh, brought forth an exceptionally dramatic climax."[33]

"The Grey Wolf" was dedicated to the talented Mary Jordan (1879-1961), a native of Cardiff, Wales, who debuted in 1911 with the Boston Opera Company, becoming most famous for her roles as

Amneris in *Aïda* and Azucena in *Il Trovatore*. During the war years she gave numerous benefit performances, for which service she was decorated in 1917 by Mrs. Woodrow Wilson with a token of the first lady's appreciation, a handsome lyre pin. In the 1920s she soloed with leading U.S. orchestras. Later she toured, performed, and taught in the Philippines when her husband was stationed there. Skilled in five languages, she was contralto soloist at Temple Emanu-El for twelve years. At the time of her death in San Antonio, Texas, Jordan was the widow of Col. Charles C. Cresson and a retired vocal teacher.[34]

Another stunningly dramatic song of 1915, one of Burleigh's longer ones and also later orchestrated, was "Ethiopia Saluting the Colors" (M.M. quarter=116). The "colors," yellow, red, and green, are those of the Ethiopian flag. Walt Whitman's narrative, which well lends itself to both musical setting and interpretation, describes a black slave woman, Ethiopia, being watched by a soldier as she herself watches part of General Grant's army passing in review. The martially precise accompaniment represents feet marching to drum beats. In minor mode, it becomes a dialogue between the soldier and the old crone, separated by piano interludes, each of which leads skillfully to the next vocal utterance. A five-measure passage of accented tremolos adds flavor to the soldier's recitative, which he expresses in octave skips. Pert interludes with the tune "Marching Through Georgia" are almost comical. The piece ends quietly with more drum beats from the piano, signifying that the troops have come and gone. (See Musical Examples Nos. 4-7.)

Walt Whitman (1819-1892) would probably have appreciated Burleigh's efforts. As a nurse in army hospitals in Washington, DC, during the Civil War, he knew whereof he spoke concerning attitudes on war. During active careers as a teacher, typesetter, and editor of the *Brooklyn Eagle*, he wrote freely. His best known volume is *Leaves of Grass*, at first publication controversial for its sexual frankness. "Ethiopia" was originally a part of *Drum Taps* (1865) and later included in *Leaves of Grass* which had gone into a tenth edition by the time of Whitman's death. An incapacitating stroke in 1873 somewhat curtailed this vigorous man's activities, but he continued to write, lecture, and enjoy friends at his home in Camden, New Jersey. He was called "the Good Grey Poet."[35]

Dedicatee Herbert Witherspoon's first performance of "Ethiopia Saluting the Colors" on November 23, 1915, at Carnegie Hall in New York was reviewed in the *New York Times* the following day:

> Mr. Burleigh has employed picturesque devices to illustrate this impressive poem – the rhythm of drum beats are heard; there are strains of characteristic negro rhythm and negro melody and there is the employment of "Marching Through Georgia." It is artistically conceived and skillfully executed – the work of a true musician deeply felt – and it has impressiveness, as the poem has. It was natural that Mr. Witherspoon should devote much care to Mr. Burleigh's fine composition, and he sang it with a pathos that rang through with a poignant intensity.

A *Courier* report of the same concert stated:

> Many of the songs on the Witherspoon program were heard for the first time in New York, a fact which is further proof of the fact already known that he is an unceasing student and a constant searcher after the best in his field of music.[36]

A. W. Kramer's praise of "Ethiopia" was quoted in the *New York Age*, May 18, 1916:

> No composer . . . is as well equipped to set the magnificent Whitman lines as Mr. Burleigh. . . . There are not a hundred pages by this country's composers that can rank with the final section beginning "Are the things so strange."

Another critic who approved of such an "extended piece" called it "moving tableaux, ably depicted, and admirably suited to the declamatory talent of . . . Mr. Witherspoon."[37]

Frederick H. Martens (1874-1932), a charter member and later director of ASCAP, was Burleigh's collaborator on "He Sent Me You" (1915). Martens was the author of at least six books, three of which concerned opera, and one a biography of Leo Ornstein, another of his collaborators. As a librettist and instrumental composer he also wrote for music journals, as well as the more popular magazines, *Vogue* and *Vanity Fair*.[38]

Musical Example No. 4, "Ethiopia Saluting the Colors," measures 24-31, shows Burleigh's use of the "Marching Through Georgia" theme, as do examples 5 and 6.

Musical Example No. 5, "Ethiopia Saluting the Colors," measures 36-43.

Musical Example No. 6, "Ethiopia Saluting the Colors," measures 86-89.

Musical Example No. 7, "Ethiopia Saluting the Colors," measures 95-103.

"Just You" (1915), popularized by Lucrezia Bori, Paul Althouse, and most other singers of the decade, has no dramatic intent. It is rather overly sentimental, but the yearning is heartfelt. Used widely as an encore piece, Madge Marie Miller's short love song with simple accompaniment by Burleigh reads:

> What are my thoughts tonight? They're of you.
> Where is my heart tonight? Gone with you.
> Where is my hope tonight? It's in you.
> What is my prayer tonight? 'Tis for you.
>
> How can I live tonight? not seeing you.
> Why do I weep tonight? Cause of you.
> Why burn my lips tonight? Kisses for you.
> Who seeks my soul tonight? You, just you, just you.

Ending on a high A flat, no doubt it was a crowd pleaser when rendered by the dazzling opera star Signorina Bori, to whom it was "most respectfully dedicated." Althouse sang "The Young Warrior" and "Just You" at the first musicale of the Harlem Philharmonic Society of New York on November 16, 1916.[39]

A bold flyer from Ricordi advertised "Just You," with its dedication to Bori, and the song "He Sent Me You." Though the ad bore no date, it probably was circulated widely during 1916-17.[40]

1916

In 1916, also a highly productive year, another song to text by Symons was destined to be well received. In "By the Pool at the Third Rosses," dedicated to John McCormack, a pickup note for the singer follows the four-measure piano introduction of arpeggios with a pedal-point D flat, lending an appropriate calm to the opening words "I heard the sighing of the reeds." The nostalgia of the song is an attempt to conjure up peaceful memories. Its consistently high tessitura would not suit a heavy voice, even if the range were comfortable.[41]

Rupert Brooke's more stirring poem "The Soldier" caught Burleigh's attention this year and appealed to his patriotic inclinations. It was quite popular during the remainder of the war. Brooke, a colorful, wholesome Englishman, was born in Rugby, Warwickshire, in

1887. He was a sports enthusiast, a spontaneous singer, and enjoyed reading to his schoolmates. After wandering over the United States, Canada, and the South Seas in 1913-14, he accepted a commission in the Royal Navy. Septicemia precipitated his tragic death on a hospital ship off Skyros, when he was en route to the Dardanelles. "He was buried at midnight by the light of torches on the island of Lemnos, making that corner of a foreign field forever England."[42]

Though Brooke had written poetry since 1905, his most worthy volume was titled *1914*, a collection of wartime sonnets. They expressed an idealistic attitude in the face of death, in strong contrast to his later poetry about war in the trenches. "The Soldier" was one of his best-known poems.

The song's somber beginning in A minor is marked "quasi una marcia funebre." The tympani-like piano introduction suggests extreme gloom. High Gs and Fs in the vocal line give a doleful, wailing quality, embellished with trills in the accompaniment. A happier mood emerges in a B-flat major section toward the close of the piece, lauding the beauties of England and ending on a high B flat on the word "Heav'n." The vocal line is punctuated by dotted rhythms in the accompaniment.

A. Walter Kramer was enthusiastic about the work, but one critic who spoke favorably of "The Soldier" still had some reservations:

> . . . the use of thematic snatches is less artistic, being chiefly confined to quotations from English popular songs. But it is highly effective and is by no means without artistry in its management. It is a song of a soldier about to die, and the tramp of the funeral march is never long absent from the accompaniment. "Rule Britannia," the "British Grenadiers," and the English national anthem appear now and again in the voice part of the accompaniment. But more effective still is the brief theme of four notes, which is Mr. Burleigh's own. Here again, though the musical material lacks the final mark of distinction, the structure is so canny and well artified that the song must be regarded as an able achievement.[43]

"Three Shadows" (1916) is Burleigh's setting of a subjective, intimate, beautifully romantic poem by Dante Gabriel Rossetti. It was not specifically dedicated to McCormack, who popularized it, though the cover does state "Sung by John McCormack." During the years preceding the 1920s singers successfully used this type of song as an encore, bringing roars of appreciation when done with McCormack's aplomb.

"Three Shadows" is worthy of programming, both in length and content. Its vocal line goes up to a high B flat (in the high key), preceded by high Gs, and just at the end Burleigh wrote a high A flat, perfect for holding, depending on the prowess of the singer. Using a device at which he was apt, Burleigh wrote a contrapuntal melody in the accompaniment which varies from stanza to stanza. The interludes are lush and expressive. Though the style of "Three Shadows" might be considered passé in the present day, its warmth, sentimental appeal, and excellent composition are irresistible.

Rossetti's three shadows were hair, eyes, and heart. What more romantic verse could be wished? A few of the words are:

> I looked and saw your heart
> In the shadow of your eyes,
> As a seeker sees the gold
> In the shadow of the stream;

The rhyme scheme within each stanza is "abcd, abcd." Burleigh did not alter the words except to repeat a line of the last stanza, "You can love true girl."

Rossetti (1828-1882), brother of poet Christina Rossetti, was one of the leaders of the Pre-Raphaelites who rebelled against formal artistic standards. His poetry and paintings were highly imaginative, symbolic, and sensual. As a teacher and scholar of Italian he translated Dante. Distressed by his wife's death from an overdose of laudanum he buried some of his unpublished poems with her, later exhuming them for publication. In mid-life, tortured by his passion for a married woman, he began a marathon of dissipation, using drugs and alcohol excessively.

"One Year, 1914-1915," with words by Margaret M. Harlan, was Burleigh's last "war song," except for "The Victor" in 1919. Apparently Harlan was not well known as a writer or poet, but may have been a personal friend of Burleigh. The words of this short war love song are:

1914.   Dark pines 'gainst the blue;
           Clean winds, a wide view;
           Two arms and a kiss;
           One moment of bliss: −
           'Tis a thing to remember for years,
           To remember with tears.

1915.   Battle birds in the sky;
           Shriek of gun as they die;
           Crash − and roar, bloody drench;
           Black death in the trench; −
           What a thing forever to miss
           Ah, My God! her kiss − and *this*!

Introductory chime-like chords in the key of A-natural minor presage a later chorale tune, "Praise to the Lord," in A major. The 1915 section is marked "più mosso" and introduced with a trill, building to a climax at the words "black death." The chorale tune begins quietly, then the vocal line reenters, ending on a sustained high G in the final words, "Ah, My God! her kiss."

1917

As if the successes of the past two years had not been ample, Burleigh, the composer, continued to blossom even more abundantly in 1917. Other than the thirteen spirituals published by Ricordi that year, eight art songs were also issued.

Dedicated to McCormack, "Little Mother of Mine," another perfect encore piece, nearly always brought the house down. A. Walter Kramer's aptly put phrase, "The song is being sung by John McCormack at all his concerts this season," was a kudo of the highest order. Kramer predicted that within a few months after publication this "heart-song" should be a hit. Full of human interest, "touching the universal statement of Mother love, it has undeniable appeal," with a "flowing sweet melody that anyone can sing." Every measure was marked by Burleigh's "excellent workmanship," with a finish "which the average writer of ballads cannot command."[44] The song was a smash hit, a staple not only in McCormack's encore repertoire, but appealing to nearly all concert performers and their audiences.

At first glance the song looks like an innocuous waltz tune, from the simplicity of both accompaniment and vocal line, but its essence and impact merit deeper study. Burleigh's modicum of expressive markings leaves the schmaltz to the singer's discretion. It can hardly be overdone by a capable artist.

Walter H. Brown, whose words Burleigh set for "Little Mother of Mine," has not been suitably identified. One Walter H. Brown, mentioned in a *New York Times* obituary (November 5, 1945), was a retired dairy farmer of Cornwall, New York, and president of a Horse Thief Detecting Society. He would seem an unlikely collaborator. Burleigh's Brown may have been a church friend or a ships-that-pass-in-the-night acquaintance. In any case, it certainly proved a profitable mutual effort.

"The Dove and the Lily" (M.M. quarter = 44), a charming Swedish folk song set in 1917, was first presented by Oscar Seagle on a concert for the choir boys at the Cathedral of St. John the Divine in New York on May 16, 1917. His performance, given with "a fidelity to the text and a mastery of the vocal line that thrilled," also included a group of Burleigh's spirituals. Of Seagle's Aeolian Hall concert later that year a *New York Times* reviewer wrote:

> There were tenderer moments, and for variety there might have been more of these such as . . . a Swedish folksong of "The Dove and the Lily" and a group of Negro spirituals, "camp meeting songs," that Mr. Seagle gave with a Southern relish.

Though composers Dvorak and Emile Paladilhe were mentioned in the review, Burleigh was not.[45]

Conceived in true folk song idiom, the charm of "The Dove and the Lily" is undeniable. The vocal line's strophic style is relieved only by Burleigh's inventive accompaniment, which changes with each verse like a delightfully guileless set of piano variations. Mozart or Schubert could not have done better. Range of the vocal line encompasses only an octave. A special touch is added by chords in open fifths under the words "But clear rang the bells from the Heav'nly height." This appears to be one of Burleigh's best artistic efforts.

Three songs in particular gained some recognition in 1917, partially due to Burleigh's astuteness in dedicatory matters. Two of them, "The Sailor's Wife" and "On Inishmaan: Isles of Aran," were written for Christine Miller when she was at peak popularity. She often programmed some of Burleigh's spirituals, along with his art songs, and probably was as responsible as anyone for making him known as a composer and arranger.

Words of "The Sailor's Wife," an especially beautiful work, were written by Mary Stewart Cutting (1850-1924), New York State novelist and writer of short stories pertaining to married life. Her work was frequently published in *McClure's Magazine*. Some of her books were *Little Stories of Married Life*, *Some of Us Are Married*, and *Refractory Husbands*.[46]

"The Sailor's Wife," a poignant cry of loneliness from a wife whose sailor husband is away, is ripe with ninth chords, Lisztian rumbles of left-hand octaves, and a real bravura passage, followed by a recitative of musing by the wife as she sings "Cold, cold, upon the wet sands beat the waves that thunder at my feet. And are you cold, my sailor, too?" Triplet figures in the accompaniment against the vocal line's basically duple feeling, suggest the movement of waves. Miller, the gorgeous charmer, must have acted her convincing best in performing this superb piece.

Less dramatic, but pleasant, is "On Inishmaan: Isles of Aran," also dedicated to Miller. Echoing Arthur Symons's imagery, a quietly rocking 6/8 rhythm is supplied by the accompaniment. Generally the range is low. Miller had premiered this song the previous October in Chicago.[47]

Mary Jordan premiered "In the Wood of Finvara," with text by Symons, at Aeolian Hall in February 1917. She again exposed this song the following April 20 at a Biltmore Hotel concert in New York for a Red Cross Ambulance benefit:

> The list of patrons included Governor and Mrs. Whitman, Mayor and Mrs. Mitchell, Maj. Gen. and Mrs. Leonard Wood, the Hon. and Mrs. James W. Gerard, and many others prominent in metropolitan social life.[48]

Burleigh's chordal introduction in "Finvara" continues through the first two phrases and then bursts into a rhapsodic interlude. He set only three of Symons's four verses. The idyllic text speaks of escaping life's torments, especially love, in a fairy wood retreat. A trill by the piano suggests bird song. The dynamic markings of *pianissimo* must be strictly observed for contrast of mood.

A review in *Musical America* of "Finvara" was exciting:

> Mr. Burleigh's songs are continually becoming finer and finer. Each new one is bigger and more original than the last. . . . "Wood" shows a tenser emotionalism, a subtler touch . . . a deep symphonic feeling, culminating in the big climax on the third page, where after developing a figure based on the opening measures of the voice part Mr. Burleigh takes us in contrary motion up to a *fortissimo* on "its flames aspire." The epilogue . . . is one of the most delectable things in new music; here is poesy, here is imagination! And the Adagio that closes the song only adds to its loveliness. . . . a masterpiece. . . . Mr. Burleigh writes practically nothing today that does not fall into this class. . . . This song seems . . . a series of inspired moments.[49]

Another critic writing in 1917 summed up Burleigh's work to date, recognizing in it

> the earnest and talented musician. His choice of texts for his songs indicates a refinement of taste which is revealed again in his selection and moulding of his best themes. The robust spirit that dictated "Ethiopia Saluting the Colors" is one that is much needed to lift American song-literature from the deadly average of mediocrity which now holds it fast. Better things can be expected of Mr. Burleigh than those which he has thus far done. He has visibly grown in musical stature in the last five years, the later songs being so much better in workmanship than the earlier ones that they seem the result of new inspiration. If he persists in the mood of his more ambitious undertakings he may prove a force as stimulating to musical composition as he has been charming to concert audiences.[50]

1918

Burleigh's 1918 output was comprised of spirituals except for "Under a Blazing Star," which became a favorite in 1919 of tenor Charles Harrison, then travelling the concert circuit with the Columbia Stellar Quartet. Harrison was frequently a soloist with such groups as the Toronto Male Chorus.[51]

Mildred Seitz, poet of "Blazing Star," known in Brooklyn for philanthropic activities, was the wife of business manager Seitz of the *New York World*. Her chief interest as President of helping-hand organization the Chiropean Club was finding foster homes for orphans, having adopted four of her own.[52]

1919

One of seven art songs published in 1919, Burleigh's "A Song of Rest," with text by Fred G. Bowles (*Saracen Songs*), was dedicated to Harrison. A copy of the manuscript was received by the writer, courtesy of the Erie County Historical Society Library. Except for two bars struck through by Burleigh, the tidiness and clarity of the manuscript are impeccable. Unfortunately, the copying process for reproduction lost this clarity. There is no evidence that the song has been copyrighted or published.

There is no accurate information on George O'Connell, poet for Burleigh's "Down by the Sea" and "The Victor" of 1919 – and "Love Watches" (1920). The score of "Down by the Sea" (M.M. quarter = 60) reveals a lonely woman awaiting the return of her sailor son and remembering him as a boy playing on the shore. The accompaniment is skillfully constructed with repeated syncopation, augmented chords, and a chromatic bass line, all characteristic of Burleigh, not trite, the whole creating a little gem.[53]

A far better known poet, Jessie Fauset, later Jessie Fauset Harris (1885-1961), was an editor for *Crisis* in the mid 1920s and also the author of at least four novels, among them *Plum Bum* and *There Is Confusion*. Catering in subject matter toward racial discrimination, they usually portrayed blacks of background and ambition. Fauset was the only Afro-American in her class when she entered a Philadelphia public school. In 1905 she graduated from Cornell where she was the first black female student to win Phi Beta Kappa honors. She received a Master's degree at the University of Pennsylvania and later studied at the Sorbonne. A teacher of classical languages and French in Washington, DC, and at DeWitt Clinton High School in New York City, Fauset published poems in numerous anthologies. It is highly probable that Burleigh knew her personally. He set her poem "Fragment" as "Fragments."[54]

Though "Fragment" is a heartbreakingly touching poem, Burleigh did alter a few of the lines, probably for smoother vocal execution. Fauset's first line reads: "The breath of life imbued those few dim days," which Burleigh changed to "How sweet the memr'y of those few dim days." The first line of Fauset's second stanza, "Blank futile death inheres these years between," quite a mouthful for the singer, was changed to "How sad the memr'y of these years between." Fauset's poem ends: "But frozen tears and stifled words, and once a sharp caught cry"; the song ends, "But unshed tears and unsaid words and once a stifled cry."

Burleigh uses the same melody for the vocal line in both stanzas, while varying the accompaniment, not harmonically but by a fuller treatment. This pleasant two-page piece is not difficult and would make an effective encore.

Another song of 1919 was Arthur Symons's "I Remember All," built on a four-note motif and introduced by Sophie Braslau, an active and well-known operatic contralto of that decade.[55] Braslau (1892-1935), a student of both Marcella Sembrich and Herbert Witherspoon, debuted with the Metropolitan Opera in 1914 in *Parsifal*. After leaving this company in 1920 she sang extensively in the United States and Europe and was the contralto of the Victor Quartet, a group which made operatic and popular records around 1916.

The four verses of Georgia Douglas Johnson's intense "I Want to Die While You Love Me," are similar in content to this one:

> I want to die while you love me
> Oh, who would care to live
> Till love has nothing more to ask
> And nothing more to give?[56]

Johnson (1886-1966), who received honorable mention in literature for the 1928 Harmon Award and authored several volumes of verse, including *The Heart of a Woman* and *Bronze*, was the wife of Henry

Lincoln Johnson, at that time Republican National Committeeman from Georgia. In 1926 Mrs. Johnson was named as a special field worker for the Bureau of Conciliation. She was the first black woman, after Frances Harper, to gain recognition as a poet.[57]

"In the Great Somewhere," with words by Harold Robé, was frequently performed by McCormack during the next two years. Robé (1881-1946), a song writer himself as well as a character actor, stage manager, and member of ASCAP, later arranged some of Burleigh's spirituals. As a boy he sang soprano in St. Paul's Episcopal Church in Buffalo. Two of his more famous tunes with other collaborators were "Dear Old Pal of Mine" and "I Hear You Calling Me." Another of his songs with Burleigh, "The Prayer I Make for You," was published in 1921.[58]

Harriet E. Gaylord (d. 1947), whose poem "Oh, My Love!" Burleigh set in 1919, was a writer of short stories on English country life and of lyrics for composers. She also authored a longer work on the life of the Brownings, *Pompilia and Her Poet*. She taught English literature in New York high schools for thirty years.[59]

On December 15, 1919, John McCormack introduced "Were I a Star" at the Hippodrome. The accompaniment of this short song (M.M. quarter = 60) to words by A. Musgrove Robarts uses an arpeggiated figure in the right hand, adding to its dreamy mood.

The 1920s

In 1920 three of Burleigh's art songs were composed to poems by previous collaborators: George O'Connell ("Love Watches," an Irish fragment); George Hobart ("Southern Lullaby"); Fred G. Bowles ("Tell Me Once More"); and Paul Laurence Dunbar ("A Corn Song"). Burleigh dedicated his SATB arrangement, with soprano solo, of "Southern Lullaby" to the Burleigh Glee Club of New Bedford, Massachusetts, organized and directed at that time by Mrs. Addie R. Covell. Coleridge-Taylor's setting of "A Corn Song" by Dunbar seems to have enjoyed more performances than Burleigh's.

This year, too, ASCAP member Gordon Johnstone whom Burleigh probably knew personally, collaborated on "Have You Been to Lons?" Johnstone (1876-1926), who rode with Teddy Roosevelt's Rough Riders, was a Broadway actor and author of *There Is No*

Death. His songs with other composers include "The Living God," "The New Christ," and "Laddie O' Mine." He was working on an opera libretto at the time of his death.[60]

The title "Listen to Yo' Gyarden Angel" might suggest a spiritual type setting, but the poem by Robert Underwood Johnson was rather a comical ditty in dialect. Johnson (1853-1937), the "Unofficial Laureate" of the United States, was editor of *Century Magazine*, instrumental in the American Academy of Arts and Letters, an active diplomat working in Italy in World War I for the relief fund, and head of the Hall of Fame at New York University. He spontaneously wrote odes and sonnets for an occasion of the moment. He published his volumes of poetry himself.[61]

One outstanding choral piece published in 1921, "Ethiopia's Paean of Exultation," was composed to words by Anna Julia Cooper. Quite a brilliant lady, Cooper (1859-1964) lived a long and full life. Born in North Carolina, she studied at Oberlin, Columbia, and at the Sorbonne in Paris. She taught French, German, Latin, Greek and mathematics in several states. It is likely that she taught Alston Burleigh during her tenure at Dunbar High School in Washington, DC. Cooper later became president of Frelinghuysen University, a school for employed blacks, which she managed from her home.[62]

The following April 1, 1922, Mrs. Daisy Tapley's chorus performed at Carnegie Hall. "The highlight of the evening from a musical standpoint was really the Burleigh number, the Ethiopian paean," according to the *Age* critic, who saw flaws only in the imbalance of too many women's voices over those of the men.

A lesser ensemble piece set by Burleigh in 1921, "De Ha'nt," is suggestive of the dialect word *haint* (haunt). The poem, based on an Afro-American folk tale, is by James W. Pryor, probably a parishioner at St. George's and an acquaintance of Burleigh's. Pryor (1877-1924), an attorney in Flushing, New York, was active in the Boy Scout movement. Burleigh may have sung for his funeral, which was held at St. George's.[63] Ricordi published an arrangement of "Just You" for male voices, dedicated to the Howard University Glee Club in 1921.

From 1921 there was also "He Met Her in the Meadow," a solo for male voice (See Musical Example No. 8.), with arrangements for mixed voices and female voices following the next year. Words are by Burleigh though he did not credit himself on the score as author. The music is unashamedly corny. Every measure of this song drips with saccharin, resembling vocal selections of the old-time hearts-and-flowers vintage. The serious marking *Andante con molto sentimento* in no way divulges the hysterically funny ending of the piece. Three cheers for Mr. Burleigh's sense of humor! It would make a great encore number –

> He met her in the meadow as the sun was sinking low
> They walked along together in the twilight's afterglow.
> She waited until patiently he had lower'd all the bars,
> Her soft eyes bent upon him as radiant as the stars.
>
> She neither smiled nor thanked him, in fact she knew
>   not how,
> For he was a

Musical Example No. 8, "He Met Her in the Meadow," measures 25-30.

"Before Meeting," another poem by Arthur Symons, written in 1894 about an imaginary child of his dreams, was set by Burleigh in 1921. The poem was part of Symons's cycle *Celeste*, in which the child becomes his love, then his lost love in the course of the seven poems.

"Little House of Dreams" by Arthur Wallace Peach, a contributor to the *Age*, "Exile" by unknown Inez Maree Richardson, and "Love Found the Way" by Jesse Winne were set in 1922. "Exile" is a little gem, which could seem fragmented if performed perfunctorily by an unfeeling singer with an insensitive accompanist. The accompaniment with its independent melody could stand alone as a salon solo. Its chord progressions have the flavor of Cyril Scott's "Lento" for piano and a fascinating chromaticism suggestive of Scriabin's shorter pieces. A sentimental song, it is also a sophisticated one. Burleigh's augmentation of the short poem with brief interludes and two meter changes (from 3/4 to 9/8 to 3/4) is ingenious. Richardson's poem reads:

> My lonely heart and I waited for spring:
> Waited for spring: by the side of the road,
> And spring pass'd us by!
> We could not share her loveliness;
> The lilting song, the blue sky
> Exiled in our wilderness:
> My lonely heart and I!

Its mood of introspection should be sustained by strict observance of Burleigh's dynamics, the climax falling on the word "exiled," marked *mezzo forte*, the loudest level in the song.

Jesse Winne (1875-1964), a charter member of ASCAP, was fairly well known as a composer, author, and organist. He worked for various music publishing houses and found time to travel with theatrical companies. He also collaborated with Geoffrey O'Hara.[64]

In his dissertation Roland Lewis Allison lists only two Burleigh songs published in 1923. The poems were "The Dream of Love" by Alexander Groves, whose "Hour Glass" has been discussed, and "The Trees Have Grown So" by John Hanlon.

The nostalgic Hanlon poem bemoans the fact that the tall, graceful trees, once a trysting place for lovers, kept growing, while the lovers drifted apart. The climax of the piece is sustained on a high A in the vocal part, ending firmly but somberly with a heart-breaking *portamento* between the words "Oh, God!" a direction seldom written in by Burleigh. The accompaniment then diminishes to *ppp*. The accompanimental melody follows the vocal line closely, beginning with sequential phrases, which the voice repeats in the second stanza.

The September 1923 *Musical Forecast* reviewed "The Trees Have Grown So," contrasting it vividly with six songs of other composers published by Theodore Presser Co. which were dismissed as "hopeless drivel" and "without a single saving quality."

> Having worked off our venom on these aforementioned luckless songs, we will bring to notice a new Burleigh song which is one of the finest of its type that has appeared for a long time. Burleigh is without doubt among the most gifted song-writers in America, and he has reached one of the high spots in this composition. It is of a popular appeal – a sort of glorified ballad; but this enhances, rather than detracts from its interest. . . . Burleigh's setting is simple, but deeply emotional. It is a song which should meet with instant response from an audience, and one which will be widely used during the coming season.[65]

In addition to the high praise for this particular song, the reviewer showed familiarity with Burleigh's work in general.

Burleigh devoted the period 1924-26 to the arranging and publication of spirituals, some for solo voice and others for vocal ensembles. In 1927 a new collaborator but old acquaintance, William Pickens, enlisted Burleigh's aid on "Fair Talladega," adopted as one of that institution's three school songs. A letter to the writer from Dr. J. Roland Braithwaite, Head of Talladega's Music Department clarified current use of the song:

> In answer to your question – Is it our school song? Yes, in a sense. It is one of three that are school songs. However, it never replaced an older song the words of which were also written by William Pickens. The earlier song is generally considered as *the* school song. In the time when week day chapel assemblies were required there were frequent enough

Fair Talladega

Alma Mater Song Of Talladega College

Words by
WILLIAM PICKENS '02

Music by
H.T.BURLEIGH

On Thee, fair Tal - la - de - ga, With

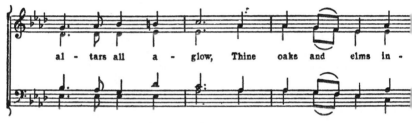

al - tars all a - glow, Thine oaks and elms in -

vit - ing, Our prais - es we be - stow; O,

AL - MA MA - TER dear, Our ears will ev - er

4

hear, Thy voice a-call-ing us, Where
ev-er we may go. Thy voice a-call-ing
us, Where ev-er we may go.

(small notes for piano or organ)

Unison

Harmony

rall.

2 Thou castle of the bravest,
   Of truest hearts the home,
   Wherever thou dost call us,
   Fond children we will come;
   O, ALMA MATER dear,
   Our hearts will ever hear
   Thy voice a-calling us,
   Wherever we may go.

3 At thy great burning beacon
   We do our torches light;
   And heartened by thy vict'ry,
   Our lesser battles fight;
   O, ALMA MATER dear,
   Our spirits ever hear
   Thy voice a-calling us,
   Wherever we may go.

Musical Example No. 9, used by permission of Talladega College, Talladega, Alabama.

occasions for us to rotate all three of the songs. Now, the Burleigh song is never used, mostly because choir directors since the retirement of Prof. Frank Harrison (a long time member of the faculty and head of the Music Department) in the late '60s have not taken the time to teach it to the choir, and through choir use project it to the student body. In short, the memory of the song has been lost because of changes in personnel and because of the fewer occasions on which school songs would be sung. But the music is still here and I hope to encourage our current choir director to use it. Musically, it is far superior to the one generally accepted and commonly used.

I do not know of the circumstances of its adoption. Frank Harrison did comment that it was never able to re-place the old song in the hearts of the old alumni. This suggests that some attempt was made to make it the *alma mater*. By the time I came here (1952) all three songs were in common use and remained so until the 1960's.[66]

"Fair Talladega" (see Musical Example No. 9) is reprinted by permission of Talladega's president, Paul B. Mohr, Sr.

Dr. Pickens (1881-1954), a well-educated South Carolinian raised in Arkansas, held degrees from Fisk, Selma, and Yale universities. At Yale he was a Phi Beta Kappa. In 1920 he became the Field Secretary of the NAACP. Pickens's teaching experience was gained at Wiley and Talladega colleges and at Morgan State. He was the latter's first black Vice-President and later became its Dean. Author of three books about Afro-Americans, the verbally gifted Dr. Pickens was a go-getter in every endeavor. With the Spingarns he helped establish the first black officers' training camps. His untimely death from a heart attack occurred aboard ship as he was returning to New York from a Caribbean cruise.[67]

Burleigh's songs in 1928 number only three: "A Fatuous Trage-dy" with words by Homer Brewer; "Are You Smiling," words by Hector MacCarthy; and "Passing By," an anonymous poem errone-ously attributed to Robert Herrick. Though no information has come to light on Brewer or his poem, its title suggests humor. Canadian-born MacCarthy (1888-1973), who was later to set Burleigh's solo arrangements of spirituals for ensemble, was a member of ASCAP, a composer, author, pianist, and writer in the field of music education. He studied at Juilliard and with voice professor Dudley Buck. As a singer and accompanist he toured with the Metropolitan Opera Company.[68] "Passing By" has invited musical setting by several composers, including Norman Dello Joio, who titled his song "A Lady Sweet and Kind" (1948).

The 1930s

Burleigh's next published art song of consequence was "Lovely Dark and Lonely One" (1935), a true jewel in both text and music. The text is by Langston Hughes (1902-1967), a poem from his collection, *The Dream Keeper* (1932). The work has been said to represent the "consummation of Burleigh's creative powers" and, more abstract in conception, to avoid the "tedious heaviness characteristic of his earlier ballads."[69]

Two simple bars of C major arpeggio, sustained by pedal and ending with a fermata, introduce the two-page piece. The vocal line might present problems to an inexperienced singer in its unexpected intervals, supported nobly and richly by the constantly shifting harmonic structure of the accompaniment. An effective high G on the word "wait," preceded by a dramatic passage leading to it, is the song's high point.

Poet Hughes made quite a name for himself, not only in literary circles, but as the founder of Harlem Suitcase Theater (1938) and the Negro Theater in Los Angeles (1939). A constructive worker against racial oppression, he received the Harmon Gold Medal for Literature in 1930, a Guggenheim Fellowship in 1935, the American Academy and Institute of Arts and Letters Award in 1946, the Anisfield-Wolf Award in 1953, and the Spingarn Medal in 1960. Other of Hughes's better known volumes are *The Weary Blues and Other Poems* (1926) and *Scottsboro Limited* (1932), including four poems and a play. His poems have been translated into German, French, Spanish, Russian, Yiddish and Czech, and set by many composers, including William Grant Still and John Alden Carpenter.[70]

During 1936-38 none of Burleigh's compositions were published, though he did arrange "Greeting" for the Burleigh Glee Club, founded and directed by Ella Belle Davis. In 1939 Burleigh collaborated on another college song, "Dear Ol' N.C.C." (North Carolina College, now North Carolina Central University), with Annie Day Shepard. Known principally as a lyricist and collaborator with Gene Autry, Shepard wrote a few compositions of her own. Burleigh likely knew her at this time as Ann Shepard Mazlen, member of ASCAP. Born in 1918, she was still living as late as January of 1986 but did not answer queries on her connection with Burleigh. The tune, published by North Carolina College, was later revised by Alston Burleigh. According to the *Age*, July 5, 1941, Annie Day Shepard was the daughter of Dr. James Shepard, President of North Carolina College at the time.

The 1940s

In 1940 another female member of ASCAP, Beatrice Fenner (1904-85), offered words to Burleigh for "I Wonder." Fenner, trained at Juilliard, composed a number of songs and a few instrumental works. Later she became a foster mother for handicapped infants. A letter to the author dated March 18, 1986, from Fenner's niece, Mrs. Barbara Stoner of Rancho Santa Fe, California, official administratrix of Fenner's estate, explained:

> We have not begun to go through her music files yet, but I do plan to go to her house in Los Angeles in the next two weeks to do some more packing and organizing. Be assured that if I come across any files on Burleigh or sheet music, I'll gladly pass them on to you. We'll watch for "I Wonder" especially.

Unfortunately this particular song was not located during a later examination by Mrs. Stoner of Fenner's sheet music, though some further details on the poet were found. Fenner's photo with John Charles Thomas was on the cover of a 1940 issue of *Pacific Coast Musician*, which also carried an article about her. Fenner authored a volume of poems titled *Blue Laughter*. Though Ricordi published some of her songs, she later established Fenner Publications in Los Angeles. Her own "I Wonder" (1925) was often sung by Amelita Galli-Curci and Claire Dux.

Afflicted by congenital blindness, Fenner was a remarkable and courageous woman. While she was at Juilliard a Professor Nobel had special paper printed for her, which he described as having "lines more than an inch apart. She measured with her finger from the top of the paper down – and with large whole notes wrote out her counterpoint." Legally blind by the early 1930s, she sat at the piano and played her songs to Galen Lurwick, a pianist-accompanist friend, who notated them. Lurwick wrote:

> Her vision was less than 10%. . . . She sat at the piano and played them and I wrote them down. She knew exactly what she wanted. I merely put it on paper – that was all.[71]

Two of Fenner's better-known songs were "Reciprocation" (1939) and one recorded by John Charles Thomas, "When Children Pray." Her poems, some of which she read and recorded herself, were said to have "a distinct individuality, yet represent widely different moods and shades of meaning . . . delicate pastels of tenderness and beauty."[72]

The last five of Burleigh's vocal compositions and arrangements (1941-49) were sacred in content. By this time, considering his age and approaching senility, a decline in compositional output was inevitable.

An Overview of Burleigh's Art Songs

To date none of Burleigh's art songs have been included in an anthology or compilation of similar works. Willis C. Patterson, editor of *Anthology of Art Songs by Black American Composers*, attempts to explain his exclusion of Burleigh in this particular collection by pointing out Burleigh's previous wide publication, both as an art song composer and an arranger. Nevertheless, one token song by Burleigh in this ambitious and selective anthology of twenty-four representative composers would have been respectful, since Burleigh was the first black American to win critical acclaim for his art songs.[73]

An examination of Burleigh's art songs from 1898 through 1940 indicates that he developed his own style. There is practically no borrowing of compositional tools from European composers. Burleigh has infrequently been compared to Schubert, but not as a copier of him. Burleigh's use, though sparse, of accompanimental triplet passages might resemble Schubert or Beethoven, but other similarities are not particularly noticeable, except perhaps the subject matter, of course, such as Love, Nature and the like, which every composer and writer has drawn on since time began. He used trills and tremolos sparingly.

Professor Richard Crawford of the University of Michigan divides American composers into those reticent to shuck European tradition and others more experimental, who probe American musical roots and tradition, taking inspiration therefrom. Reasoning of the first group has stemmed in part from insecurity, fearing nonacceptance of anything too drastically nouveau. There has been safety in the womb of European tradition.

In the other camp Burleigh certainly explored Negro spirituals to the fullest and was unprecedented in his treatment of them, as well as his innovations in the field of the art song. They are tasteful but simple, not made ludicrous by attempts to jazz them up for saleability.[74] On the subject of the German influence dominating American composers past the turn of the century, Dominique René De Lerma states:

> Dvorak knew this and he was also aware that this cultural inferiority complex and that racial prejudice prevented white America from acknowledging its distinct cultural heritage in Black music. . . . Under Burleigh's direct stimulus this Czech tried to awaken Whites to their Black potentials. The fact that the *New World Symphony* is more Czech than Black is irrelevant.[75]

Nor do Burleigh's art songs resemble the more brooding ones by his European contemporaries Strauss (1864-1949), Mahler (1860-1911) and Rachmaninoff (1873-1943). Burleigh's song cycles, less emotionally draining, are also less complex in construction. Only in a few of his songs does one hear an imaginary orchestra in the accompaniment. Strauss's heavier-textured vocal works sound operatically and/or orchestrally conceived; Mahler's subject matter is often depressing, for he was not a particularly happy man; and Rachmaninoff's chronic bouts of mental depression were sometimes reflected in his music.

Only in the *Hope* cycle and *Saracen Songs* is there any hint of impressionism, and that a far cry from Debussy and Ravel. Burleigh was his own man. Only in small degree did he inject his personality into his songs. Neither do they have a black sound, one which he instinctively reserved for his arrangements of the spirituals.

Burleigh's Instrumental Works

It is not certain that Burleigh's *Six Plantation Melodies for Violin and Piano* (1901) was ever published. Nor does *The National Union Catalog Pre-1956 Imprints* list the pieces as having been copyrighted. A search for the manuscript is still in progress, however.

Suite of Piano Sketches

Some authorities date the publication of *From the Southland*, a suite of six piano sketches, as 1907. Actually, according to a score of the work obtained from Jean Snyder, a Burleigh scholar at the University of Pittsburgh, it was first published in 1910 by the William Maxwell Company. The copyright was transferred to Theodore Presser, who reissued it in 1914. Burleigh dedicated it: "To my friend S. Coleridge-Taylor, Esq. London, England."

Inspired by some dialect poems of Louise Burleigh, each piece is prefaced by one of her verses, signed "L. A. B." The very expressive first piece "Through Moanin' Pines" reads:

> Along de desolate roads we pass
> Thro' lonely pines and wither'd grass: –
> De win' moans in de branches tall
> An' a heavy sadness broods o'er all!

Burleigh's *Andante Semplice* marking (M.M. quarter=66) well suits its key of F-sharp minor; its lush chords could be arranged interestingly for string ensemble. In ABA form, the two-page piece ends in a major key. The melody of the last A section is written up an octave with added voices and a louder dynamic marking.

"The Frolic" is definitely dance-like, as the poem dictates:

> Clean de ba'n an' sweep de flo'
> Ring my banjo – Ring!

> We's gwine dance dis ebenin' sho'
> Sing my banjo sing!
>
> All day long in de burnin' sun
> We wuk'd an' toil'd, lost an' won
> Now de ebenin' shadders come
> Now de bendin' wuk is done!
>
> Den come 'long Nancy – come 'long Sue
> We'll dance down care de whol' night thoo.

It is a charming piece, full of syncopated patterns and clever key changes, beginning in F minor, going into A-flat major. After a pensive middle section, *andante tristezza*, the opening sections are repeated. The M.M. markings are quarter = 76, quarter = 120, and quarter = 88. Its saucy ragtime quality should appeal to a disinterested younger student.

The mood of the third piece, "In de Col' Moonlight," is Chopinlike in its somberness. Set in F minor (M.M. quarter = 60, quarter = 44), the yearning words are well reflected in this lovely short sketch, pleasantly expressive with phrases of this rhythmic pattern:

The left hand has several reaches of tenths, not designated as rolled or broken chords, sonorities best executed by a pianist with a large reach. Ending the piece in F major is a cadenza-like measure followed by two *ppp* chords of half-note duration. The poem is:

> Just a tender heart repinin': –
> 'Cased – yet 'scapes its bindin'
> And in mem'ry of a home
> Forgets it's not its own.
>
> Toil on seeker – stumble, cry
> Never know de reason why!
> Alone in de moonlight call to de sky
> Listen for de col' reply!

The text which inspired the more joyous "A Jubilee" reads:

Altho' you see me go 'long so,
Ma spirit's boun' fo' de Hebbenly sho'
Gwine walk right up to de golden do'
To ma home in de New Jerusalem.

This Burleigh piece, which includes more tenths for the left hand, calls for added technical facility not required by the preceding sketches. Some of the left-hand passages of stride bass accompany a restatement of the theme in octaves. Musical Example No. 10 (M.M. quarter=60), illustrates a chromatic progression in the bass line, an effective technique often used by Burleigh in his accompaniments. Two fragments of "Old Folks at Home" are used within the piece. (See Musical Example No. 11.)

The few lines of Louise Burleigh's "On Bended Knees"

Oh, I look away yonder – what do I see?
A band of angels after me.
Come to tote me away from de fiel's all green
'Cause nobody knows de trouble I've seen!

evidently stirred the composer, since he marked this piece *Andante con gran espressione* (Musical Examples Nos. 12 and 13, M.M. dotted quarter=40, then half note=dotted quarter). Previously in orchestral arrangement, "On Bended Knees" is another ABA structure, the A sections in G minor in 6/8 meter reminiscent of a cello solo with accompaniment. The B section, in G major and 4/4 meter, is a beautiful chordal harmonization of "Nobody Knows de Trouble I've Seen." Musical Example No. 12 again shows a descending chromatic line in the left hand. Returning, the A section in 6/8 is varied by a syncopated left-hand figure for its last five measures, culminating in a rather dissonant chord sustained by a fermata. A three-measure coda repeating a fragment of "Nobody Knows the Trouble I've Seen" ends the piece. (See Musical Example No. 13)

The opening measures of "A New Hidin'-Place," the last part of *From the Southland*, boldly state the theme of "My Lord What a Morning," which is followed by another old Negro tune. (See Musical Example No. 14 for the themes.) The poem reads in part:

> My Lord, what a mornin' –
> When de stars begin to fall!
> De rocks an' de mountains shall all flee away;
> But you shall have a new hidin'-place dat day.

The change in metronome markings (M.M. quarter = 56 to quarter = 96), as well as the difference of moods, is definitely noticeable. The second theme gives way to a four-measure transitional passage of sixteenth notes, a notation uncommonly used by Burleigh. In Musical Example No. 15 the original theme returns and is entwined with the second strain.

Finally, as if the whole orchestra is playing, heavier chords marked *fff*, several with added accents, continue for the last sixteen measures of the piece, making a splendid ending for the suite.

New York Age critic Lester Walton, in response to a comment by John Philip Sousa that ragtime was dead, wrote in the fall of 1910:

> Harry T. Burleigh, one of the greatest Negro composers America has produced, has just finished a piano cycle, the theme of which is taken from Darky folk-songs with syncopated rhythms. I feel confident in saying that Mr. Sousa, after reading the score of Mr. Burleigh's cycle, would know that it was, and shall never cease to be pleasing to the ear of a music-loving public.

Geneva Southall described the "Jubilee" as reflecting "the more spirited expressions of the ex-slaves" and one which pointed to the "growing influence of the then-popular ragtime on religious music."[76]

But from the sparse information about *From the Southland* it would seem to have been completely forgotten or at best, neglected. Not an earthshaking set of pieces, it is nevertheless worthy of examination. Compared to Nathaniel Dett's *In the Bottoms Suite* (1913), it might present less of a challenge to the pianist, but is certainly more concise in content and equally listenable. Perhaps if Burleigh, a capable pianist himself, had chosen to perform this work on as many occasions as Dett presented his own keyboard works, it would have received wider recognition. Burleigh's pieces, well-conceived pianistically, lie comfortably for the instrument. The total lack of

Musical Example No. 10, "A Jubilee," measures 66-69, showing chromatic progression in bass line; measures 70-77, stride bass with melody in octaves.

Musical Example No. 11, "A Jubilee," measures 86-92, "Old Folks at Home" theme.

Musical Example No. 12, "On Bended Knees," measures 14-17.

Musical Example No. 12, "On Bended Knees," measures 29-35, showing chromatic progression in bass line.

Musical Example No. 13, "On Bended Knees," measures 39 (with pickup)-43.

Musical Example No. 13, "On Bended Knees," measures 50-52 (Coda).

VI.

A NEW HIDIN'- PLACE

Musical Example No. 14, "A New Hidin'-Place," measures 1-10.

Musical Example No. 14, "A New Hidin'-Place," measures 14-17.

Musical Example No. 15, "A New Hidin'-Place," measures 22-24, transitional passage of sixteenth notes; measures 27-31, themes combined.

pedal markings indicates some amount of flexibility in interpretation. All six segments can be performed in approximately fifteen minutes.

Suite for Violin and Piano

Ricordi published *Southland Sketches*, Burleigh's pieces for violin and piano, in 1916. Based on Afro-American themes, they were described by H. K. M. as "an attempt to set in relief the negroid musical characteristics," the third piece, "Allegretto grazioso," recalling to him Dvorak's "Humoresque."[77] The names of the movements, "Andante," "Adagio ma non troppo," "Allegretto grazioso," and "Allegro," somewhat belie their fanciful, syncopated nature. One wishes that Burleigh had given them more programmatic titles.

There is no evidence that *Southland Sketches* has been recorded. Parts of it were performed a few times at St. George's on their annual program of spirituals. Along with half a dozen of Burleigh's art songs and spirituals, it was scheduled for a projected concert tour, sponsored by Indiana University, covering various American cities during the period 1969-72.[78]

An overview of *Southland Sketches* reveals that the four pieces of the suite have been expertly put together. Not difficult, they would make excellent teaching pieces for a young violinist. Burleigh's carefully marked phrasing and bowings show an awareness of string playing techniques. The unobtrusive accompaniments are not as imaginative as those of his art songs, but well crafted. Some clever effects are achieved with syncopation in "Andante," the opening movement. (See Musical Example No. 16.) In the "Adagio" the piano announces the theme, which is then taken by the violin. These statements are followed by an echo effect between the instruments. (See Musical Example No. 17.) A similar opening is found in the third segment, "Allegretto grazioso," and when the theme is repeated Burleigh alters the accompanimental harmonies. (See Musical Example No. 18.) The lively theme of "Allegro," the last movement, stated in G minor, closes with a pizzicato chord of that key. After a fermata a second section in B-flat major, marked *Meno mosso*, continues for fifty-three measures. Then the first theme returns, *a tempo*, ending the piece with a flourish. Some of the selected passages can be seen in Musical Examples Nos. 19a, b, and c.[79]

Musical Example No. 16, "Andante" from *Southland Sketches*, measures 59-66.

By his own statement Burleigh was strongly drawn to song composing and arranging, rather than to solo instrumental composition or such larger forms as opera, chamber music, and symphonic works. Due in part to salability, but in a broader sense to settling into a comfortable genre, he did not seem to regret non-distinction as a composer in these other areas.

Just as waning popularity befell *From the Southland, Southland Sketches* also went out of print, confirmed by the fact that it is not listed in Margaret K. Farish's definitive compendium *String Music in Print* published in New York in 1973 by R. R. Bowker.[80]

Musical Example No. 17, "Adagio ma non troppo" from *Southland Sketches*, measures 1-12.

№ III.
Southland Sketches

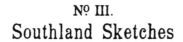

Musical Example No. 18, "Allegretto grazioso," *Southland Sketches*, measures 1-20.

Nº IV.
Southland Sketches

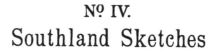

Musical Example No. 19a, "Allegro," *Southland Sketches*, measures 1-14.

Musical Example No. 19b, "Allegro," *Southland Sketches*, measures 33-44.

Musical Example No. 19c, "Allegro," *Southland Sketches*, measures 117-128.

CHAPTER V

Spirituals and Negro Folk Songs

♪

The name Harry T. Burleigh often calls to mind the topic of Negro spirituals. Rarely does a writer speak of him without mentioning his innovative efforts in arranging dozens of these pieces as solos for the concert audience. Before Burleigh's stunning success with a revised arrangement of "Deep River" in 1917, his settings of Negro songs had been demonstrated with *Plantation Melodies, Old and New* (1901, G. Schirmer, Inc.), *Plantation Songs* (1902, G. Schirmer, Inc.), and *Two Plantation Songs* (1907, William Maxwell Company). Called by Charlotte Murray "modest chordal settings" which "do not foreshadow the highly sensitive spiritual arrangements" of later years, these simple beginnings were, nevertheless, a giant step toward bringing the public in contact with theretofore unexplored lore.[1]

As a broader view developed of the unique place of Afro-American music, a genuine love for it was established, largely due to Burleigh's maintenance of the inherent dignity and pathos of the songs. It is estimated that Burleigh produced solo arrangements of over seventy spirituals and Negro folk songs. Approximately sixty of those derived from Negro tunes were arranged by Burleigh or his contemporaries, probably the most prolific representation of any composer in this field. This chapter also includes Burleigh's songs of a religious nature not discussed previously.

Background of the Spirituals

In the early 1870s the Fisk Jubilee Singers first popularized ensemble arrangements of Negro folk songs through their extensive concert tours as a fund-raising venture for Fisk Institute. Instrumental in organizing their international tours was Fisk Institute Treasurer George L. White, who "strove for an art presentation, not a caricature of atmosphere." Dialect was rarely sung and only for specific effects. The Fisk repertoire became known categorically as Jubilee Songs.[2] Other black schools, including Howard and Hampton, later followed suit, but not with as long-term positive effect, and it is doubtful that their profits equalled the $150,000 raised by the Fisk Jubilee Singers.

Geneva Southall deems the legacy of the Fisk Jubilee Singers the prototype for both black and white composers' settings and arrangements of spirituals in later years. She shares the sentiments of W. E. B. DuBois and Frederick Douglass that slave songs are those of sorrow, that they "represent the unconscious efforts of the slave to make sense of a shattering life situation" by expressing "weariness, loneliness, sorrow, hope, determination and assurance." Douglass called them "tones, loud, long and deep, breathing the prayer and complaint of souls boiling over with the bitterest anguish."[3]

The fact that Burleigh as a soloist sang some of the Negro melodies in the early 1900s while touring with Booker T. Washington in behalf of Tuskegee Institute may have been a first test of their acceptance. But apparently the solo spirituals were not in immediate demand with every audience, according to *Coronet* writer Henry Lee, who spoke of Burleigh and the increasing appeal of the songs.

> Mocked once because he wanted to sing old songs, he now stands recognized as one of the foremost musical pioneers of his people. Wherever folks heed God and own a piano, you will hear his arrangements of America's well-loved spirituals.[4]

In light of their long association and mutual efforts it is inconceivable that Washington neglected to mention Burleigh's early attempts in the Negro folksong field in his article reprinted in the *Musical Courier* in 1915. One of Washington's last writings, the article dealt with development and value of black themes for which he specifically cited only composers Dvorak and Coleridge-Taylor.[5]

Coleridge-Taylor's collection of piano pieces, titled *Twenty-Four Negro Melodies*, was published in 1905. He preferred to speak of them not as arranged but amplified, due to their brevity. A few of the better-known composers who followed Burleigh's example were James Weldon and J.Rosamond Johnson, Hall Johnson, Nathaniel Dett, Carl Diton, and Roland Hayes, though Burleigh's consummate artistry remains unchallenged.

History, Controversy, and Problems

Several facets in the history of Negro folk songs continue to remain in dispute. John W. Work presents an overview of their development in his *American Negro Songs*, dating the first successful attempt to collect them around 1840. Perhaps the first significant publication of them was William Francis Allen's *Slave Songs of the United States* (1867) with co-authors Lucy M. Garrison and Charles Ware. As early as 1819, however, John Fanning Watson wrote of "the colored people" gathering at camp meetings which ran into hours of prayers, affirmations, pledges, and the like, made longer by repeated choruses. They were "all sung in the merry chorus-manner of the southern harvest field, or husking-frolic method of the slave blacks." Elements of improvised song were evident, though the group could not read or write.[6]

Gradually a uniform body of Negro song was welded by social conditions and Christianity through the interchange of slaves among the colonies. Collecting and notating the songs have been a problem, due to their free style, which embraces portamenta, slurs, and the spontaneity of extra notes and beats.

A system of notation, particularly one for the call-and-response style, was desperately needed. The songs were especially difficult to transcribe from live performances, even the less formal ones, due to "odd turns in the throat and the curious rhythmic effect produced by single voices chiming in at different irregular intervals." William Francis Allen wrote:

> The intonation and delicate variations of even one singer cannot be reproduced on paper. The sounds abound in slides from one note to another, and turns and cadences not in articulate notes. . . . There are also apparent irregularities in the time . . . difficult to express accurately.[7]

Additionally, the lack of portable, efficient recording equipment made taping from the source unfeasible or inaccurate.

Until the early 1890s it was assumed that spirituals were of Afro-American origins. But in 1893 Dr. Richard Wallaschek, in his *Primitive Music*, belittled them as having no place, as overrated, and as wholly derived from European and other white folk music. And further, Wallaschek, who incidentally had never been to America, made no distinction between minstrel songs and spirituals. His book is both unreliable and passé. Henry E. Krehbiel, scholar of folk music and doyen of American musical critics, attests to Wallaschek's imperviousness on the subject:

> It is plain that Dr. Wallaschek never took the trouble to acquaint himself with the environment of the black slaves in the United States. . . . The truth is that, like many another complacent German savant, Dr. Wallaschek thinks Americans are barbarians. He is welcome to his opinion which can harm no one but himself.[8]

Transcriptional deficiencies were overlooked until around 1920. The folk songs had theretofore looked pretty much like German *lieder* rather than simple folk tunes, even the spirituals set by the Johnsons in 1925 (*The Book of American Negro Spirituals*). German professor Erich von Hornbostel, head of Phonogrammarchiv in Berlin, had heard both African and American music. In 1926 he wrote that to the eye the scoring resembled that of European folk songs (particularly Scotch, English, or French and Spanish Creole), though they did not sound similar. Though he admitted the evidence in European songs of the call-and-response idea, it was far from the only method used. On the other hand, it was the one most usually found in African songs. One of von Hornbostel's astute summations of the matter was aptly put:

The great mass of the songs now in vogue are real folk songs of American negro origin. . . . The American negro songs are European in style and pattern, they are American folk songs as far as they have originated amidst American folk and culture, and they are African when sung by negroes.[9]

Another shrewd observation on Negro folk song origins has been offered by Colonel Thomas Wentworth Higginson, scholar and writer in the field. Higginson printed texts and analyses of several Negro songs in *The Atlantic Monthly*, June 1867. W. J. Henderson wrote:

The manner in which the negro sometimes produced his song was discovered by Col. Thomas Wentworth Higginson to his own delight. He asked a negro boatman in the southern islands how songs came to be, and the man replied: "Some good speritfrom are start jess out o' curiosity. I benn raise a sing myself once. Once we boys went for tote some rice, and de nigger-driver he keep a callin' on us; an' I say, 'O de ole nigger-driver!' Den annuder said, 'Fust ting my mammy told me was, notin' so bad as nigger-drivers.' Den I made a sing, just puttin' a word and den anudder word."

Then, to illustrate his description, he began to sing and the other men after listening a moment joined in the chorus as if it were an old friend, though they had evidently never heard it before. Thus Colonel Higginson saw how a negro song originated and took root. But the process should have sufficed to satisfy him that the negro was merely reproducing in a crude and disfigured form some phrases, possibly not all from the same melody, which he had picked up while hearing the band at the military post in the evening or his mistress at her piano in the morning.[10]

Vanderbilt professor George Pullen Jackson, long-time scholar and prolific writer on spirituals, denied nearly all black origins, saying that Afro-Americans copied white gospel hymns, a view supported also by Drs. Guy Johnson and Newman I. White. Jackson gives credit to blacks only for "Steal Away," "Deep River," and "Swing Low, Sweet Chariot."

No reasonable person denies that the Negroes made *some* songs, and I shall not, until I find concrete evidence to the contrary . . . deny that. But were not the whites on the mountains and the hard-scrabble hill country also musical and oppressed? . . . If their condition was any more tolerable than that of the Negroes, one certainly does not get that impression from any of their songs of release and escape.

One may even admit that the specific Negro spiritual is in some instances more beautiful than its known white ancestor and still ask how much of this superiority is due to the difference between the recording ability of the singing-school master of a hundred years ago and that of the skilled folklorist or caterer to the concert singer of today. To be sure, the Negro *seems* to have loosened up the white man's metrical patterns, limbered up his harmony-determined pitch intervals, and injected a wealth of emotion which was not there before. But who can prove that he really did so? Who knows how the rustic whites actually sang four generations ago? Do we quite realize the width of the chasm which yawns between the recorded, arranged, harmonized, piano-broke and printed composition which goes by the name of Negro spiritual today, and the actual "wild chant" of the remote Southern Negro camp-meeting? The Aframerican's contribution to the white man's primitive song cannot be appreciated until the student crosses that chasm. May not even then. For there is still that other chasm of a hundred years of elapsed time.[11]

Balancing this debatable idea have been the opinions of Henry E. Krehbiel, James Weldon Johnson and Dr. John F. Garst, firm exponents of black origins.[12] Many other scholars in the field have continued to keep the unresolved battle going.

One such spokesman, John W. Work, felt that Afro-Americans were critical of gospel hymns, tending to redo them to suit themselves; because the spirituals served as both work and social songs, particularly those traceable to minstrel origins, their religious significance diminished. Lack of articulation made the spirituals more important musically than textually. Work maintains that "from the standpoint of form, melodic variety, and emotional expressiveness the spiritual is the most highly developed of the Negro folk-songs."[13]

Conflicts within the Afro-American's soul often arose through fear. Song texts rarely contained actual copying of biblical words, but rather blacks' own interpretation of them, often in narrative form. The strong wording of biblical messages, especially those concerning punishment by Satan, prompted blacks to join either the Methodist or Baptist church. In early rural churches the spirituals were sung fairly straight and unembellished, with few dynamics and no ritards anticipating the closing cadences. The leader established and maintained the tempo. These unaccompanied songs, which often glorified the preacher, the elder, or the deacon, were rarely in more than two parts.

Work gives as one basic characteristic of the spiritual an unconscious avoidance of the fourth and seventh major scale steps, making the scale pentatonic. Another is the use of the flatted third and seventh, common to blues. In various spirituals the end result is modal, usually Dorian or Phrygian.

Three types of Afro-American songs are clarified by Work: (1) the unquestionably African call-and-response chant, whose main feature is a "melodic fragment sung repeatedly by the chorus as an answer to the challenging lines of the leader which usually change." The fragment may vary from two words to several. The examples "Great Camp Meeting," "Shout for Joy," "Good Morning Everybody," "Swing Low, Sweet Chariot," and "Sittin' Down Beside the Lamb" exemplify call-and-response. (2) Not as common as call-and-response, the slower ones have long sustained phrases, for example "Deep River," "Nobody Knows the Trouble I've Seen," "My Lord, What a Morning," and "Were You There?" The texts are usually in long phrases or complete sentences. (3) The more popular faster ones stimulate body movement. They appear segmented and the rhythm is syncopated, or else features a "pulse note." An unusual distribution of notes within a pattern often occurs, one never altered, illustrating the fundamental importance of note over word. Prosody in these songs, which occurs frequently, does not disturb the singers, because the repeated rhythm seems to carry the words effortlessly.[14]

John E. Taylor, choral professor, North Dakota State University, considers influences and origins from both white and black cultures:

African beliefs and customs were preserved in the spirituals, particularly in their acute concern with the "everyday." Also the way in which Africans passed on the traditions of their ancestors from one generation to another through music, and through rhythm or dancing and emotionalism was clearly evident.

White songs and hymns of the European tradition also influenced the spiritual texts. The psalm paraphrases and hymns of Isaac Watts, and the songs of Charles Wesley, and others (especially the composers of the white "gospel" songs) helped to create waves of revivalism. The impact of these hymns was particularly felt upon the theology, vocabulary and melodies which the Negroes used in the creation of their spirituals.[15]

Burleigh Credited

The progress of black musicians received almost no publicity in the *Musical Courier* in the early years of 1900. In 1915, before Burleigh's "Negro music" became recognized, the begrudging Leonard Liebling, that journal's four-decade editor, wrote a rather scornful article after touring a few Southern college and universities that year.In part it read:

What is Negro music at its best like? No doubt it has melody of a peculiar kind and rhythm of a pronounced type, but of its capability of expansion into the thousand and one expressions of grand opera and the epic grandeur and contrapuntal profundities of oratorio, we are not so sure.[16]

Another of his barbs in a 1919 *Courier* was slightly mellower though snobbish:

The Indian and the negro started as savages, but musically the negro forged far ahead of his red brother. What is the answer? Personally, we like Indian music, but think that the negro examples easily have the bigger future. Rhythm was the outstanding characteristic of primitive

Indian music and yet the negro has developed infinitely more complex, resourceful, and interesting rhythms. Also, he has kept his ear cocked for the tonal hues and harmonic combinations of the white man's tunes, especially where they copy the Oriental color, sequences, and atmosphere. Altogether, the cullud pussons bear watching in the melodious art, as Dvorak pointed out to our native musicians long ago.[17]

Nathaniel Dett's "The Ordering of Moses" (1937) and William Grant Still's "And They Lynched Him to a Tree" (1940) proved beyond a doubt that black composers could write sensational oratorio. And another coup which captured for Still one of his many "firsts" was the 1941 premiere of *Troubled Island* by the New York City Center Opera. One hopes that Liebling was able to accept these successes graciously.

Outweighing this prejudice and negativism has been maximum praise for Burleigh as the composer who put Negro spirituals on the concert map. James Weldon Johnson wrote:

> Today the public buys the Spirituals, takes them home and plays and sings them . . . because the songs have been put into a form that makes them available for singers and music lovers. The principal factor in reaching this stage has been H. T. Burleigh, the eminent colored musician and composer. Mr. Burleigh was the pioneer in making arrangements for the Spirituals that widened their appeal and extended their use to singers and the general music public.[18]

Several writers, including Eileen Southern, have attributed Burleigh's success in setting the spirituals to Dvorak's influence and his faith in the importance of exploring America's untapped musical lore. Some critics feel that without his work the spirituals, theretofore handed down orally, might have been lost, because many blacks wanted to forget them and the oppressive conditions from which they were spawned.

Lucien White, music critic for the *New York Age*, reviewed one of Burleigh's broadcasts for the Frigidaire Program in 1928. He wrote of the composer:

He is given full credit in the world of music for having saved the now famous Negro folksongs and Spirituals from oblivion. Years of research and study of the music of his own people have resulted in the composition and arrangement by him of one hundred and thirty-five of these songs, whose beginnings go back to days of antiquity from the black tribes of Africa. His best known composition of this nature is "Deep River."[19]

But notice of Burleigh's efforts had been taken even earlier (1926) by the new and sophisticated *New Yorker* magazine, limned in an article on Negro folk songs and their singers:

Curiously enough, the most skilled worker in the field of negro music has been partly obscured by the array of new talent. We refer of course to Harry T. Burleigh, whose arrangements of spirituals and other negro songs have not been surpassed and are not likely to be. Probably the genius [sic] interest which has been created pleases no one more than it pleases Mr. Burleigh, but we believe that he has not had complete justice from those who are engaged in the pursuit of calling attention to native airs. To expound this theme would embarrass Mr. Burleigh, who is a singularly modest musician; therefore, we content ourselves with suggesting that if anybody is going to do more for negro folk songs than Harry T. Burleigh has done it will be Harry T. Burleigh.[20]

Ellsworth Janifer wrote that Burleigh's

supreme ability to sustain the emotional mood of a poem in music . . . made practically every one of his spiritual settings a miniature masterpiece. . . . The high artistic standard of his spiritual arrangements was a direct result of his proven skill as a song writer.[21]

Ralph W. Bullock, quoting another music authority who feels that each of Burleigh's compositions is a classic in itself, praises the composer's "real contribution to the music world," the setting of old Negro melodies to music accompaniment. Previously Southerners, in particular,

regarded negro songs as a joke, and laughed over them until
negroes themselves grew half ashamed of their wonderful
melodies, and for a while were reluctant about singing them
in public gatherings.[22]

A similar view is shared by Maud Cuney-Hare. While crediting
Burleigh's singing ability and genuine knowledge of the song idiom as
aids in maintaining the traditional mood of the folk song, she has
been aware of troubled waters, in particular the 1909 strike at
Howard University against singing Negro songs.

> Until today the extensive use of the old plantation
> melodies has been repugnant to many people of African
> descent. Not having felt nor undergone the hardships of
> vassalage, they were too far removed in freedom of spirit
> and not far enough separated by duration of time to wel-
> come the allusion to slavery and felt that the plantation
> hymns were but a reminder of the misfortunes of a race.
> They resented, too, the attitude of many Caucasians in their
> wish to restrict Negro singers to folk songs and in their
> expressed desire to hear students in Negro schools sing
> plantation hymns to the exclusion of other music.[23]

Though several scholars, including Edith Borroff, have pointed
out the difference between Burleigh's and Dett's arrangements, each
finding added chromatic harmonies in the arrangements of Dett and
Hall Johnson, John Tasker Howard seemed to desire an even purer,
less enhanced setting than Burleigh's. His statement is open to
interpretation:

> Strange to say, though he is a negro, his harmonizations
> and treatment are far from negroid. He brings to the melo-
> dies a sophistication of treatment, chromatic harmonies and
> the like, which lifts them from their native element. The
> results may be satisfying musically, but they are not always
> in keeping with the original.[24]

In further praise of Burleigh, Henry T. Finck, brilliant journalist
and music editor of the *New York Evening Post*, deplored the fact that
Chinese music had not been made as accessible to white audiences

as black folk music had been. Burleigh had attended Finck's music history lectures at the National Conservatory of Music in New York. Finck remarked: "I never had a student who passed a better examination. . . . China needs a Harry T. Burleigh. . . . He is one of the two best colored composers in the country."[25]

Henry Lee wrote in *Coronet*, July, 1947:

> . . . when you sing Negro spirituals, you sing them *gladly*. You sing them not from the heart but from the soul. That is the way Harry Burleigh interprets the bittersweet melodies of his race. And he should know because, for half a century he has been America's greatest singer and composer of spirituals.[26]

Alain Locke lauded Burleigh eloquently:

> Mr. Burleigh not only sang the spirituals into favor with a more select audience than they had hitherto reached, but by his refined arrangements of them, made them standard favorites with concert artists and their audiences. This was yeoman service. . . . More than any single other person, Mr. Burleigh . . . played the role of a path-breaking ambassador of Negro music to the musically elect.[27]

Later Locke called Burleigh the "father of the art spiritual . . . even though some of his settings have overlaid the folk spirit with concert furbelows and alien florid adornments."[28]

Burleigh's Views on the Negro Spiritual

The foregoing material, largely the testimony of others, has established Burleigh's spiritual arrangements as a viable song form and secured their place in concert vocal repertoire. But what did Burleigh himself feel and relate about his work in this genre?

Though W. C. Handy recalled Burleigh's saying that "the blues and spirituals are first cousins,"[29] Burleigh felt strongly that the spirituals owed their origins to religious impulse, that their dignity and sublimity expressed both tragedy and sadness. He was not considered the conscious leader of a black Renaissance, but he was a standard-bearer for the renascence of the Negro spiritual. A part of the spiritual's charm was its whimsical, sometimes garbled language, a result of the groping black's heartbreaks experienced in a white man's world. However, he detected no anger, malice, or retaliation in the songs, only hope.

There is no better way to convey Burleigh's attitudes than to quote his own words from excerpts found in broadcasts, interviews, and lectures. His preface to *Album of Negro Spirituals*, published by Franco Colombo Publications in 1917, again prefaced a larger collection, *The Spirituals of Harry T. Burleigh*, issued by Belwin-Mills Publishing Corporation in 1984.

> The plantation songs known as "spirituals" are the spontaneous outbursts of intense religious fervor, and had their origin chiefly in camp meetings, revivals and other religious exercises.
>
> They were never "composed," but sprang into life, ready made, from the white heat of religious fervor during some protracted meeting in camp or church, as the simple, ecstatic utterance of wholly untutored minds, and are practically the only music in America which meets the scientific definition of Folk Song.
>
> Success in singing these Folk Songs is primarily dependent upon deep spiritual feeling. The voice is not nearly so important as the spirit; and then rhythm, for the Negro's soul is linked with rhythm, and it is an essential characteristic of most all the Folk Songs.
>
> It is a serious misconception of their meaning and value to treat them as "minstrel" songs, or to try to make them funny by a too literal attempt to imitate the manner of the Negro in singing them, by swaying the body, clapping the hands, or striving to make the peculiar inflections of voice that are natural with the colored people. Their worth is weakened unless they are done impressively, for through all these songs there breathes a hope, a faith in the ultimate justice and brotherhood of man. The cadences of sorrow invariably turn to joy, and the message is ever manifest that eventually deliverance from all that hinders and oppresses the soul will come, and man – every man – will be free.[30]

In mid-June of 1917 Burleigh sang to a packed house of between 1,200 and 1,400 at Bethel A. M. E. Church in Baltimore, where he was presented by the Cosmopolitan Choral Society. "Before singing his last songs," according to Alain Locke, "Mr. Burleigh spoke for a few minutes about Folk songs":

> Negro Folk songs, or plantation melodies, as they are sometimes called are not the sole, but the most beautiful expression of experience in song this side of the Atlantic. I don't know whether or not I should apologise for singing them before this audience, but in my annual trips with the late Dr. Booker T. Washington, in the interest of Tuskegee Institute, audiences in Boston and Cleveland criticised me severely for singing these songs before white people.
>
> Perhaps they did it because they connected it with ragtime, which is the old plantation melody caricatured and debased. Every race is proud of its Folk songs. The Negro is not proud because they are associated with the so-called coon songs. Some say these melodies are not American, but they are indigenous to the soil. They are the experience in song of the people, who were in America, when Balboa discovered the Pacific Ocean. If the Negro is not American, I do not know who is. These songs are our heritage, and ought to be preserved, studied and idealized.
>
> I have given the songs the melodies that they had in former times. There is a rhythm about them that is unmistakable, but I hope you will still remember that they are spirituals.[31]

Apparently always eager to speak about the spirituals, Burleigh preceded his recital on Cheyney Day, October 14, 1922, at the Cheyney Training School with another discussion of them.

> Mr. Burleigh stressed the necessity of a racial aristocracy in the colored race and the cultivation of the aesthetic sense in order that Negro folk literature may live. He felt that this folk literature, the most precious heritage of the race, ought to be cherished and cultivated because it reveals the spiritual

reaction of a transplanted people, subjected in their new environment to bitter experiences. Their harmonies, he said, have no trace of bitterness, and were "more tender than tears."[32]

A few weeks later Burleigh's lengthy letter to the NAACP, urging the cooperation of blacks and whites in preserving the spirituals from debasement in jazz, appeared in the *Courier*. In part it said:

> The growing tendency of some of our musicians to utilize the melodies of our Spirituals for fox trots, dance numbers and semi-sentimental songs is, I feel, a serious menace to the artistic standing and development of the race.
>
> These melodies are our prized possession. They were created for a definite purpose and are designed to demonstrate and perpetuate the deepest aesthetic endowment of the race. They are the only legacy of slavery days that we can be proud of; our one, priceless contribution to the vast musical product of the United States.
>
> In them we have a mine of musical wealth that is everlasting. Into their making was poured the aspiration of a race in bondage whose religion – intensely felt – was their whole hope and comfort, and the only vehicle through which their inner spirits soared free. They rank with the great folk music of the world and are among the loveliest of chanted prayers.
>
> Now, since this body of folk song expresses the soul of a race it is a holy thing. To use it and not artificialize or cheapen it calls for reverence and true devotion to its spiritual significance. Yet these delinquent musicians contemptuously disregard these traditions for personal, commercial gain.
>
> Their use of the melodies debases the pure meaning of the tunes, converting and perverting them into tawdry dance measures or maudlin popular songs. Their work is meretricious, sacrilegious and wantonly destructive. It offends the aesthetic feelings of all true musicians – white and black – and because some of us have endeavored never to sink the high standard of our art nor commercialize the sacred heri-

tage of our people's songs but rather to revere and exalt it
as a vital proof of the Negro's spiritual ascendancy over
oppression and humiliation, we feel, deeply that the willful,
persistent, superficial distortion of our folk songs is shocking-
ly reprehensible.

Skilled musicians can detect instantly the flagrant misap-
propriation, the amateurish perversion. There are others, the
unskilled musicians and particularly our young people who
cannot detect the misuse of these prayer songs, who cannot
distinguish the false from the true, the makeshift from the
real, the spurious from the genuine, the theatric from the
spiritual, and who are thus being fed with a wrong idea, a
false valuation of all our beautiful melodic inheritance –
unless this pernicious trickery is stopped.

How can it be stopped? These gentlemen seem not to
realize that they offend the deepest sentiments of the race.
They seem incapable of comprehending the enormity of the
offense and the far-reaching effect upon future generations.
True, these melodies are public property and there is no real
means of protecting them except through race pride.

Have these men sufficient race pride to forego the cheap
success and the easy money? Have they sufficient racial pride
to refuse to prostitute the inherent religious beauty of our
Spirituals? Can we not convince them that it is all in bad
taste; that it is like polluting a great, free fountain of pure
melody?

In the interests of millions of colored people who love
and revere the Spirituals and who believe these old melodies
can be an essential factor in the cultural evolution of the
race as well as a powerful stimulus to its higher artistic
development – and in the interest of millions of white people
who love and revere the Spirituals and who believe that the
"Negro stands at the gates of human culture with hands
laden full with musical gifts," I earnestly solicit your help and
cooperation in a determined effort to persuade our misguid-
ed friends to cease their desecrating work and to join with us
in honoring and protecting from any secular or degenerate
use the Negro Spirituals – the only songs in America that

conform to the scientific definition of folk songs. I have the
honor to remain,

Very truly yours,
H. T. Burleigh[33]

When St. George's paid tribute to Burleigh on his thirtieth anniversary there (March 1924) with a service of spirituals, the composer
was genuinely moved. A second service, with identical program, was
scheduled a few Sundays later to accommodate the crowds unable to
be seated for the first one. The occasion was reported in at least two
articles, both lengthy. *Musical America* quoted Burleigh:

> You know, when they sang "My Lord, what a morning
> when the stars begin to fall," it stifled me. I was completely
> overwhelmed. What an idea! You can't see it. I can't see it.
> But the old Negroes working on the plantations knew what
> it meant. They could see the morning when the stars began
> to fall. The choir sang it so beautifully at the service. It was
> a big moment for me. I couldn't even answer them to thank
> them for it, my heart was so full. I've written them a letter,
> though.

The article quotes Burleigh's letter:

> In honoring me so significantly, you also honored and
> exalted my race – from whose sorrowful hearts came these
> matchless prayer and praise songs – in which the Negro
> voices a religious security as old as creation, older than hope,
> deeper than grief, more tender than tears; the utterance of
> a race unshaken in faith. They are the Negro's free contribu-
> tion to the art values of the world, a living proof of the race's
> spiritual ascendancy over oppression and humiliation.
>
> For many years now the spirituals have been hidden un-
> der the mass of Negro minstrel songs. People thought that
> the minstrel songs of the Negro are cheaper, more popular.
> They are gay and attractive. They have a certain rhythm, but
> they are not really music. The mistake was partly the fault of
> the Negroes, partly the result of economic pressure. After
> the Jubilee Singers came back from Europe, some good
> showmen took up the idea of Negro songs, and they had

troupes of black-face comedians and minstrels wandering all over the world. Everyone hummed the minstrel songs and forgot the spirituals. They produced jazz. They made the world believe that was Negro music. We are just beginning to rescue the spirituals.

In the old form the spirituals were just simple tunes. Only the Negroes could sing them because they understood, instinctively, the rhythms. They could harmonize them with their voices and produce some of the strangest, most subtle effects. They had no accompaniments. There was nothing in the tune to guide the singers. No one else could understand them. They were really hidden from the world. You know they have been in print for years, but it is only since they were arranged that they have become widely known.

Dvorak of course used part of Swing Low, Sweet Chariot, note for note, in the second theme of the first movement of the New World Symphony. It was not an accident. He did it quite consciously. . . . He tried to combine Negro and Indian themes. The Largo movement he wrote after he had read the famine scene in Longfellow's Hiawatha. It had a great effect on him and he wanted to interpret it musically.

We talk of American composers. Why are they American? You cannot listen to their music and immediately mark it American. But you can recognize an Irish lilt or a Russian rhythm. We have not developed a distinctive national literature or art; we have not made American music. It will come, but it will take a long time. When it does, I think it will show the influence of the Negro spirituals. They are the only American folk-music. They are the product of a homogeneous people. They have not yet affected American music. They will not, until America is willing to admit that Negroes can be artists.

The journalist commented,

There is a simplicity in Mr. Burleigh's plea for the music of his race and modesty, but both contribute to a supreme faith in the value of the spirituals, a sincere hope for the music that will come from them. There is a naïveté in

Mr. Burleigh's music and there is a supreme sophistication. He does not mix his genres.[34]

And in another article, largely biographical, Burleigh answered the question by Lester A. Walton of the *New York Age*, "In what do you take more pride – being a singer, or composer?"

> I hope to make my greatest reputation as an arranger of Negro spirituals. In them my race has pure gold, and they should be taken as the Negro's contribution to artistic possessions. In them we show a spiritual security as old as the ages.
>
> These songs always denote a personal relationship. It is "my Savior," "my sorrow," "my kingdom." The personal note is ever present. America's only original and distinctive style of music is destined to be appreciated more and more.[35]

A radio broadcast by Burleigh, probably between 1924 and 1928, was reprinted in Hazel Gertrude Kinscella's *Music on the Air*. It is a comprehensive summation of Burleigh's views. Titled "The Negro and His Song," it reads as follows:

> The story of the Negro is told in his music for, from its beginning to its end, his life is attuned to song. The history of Negro song in America is comparatively short, no successful attempt having been made to collect it before 1830, from which time a few letters or articles describing it have been preserved. Best known to the world are the plantation songs known as Spirituals, which, on account of their great number, their lovely melodies, compelling rhythms and deeply emotional content, are unique examples of folk song.
>
> The origin of the Negro's song is problematic, and to attempt to trace its history is to venture upon controversial ground. I differ with some musicians who think it a form of the German chorale, and also with others who feel that the Spirituals are derived entirely from the hymns the Negro heard in the religious services of the white people. The songs are entities in themselves, influenced in some instances, no doubt, in their form and substance, by the songs which the colored people heard from itinerant missionaries; and if at

all African, resemble more the exalted beauty of the songs of the Israelites than the barbaric yells and rhythms of the Negroes of Africa, the latter probably the result of structural peculiarities of African languages. Who can tell, a beautiful melody sung by the Hebrews in those far-off days recorded in the Old Testament may have come, by being overheard by African Negroes and carried through centuries of trials and countless mutations, to flower on American soil!

White critics, and some of the Negroes as well, classify the songs as Spirituals, "work" songs ("John Henry" songs), the "blues," and the social songs. As to the so-called "work" songs, they are a very small minority of the whole mass of Negro song, and I call them "dialect" songs. Very few white people have heard the Negro really singing at work, what songs they have heard have been, rather, rhythmic improvisations. The "blues" have a characteristic syncopation which, if not overdone, is very fascinating, but which, in its abuse, forms the dominating element of jazz.

The main feature of the most intimate and finest of the Negro's songs is its simplicity, for, like the colorful folk music of Russia, it is usually made up of just one idea repeated over and over in the stress of deep fervor in an effort to give some expression to an inner emotion. The Negro just takes a few simple words, and about their rhythm creates a beautiful musical picture. When given the right interpretation this reiteration does not produce monotony, but seems absolutely inspired, as illustrated in the appealing "De Blin' Man Stood on de Road an' Cried," where a simple phrase is repeated sixteen times.

Many of the songs are in the five-toned (pentatonic) scale which has been used by all races who have been in bondage, including the Hebrews. It is so old that no one knows its origin. The Scotch use it in their folk songs, and it has always been heard in music of the Orient. If one sings the common major scale, omitting the fourth and seventh tones, he has the pentatonic scale.

There is also a fondness in Negro song for the use of either the major or minor scale with a flat seventh tone. This gives a peculiarly poignant quality. Dvorak, in his *New World Symphony*, made great use of the flat seventh in the minor. This great master literally saturated himself with Negro song before he wrote the *New World*, and I myself, while never a student of Dvorak, not being far enough advanced at that time to be in his classes, was constantly associated with him during the two years that he taught in the National Conservatory in New York. I sang our Negro songs for him very often and, before he wrote his own themes, he filled himself with the spirit of the old Spirituals. I also helped to copy parts of the original score. A study of the musical material of which the *New World* is made will reveal the influence of Negro song upon it.

The introduction of the Symphony is pervaded with syncopation common to Negro song, and by a use of the flat seventh in the minor mode. This is suggestive of the strangeness of the new country. The syncopation is even more marked in the first theme of the opening movement which is followed by a four-measure subsidiary theme of real charm in which Dvorak employed the lowered, or flat, seventh. Then comes the second theme with its open reference to the beloved Spiritual "Swing Low, Sweet Chariot" of which Dvorak used the second and third measures almost note for note, as a comparison will show. The colorfulness of this entire movement, as well as that of the final movement, lies largely in the use of the flat seventh in the harmonization, this remark in no way belittling Dvorak's superb gift for instrumentation.

Negro Spirituals may be classified as narrative songs, songs of admonition, songs of inspiration, of tribulation, of death, and of play. Of the latter none is so gay as "Lil' Liza Jane," of the Mississippi levees. The tribulation songs, strangely, are not all melancholy. Many of the Negro's best songs vacillate oddly, sometimes within a single phrase, between major and minor. But even when entirely in the minor, they are not always sad: poignant and appealing, yes, but never melancholy.

No songs in the world have a greater or more deserved popularity than those Spirituals which tell of the universal striving and weariness of all men, not alone of the Negro race. There is the tender "Somebody's Knockin' at Yo' Door," and "I Bin in de Storm So Long," the imploring "I Want to Be Ready," and "Standin' in de Need of Prayer," this latter song being used, with modifications, by Louis Gruenberg, in his *Emperor Jones*; and the truly exquisite "Deep River."

In the narrative Spirituals, the Negro has translated the marvelous stories of the Old Testament into simple home language, each tale, in his telling, being colored by his own exaltation and understanding of the Scriptures. Here we find "De Gospel Train," "Didn't It Rain," "Who Built de Ark," and "Ezekiel Saw de Wheel."

Many modern composers see in the piquant rhythms of Negro song, and its simple but expressive melodies, material to use in a thematic way in the writing of great art works. The week that Dvorak sailed back to his Old World home, after two years spent as a teacher in New York, a prominent journal commented by saying that "no sum of money was large enough to keep Antonin Dvorak in the New World. He left us his *New World Symphony* and his *American Quartet*, but he took himself away."

But even if he did he left behind a richer appreciation of the beauties of Negro song, of its peculiar flavor, its sometimes mystical atmosphere, its whimsical piquancy, and its individual idiom, from all of which many other splendid artists have already drawn inspiration.[36]

The *New York World*, October 25, 1924, quoted Burleigh on his purpose for the spirituals: "My desire was to preserve them in harmonies that belong to the modern methods of tonal progression without robbing the melodies of their racial flavor."

Burleigh's work was most popular in the mid 1920s when a controversy arose over whether the spirituals should be presented in their simplistic state or in modern arrangement. Through a depth of harmonic effect imparted to them by Burleigh they carried a universal appeal, attractive to a wide public.

Twenty years later, after his last concert in Erie (1944), Burleigh remarked: "Under the inspiration of Dvorak I became convinced that the spirituals were not meant for the colored people, but for all people."[37] In reporting on this concert the *Erie Daily Herald*, June 9, 1944, said that Burleigh sang with his eyes closed and a reverent smile on his face, feeling every note with sincerity.

Early Settings of Folk and Religious Songs, 1900-1913

Burleigh's seven *Plantation Melodies Old and New*, published in 1901 by G. Schirmer, Inc., included dialectical poems by three authors. No information has been found on R. E. Phillips, poet of four of them: "I Doan' Want Fu' t' Stay Hyeah No Longah," "Ma Lawd's A-Writing down Time," "When de Debble Comes 'Round," and "De Blackbird an' de Crow."

Two other poems of the set, "My Merlindy Brown" and "Negro Lullaby," were by Ohioan James E. Campbell (1867-1905), who served as principal of West Virginia Colored Institute from 1890 to 1900, was journalist for the *Chicago Times Herald*, contributed to *Four O'Clock* magazine, and was one of the first blacks to write dialect poetry. Poems from his two volumes, *Driftings and Gleanings* and *Echoes from the Cabin and Elsewhere*, have been published separately in various anthologies.

Campbell's text for "Ring, My Bawnjer, Ring" was one of two Burleigh used in *Plantation Songs* (1902). They were to collaborate later on "Heigh-Ho!" (1904).[38]

Paul Laurence Dunbar, whose lengthy "An Ante-Bellum Sermon" is the last of the *Plantation Melodies*, was a New York acquaintance of Burleigh in the 1890s. Dunbar, a much-loved reader and poet, both in the United States and abroad, was editor of the *Indianapolis World* in 1895. Clearly an advocate of aggressive community social action, he desired to defend as well as promote his people. He was an assistant in the Library of Congress for two years, preceding the contraction of tuberculosis in 1899, which took his life in 1906. His literary output totalled three dozen volumes, including several books of poetry, a novel, and short stories.

The five verses and refrain of Dunbar's "A Corn Song" were set by both Coleridge-Taylor (1896) and Burleigh (1920). One of Burleigh's finest art songs, "Lovely Dark and Lonely One" (1935), was set to Dunbar's words. Dunbar, as a reader of his own poems, has been described by W. E. Berwick Sayers:

> He sang as naturally and as simply as the lark. . . . It was remarked that the appearance of Dunbar was somewhat repulsive, but that when he rose to read, the beauty of his voice and the dramatic reality of his delivery quickly cancelled the earlier impression, and left only the . . . naturally noble soul working behind the unattractive features.[39]

The following year, 1902, Schirmer issued *Plantation Songs*. Besides Campbell's "Ring, My Bawnjer, Ring," Frank L. Stanton's "You'll Git Dar in de Mornin'" suggested another dialectal treatment. Stanton was subsequently to collaborate with Burleigh on some art songs, the best known of which was "Jean" (1903).

Burleigh set three anonymous religious poems, titled "O Why Art Thou Not Near Me," "We Would See Jesus," and "Father to Thee," and "While Shepherds Watched Their Flocks," with text by Nahum Tate, all published in 1904 by the William Maxwell Company.

Between 1905 and 1909 similar pieces published by Maxwell were with lesser known collaborators: "Through Peace to Light," 1905, Adelaide Proctor; "Once in Royal David's City," 1905, C. F. Alexander; arrangements for men's and women's voices of the traditional "Rockin' in de Win'," 1906; "Come Unto Me," 1906, from Matthew 2:28; and "Savior Divine," 1907, R. Palmer.

The words for *Two Plantation Songs* (1907), "I'll Be Dar to Meet Yo'" and "Keep a Good Grip on de Hoe," were supplied by Beverly Garrison and Howard Weeden. It is unknown whether Garrison was male or female, but, curiously, Howard Weeden was a woman. Weeden (1847-1905), whose specialty was Afro-American subjects, was from Huntsville, Alabama. Born into an old family of slave holders and cotton planters, she later became known as the author and illustrator of several volumes of Southern poetry, *Bandana Ballads*, *Shadows on the Wall*, *Songs of the Old South*, *Old Voices*, and

Plantation Ballads. Most anthologies of black poetry contain some of her poems.[40] "Keep a Good Grip on de Hoe," not found in *Bandana Ballads* nor *Shadows on the Wall*, is likely included in Weeden's *Songs of the South* or *Plantation Ballads*.

Schirmer's publication date of *Negro Minstrel Melodies*, a collection of twenty-one songs with piano accompaniment edited by Burleigh, is assumed by several writers as 1910, but 1909 is the date given on the volume's cover. The compilation includes:

Angel Gabriel	James E. Stewart
Angels, Meet Me at the Cross-Roads	Will S. Hays
Balm of Gilead	H. T. Bryant
Come Where My Love Lies Dreaming	Stephen C. Foster
Darling Nellie Gray	B. R. Hanby
Dearest Mae	L. V. H. Crosby
De Camptown Races (Gwine to Run All Night)	Stephen C. Foster
Jim Along Josey	Author unknown
Kingdom Coming	Henry C. Work
Massa's in de Col', Col' Ground	Stephen C. Foster
My Old Kentucky Home	Stephen C. Foster
Nellie Was a Lady	Stephen C. Foster
Nelly Bly	Stephen C. Foster
Oh! Dem Golden Slippers!	James A. Bland
Oh! Susanna	Stephen C. Foster
Old Black Joe	Stephen C. Foster
Old Cabin Home, The	Author unknown
Old Folks at Home	Stephen C. Foster
Shine On	Luke Schoolcraft
Tom-Big-Bee River (Gum-Tree Canoe)	S. S. Steele
Wake Nicodemus	Henry C. Work

Stephen C. Foster (1826-1864) is well-known as an American song composer. Edwin P. Christy organized "Christy's Minstrels," the most successful of the early minstrel shows, in 1842 in Buffalo. This group, which used many of Foster's tunes, played to packed houses in England and America for a decade.[41]

W. J. Henderson, in his preface to *Negro Minstrel Melodies*, comments:

. . . Jas. A. Bland and Luke Schoolcraft were minstrel performers, and turned out their songs in what might be called the ordinary course of business. But these men had that priceless faculty, imagination. . . . The result was that they created a genre which cannot be described as folk-song nor yet merely as popular ballad. The negro minstrel song of twenty, thirty, forty years ago stands entirely alone in the literature of vocal music. . . . An examination of the songs of Foster and of the other early writers of minstrel music, will suffice to convince the most casual observer that they bear no resemblance to the so-called negro music of to-day.[42]

New Orleans-born Luke Schoolcraft (1847-1893), "clever black-face performer, but a gifted character actor," was the son of Henry Schoolcraft, a singing comedian. After Henry's death, Luke's mother worked as wardrobe mistress for the New Orleans Academy of Music. Of limited financial means, Luke struggled to become a responsible and successful performer with several minstrel troupes. One of his comedic specialties was German dialect.[43]

Henry Clay Work, a self-taught musician from Connecticut, was a printer by trade. His two songs, "Kingdom Coming" and "Wake Nicodemus," which Burleigh selected for this collection, came out of the Civil War. W. S. (William Shakespeare) Hays (1837-1907) published nearly 300 songs which sold several million copies. The best known of these were "Molly Darling," "My Southern Sunny Home," and "Evangeline."[44]

James A. Bland (1854-1911), the composer of "Carry Me Back to Old Virginny," adopted as Virginia's state song, is also famous for "Hand Me Down My Walking Cane," and "In the Evening by the Moonlight," just a few of his 600 songs of all types. Bland attended Howard University but left to become a professional minstrel. A self-taught banjo player and singer, he was socially in demand in Washington, DC.

Benjamin R. Hanby (1833-1867) was born in Rushville, Ohio, attended Otterbein College, and then settled in Westerville, Ohio. In 1937 the Hanby Memorial Association of that city engaged the WPA to restore Hanby's old home, with the purpose of dedicating it as a museum and shrine. "The old desk at which Hanby sat when he wrote the song ["Darling Nellie Gray"] in 1855 and other furniture have been collected as a permanent exhibit." It is commonly believed that "Darling Nellie Gray" never made him a cent.[45]

No supportive information has been found on S. S. Steele, L. V. H. Crosby, H. T. Bryant, or James E. Stewart, except that they were not of the New Orleans area. Bryant might have been the son of Dan, Jerry, or Neil Bryant whose successful Bryant's Minstrels troupe was organized in 1857. Crosby, similarly, may have been the progeny of Dug or Tom Crosby, minstrels with Gales and Hagger's Minstrels out of Cincinnati in 1884. An "Ed" Stewart is listed with Hart's Alabama Minstrels (1872), an Evansville, Indiana company.[46]

In 1911 and 1912 Burleigh is credited with two publications of a religious nature, one with an anonymous text, "Child Jesus Comes from Heav'nly Height" (1911). "Tarry With Me, O My Savior!" (1912) with words by C. L. Smith – likely Clay Smith (1877-1920), an author, musician, and composer of songs – was the first of Burleigh's works to be published by Ricordi and Company, the year before he became its editor in 1913.

The year 1913 marked Burleigh's first arrangement of "Deep River," which was made for unaccompanied chorus and published by G. Schirmer, Inc., in a compilation edited by Burleigh titled *Jubilee Songs of the U.S.A.*[47] Though useful at the time in choir and ensemble repertoire this version of "Deep River" did not create the stir that the solo arrangement did in 1917.

The Burleigh-Krehbiel Folk Song Collaboration (1913-1914)

The inclusion of eleven arrangements by Burleigh in Henry E. Krehbiel's *Afro-American Folksongs* (1914) was a prestigious distinction for Burleigh. Krehbiel (1854-1923), long-time scholar of folk songs and music critic for the *New York Tribune*, also authored and edited several books on musical subjects. Other arrangers in Krehbiel's volume are Arthur Mees, choral conductor and composer; Henry Holden Huss, composer and pianist; and John A. van Broekhoven, conductor, teacher, and composer. For their work and Burleigh's Krehbiel wrote in his preface: "I am deeply beholden."

Two of Burleigh's arrangements, the Mississippi River songs "Oh Rock Me, Julie" and "I'm Gwine to Alabamy," have exclamatory cadenzas on the word *Oh*. Their structure also resembles a stereotyped formula found in Native American music, beginning with a high melodic motif and then repeated in a lower range. The whole tone scale is easily detectable in "Julie," which is sectioned for "solo" and "chorus," suggestive of a call-and-response treatment. "I'm Gwine to Alabamy" was called by William Francis Allen, collector of *Slave Songs of the United States*, "a very good specimen . . . of the strange barbaric songs that one hears upon the Western steam boats."[48] Krehbiel gives generous musical examples of each Burleigh arrangement. These accompaniments were expanded by Burleigh in his later arrangements of the same tunes.

Krehbiel spoke of "Acadian Boatmen's Song" as "intrinsically interesting as a relic of the Acadian period in Louisiana," though its words were given to him in Parisian French by a New Orleans woman. "Cajun" French in written form was almost nonexistent until recent years, but Burleigh, nevertheless, captured the flavor of this somewhat humorous song, which in translation reads:

> The mosquitoes sting us, we must paddle.
> One's life is not all passed in paddling.
> Paddle, paddle, paddle, my boy.
>
> All the week we eat sacamité
> And on Sundays for good cheer
> We eat gombo filé.
> Paddle, paddle, paddle, my boy.

Sacamité is a thick soup made of corn and milk. Gombo, or gumbo, a staple in the Cajun diet, is a thinner concoction, usually containing okra and chicken, sausage, or seafood, eaten over rice. Filé, made of crushed sassafras leaves, is sprinkled on top of the gumbo. Burleigh's accompaniment in D minor uses some subtle chord changes in the brief twelve-measure piece.

The accompaniment of "Nobody Knows de Trouble I've Seen" follows the vocal line exactly, in both melody and rhythm. The tune, taken from *Slave Songs of the United States*, is strictly pentatonic, avoiding the fourth and seventh scale tones. Burleigh's later arrangement is fuller and has a more interesting accompaniment.

Illustrating the raised or major sixth in songs of minor key Krehbiel cites "You May Bury Me in de Eas'." Burleigh creates a short recitative effect in the first two bars with sustained chords only under the words "bury" and "Eas'," then under "bury" and "Wes'." He goes from a G-major chord to an F-major one to highlight the raised sixth, marked by a crescendo. Heavier chords are noticeable in this particular accompaniment. The melody came from one of J. B. T. Marsh's dozen or more editions between 1875 and 1903 of *The Story of the Jubilee Singers*.

In G minor, "Father Abraham" ("Tell It") is a good example of the Oriental interval called by Krehbiel the augmented or superfluous second, in this case a C sharp descending directly to a B flat. Burleigh, by writing two eighth-note chords for the left hand, interpolated a choral-like effect, using the urgent short phrase "tell it." He had actually retained the effect of a unique choral accompaniment as sung at the Calhoun School, Lowndes County, Alabama. Krehbiel states:

> Notable, too, in this song is the appreciation of tone-painting exemplified in the depiction of the sojourn on the mountain-top by persistent reiteration of the highest note reached by the melody.[49]

"Father Abraham," with seven verses, was one of the songs included in Emily Hallowell's *Calhoun Plantation Songs* (1905). Burleigh suggested that black singers held the high G in "Father Abraham" to show the feeling of being in heaven with Abraham.[50]

Krehbiel's section on funeral music includes three doleful songs arranged by Burleigh. One noticeable characteristic is the strict adherence of chords to the vocal line. Burleigh's melodic accompaniment follows it exactly, lending a seriousness of an almost frugal quality. The skillful transition from A flat major to F minor in "O Graveyard" from *Slave Songs of the United States* lends a perfect somber mood. The first of the three short verses of "O Graveyard" reads:

> O graveyard, O, graveyard!
> I'm walkin' troo de graveyard
> Lay dis body down.

"Dig My Grave," supposedly surviving from ancient ceremonies connected with death and burial, is from the Bahamas "where the songs, though they have much community of both poetical and musical phrase with them, . . . show a higher development than do the slave songs of the States." This song, going from a "Largo" marking in 4/4 meter to "Poco più mosso" in 2/4, then ending with a ritard, Krehbiel calls "tripartite" and "Schumanesque in breadth and dignity."[51]

The third funereal song, "I Look o'er Yander," derives a unique interest from its associated ceremony. It had often been used as a nocturnal chant for the dying or the dead, some singers taking the melody and others, harmonic parts. Such a custom is said to have prevailed in South Carolina, especially attending the death of the father of a family.

> This function . . . I call a relic of ancient ceremonies, because, like the peculiar idioms of the melodies, it cannot have been copied from any of the funeral rites which the slaves saw among their white masters, but does show affinity with the Old World and old time ceremonies.[52]

Melody and words for both "Dig My Grave" and "I Look o'er Yander" are taken from Charles L. Edwards's *Bahama Songs and Stories* (1895), according to Krehbiel.

Krehbiel does not definitely identify the origin of the black Creole song "Pov' piti Lolotte," though it seems to have become well known in Louisiana Creole land via the West Indies. Burleigh arranged it with a coda, which incorporates the melody, a style related solely to the singing of slaves on the Good Hope Plantation in St. Charles Parish, Louisiana. "Lolotte's" African "snap" dotted rhythms on the Creole word *doulé*, likely a corruption of *douleur* (sadness), are found more frequently in "spirituals."

"Poor Little Lolotte" is a love ditty involving two girls in the early 1800s who vie for clothing given as favors by their master. Calalou, Lolotte's rival, has an embroidered petticoat and Lolotte a broken heart. Burleigh's accompaniment is in F minor with a left-hand figure in eighth notes of broken tenths, which gives the piece a "propulsive effect."[53]

In Krehbiel's appendix of ten characteristic songs, three of Burleigh's arrangements appear, all with words and melody from *Bahama Songs and Stories*. The text of "Neve' a Man Speak Like This Man" ("O! Look-a Death"), however, is actually based on John 7:45-46: "Then came the officers to the chief priests and Pharisees; and they said unto them, Why have ye not brought him? The officers answered, Never man spake like this man."

"Jesus Heal' de Sick," unlike the preceding songs, has a three-bar introduction, followed by a typical Burleigh chordal accompaniment. In "Opon de Rock" a simple pattern of syncopation (weak, strong, weak), often employed by Burleigh, sets a background for the repeated words "opon de rock," a prosodic treatment which usually gives the needed vitality to many of his slower songs.[54]

On April 25, 1923, a few weeks after Krehbiel's death, Burleigh delivered a eulogy, "Mr. Krehbiel as I Knew Him," at a joint memorial service at the New York Public Library for Krehbiel and Natalie Curtis Burlin (1875-1921), another scholar and writer on folk music. The ceremony was reported in the *New York Age*, May 5, 1923:

> Mr. Burleigh's talk was intensely interesting because his had been a peculiarly intimate association with the late dean of New York's music editors, and he told of incidents of that association that stirred his hearers. Several letters he had received from Mr. Krehbiel during the years of their intercourse shed an illuminating insight into the character of the deceased, and at the same time brought out indirectly attributes of our own artist that are usually kept modestly hidden.

An Interim

In 1916 Schirmer published Burleigh's more complete arrangement of "Father Abraham," along with "So Sad," another Negro spiritual from Calhoun, Lowndes County, Alabama, and "Didn't My Lord Deliver Daniel?" taken from Burleigh's own collection, *Jubilee Songs of the U.S.A.* "So Sad" bemoans the grief and loneliness of dying by oneself. "Daniel," probably originally from Kentucky or Florida, is found in *Jubilee Songs* (1872), *Slave Songs of the United States* (1874), and *The Story of the Jubilee Singers* (1875). "Didn't Old

Pharaoh Get Lost" is a Kentucky variant of the song. The Daniel of the Old Testament was a frequent character of the freedom spirituals with whose trial and deliverance the Afro-American could identify.

Burleigh retained the key of G minor for "Daniel" and sprinkled it effectively with the "snap" rhythm, first announced in the piano's introductory measures. Alternating between G minor and B-flat major, "Daniel" allows the singer not a single measure of rest during the four verses. The accompanimental texture, at first in octaves following the voice line, thickens with each verse. An urgency is compounded by the insertion of a measure of 2/8 time which ends three different phrases, going on at once to the established 4/8 meter. The G-major ending rollicks with big chords marked *forte* and *fortissimo*.

A Marathon of Spirituals

Between 1917 and 1924 Ricordi published separately almost four dozen of Burleigh's solo arrangements of Negro spirituals.[55] Among the first of these was "Deep River" (1917). Arranged for both solo and male chorus, it soon proved to be Burleigh's most famous work and was widely adopted by many celebrated singers of the day. This spiritual originated in Guilford County, North Carolina, in connection with the shipping of slaves back to Africa as early as 1820.[56]

Dedicated to Mary Jordan, who made extensive use of it in her concerts, "Deep River" was popularized also by John McCormack, Oscar Seagle, Marcella Sembrich, Roland Hayes, a host of other concert singers and choirs, and later Marian Anderson. The prestigious all-black Clef Club performed "Deep River" frequently in subsequent years, once at the Selwyn Theater in 1918, a concert conducted by Fred M. Bryan.[57]

Of the dedication to Mary Jordan of this "camp meeting song" the *Musical Courier* wrote: "The song expresses the haunting, melancholy fervor of old darky days and the contralto considers it one of the most effective in her repertoire."[58] Earlier the *Courier*, reporting on McCormack's January 14, 1917, performance at the Brooklyn Academy of Music, stated: "Deep River has been done frequently this season, but McCormack's version of it surpasses all."[59]

Burleigh, too, often sang the spirituals in recitals while accompanying himself at the piano. One such instance occurred in mid-

June of 1917 in Baltimore at the Bethel A. M. E. Church at a concert
sponsored by the Cosmopolitan Choral Society.

This time his own accompanist, Mr. Burleigh sang his
arrangements of "Swing Low, Sweet Chariot," "Dig My
Grave Long and Narrow," as it is sung in the Bahama
Islands, "Sinner Don't Let de Harves' Pass," frequently used
as a revival song in Tennessee, and "I Don't Feel No-Ways
Tired." The Cosmopolitan Choral Society, directed by
Rev. Charles E. Stewart, also sang "Father Abraham" and
"Deep River" as arranged by Mr. Burleigh.[60]

The critics did indeed notice "Deep River's" appearance on the
concert scene. H. K. M. of the *Boston Evening Transcript* wrote:

The rune-like two-line melody of "Deep River" was
Coleridge-Taylor's favorite "spiritual," and Mr. Burleigh was
far-visioned enough to appreciate its availability for the
concert hall. Supplying a very simple middle section, he built
the tune into a song as compactly organized as one of Schubert's. The moving climax is hardly surpassed in emotional
intensity in many a renowned song. Mr. Burleigh's accompaniment, however, is neither difficult nor unusual. It makes no
attempt at exotic or racial effect. For Mr. Burleigh has little
faith in the availability of the negro tones as a basis for a
special style or "School" of music. Although he has interested himself to the extent of making choral arrangements of
some of the "spirituals," no one in studying the songs would
guess the composer's race. Some may wish that "Deep
River" had been arranged with a view to carrying out the
negro elements of the melody, but none could ask for a
more effective piece for the concert hall.[61]

According to scholar-composer Edith Borroff "Deep River" was
part of the collection *Story of the Jubilee Singers*, published in 1875 by
the Jubilee Singers. Speaking of Burleigh's harmonizations of the solo
line she says:

In Burleigh's harmonization of "Deep River" . . . the
elements were the same, but their relationship was reversed

from the original. . . . In "Deep River" the harmony was basic, the essential fabric was the "oneness" of the choir, the blue notes sacrificed to those twelve piano pitches, and the rhythm flattened out to let the harmony sound. But the melody was exquisite and Burleigh's harmony tremendously skillful; few choral works are more beautiful.[62]

One writer, who said that "Deep River" was a "successful venture" which "ushered in a new era for this type of music literature," quotes Burleigh as saying:

> In the old forms spirituals were just simple tunes and only the negroes could sing them because they understood the rhythms. They could harmonize and get strange subtle effects but they were really hidden from the world. They had been in print for years but only since they were arranged have they become known.[63]

At least two reviews of the 1917 revised version of "Deep River" were carried in *Musical America* that year. In one, A. Walter Kramer noted the improvements of a simpler harmonic accompaniment (i.e., the use of sixths and thirds), thereby creating a truer spirit of the folk song. William Arms Fisher, editor of *Seventy Negro Spirituals* (1926), called it the "most conspicuous success of the song recitalists offerings" and the one most frequently appearing on New York recital programs.[64]

The following musical example from the vocal solo version of "Deep River" is characteristic of Burleigh's adaptation of accompaniment to suit the text. The A-minor section which follows the first tranquil one has a feeling of urgency. (See Musical Example No. 20.)

A manuscript of "Deep River" dated 1926 is a part of the Mary Flagler Cary Music Collection given to the Pierpont Morgan Library in New York City in 1968. Mrs. Cary's husband, Melbert B. Cary, Jr., founder and owner of a private press, had also been a collector of fine printing. After his death in 1941, Mrs. Cary, with her father's help, continued to collect musical manuscripts. The first public showing of the Cary Music Collection was held from November 17, 1970, to January 31, 1971. Mrs. Cary purchased the "Deep River" arrangement in March of 1950 from Paul F. Hoag, an autograph

Musical Example No. 20, "Deep River," measures 15-21.

dealer in Gilmanton, New Hampshire. Mrs. Cary died in 1967.[65] Scholars are curious as to the whereabouts of a 1917 manuscript of "Deep River."

Transcriptions of "Deep River" have been countless. Among the more well-known versions during the 1920s was one for string quartet by A. Walter Kramer, played by the Zoellner Quartet; one for organ, played by E. Power Biggs; one for violin and piano, played by Mischa Elman; another for organ by James H. Rogers; another for violin by Maud Powell; one for cello by Karl Rissland; and one in 1929 for the Monarch Band by its bandmaster Lt. Fred W. Simpson.[66]

An orchestral arrangement was made of "Deep River" by Burleigh and Agide Jacchia in 1923 in Boston. From an examination of a copy of the unpublished manuscript, the score was not notated in Burleigh's hand. It is the only orchestral work by Burleigh in manuscript listed in the card catalog in the Music Division of the

Boston, Friday, May 11, 1923	Orchestra of Symphony Players AGIDE JACCHIA, Conductor	No. 3

W. H. BRENNAN, Mgr.	G. E. JUDD, Asst. Mgr.	A. M. WIGGIN, Treas.

FRIDAY, MAY 11, 1923
SOUTHERN NIGHT
PROGRAMME

1. MILITARY MARCH . . . . Schubert
2. OVERTURE to "Oberon" . . . . Weber
3. { a. DEEP RIVER . . . . Burleigh–Jacchia
   { b. DIXIE'S LAND . . . . Dan Emmett
4. FANTASIA, "Aïda" . . . . Verdi

5. SUITE, "Scènes de Ballet" . . . . Glazounov
   a. Danse Orientale   b. Valse   c. Polonaise
6. AFRO–AMERICAN FOLK SONGS . . . . . Arranged by Agide Jacchia
   a. "Bury me in de Eas'"   *b. "Musieu Bainjo"   c. "Nobody knows"
7. SCHERZO, "Midsummer Night's Dream" . . . . Mendelssohn
8. RIDE OF THE VALKYRIES . . . . Wagner

9. HUNGARIAN MARCH . . . . Berlioz
10. WALTZ, "Roses from the South" . . . . Strauss
11. SELECTION of Southern Airs . . . . Bendix

*This Creole song from Louisiana has been translated as follows: Look at that darky there, Mr. Banjo, doesn't he put on airs!
Hat cocked on one side, Mr. Banjo, walking-stick in hand, Mr. Banjo, boots that go "creak, creak," Mr. Banjo.
Look at that darky there, Mr. Banjo, doesn't he put on airs!
(There is a pun on the words *mulet*, "mule" and *muldtre*, "mulatto.")

RUSSIAN-TCHAIKOVSKY PROGRAMME . . . . . Sunday, May 13
RADCLIFFE COLLEGE NIGHT . . . . . Tuesday, May 15
NORTHEASTERN UNIVERSITY NIGHT . . . . . Wednesday, May 16
(All Nights Open to the Public)

FOR LIST OF REFRESHMENTS AND CIGARS SEE PAGES 8 AND 9

1

Program copies courtesy of Eleanor McGourty of the Boston Symphony Orchestra Program Office.

Boston, Wednesday, June 13, 1923 — Orchestra of Symphony Players AGIDE JACCHIA, Conductor — No. 16

W. H. BRENNAN, Mgr.   G. E. JUDD, Asst. Mgr.   A. M. WIGGIN, Treas.

WEDNESDAY, JUNE 13, 1923
DARTMOUTH NIGHT
PROGRAMME

1. *OVERTURE to "The Sicilian Vespers" . . . . Verdi
2. WALTZ, "Vienna Bonbons" . . . . Strauss
3. DEEP RIVER . . . . Burleigh-Jacchia
4. FANTASIA, "L'Oracolo" . . . . Leoni

5. PRELUDE AND SICILIANA, "Cavalleria Rusticana" . . . Mascagni
(Solo Horn, MAX HESS)
6. TURKISH PATROL . . . . Michaelis
7. SEXTETTE from "Lucia di Lammermoor" . . . . . Donizetti
8. WOTAN'S FAREWELL AND MAGIC FIRE SCENE, "The Valkyrie" Wagner

STEIN SONG

9. "THE SHAMROCK," Selection of Irish Airs . . . . . Myddleton
10. PANAMERICANA . . . . Herbert
11. FIFTH HUNGARIAN DANCE . . . . Brahms

THE DARTMOUTH SONG
MASON & HAMLIN PIANO USED

*Verdi wrote "Les Vêpres Siciliennes" for Paris, where it was produced on June 13, 1855. The Austrian police in Italy frowned upon the rebellious subject of a Sicilian uprising, and forced it to be changed to "Giovanna di Guzman." This was not Verdi's only encounter with oppressive officialdom. He stood for a long while against the censorship of "A Masked Ball," which was originally called "Gustavus III," and alluded to Napoleon III. Naples, taking up his cause, resounded with the cryptic slogan of "Viva VERDI" ("Vittorio Emmanuele Re D'Italia"). Verdi finally made peace by changing the scene to the most remote place he could think of. So the character of "Gustavus III" became "Richard, Governor of Boston. U.S.A."

BOSTON UNIVERSITY NIGHT . . . . Monday, June 18
SPECIAL PROGRAMME OF DANCE MUSIC . . . . . Tuesday, June 19
LAST SUNDAY CONCERT (Russian-Tchaikovsky Programme) . . Sunday, June 24
ANNUAL REQUEST NIGHT (See opposite page 16) . . . Wednesday, June 27
(All Nights Open to the Public)

FOR LIST OF REFRESHMENTS AND CIGARS SEE PAGES 8 AND 9

1

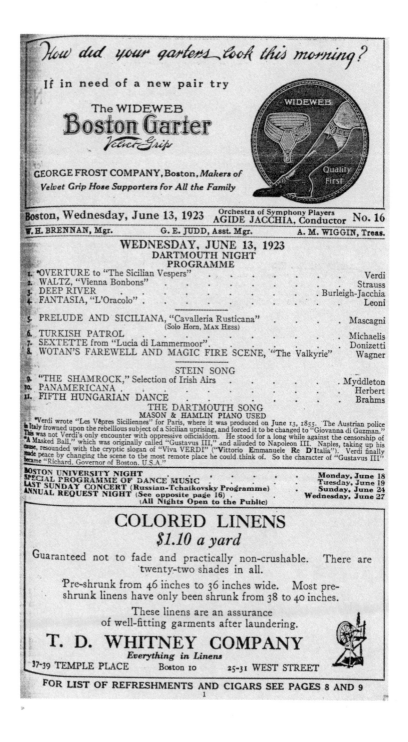

SATURDAY, JULY 7, 1923

CLOSING NIGHT

1.	FIRST SLAVONIC DANCE	Dvořák
2.	PRELUDE to "The Mastersingers"	Wagner
3.	LOVE'S DREAM AFTER THE BALL	Czibulka
4.	FANTASIA, "L'Oracolo"	Leoni
5.	FIRST HUNGARIAN RHAPSODY	Liszt
6.	DEEP RIVER	Burleigh-Jacchia
7.	*SERENADE	Schubert
	Arranged by Agide Jacchia	
8.	MARCHE SLAVE	Tchaikovsky
9.	SELECTION, "Cavalleria Rusticana"	Mascagni
10.	WALTZ, "España"	Waldteufel
11.	STARS AND STRIPES FOREVER	Sousa

AULD LANG SYNE

*Schubert wrote his songs with such marvelous ease and speed, that his friend the tenor, Vogel, believed the act of creation to be, with him, a matter of clairvoyance. Once, in a beer garden, he suddenly exclaimed, "Such a lovely melody has come to me: if I only had a sheet of music paper!" His friend Doppler drew some staves on the back of a bill of fare, and amid the confusion of clanking glasses and skittles, the immortal song, "Hark, Hark, the Lark" came into being. Schubert wrote the "Serenade" in the last year of his life.

FOR "POP" TICKETS TELEPHONE BACK BAY 1492

Manuscript: "Deep River," dated 1926. Reprinted by permission of Library and Archives, Erie County Historical Society, Erie, Pennsylvania.

Oh don't you want to go— to that gos — pel — feast;— That prom — is'd land— where all — is peace? Oh deep— riv - er, Lord, I want to cross o - ver in - to camp-ground.—

G. Ricordi & Co. — No. 9

Aug. 1926

Library of Congress. The opening theme, stated by the English horn and violins, is given to the flutes in the second section. Full instrumentation, including organ, indicates a sonorous version of the spiritual, though the brass scoring is intermittent.[67] Jacchia (1875-1932), Italian flutist and conductor, accompanied Mascagni to America in 1902, returning for another tour as conductor of the Milan Opera in 1907-09. For the next three years he conducted the Montreal Opera Company, and was two years with the Boston National Opera. From 1918 to 1926 Jacchia was conductor of the Boston Pops Orchestra and then returned to Italy.

In 1922, by which time performance transcriptions of "Deep River" had peaked, some the worse for wear, Burleigh champion Lucien White of the *New York Age* wrote at length on the subject, deploring the piece's increasing corruption. He lamented the fact that jazz versions and frequent use of syncopation had destroyed "Deep River's" serious nature. The manager of Fox Theaters of Greater New York came to the rescue, requesting Burleigh's version of it to be performed by Mrs. Jessie Andrews Zachery, coloratura, the first black singer ever booked into these theaters. "Letters to the Editor" followed, even by white supporters of the idea.[68]

Other Spirituals in 1917 After "Deep River"

All twelve of the single arrangements published by Ricordi in 1917 were reissued by Belwin-Mills in 1984 (*The Spirituals of Harry T. Burleigh*), along with three dozen other spirituals, a biographical sketch by Dr. Harry T. Burleigh II, Burleigh's grandson, and Burleigh's own preface that had been included with the 1917 issues. Several of the representative ones merit discussion.

A. W. Kramer was enthusiastic enough about these 1917 spirituals to call them "all little masterpieces," crediting Burleigh's penetrative abilities as surpassed by no other living composer. He calls the accompaniments "harmonically elusive," with distinct interest and quaint phraseology characteristic of the plantation Negro. "You May Bury Me in de Eas'," "epic in its significance," has been treated almost symphonically. In "Swing Low, Sweet Chariot" "he has outdone himself. . . . The harmonies fairly melt in this setting, and yet form just the background. . . . Bravo again, Mr. Burleigh!"[69]

Burleigh used one of the same tunes in "By an' By" that is given in Work's *American Negro Songs*, but added an accompaniment. "By an' By" is one of the same two dozen or so spirituals set by both Burleigh and J. Rosamond Johnson. An overall comparison of the two actually reveals a similarity in style, but a distinct individuality in rhythmic patterns. Too, most of Johnson's arrangements are dedicated to persons, whereas only a few of Burleigh's are. "By an' By," aptly classified by Work as a "Song of Patience," expresses a desire for the good life, free of burden, as it repeats "I'm goin' to lay down dis heavy load, by an' by." In 1917 Burleigh not only made a solo arrangement of this spiritual but also one for unison voices.

The text of "Go Down Moses," a Bahama song, is taken from Exodus 8. Marked *Lento* and in G minor, it is interesting more for its accompaniment than its vocal line. The "snap" rhythm punctuates effectively the words *tell* and *lan'*. This is one of the few spirituals that has a piano interlude between verses, in this case a repetition of the introduction varied rhythmically by using two sixteenths rather than an eighth note. (See Musical Example No. 21.) These devices hint at the Egyptian essence. As in the art songs Burleigh's step-wise descending and ascending bass line is evident, in this particular piece alternating with a pedal tone on G.

Once after Burleigh had sung "Go Down Moses" to Dvorak, the Czech master said, "Burleigh, that is as great as a Beethoven theme."[70] Cuney-Hare calls "Moses" an "interpretation of Hebrew history with variants from Virginia and the Bahamas."[71]

"Go Down Moses," "Didn't It Rain," "Little David Play on Your Harp," and "Standing in the Need of Prayer" were all found in North Carolina, according to Frank C. Brown, author of *North Carolina Folklore, The Music of the Folksongs*.[72]

"Swing Low, Sweet Chariot" is a famous old spiritual which Burleigh probably learned from his grandfather, Hamilton Waters, and later sang to Dvorak. According to Harriet Tubman's biographer, Sarah Bradford, "Swing Low" was probably the most famous spiritual with reference to Tubman and her work, used primarily as a signal or code.

Musical Example No. 21, "Go Down Moses," measures 1-2, 21-22, 25-26, and 29-30. Each two-measure passage shows added rhythmic interest in the accompaniment.

Slaves must not be seen talking together, and so it came about that this communication was often made by singing, the words of their hymns, telling of the heavenly journey, and the land of Canaan, while they did not attract the attention of the masters, conveyed to their brethern and sisters in bondage something more than met the ear.[73]

Certain spirituals, including "Swing Low," "De Gospel Train" ("Get on Board, Little Children"), "Don't Be Weary Traveler," and "Sinner, Please Don't Let This Harvest Pass" are said to have referred specifically to the Underground Railroad and various other means of escape. "Nobody Knows the Trouble I've Seen" and "Hard Trials" depict self-pity.

Taken from II Kings, Chapters 2 and 11, "Swing Low" has not only been depicted in song and sculpture but in a painting by Marjorie Wintermute, which in 1932 was hung in the Anderson Gallery in Richmond, Virginia. William Arms Fisher places the origin of "Swing Low" in Rhodesia, where Bishop Frederick Fisher heard the natives sing a similar melody as a farewell chant to the dead. Nathaniel Dett relates it to Old China and Amerindian culture.

The song, pentatonic, was introduced by the Fisk Jubilee Singers in 1871, and was included in their first edition of *Jubilee Songs*.[74] Fisher's arrangement of "Swing Low," somewhat similar in construction to Burleigh's, has three verses to Burleigh's one. Burleigh uses extra dotted rhythms on the phrase "Comin' for to carry me," where Fisher uses all eighth notes. A high to low mood-setting effect is adroitly, but simply, carried out in Burleigh's chordal introduction and for the following eight measures.

"Nobody Knows de Trouble I've Seen" has been traced by Cuney-Hare to Charleston, South Carolina, earlier than 1865. From there it spread to the Sea Islands, a low-lying chain in the Atlantic Ocean off the coasts of South Carolina, Georgia, and northern Florida. In the eighteenth century the English and Spanish had contended for the islands. After the Civil War, freed slaves received land there and their descendants, called Gullah, remained in the area. This spiritual of slavery can be found in nearly all the standard collections.

It is written in the pentatonic scale, and was heard in the Sea Islands when the Government had failed to carry out its promise in regard to the allotment of land to the freedmen. Gen. Howard, called to address the gathering of colored people, asked them to sing. The sad strains of the old song as it broke forth from the throat of an old woman, deeply affected the speaker. Mr. Krehbiel declares that the two emotional poles, despair and hopefulness, are touched in this song.[75]

"Nobody Knows de Trouble I've Seen" in the original version has also been arranged as a solo by Clarence Cameron White. Other solo versions with a slight variation in title have been by James Weldon Johnson ("Nobody Knows de Trouble I See") and Henry E. Krehbiel ("Nobody Knows de Trouble I See, Lord") and for men's chorus by Arthur Mees.[76]

Though there is no indication on the score that Burleigh dedicated "Nobody Knows" to Mary Jordan, an item in the *Musical Courier* in 1918 mentioned that this spiritual, as well as "I Want to Be Ready," "You May Bury Me in the Eas'" and "Oh Peter Go Ring-a Dem Bells" were also dedicated to her.[77]

Burleigh's simple but beautifully fitting accompaniment for "Nobody Knows" cannot be faulted. The variance in harmonization of the verses is less prominent than in some of the other spirituals. Sparing but strategic use of augmented chords on the word "seen" gives a pang of sadness. A lively accompanimental pattern in the left hand in the happier sections is well conceived.

Several of the spirituals which Burleigh set were taken from biblical texts. "I Don't Feel No-Ways Tired" (1917) relates man's desire for a better place promised by God and is based on Hebrews 11:14 and 16. The "snap" rhythm really moves the piece along with an almost jazzy energy. (See Musical Example No. 22.) This spiritual was one of Burleigh's own favorites to sing. It is one of seventeen included in *The Spirituals of Harry T. Burleigh* (1984) that Burleigh arranged in only one key. The others were in two and often three keys.

Burleigh gives a similar musical treatment to "I Want to Be Ready" or "Walk in Jerusalem Jus' Like John" (1917), based on the second chapter of Acts and on Revelation 21:16. Another of the

Musical Example No. 22, "I Don't Feel Noways Tired," measures 37-48.

spirituals arranged in only one key, it tells of Peter's "preachin' at Pentecost," and describes Jerusalem as "jus' four-square," whereas the verse from Revelation says "And the city lieth foursquare. . . . The length and the breadth and the height of it are equal." The words "Walk in Jerusalem, jus' like John" are used seven times within this three-page joyous spiritual. According to Cuney-Hare (p. 70) "I Want to Be Ready," from Kentucky, is also similar to "Walk Jerusalem Jes Like John," "Walk into Jerusalem Jes Like John," and "When I Come to Die."

Burleigh's note in the last measure of "John's Gone Down on de Island" (1917) reads: "Shearer Cottage, Oak Bluffs, Mass., Aug. 16th 1917." Taken from a tiny reference in Revelation 1:9 to John's stay on the Aegean island of Patmos near Turkey, the song text paints a glowing picture of life there resembling Heaven, where "de streets are pearl and de gates are gold." Set in F minor, the piano introduction alternates subtly from 4/4 to 3/4 to 4/4. Without accidentals the vocal line adheres strictly to the natural minor mode, though the chordal accompaniment uses several C-major and C-major-seventh chords with the raised seventh scale step of E natural. An interlude repeating the introduction separates the two verses. A harp-like figure in the right hand of the accompaniment conjures Heaven, the pearly gates and golden streets.[78]

"Weepin' Mary" (1917), exquisite in its simplicity, is based on John 20:11: "But Mary stood without at the sepulchre weeping: and as she wept, she stooped down, and looked into the sepulchre." In only two pages Burleigh perfectly captures the touching scene. Working tonally in D minor and in AAB form, Burleigh adds interest to the vocal line's exact repetition of the A sections by placing the

Musical Example No. 23, "Weepin' Mary," measures 17-21, 25-26.

accompaniment up an octave and using suspensions and a few altered chords. All of the would-be B flats in the vocal line are raised to B naturals. (See Musical Example No. 23.) The piece ends on a sustained A major chord. The accompaniment would be suitable for organ as well as piano.

First Corinthians 15:52, a text much used by oratorio composers, states: "In a moment, in the twinkling of an eye, at the last trump: for the trumpet shall sound, and the dead shall be raised incorruptible, and we shall be changed." Burleigh fashioned these thoughts into "You May Bury Me in de Eas'," a spiritual of faith in which, like "Weepin' Mary," he used the major sixth in the minor mode. The introduction with broken octaves in the left hand (written as grace notes) ominously states the coming opening theme of the vocal line, then embarks on a melody of its own in intervals higher than the voice part. In both verses the skip of an octave (F down to F) is written for the voice on the word "mornin'" as if to effect a wail or moan. Though not marked with a slur or portamenta, the accompaniment under it in descending sixths intensifies its mournful quality. The rather rhapsodic accompaniment would almost stand alone as a piano solo. It ends on an F-major chord. Though Burleigh's words did not adhere to the biblical text, he did point up, with accents, the "trumpet soun'."

The other two spirituals published in 1917, "My Way's Cloudy," commonly known in the Southern states, and "Sinner, Please Doan Let Dis Harves' Pass" from Tennessee, were written in only one key. Curiously, Burleigh has not marked a single rest in the voice parts of either song. The *Lento* tempo for "My Way's Cloudy" seems unsuitable for the animated vocal line. Opening with a single A flat by the piano the accompaniment, suggesting a sustained rocking motion, breaks into a livelier banjo pattern. Breath support and proper phrasing are of the essence in this spiritual. The accompaniment in both verses of "My Way's Cloudy" is the same, a rarity in Burleigh's compositions.

"Doan Let Dis Harves' Pass" begins in E minor, then without transition breaks abruptly into a happier G major section on the phrase "I know that my Redeemer lives" which is repeated on the words "My God is a mighty man of war." A four-measure reiteration of the opening E-minor theme separates the sections and is again used to end the spiritual. A rhythmic figure of short-short- long, short-short-long, uncommon in Burleigh's songs, suggests a war-like chant or dance, perhaps to stress the strong rhythm prevalent in Negro work songs. This is the type of song that expressed the Afro-American's emotional and mental confusion at his own plight.

The Spirituals of 1918

The joyous "Oh Peter Go Ring-a Dem Bells" was arranged by Burleigh for both solo and unison voices in 1918. More suited for high voice, in the key of F major, the song's ambit is that of middle C up to a high F, which is marked with a *ritard*. Burleigh's step-wise crescendoing bass line is used to great effect. Accented chords of open fifths give the hollow, yet ringing effect of bells, especially the left hand's pedal tone of a fifth (low F up to C). It is a rangy, raucous, clangy accompaniment in contrast to the introspective one for "Weepin' Mary." (See Musical Example No. 24.) The piece ends quietly on the F-to-C fifth.

Incorporating in part the sameness of the hymn tune "Standing in the Need of Prayer," Burleigh's "T'is Me, O Lord" (1918, reissued in 1924) is fairly free in style. The accompaniment is reminiscent of the old-timey revival piano-player, with near jazzy fillers under the voice's sustained notes. "I Stood on the Ribber ob Jerdon" is ar-ranged in two verses. Burleigh reins the accompaniment through half of the first one, then gradually lets it grow more active by adding eighth note figures. As the second verse begins the accompaniment moves up an octave, then back to the range of the voice line, growing louder with heavier chords on the off beats, leading to an optional high F at the climax. Then a measure of three accented ninth chords (G, F and E flat) precedes an unexpected D-flat major chord. This is followed by the four-bar ending, which resolves in a series of descending F-major chords marked *pianissimo*, under the last soft words "I Stood on de ribber ob Jerdon."

It is inexplicable that Burleigh's name is mentioned but once in Marian Anderson's autobiography, *My Lord, What a Morning*. Though "Deep River" and other Burleigh spirituals which Anderson sang were mentioned, "My Lord, What a Mornin'" (1918) undoubtedly

Musical Example No. 24, "Oh Peter Go Ring-a Dem Bells," measures 1-4.
Below: Measures 18-24 show the effectiveness of Burleigh's descending,
crescendoing bass line.

among them, Burleigh was not credited as their arranger. The theme of "My Lord, What a Mornin'" was used in "A New Hidin' Place," a segment of Burleigh's piano suite *From the Southland* (1914). Its text, taken from a fragment of Revelation 8:10, "and there fell a great star from Heaven," became in Burleigh's words "When de stars begin to fall." In one of the earliest editions of the Jubilee songs and in *Plantation Songs* (1887) "mornin'" was "mournin'."

Cuney-Hare calls the song a variant of "Wrestling Jacob," tracing it to the Southeastern slave states, an assumption also noted in *Jubilee Songs* (1892).

> A variant, "Stars begin to fall," noted in *Slave Songs of the United States*, 1867, comes from Edisto Island and a version, "My Lord What a Morning," is found in *Cabin and Plantation Songs*, Hampton, 1890-1901.[79]

Burleigh's version in D-flat major and in AABA form, marked *Adagio non tanto*, has a two-measure chordal introduction. Its ten-measure melody of the first section is repeated, underlaid by an arpeggiated and chordal accompaniment. The B section, marked *poco più mosso*, is arrived at smoothly via one F seventh modulatory chord from D-flat major to B-flat minor. Within this section Burleigh again uses a pedal tone, doubles rhythms on the off beats, and sustains a crescendoing step-wise bass line to good effect for four measures before returning to the A section.

Perhaps one of Burleigh's most touching arrangements of 1918, or any time, was "Sometimes I Feel Like a Motherless Child." In spite of the title, the song's text retains the usage "chile." Burleigh altered the rhythm on the words "motherless chile" from the original triplet figure followed by an eighth note to four even eighths. The tune croons, it moans, it cries, it hums, it lulls. The vocal range is an octave. The accompaniment is chordal and sedate. Burleigh arranged the spiritual for female voices in 1919. It came from Mississippi, according to Cuney-Hare, and was noted in the standard collections as early as 1874. A variant titled "Moanin' Dove" was found in Beaufort County, South Carolina.[80]

1919

Burleigh's productivity during World War I years did not diminish toward that decade's close. In 1919 six more solo arrangements of spirituals, some also expanded for ensemble, were published by Ricordi. Four of these were based on biblical texts. "Hard Trials" (Matthew 24:21 and 8:20) borders on the comical, with its whimsical talk of "Methodis'" and "Piscopal" sides and "de debbil," enhanced

Musical Example No. 25, "Hard Trials," measures 67-74, showing descending bass line.

by suspenseful fermatas and Burleigh's frolicky accompaniment. (See Musical Example No. 25 for descending bass line.) Instead of Matthew's words (8:20) "But the Son of Man hath not where to lay his head," Burleigh's bemoan the po' sinners' lack of a hiding place. But the "great tribulation," presaged by Matthew, Burleigh kept as written.

"Oh Didn't It Rain?" originating in the Bahamas, was one of the spirituals sung frequently at the Calhoun School in Lowndes County, Alabama. Emily Hallowell, author of *Calhoun Plantation Songs*, described this institution, which opened in 1892, as being

> . . . in the blackest part of the Black Belt in Alabama where the colored people out number the whites by seven to one. The negroes are more primitive perhaps than those of any Southern state and their songs more nearly represent the unalloyed, unmodified plantation slave than those of less aboriginal communities.[81]

Hallowell's unaccompanied versions for chorus better lend themselves to multiple verses than do Burleigh's accompanied solo arrangements. Burleigh's tune for "Oh Didn't It Rain?" does not resemble Hallowell's, and he substitutes "Noah" for her "Nora." The text was taken from Genesis 7:4, concerning the rain of forty days and nights. This was one of Burleigh's spirituals with which Roland Hayes charmed his formal Aeolian Hall audience when he debuted there in January of 1919. Accompanied by Burleigh, he had to repeat the song.

Solo arrangements of "Let Us Cheer the Weary Traveller," "Balm in Gilead," "Don't You Weep When I Am Gone," and "He's Jus' de Same Today," plus an arrangement for female voices of "Sometimes I Feel Like a Motherless Child," completed the spirituals published in 1919. "Let Us Cheer the Weary Traveller" is described by Cuney-Hare as "a slave song of hope" from Kentucky.[82] Its accompaniment is rather hymn-like and stately, but becomes heavier and more martial toward the end.

"Balm in Gilead," based on Jeremiah 8:22, was dedicated by Burleigh to "Prof. John Wesley Work, Fisk University, Nashville, Tennessee." As a faculty member there from 1898 to 1923, Work reorganized Fisk singing groups for tours. Work himself was a singer of oratorio. In 1923 he accepted the presidency of Roger Williams

University in Nashville. His treatise *Folk Songs of the American Negro* was published in 1915. John W. Work III, his son, carried on the father's interest in Negro spirituals and folk songs, and later succeeded him as a professor at Fisk. Burleigh's setting of the song is rather calm, using a sustained pedal tone on G through much of the accompaniment. The Bible verse asks: "Is there no balm in Gilead?" Burleigh's text, more positive, reads "There is a balm in Gilead."

Taken from another verse of Jeremiah (22:10), the gist of "Don't You Weep When I'm Gone" is "Do not weep for one who dies, but rather for me who goes away and can never return to his native land." The Bahama equivalent is titled "Don't You Weep After Me." Burleigh treats the somber text with an appropriate syncopated movement in the key of G flat, an unusual one for him. The rondo-like form is ABABA.

In "He's Jus' de Same To-Day" Burleigh followed the Calhoun melody fairly closely, even to using the lowered third (B flat in the key of G major). It is a more joyous song than some, from Exodus 14:22 and I Samuel 17:49, which say that God is unchanging. Burleigh specifies on the score that "today" be pronounced "toe-day."

Spirituals and Folksongs, 1920-1925

Three Negro folk songs, as opposed to spirituals, were arranged for solo voice in 1921 by Burleigh: "Oh! Rock Me Julie," a departure from the Krehbiel setting in 1913; "Scandalize My Name," another popular song from Calhoun, Alabama, with rather comical words; and "Don't You Dream of Turnin' Back," which may possibly be a version of "Don't You Let Nobody Turn You Roun'," a caution to stay on the straight and narrow path.[83] His arrangement of "The Lord's Prayer" (Matthew 6:9-13) was also published in 1921.

Burleigh's spiritual arrangements issued by Ricordi in 1921 were "Little David, Play on Your Harp," another edition of "Didn't My Lord Deliver Daniel?" "De Gospel Train" (for solo and male chorus), "Heav'n, Heav'n" (for solo and mixed voices), and "Steal Away." "Little David" was dedicated "To Mr. George Hamlin," the famous tenor to whom Burleigh had earlier dedicated "The Glory of the Day Was in Her Face" from the cycle *Passionale*. The A sections of the ABABA form gather interest by accompanimental variations; the B sections are marked *quasi recitando, slower*. Pedal points on F and D form much of the bass line. In the phrases "O Lord" and "O Little David," "O" falls on the strong beat, giving the piece a sense of urgency. Overall "Little David" moves swiftly, allowing the singer little rest.

"De Gospel Train," a revival song in pentatonic mode, is a variant of "Get on Board" from the Bahama Islands, noted in Charles Edwards's *Songs and Stories* (1895), and of "From Every Graveyard" and "Git on Board Little Children" (*Hampton Cabin and Plantation Songs, 1901*). It also appears in *Jubilee Songs* (1872) and in *Jubilee and Plantation Songs* (1887). A "Gospel Train," attributed to Oscar Buckner, a black slave who saw the conductor and brakeman as biblical characters, might also have been a partial source.[84]

Burleigh definitely projects the image of train wheels in motion in the left hand of the accompaniment. For all its energy the ambit of the entire tune is a major sixth (from E flat up to C). The accompaniment becomes fuller and augmented in range with each repeated phrase. The piece ends *pianissimo* with two "toot-toot" chords in the right hand on E and A naturals against a sustained A-flat chord. Still a favorite in 1928, "De Gospel Train" had to be repeated by Marian Anderson in a Carnegie Hall recital on December 30 of that year.[85]

According to Newman I. White there are many Afro-American train or railroad songs, and this particular one is not confined to blacks but used equally at white revival meetings. Origins are cited in Shelby County, Alabama; Durham, North Carolina; the Bahamas; and Texas, Louisiana, and South Carolina.[86]

Burleigh dedicated "De Gospel Train" (1921) to Royal Dadmun, an American baritone and vocal teacher from Massachusetts whose wife, Christine Schutz, was also a singer and teacher. During World War I Dadmun was popular as an oratorio singer and recitalist. He was soloist with several top orchestras, including the New York Philharmonic and the Boston Symphony, and with the New York Oratorio Society and the Toronto Mendelssohn Choir. During a spring tour in 1916

> he was highly commended and has a big recital season already booked in the cities where he was thus heard during the latter part of last season. The demand for his return in

these cities is ample testimony to the satisfaction which his singing gave to the music lovers there.[87]

On December 12, 1918, Dadmun was baritone soloist for a Singer's Club concert in Cleveland at Gray's Armory where "he was at his best in the four negro spirituals arranged by H. T. Burleigh."[88]

Marian Anderson, perhaps more than any other singer, helped popularize "Heav'n, Heav'n" (1921), though the score bears no dedication. One of Burleigh's very few compositions which he marked "Joyfully, but not too fast," "Heav'n, Heav'n," with the second syllable "like a hum," has a delightfully varied and jubilant accompaniment. Under the words "All of God's children got a harp," Burleigh uses one of his rare trills. The ending, marked "ecstatically but not loudly," shows more of Burleigh's accompanimental big-chord treatment. The range of "Heav'n, Heav'n" (key of A-flat major) like that of "De Gospel Train," is within a major sixth. This tune with numerous verses is listed by Hallowell as "Gwine to Shout All Over God's Heaven" from Lowndes County, Alabama (p. 58).

To Melville Charlton, Burleigh's superb accompanist and "devoted friend" for many years, he dedicated "Steal Away." The mood of the piece, again within the range of a sixth, is subdued. Burleigh's accompaniment subtly images "the trumpet sounds" with some special accents and the bending trees with moving eighth notes. (See Musical Example No. 26.)

Charlton died in 1973 at the age of ninety-three. He was an active and much in-demand organist, pianist, and teacher in both religious and social circles, and was the first black to qualify for the American Guild of Organists (1915). It is a pity that Burleigh was not mentioned as one of Charlton's associates in an obituary from *The Diapason* of January, 1974. Periodically Charlton submitted items of musical interest to the *New York Age*. In one of them he spoke of the evolution of the spiritual with native tom-tom accompaniment to its later contrapuntal emanations and other classic features.[89]

Roland Hayes, who also arranged "Steal Away," was the great-grandson of a slave. He believed that the Bible lore of the slaves was "mated to music brought from Africa, or improvised in similar mold."

The song "Steal Away" is said to be so inspired and was born in a cotton field where there were a great number of

Musical Example No. 26, "Steal Away," measures 29-35.

slaves hoeing cotton. The leader who always planned the date when the slaves would go secretly, after nightfall, to hear a Northern white clergyman preach the gospel of salvation through Christ would first whisper, "Steal away," to the slave next in line to him. This whispered word, spoken over rhythmic measures of hoe strokes of the choppers, was passed along the line until it reached the last individual. Work, of course, took on a more lively gait from this moment. Then the spoken word gradually took on melody which surged forth increasingly on the rhythmic verve of spirited melody of a decidedly African idiomatic pattern. The hoes were simply playing an ecstatic rhythm as an accompaniment background to the song. Now and again, the leader would halt the flow of a smoothly conceived legato to introduce a sort of recitative occasioned by the oncoming of wind or a threatened storm, which he used to stress the urgent call to the meeting. This kind of spirited melody kept up until the end of the workday. Thus the plan of the slaves to attend the religious services secretly, after nightfall, was effectively hidden from the master.[90]

Courageous "Prophet" Nat Turner is said by one scholar to have composed "Steal Away" in connection with his slave insurrection in Jerusalem (now Courtland), Southhampton County, Virginia.[91]

Burleigh's autograph on a copy of "Steal Away" for Reverend Cornelius Greenway in 1941 read: "To Rev. Cornelius Greenway Copliments [sic] of H. T. Burleigh New York 1941 Xmas." Greenway (1897-1968), an avid collector of autographs of famous people, was pastor of All Souls Church in Brooklyn.[92]

Burleigh's best known settings of spirituals in 1922 included "Couldn't Hear Nobody Pray" (solo and mixed voices), "Ain't Goin' to Study War No More," and "Oh, Rocks, Don't Fall on Me." There is a noticeable amount of expressive markings in the score of "Couldn't Hear Nobody Pray," dedicated to Nathaniel Dett of Hampton Institute. Dett (1881-1943) was an indefatigable teacher, pianist and composer whose own arrangements of spirituals achieved considerable recognition. There is no evidence that the two were close friends, though mutual respect is almost certain. As a young pianist Dett was one of the few blacks who got adequate publicity. John W. Work's version of "I Couldn't Hear Nobody Pray" calls for a leader and chorus.[93]

Another well-known person, Dr. J. Stanley Durkee (1867-1951), was the dedicatee of "Ain't Goin' to Study War No More," one of Burleigh's longer arrangements. The words of the spiritual are quite repetitive, but Burleigh makes the piece interesting by skillful embellishments in the consecutive verses, a departure from the more staid

Ain't Gonna Study War No Mo'

Negro Spiritual

arranged by

H. Burleigh

Ms. "Ain't Gonna Study War No Mo' " by Harry Burleigh. Reprinted by permission of Library & Archives, Erie County Historical Society, Erie, Pennsylvania.

Ain't Gonna Study War No Mo'

Arranged by
H. T. Burleigh

1. I'm gon-na lay down my bur-den, Down by the riv-er side,
2. " " " swod an' spear

Down by the riv-er side, Down by the riv-er side, Gon-na lay down my

bur-den, Down by the riv-er side, Ain't gon-na stud-y — war no
swo'd an' spear " " " " "

mo' Ain't gon-na stud-y war no mo' Stud-y war no

Style No. 12—12 Staves
Printed in the U. S. A.

G. Schirmer (Inc.) New York

original manuscript. From 1918 to 1926 Durkee was president of Howard University where he received an honorary LL.D. Later as a pastor at Plymouth Church of the Pilgrims in Brooklyn, he had a radio program, wrote poetry, and authored five books on religion.[94]

"O Rocks, Don't Fall on Me" was dedicated to American tenor Judson House (1894-1945). Often featured with orchestras, House was also soloist at St. Bartholomew's Church and Temple Emanu-El in New York. He received three citations for valor in World War I. After his debut with the New York Symphony Orchestra in Saratoga Springs in 1915 a reviewer called him

> one of the finest tenors appearing before the American public. . . . Mr. House commands a sweetness of tone that is quite entrancing and he held his hearers spellbound during every number of this quality.[95]

Burleigh accompanied House in a New York art song recital in late September 1920, when both men were with Temple Emanu-El.[96]

One of Burleigh's most timeless and beautiful arrangements, "Were You There?" (solo and mixed voices), was published by Ricordi in 1924. Conceived with the utmost simplicity, this spiritual, unlike nearly all of the others which Burleigh set, uses no words in dialect, as its touching and somber mood does not call for such a treatment. Rather than short phrases complete sentences are used. One of Burleigh's very effective devices is the chromatic and stepwise movement of the accompaniment's inner voices. When the word *Oh* is repeated, Burleigh's harmony changes to accommodate the lowered sixth. (See Musical Example No. 27.)

According to David Cantrell "Were You There?" was one of Burleigh's personal preferences which he felt to be appropriate in any church. Though "Deep River" was Burleigh's favorite choral arrangement (also according to Cantrell), "Were You There?" outsold it; it was reissued in 1925, 1926, and 1927.[97]

The longer "Oh, Wasn't Dat a Wide Ribber?" also issued by Ricordi in 1924, is a contrast with its dialect and more complex accompaniment, giving way to a bravura ending marked "maestoso." Burleigh instructs the singer to pronounce "wasn't" as "wazzun."

In 1925 only three of Burleigh's new arrangements were published. Two of them, "Ev'ry Time I Feel de Spirit" and "Wade in de

Musical Example No. 27, "Were You There?" measures 12-13 and 31-32.

Water," were for both solo and mixed voices; but "I Know de Lord's Laid His Hand on Me" was for solo voice only. Burleigh often included the latter, a Lowndes County spiritual, in his recitals. Its words were taken from Matthew 19:15 and Acts 8:17 and 19:6. "Ev'ry Time" has several meter changes, perhaps for phrasing purposes. "Wade in de Water," likely published as early as 1922 though Burleigh authority Roland Lewis Allison gives the date as 1925, is of Georgia Sea Islands origin, sometimes titled "Wade in Nuh Watuh, Childun."

Spirituals Arranged Between 1925 and 1930

In 1924 St. George's had begun its annual service of Negro spirituals in Burleigh's honor. His style in arranging did not vary noticeably from this period on, but neither did he fail to convey the essence of each spiritual in a tasteful way. Though he had arrived at some workable techniques, no triteness was involved.

Around the mid-1920s the Ricordi office in London issued a "Thematic Booklet of the Celebrated Negro Spirituals by H. T. Burleigh," claiming that over thirty were now in print and selling at two shillings each. The frontispiece of the booklet also listed ten singers and singing groups who were popularizing the spirituals, among them Dame Nellie Melba, Mr. Ben Davies, Mr. John McCormack, Mr. Roland Hayes, the Fisk Jubilee Singers, and the De Reszke Singers.

Besides the reissue of "Were You There?" in 1926, Burleigh's published spirituals numbered four others by Ricordi, and two by Oliver Ditson Company: "Dar's a Meeting Here Tonight" and "Run to Jesus." William Arms Fisher was responsible for including these last two in *Seventy Negro Spirituals*,[98] a collection which he edited for Ditson. The first, "Dar's a Meeting," from the Port Royal Islands, is another nonstop feat for the singer, full of saucy sixteenth-note patter, but subject to flexibility in interpretation and marked with "devotional feeling" by Burleigh. The vigorous rhythms of both words and tune suggest a camp-meeting atmosphere. Fisher's note accompanying "Run to Jesus" reads:

> This song was given to the Jubilee Singers by Hon. Frederick Douglass, at Washington, DC, with the interesting statement that it first suggested to him the thought of escaping from slavery.

The two-page setting of this Sorrow Song in D minor with one repeat is filled with dotted rhythms. The accompaniment follows the voice line exactly throughout. A raised minor sixth (B natural) occurs in the brief coda on a hum ("Hm").

"I Got a Home in-a Dat Rock" (1926) is unique in that Burleigh asks for a *parlando* passage at the end, immediately following a brief *stringendo*, to be spoken rather than sung. "Go Down in the Lonesome Valley" (1926), probably from the Port Royal Islands ("The Lonesome Valley"), was sung by Burleigh in 1935 at his forty-first anniversary with St. George's. Another lesser-known publication of this year was "Give Me Jesus," a sustained spiritual both in the vocal line and the chordal accompaniment.

"Stan' Still, Jordan" (1926), one of Burleigh's longer arrangements, was dedicated to the famous black tenor Roland Hayes (1887-1976), who by this time had made quite a name for himself abroad as well as in the United States. Beginning in 1919 the *Musical Courier* chose periodically to mention his singing of Burleigh's arrangements, sometimes even including reviews by Paris critics.

Burleigh and Hayes first met in 1914, at which time they sang duets while travelling with Booker T. Washington.[99] When Hayes was awarded the Spingarn Medal in 1924, Burleigh accepted it for him since the tenor was abroad on tour. In addition to singing, Hayes attempted to educate audiences on the value of Negro music. He said in an interview in 1919 that

> the essence of Negro music is the voice. The spirituals and shouts were meant to be sung, indeed, never anything else. The Negro . . . had something to say and he chose to say it in song. . . . I am endeavoring to carry the message of my people.[100]

In 1948 Hayes's *My Songs*, a collection of his own arrangements of Negro folk songs and spirituals, was published in Boston by Little, Brown and Company.

Again, a few years later when touring Russia, Hayes was asked in Moscow his own meaning of the spirituals. In replying he hoped to discredit the Russian idea that they grew solely from the "Negro's effort to liberate himself from slavery." "Deep River," he said, "had become, in proletariat hands, a dreary narrative about negroes picnicking on the banks of the Jordan river."[101]

As a welcome and useful addition to St. George's services Burleigh wrote "Six Responses" in 1926. These short pieces carefully balanced speech and rhythms.

"Ezekiel Saw de Wheel," not included in *The Spirituals of Harry T. Burleigh* (1984), was arranged for male and female voices in 1927 and as a solo in 1928. Other new arrangements in 1927 were of "I've

Been in de Storm So Long" and "Hear de Lambs A-Crying." Unusual chord changes and chromaticism of the accompaniment's inner voices in "I've Been in de Storm So Long" indicate unrest and need for the soothing comforts of prayer. "Hear de Lambs" was dedicated to Mr. and Mrs. James A. Myers, singers with various Fisk University choral groups. In 1916 Mr. Myers was a member of the Fisk University Sextet. The tranquil accompaniment of "Hear de Lambs" begins and ends with an A-minor sixth chord, not a common one for Burleigh, but a fitting dissonance for the song's theme.

In 1928 Burleigh produced two more spirituals: "De Blin' Man Stood on de Road an' Cried" and "Don't Be Weary Traveler" (arranged for both solo and mixed voices). The first, pronounced by Burleigh as "Duh Blin' Man Stood on duh Road an' Cried," is from Mark 10:46 and 52, and concerns the blind Bartimeus, who regained

Musical Example No. 28, "Don't Be Weary Traveler," measures 34-39.

his sight through faith. "Don't Be Weary Traveler" is a slave song from Virginia.[102] Neither of the spirituals is given an elaborate musical treatment by Burleigh, though he wrote a step-wise passage near the end of "Traveller" with repetitive octaves resembling tramping feet. (See Musical Example No. 28.)

Burleigh set the Christmas spiritual "Behold That Star" in 1928, and subsequently in 1943 and 1944. It was chosen from a collection by Thomas W. Talley (1868-1952), a professor at Fisk University who was interested in folk rhymes. His book *Negro Folk Rhymes, Wise and Otherwise* was published in 1922, but it is highly likely that "Behold That Star" was found after this publication, since it was not included in it. The words celebrate the birth of Jesus and the Star of Bethlehem. The introduction is repeated by the piano at the end of the song. In the sections which depart from the hymn-like treatment, Burleigh does not choose to follow the vocal line, giving an obligato effect. Heavier chords reinforce the closing measures forcefully. (See Musical Example No. 29.)

Hall Johnson's "Ride On, King Jesus" (1951) probably became as popular as Burleigh's arrangement published in 1929. Actually their versions are similar in strength, brio and bravura. Biblical references for the text are found in Psalm 45:4 and Revelation 6:2. Burleigh's setting, marked *maestoso*, is punctuated with strategic staccato notes and deliberate rests, neither device commonly used by him. The "white horse" of Revelation was embellished by Burleigh to read "milk-white horse," and he referred to the roaring "troubled waters" of the psalm as "de ribber of Jordan." In the song there is no mention of the crown which the biblical equestrian wore.[103]

Also in 1929 Burleigh composed "Christ Be with Me" with words taken from an anonymous poem, "St. Patrick's Breast Plate." They may have been similar to those on St. Patrick's badge, which, translated from the original Latin, "Quis separabit," mean "one who will separate." "Go Tell It on de Mountains," with Christmas text, a typical seasonal song heard on many plantations, was also set this year.

Burleigh's largest work of 1929 was the *Old Songs Hymnal* in collaboration with Dorothy G. Bolton, a Georgia white woman, according to *Crisis* magazine, December 1929, but whom many scholars assumed to have been black. Dr. John F. Garst, a professor at the University of Georgia wrote:

Musical Example No. 29, "Behold That Star," measures 44-53. Rhythmic placement of the word *glory* in measures 45-46 shows prosodic treatment.

The tone of the introduction in the book is that it is an
effort to preserve the old songs for "our people," or some
such. To me, this is a direct implication that Bolton is black.
I think it must be so, unless she was deliberately hiding her
whiteness in the foreword to the book.[104]

Old Songs Hymnal, published by the Century Company in 1929,
includes 187 settings by Burleigh of hymns found in Georgia by
Bolton. The table of contents divides them into Folksongs in the
Making; Narrative Songs; Songs of Admonition; Songs of Striving,
Weariness and Aspiration; Songs of Conversion; Songs of Devil and
Hell; Songs of Death; and Songs of Judgment, Resurrection and Re-
ward. Existing copies of the hymnal are not plentiful but there are
at least a dozen in U.S. libraries.

According to Dr. David Cantrell, a Burleigh scholar, many of the
songs were originally contributed by former slaves. "De Gospel
Train," one typical example, shows a simple, singable four-part
arrangement in the comfortable range of C major. Extra verses are
not added between the staves under the first verse, but at the bottom
of the page. The Foreword to *Old Songs Hymnal*, signed by both Burleigh and Bolton reads:

> Whenever one of these old hymns is sung in church or
> Sunday school a deeper emotion wells up in us all and a
> more intense religious fervor seems to descend upon us.
> Until now we have had to depend upon memory alone to
> sing them, and when the minister could not "line" them for
> us some old brother or sister would undertake to lead them.
> All these older ones will soon have passed over the border
> and very few of the present generation know these songs.
> They know the tunes and a verse here and there so that they
> can join in when some one else leads, but they do not know
> them well enough to continue singing them in church when
> the old folk have passed on.
>
> There are many beautiful collections of these songs, but
> all with accompaniments too difficult for the average person
> to play at sight, and so we present this volume as a hymn-
> book with the music as simple as possible, hoping that it will

be used in church and home and school, preserving to us this precious heritage.

The lines of these hymns are of unequal length, and while we have selected for the music the best known verse, the words of the other verses must be adjusted to the music with the greatest freedom by the individual singer. The natural sense of rhythm of the old folk found no difficulty in doing this, and so we have not attempted to bring the words into proper alignment with the music, but give them verbatim as we have heard them sung.

We offer this book with the hope that in these songs the human heart will continue to find expression for its deepest emotions of joy, of sorrow, of inspiration and that exaltation of the soul which gave them the name – spirituals.[105]

The 1930s

Between 1930 and 1934 Burleigh's output of folk songs and spirituals was noticeably slimmer than previously. It included another issue of "Nobody Knows de Trouble I've Seen" (1930); "Dry Bones" and "Who Dat Yondah?" (1931); "Little Child of Mary" (1932); and a choral setting of "Mister Banjo" (1934) to words by Alston Burleigh.

The Creole song "Musieu Bainjo" ("Mister Banjo"), from St. Charles Parish in Louisiana, was first printed in *Slave Songs of the United States*. Satirical in nature, this is another song in which Burleigh used the African "snap" on the words "Look at" and "Doesn't" in the opening bars. In *Slave Songs* editor William Francis Allen calls "Mr. Banjo" an attempt of some enterprising Afro-American to write a "French song." Translated, the jaunty words of "Mister Banjo" are:

Look at that darkey there, Mister Banjo,
Doesn't he put on airs!
Hat cock'd on one side, Mister Banjo,
Walking stick in hand, Mister Banjo
Boots that go "crank, crank," Mister Banjo;
Look at that darkey there, Mister Banjo,
Doesn't he put on airs!

In 1934 Ricordi published an SATB arrangement, a cappella, of "Mister Banjo," one still available through Belwin-Mills. With second and third verses by Alston Burleigh, the piece was dedicated to the Westminster Choir, which first performed it in 1934 under the direction of Dr. John Finley Richardson.

The text of "Dry Bones," usually comically interpreted, came from Ezekiel 37 and deals with the resurrection of life from the bones of the dead. Roland Hayes described "Dry Bones," a spiritual he also set, as

> an example of how the gifted Aframerican preacher adapted himself to the limitations of the congregation. To heighten the effect and to ease the way to the understanding of his flock he impersonates the questioning layman in his congregation: "Tell me, how did de bones get together wid de leg bone?"[106]

In 1931 Burleigh arranged an organ accompaniment of "Who Dat Yondah?" for Eva Jessye. This spiritual is possibly derived from "O Who Dat Coming Ober Yonder?" as sung in Calhoun in Lowndes County, Alabama. Interviewed by the writer in Ann Arbor, Michigan, in August 1986, Dr. Jessye was unable to locate a copy of the work. Dr. Jessye (b. 1895) was choral director for the premiere of *Porgy and Bess* (1935), one of the highlights in her colorful career as a professional musician.

The words of "Little Child of Mary" were adapted from a Christmas spiritual, "De New-Born Baby," from South Carolina where it was sung by the fishermen on the Atlantic Coast. One possible variant is "Mary Had a Baby" from the Atlantic Ocean island of St. Helena between South American and Africa.[107]

The Last Spirituals

Between 1935 and Burleigh's death in 1949, Allison lists the publication of only four thus far unpublished spirituals and three songs of a religious nature. "Joshua Fit de Battl' ob Jericho" (1935), based on another biblical text (Joshua 6), is unpretentious, but nevertheless stirring. Burleigh's clever miniature suggestion in the accompaniment of a trumpet fanfare is a perfect embellishment. Under the final phrase "An' de walls come tumblin' down" chords of fourths and fifths descend *precipitando* to good effect. "O Lord, Have Mercy on Me" (Ricordi), another spiritual, and "Silent Prayer" ("May the Words"), termed a "Response to Silent Prayer" (Jewish Sabbath Service, Emanu-El) were also issued in 1935.[108]

Of the spirituals of 1938 – "Hold On" ("Keep Your Hand on the Plow"), "Walk Together, Children," and "You Goin' to Reap Jus' What You Sow" – not one is included in *The Spirituals of Harry T. Burleigh,* issued by Belwin-Mills in 1984.

In 1940 Burleigh set John Oxenham's "In Christ There Is No East or West," which was published by the Protestant Episcopal Church's Pension Fund. Oxenham, whose real name was W. A. Dunkerley, was over eighty when he died in 1941. He was a prolific writer of novels, essays, and popular verse, especially poems that dealt with World War I, many of which "enjoyed a vogue as best-sellers." His "Hymn for Men at the Front" sold eight million copies.[109]

Only one of Burleigh's publications is listed after 1944 by Allison: "Lawd Whatcha Gonna Do Wid Me?" with collaborator J. C. Johnson (1949, Record Music Publishing Company). A more likely confirmation, unless the song was finished in the years before senility overtook Burleigh, was related in a letter dated June 22, 1987, to the author from Gary M. Schuster of The Song Writer's Guild. This agency became administrator of Record Music in 1979. Schuster stated: "According to ASCAP's listing of the works of J. C. Johnson the song was written by Johnson alone and published by Record Music." J. C. Johnson (1896-1981), who spent most of his adult life in New York, was best known as a jazz pianist and composer of popular songs. Some of his collaborators were Fats Waller, Fletcher Henderson, and George Whiting. In 1940 Johnson, a member of ASCAP, founded the New York Crescendo Club, an organization for black songwriters.[110]

The forty-eight spirituals in *The Spirituals of Harry T. Burleigh* are excellent representations of Burleigh's arrangements. Ideally the collection would have included each of the dedicatory inscriptions, a definite plus for those published separately by Ricordi earlier.

Philip Miller, author and critic, commented:

Purists have criticized Burleigh's arrangements as inappropriate for folk music. This misrepresents his intention. In his time the folklorists had barely begun their work. Burleigh gave us a kind of idealized spiritual, a transformation of the melodies into art songs very much in the manner of the Brahms Deutsche Volkslieder.[111]

Burleigh is quoted by Charlotte Murray as saying:

Spirituals are the only legacy of slavery of which the race can be proud. Into the making of these spirituals was poured the aspirations of a race in bondage whose religion, intensely felt, was their only hope and comfort. They rank with the great folk music of the world.[112]

Singers of the Spirituals

To large extent Burleigh as a singer popularized his own arrangements of black music. But even broader exposure was given them by John McCormack, George Hamlin, Paul Althouse, Paul Robeson, Roland Hayes, Evan Williams, Marian Anderson, Christine Miller, Mary Jordan, Oscar Seagle, and a host of other prominent singers during World War I and the two decades following.

Reviews of a recital by contralto Mary Jordan in Aeolian Hall on November 15, 1917, show that Burleigh's spirituals were treated well on a "flower bedecked stage," before a capacity audience: "An interesting part of the program was one devoted to negro spirituals arranged by H. T. Burleigh."[113]

In 1925, when Marian Anderson won an engagement to sing with the New York Philharmonic after besting 300 contestants, she included Burleigh's "Deep River" and "Heav'n, Heav'n" in the concert at Lewisohn Stadium.[114]

McCormack, Robeson, Hamlin, Hayes, Anderson and Seagle, all frequent travellers abroad, spread the word of black people's joys and sorrows through their own special talents, making this music a viable staple in concert repertoire.

By 1920 Roland Hayes had been accepted as the first gifted black concert singer, thus, in a way, breaking the ground for Robeson's emergence. Robeson's first concert was given in Greenwich Village in 1925. A powerful figure on stage, his delivery of the spirituals endeared him to large audiences everywhere.

> Robeson has sung spirituals to appreciative audiences all over the world. . . . His physical appearance, voice range and control, and tremendous emotional color and variety are only a few of the reasons why he is a spiritual singer par excellence.[115]

Alain Locke has compared Robeson's "robust and dramatic rendering" of the spirituals with Hayes's "subdued, ecstatic and mystic" delivery of them.[116] Robeson's accompanist, Lawrence Brown, who was soon to arrange spirituals himself, sometimes joined in at a concert, singing the spirituals in his high tenor voice with Robeson.

> Larry Brown, who went abroad . . . heard the great folk music of other lands and dedicated himself, as did Harry Burleigh before him, to showing that this was a great music, not just "plantation songs."[117]

Speaking of the spread of the spirituals by black concert singers, James Weldon Johnson wrote in the mid-1920s:

> The superlatively fine rendition of these songs by Roland Hayes, Paul Robeson, Marian Anderson and Julius Bledsoe has brought them to the highest point of celebrity and placed the classic stamp upon them. Today it is appropriate for any artist, however great, to program one or a group of these spirituals.[118]

The writer of an item in *The New Yorker*, January 16, 1926, seemed to feel that the situation had become too much of a Good Thing:

> The latest popular diversion of the intelligentsia seems to consist in summoning the colored hall-boy and inviting him to sing songs about Moses. . . . Certain social aspirants are exploiting every one suspected of African blood, and one wonders what a sensitive negro thinks of it.

. . . J. Rosamond Johnson's collection of negro spirituals probably started the fad, and it has not been sluggish about getting into concert halls. Roland Hayes draws huge audiences in Carnegie Hall, and Paul Robeson, assisted by that impish genius, Lawrence Brown, seems to be not far behind in popularity. Mr. Johnson, himself, paired with a young tenor named Taylor Gordon, has acquired a following, and Julius Bledsoe is almost a fetish in some circles.

. . . All of the singers of negro music are gifted with unusually beautiful voices, but some of them are beginning to show signs of contact with people who think them Just Too Wonderful. . . . If you'll pardon a bromidium, our talented colored singers will have to be saved from their friends.

Seagle the Specialist

Baritone Oscar Seagle was reputedly the first singer to include an entire group of spiritual arrangements in a significant vocal recital. He felt strongly enough about their worth to keep them in his repertoire after other, racially prejudiced white singers had dropped them. Though no written dedication to Seagle can be verified, there is some opinion that Burleigh arranged several of the spirituals especially for him.

> In the domain of the negro spiritual Seagle has been able to offer unique arrangements, inasmuch as he, and he alone, has had the opportunity to sing from manuscript the arrangements of various spirituals which H. T. Burleigh has made during the past few months. Recently Mr. Burleigh furnished him with additional arrangements which will be used during the coming season.[119]

Beginning even as early as 1916 Seagle and his accompanist Henry Doering were to continually receive abundant publicity for programming Burleigh's spirituals. Tennessee-born Seagle, who for his prowess in the sport might have become a professional baseball player, chose to sing, channeling his talents toward the wider audience of the concert stage rather than to that of the opera house.

A large advertisement in the *Courier*, October 26, 1916, mentioning Seagle's assets, praised his "inimitable" singing of Afro-American melodies. An item announcing Seagle's first Brooklyn concert in the Music Hall at the Academy of Music on March 25, 1917, gave Burleigh some recognition also, for it was the first time Seagle had used the composer's arrangements.

> Mr. Burleigh, a negro himself, knows better than any other composer how to place them in an artistic setting without violating their spirit. Mr. Seagle . . . knows the negro thoroughly, has probed the depths of his emotional life, and . . . better than any other singer, understands the interpretation of Mr. Burleigh's arrangements.[120].

A review of this concert the following week listed Burleigh's spirituals – "Father Abraham," "I Don't Feel No-Ways Tired," "I Want to Be Ready," "Dig My Grave," and "Jesus Healed the Sick" – as the "special feature" of the recital.

> Mr. Seagle's interpretation of them was splendid and he was obliged to repeat several of them in response to the hearty applause of the audience. He called upon Mr. Burleigh, who was in the audience to share the applause.[121]

A review from *Brooklyn Life* reprinted in the *Courier* without mentioning Burleigh's name nevertheless complimented his work on the spirituals. Speaking of Seagle's program of art songs the reviewer wrote:

> Yet more important than all these – at least to the inquisitive – was the group of negro spirituals. These expressions of the negro's deep religious experience form the one true body of folksong that America has produced. . . . The composer has come who can set them, making use of all the devices of civilized music but without vitiating their spirit. . . . Like all folksongs the spirituals have not been easy to record . . . so to sing them as they must be sung . . . requires

an artist who knows instinctively and from association how the negro of slavery times sang them. Such is Seagle.[122]

A summary of the same notice which praised at length vital interpreter Seagle's artistry, keen musical intelligence, and technique said:

> The most important part of the program was the group of negro spirituals. . . . In Oscar Seagle these songs have found their true interpreter. . . . Others have sung arrangements of them, but always there has been lacking what Seagle furnished – the thorough appreciation of, and the ability to convey, the deep underlying spirit of the compositions.[123]

In late April of 1917 Seagle dared to sing spirituals on a Southern formal concert. Editor Liebling of the *Courier*, aware of Seagle's appearance at a Little Rock, Arkansas, festival, wrote: "His versatility was the surprise of the evening. The old negro folksongs were rendered with unfailing truth to nature. In them he put much poetic feeling."[124] Seagle received a letter from the director of the festival, saying that the programmed spirituals had been widely discussed, with the consensus that they had made a lasting favorable impression. When asked prior to the Little Rock concert how he predicted the Southerners' estimation of the songs, Seagle replied:

> These songs were heard by them first when the old mammy crooned them to make the child sleep. They have a firm place in the heart of every true Southerner and . . . awaken all the old memories and revive the happiest days of a man's life.[125]

At a concert for the choir boys at the Cathedral of St. John the Divine in New York on May 16, 1917, Seagle combined art songs with Burleigh's spirituals,

> camp meeting songs that Mr. Seagle gave with a Southern relish. He encored "I Want to Be Ready," among the American melodies, adding at the close the beautiful "Swing Low, Sweet Chariot" twice over and "Brother Andrew, Where You Been?" songs that lay on the borderland between smiles and tears, and were much applauded.[126]

The following week Seagle performed in Kansas City for the first time, at that city's spring festival, where "he was compelled to add many extras, among them three old negro folksongs belonging to the fifties which were in his handling superior to all the folksongs of the whole world ever heard here."[127]

In an unstinting and comprehensive article entitled "The Negro Spiritual," Seagle himself defined the meaning and traced the history of the American folk song and the spiritual. He had known the songs since boyhood as the son of a lay minister and as a spectator at black revival meetings.

> There are few memories so vivid to me as those of the old darky preacher exhorting his congregation to seek salvation and leading them in deeply stirring emotional outbursts of song. Frequently in their singing they would lose control of themselves and the verses would be punctuated with cries of praise of their Maker.
>
> Although familiar with their beauty and loving them with a tenderness that only the association of youth can give, I have never been able to use them in my programs because of the lack of arrangements suitable for the recital hall. . . . Recently, however, Henry T. Burleigh submitted to me such arrangements as I considered to be just what I had been seeking for so long a time. I used them first in my Brooklyn recital this spring. The result was what I had anticipated. Their appeal was instantaneous. My audience could not get enough of them, and after repeating the five in my group I was obliged to add "Deep River."
>
> . . . Their singing has been a great joy but present certain difficulties that I want to emphasize. As I stated above, failure is reserved for the singer who in singing the spirituals would follow strictly the notation and rhythm of the modern arrangement. Their folksong character argues the presence in them of peculiarities of rhythm and interval that our inflexible notation cannot record. When, therefore, they are sung by one who has not known them in their original state, it is exceedingly hard to catch their elusive charm. Of course the singing of the negro was not an artistic effort in our

sense of the term. He sang because of the necessity for expression, for the pure joy of singing. And it is into this spirit that I try to enter when I sing them. I let myself get right into the spirit, relying upon my memory of the old revivals and striving for the same frame of mind as was the negro preacher's. In this connection few compliments have been so gratifying as Mr. Burleigh's when he said: "Seagle sings the spirituals just like a negro preacher."

Apart from the value the spirituals possess in themselves, they may ultimately serve the same purpose as have the folksongs of other countries in the development of the higher art forms. . . . The fact that rag-time took one of its elements from the spiritual does not damn the spiritual, but rather would prove its all-appealing quality.[128]

Depending on the type audience, Seagle often gave an informal talk with his presentation of the spirituals, a practice particularly suitable at the college and university level, though sometimes a brief lecture accompanied more formal concerts. Seagle concertized and taught without respite during 1917. At a November 26 recital in Aeolian Hall featuring a group of spirituals, he included Burleigh's newly-arranged "Swing Low,Sweet Chariot." Several of the spirituals had to be repeated. Of the performance one fastidious critic wrote:

The arrangements might be improved – there are rhythmic and harmonic possibilities which Mr. Burleigh has entirely failed to realize – but it would be hard to imagine anything better than Mr. Seagle's inimitable singing of the truly unique songs.[129]

Success followed success for Seagle with the spirituals. One coup d'etat was accomplished with a concert in Chattanooga on December 10, 1917, with native pianist Augusta Bates, the first time Burleigh's spirituals had been presented in that city, though Seagle had used his art songs there on a former occasion. Besides an arrangement of the folk song "The Dove and the Lily," Seagle performed "Nobody Knows the Trouble I've Seen," "Brother Andrew, Where You Been?" "I Am Seeking the Holy City," "Is Dar Anybody

Here," and "Jesus Heals the Sick." (Neither publication dates nor publishers have been traced for the last four of these.)

> The singing of the plantation melodies in their artistic new settings by the Southern baritone, accompanied by the Southern pianist was received by the Southern audience with a veritable ovation.[130]

Seagle's enthusiasm and that of other prominent singers for the spirituals continued for several years, solidifying Burleigh's place as a master arranger of what he knew best. Burleigh's spirituals, effectively used in concert for decades, have enjoyed a longer vogue than did his art songs.

The consistent programming of Burleigh's music from 1903 to 1960 in a typical American cultural city has been confirmed by Jean E. Snyder's studies at the University of Pittsburgh in the spring of 1987. Her data revealed that with rare exceptions several of Burleigh's spirituals and art songs had been presented in Pittsburgh each year throughout this time period. Leading the list was "Deep River," programmed or sung as an encore at least forty-three times.

Other Arrangers of Burleigh's Solo Spirituals

Contrary to common belief Burleigh himself was not responsible for all ensemble arrangements of the spirituals made from his solo versions. One of the most prolific arrangers was Ruggero Vené, engaged by Ricordi, whose 102 arrangements largely retained the essence and characteristics of Burleigh's work. Italian-born Vené (1897-1961) became an American citizen in 1944, having arrived in the United States in 1932. A student of Respighi, his previous education was in Italy and France. He was a choral conductor and professor at Columbia University and also on the faculty at Washington University. Some of Vené's own compositions include "Rossaccio," a symphonic poem; a string quartet; and a string quintet for piano and strings.

Another of the better-known arrangers, Canadian Geoffrey O'Hara (1882-1967), whose first career was banking, became a researcher in native Indian music for the Secretary of the Interior in

1914. Like Burleigh he was a charter member of ASCAP, and served
as its director from 1942-45. Some of his famous songs are "K-K-K-
Katy," "Give a Man a Horse He Can Ride," and "I Walked Today
Where Jesus Walked."

Among other arrangers, Deems Taylor (1885-1966), eminent
composer, writer, and music critic, made at least three arrangements
of Burleigh's solo spirituals.

Hector MacCarthy (1888-1973), also a Canadian, composer, music educator, author, and pianist, studied at Juilliard and with Dudley
Buck. He was an accompanist with the Metropolitan Opera touring
company and for tenor Craig Campbell and other prominent singers.

Victor Harris (1869-1943), song composer, author, and teacher,
was a vocal coach for the Metropolitan Opera as early as 1893. He
later organized and directed the original St. Cecilia Club concerts.

Compositions by arranger Nathaniel Clifford Page (1866-1956) include songs, cantatas, instrumental works, and stage scores. Page was
an editor for Oliver Ditson, Carl Fischer, and Theodore Presser music publishers, and taught at Columbia University from 1920 to 1928.

Lesser-known arrangers of Burleigh's spirituals and art songs are
John Hyatt Brewer, George H. Pickering, Jerry Sears, G. Ackley
Brower, and organist-pianist Carl Wiesemann. Wiesemann (d. 1954)
spent a good part of his teaching career in Texas at Baylor and Texas
Woman's Universities. An outstanding member of the American
Guild of Organists, Wiesemann was a choral conductor and organist
at St. Matthew's Protestant Episcopal Cathedral in Dallas, Texas. His
successful efforts toward accrediting the private piano teacher in
Texas will long be remembered.

The Burleigh Touch

Certain pertinent characteristics emerge clearly from an examination of Burleigh's scores. Rather than including all available verses,
Burleigh wisely knew when to quit. Brevity, in this instance, has
partially accounted for their interesting presentation. There is always
a tempo indication though the lack of metronome markings allows
some interpretive license to be taken at the individual singer's discretion. Addition of extra syllables, usually an "a" (e.g., "ring-a, "a-
trembling," "in-a," "a-rowin'," "chill-a," and the like), besides

skillfully carrying rhythm and melody forward, gives a more accurate speech pattern of the black dialect of the time. Roland Hayes called the phrase repetitions "phenomena of imaginative, poetic intoxication that . . . identifies the person with the mood."[131]

Allison, comparing the spirituals as arranged by Burleigh and others, based on vocal scoring, meter, rhythm, harmony, texture, form, and dynamics, places Burleigh midway between the outer limits of the simple and straightforward and those of the extremely sophisticated.

These songs were arranged carefully and tastefully, retaining the necessary wit, reservation, poignancy, and hopefulness that were so much a part of the Afro-American culture. Burleigh's accompaniments are enjoyably playable, clever, full of flavor, and lie well within the piano idiom. As Galen Lurwick, an experienced vocal accompanist now at Missouri Southern State College in Joplin so aptly put it, "Of course, I know H. T. Burleigh through his spirituals, and no one ever did them better than that. He was unbelievable!"[132]

PART THREE:
Catalog of Music, Discography, Bibliography

Catalog of Music

Burleigh's works, listed chronologically according to publication date, comprise three categories: Art Songs and Religious Songs (those specified by a particular poet); Spirituals and Negro Folk Songs; and Instrumental Works.

Publishers are abbreviated by the following symbols:

BM   Belwin-Mills Publishing Corp., 15800 N. W. 48th Ave., Miami FL 33014

CC   The Century Company; sole agent: Ashley Dealers, Inc., 133 Industrial Ave., Hasbrouck Heights NJ 07604

CF   Carl Fischer, Inc., 62 Cooper Square, New York NY 10003

E   Episcopal (Protestant Episcopal Church Pension Fund, New York)

EE   Congregation Emanu-El of New York City

FC   Franco Columbo, Inc.; sole agent: Belwin-Mills

GM   Galaxy Music Corporation, 131 W. 86th St., New York NY 10024

GR   G. Ricordi and Company, Inc.; sole agent: G. Schirmer, Inc.

GS   G. Schirmer, Inc., 866 3rd Ave., New York NY 10022

HVT   Harry von Tilzer Publishing Company; sole agent: Theodore Presser

NCC   North Carolina College, now North Carolina Central University, Durham NC 27707

OD   Oliver Ditson Company; sole agent: Theodore Presser

RM   Record Music Publishing Company; sole agent: Songwriters Guild, 276 5th Ave., New York NY 10001

SG   St. George's Church, 209 E. 16th St., New York NY 10003

TC   Talladega College, Talladega AL 35160

TP   Theodore Presser Company, Presser Place, Bryn Mawr PA 19010

WMC   William Maxwell Company; sole agent: Theodore Presser

Very few of the art songs and no instrumental works are now available from the original publishers. However, most of the spirituals, both for solo and ensemble, are accessible through Belwin-Mills Publishing Corporation.

Though total catalog information on each entry is not complete, copies of the works can be found at the places whose abbreviated symbols follow:

ACUP   Marian Anderson Collection, Van Pelt Library, University of Pennsylvania

ASU   Arizona State University Library

CLSU   University of Southern California Library

CLUP   Carnegie Library of Pittsburgh

CSt   Stanford University Libraries

ECHS   Erie County Historical Society Library, Erie PA

ECPL   Erie County Public Library, Erie PA

IaU   University of Iowa Library

ICN   Newberry Library of Chicago

IU   University of Illinois Library

JCY   James Weldon Johnson Collection, Yale University Library

MB   Boston Public Library

MH   Harvard University Library

MI   Michigan State University Library

MSRC   Moorland-Spingarn Research Center, Howard University

NB   Brooklyn Public Library

NBuG	Grosvenor Reference Division, Buffalo, NY, and Erie County Public Library
NcU	University of North Carolina Library
NIC	Cornell University Library
NN	New York Public Library
OCl	Cleveland Public Library
OO	Oberlin College Library
PP	Free Library of Philadelphia
PPULC	Union Library Catalogue of Pennsylvania
RPB	Brown University Library
SCNYPL	Schomburg Collection, New York Public Library
TNF	Fisk University Library
ViU	University of Virginia Library
WaU	University of Washington Library

Catalog numbers in the 784-B category, one designated in the Dewey Decimal System for Vocal Music, are used for the Schomburg Collection. Those numbered 09760– are in the Brooklyn Public Library. All V 1, 2, and 3 numbers belong to the James Weldon Johnson Collection. The Marian Anderson Collection lists Burleigh holdings by box numbers, and the Moorland-Spingarn Collection by 1, 2, 3, or 4 BV with numbers following.

Many of the spirituals arranged for choral ensemble are not listed separately in the collections at NB, but rather in general categories of SSA, SATB, TTBB, etc., bearing the numbers 0976006 through 0976010.

The Spirituals of Harry T. Burleigh (Belwin-Mills, 1984), containing forty-eight spirituals with piano accompaniment, includes all of those listed in the Catalog of Music except "Oh Rock Me Julie," "Don't You Dream of Turning Back," "Scandalize My Name," "De Creation," "Dar's a Meeting Here Tonight," "Run to Jesus," "Ezekiel saw de Wheel," "Who's Dat Yondah?," "Dry Bones," "Little Child of Mary," "Mister Banjo," "O Lord, Have Mercy Upon Me," "Hold On," and "Walk Together Children."

One spiritual and one art song are not mentioned in the Catalog of Works, due to incomplete information: "In de Lord," Box 181, ACUP; and "When the Twilight Shadows Fall," ms, JCY. The date of composition of another song, "Lawd, Whatcha Gonna Do Wid Me?" with words by J. C. Johnson, is uncertain, but according to Roland Lewis Allison was published by Record Music Company in New York in 1949. A spokesman for Songwriter's Guild, however, places the song's publication by Record as 1934, with Johnson as the sole composer.

In the following Catalog of Music, items are grouped by date of composition, which usually coincides with the date of publication. Each entry includes as much of the following as is known:

"P" or "S" indicates interest to professionals or students, based on audience appeal as well as difficulty;

"*" indicates a work well received and/or much performed during the composer's lifetime;

"**" indicates suitability for today's repertoire;

title;

tempo, MM, or expression markings;

durations cited for either the whole work, each movement, or each segment;

key and/or range (voice);

whether vocal solo, vocal ensemble, instrumental, or orchestral;

text source or poet;

"R" indicates that the work has been recorded (see Discography);

publication information including city, abbreviation of publisher, date;

premiere performance;

abbreviations of libraries or collections possessing copies with their catalog numbers where available.

Art Songs and Religious Songs

1898

1. S. *Three Songs*
   "If You But Knew;" Fervently; 5 pp.; med. in E (bar./mezzo);
   solo w/piano acc.; text trans. from French source
   ["The Martian"].
   "Life;" med. (bar./mezzo); solo w/piano acc.; John Boyle
   O'Reilly.
   "A Birthday Song;" med. (bar./mezzo); solo w/piano acc.;
   Christina Rossetti.
   New York: GS, 1898; SCNYPL (784-B), NB (0976049), MSRC
   (2BV-14.28), NN.

1901

2. S. *Plantation Melodies Old and New*; 18 pp.; med.;solos w/piano
   acc.
   "I Doan' Want Fu' t' Stay Hyeah No Longah;" R. E. Phillips.
   "My Lawd's A-writing Down Time;" R. E. Phillips.
   "When de Debble Comes 'Round;" R. E. Phillips.
   "De Blackbird an' de Crow;" R. E. Phillips.
   "My Merlindy Brown;" James E. Campbell.
   "Negro Lullaby;" James E. Campbell.
   "An Ante-Bellum Sermon;" Paul Laurence Dunbar.
   New York: GS, 1901; SCNYPL (784-B), NB (0976041), MSRC
   (4BV-16.13), JCY (V3B92P69), NN, MI, PP, MH, NCU, ViU, IU,
   PPULC, RPB.

1902

3. S. "Thy Heart;" med. or low; solo w/piano acc.; A. V. Williams
   Jackson.
   New York: GS, 1902; MSRC (2BV-14.30).

4. S. *Plantation Songs*
   "Ring, My Bawnjer, Ring;" med.; solo w/piano acc.; SSA;
   James E. Campbell.

"You'll Git Dar in de Mornin';" med.; solo w/piano acc.; SSA; Frank L. Stanton.

New York: GS, 1902; NB (0976051), MSRC (4BV-16.15 and 4BV-16.28), NN.

5. "Sleep, Li'l Chile, Go Sleep;" in G; solo w/piano acc.; George V. Hobart.

New York: HVT, 1902.

6. "Love's Garden;" 6 pp.; high; solo w/piano acc.; M. Heuchling.

New York: WMC, 1902; SCNYPL (784-B), MSRC (2BV-14.2).

1903

7. S. *"Jean;" Fervently, with good rhythm; 3 pp., 2 min.; low in B flat, med. in D, high in E flat; solo w/piano acc.; Frank L. Stanton; R.

New York: WMC, 1903; Philadelphia: TP, 1914; SCNYPL (784-B), MSRC (1BV-13.32); ECHS.

8. S. *"Mammy's Li'l Baby;" In rocking rhythm, tenderly; 3 pp., 2 min.; low in D, high in F; solo w/piano acc.; Louise Alston Burleigh.

New York: WMC, 1903; MSRC (2BV-14.8).

1904

9. "Heigh-Ho!;" low in B flat, high in D flat; solo w/piano acc.; James E. Campbell.

New York: WMC, 1904; MSRC (1BV-13.20).

10. "Love's Pleading;" low; solo w/piano acc.; Leontine Stanfield.

New York: WMC, 1904; MSRC (2BV-14.5).

11. "One Day;" med.; solo w/piano acc.; Mary Blackwell Sterling.

New York: WMC, 1904; MSRC (2BV-14.14).

12. "I Lo'e My Jean;" low in E flat, high in G; solo w/piano acc.; Robert Burns.

New York: WMC, 1904; MSRC (1BV-13.15).

13.   S. *"Just My Love and I;" Andante con moto; 4 pp., 2 min.; low in
      D, med. in F, high; solo w/piano acc.; Louise Alston Burleigh.
      New York: WMC, 1904; SCNYPL (784-B), MSRC (1BV-13.34).

14.   P.S. *,**"O Perfect Love;" 6 pp., 4 min.; low, high in F; solo
      w/piano acc.; D. F. Blomfield.
      New York: WMC, 1904; Philadelphia: TP, 1914, 1922; ECHS,
      MSRC (2BV-14.17), CLUP.

15.   "If Life Be a Dream;" 6 pp.; low in D, med. in F, high in A flat;
      solo w/piano acc.; Frank L. Stanton.
      New York: WMC, 1904; SCNYPL (784-B), MSRC (1BV-13.25).

16.   "O Why Art Thou Not Near Me;" med. in E flat, high in G; solo
      w/piano acc.; Anonymous.
      New York: WMC, 1904; MSRC (2BV-14.18).

17.   "We Would See Jesus;" Anonymous.
      New York: WMC, 1904.

18.   "While Shepherds Watched Their Flocks;" in F; mixed voices;
      Nahum Tate;
      New York: WMC, 1904.

19.   "Father to Thee;" Anonymous.
      New York: WMC, 1904.

20.   "The Way O' the World;" low in C, med., high in E flat; solo
      w/piano acc.; Frank L. Stanton.
      New York: WMC, 1904; MSRC (2BV-14.37).

21.   "Waiting;" With calm intensity; low, med. in D, high in F; solo
      w/piano acc.; Martha Gilbert Dickinson.
      New York: WMC, 1904; MSRC (2BV-14.36).

22.   "Ho-ro! My Nut Brown Maid;" solo w/piano acc.; Scottish folk-
      song.
      Unpublished.

1905

23.   "Through Peace to Light;" low in D flat, high in F; solo w/piano
        acc.; Adelaide Proctor.
        New York: WMC, 1905.

24.   "Apart;" Gravely but not too slow; low in B flat, high in D flat;
        solo w/piano acc.; Frances Bacon Paine.
        New York: WMC, 1905.

25.   "O Love of a Day;" low in E flat, high in G; solo w/piano acc.;
        Randolph Hartley.
        New York: WMC, 1905; MSRC (2BV-14.13).

26.   "Dreamland;" solo w/piano acc.; Louise Alston Burleigh.
        New York: WMC, 1905.

27.   "And As the Gulls Soar;" low in F, med., high in A flat; solo
        w/piano acc.; Frances Bacon Paine.
        New York: WMC, 1905; MSRC (1BV-13.2).

28.   P.S. *"Tide;" low in D flat, med., high in F; solo w/piano acc.;
        Frances Bacon Paine.
        New York: WMC, 1905; MSRC (2BV-14.31).

29.   "Achievement;" solo w/piano acc.; Frances Bacon Paine.
        New York: WMC, 1905.

30.   "Request;" low in E flat, high in G; solo w/piano acc.; Laurence
        Hope.
        New York: WMC, 1905.

31.   "Once in Royal David's City;" solo w/piano acc.; C. F. Alexander.
        New York: WMC, 1905.

1906

32.   "Rockin' in de Win';" women's and men's voices; Traditional.
        New York: WMC, 1906.

33.   "Just A-Wearying for You;" low in D flat, high in F; solo w/piano
        acc.; Frank L. Stanton.
        New York: WMC, 1906.

34.   "Malay Boat Song;" low in B flat, high in D; solo w/piano acc.; Laurence Hope.
       New York: WMC, 1906; MSRC (2BV-14.7).

35.   "Come Unto Me;" in F; SATB w/piano/organ acc.; text from St. Matthew 2:28.
       New York: WMC, 1906; Philadelphia: TP, n.d.

36.   "Hail to the King;" low in F, high in B flat; mixed voices w/piano/organ acc.; E. H. Sears.
       New York: WMC, 1906.

37.   S. **"Just Because;" Andante moderato; 6 pp., 3 min.; low in B flat, med., high in D; solo w/piano acc.; Harry T. Burleigh.
       New York: WMC, 1906; Philadelphia: TP, 1914; SCNYPL (784-B), MSRC (1BV-13.33).

38.   S. "Love's Dawning;" Dreamily; 3 pp., 1 min.; med. high in F, high in A; solo w/piano acc.; Louise Alston Burleigh.
       New York: WMC, 1906; MSRC (2BV-14.1), SCNYPL (784-B).

39.   S. *"Through Love's Eternity;" low in F, high in A flat; solo w/piano acc.; C. C. Stoddard.
       New York: WMC, 1906.

40.   S. *"Perhaps;" Andante cantabile; 4 pp., 3 min.; low in F, high in A flat; solo w/piano acc.; Louise Alston Burleigh.
       New York: WMC, 1906; Philadelphia: TP, 1914; printed in *The Etude*, December, 1919.

1907

41.   S. *Two Plantation Songs*
       "I'll Be Dar to Meet Yo';" 6 pp.; med.; solo w/piano acc.; Beverly Garrison.
       New York: WMC, 1907; published separately by WMC in 1905; SCNYPL (784-B), MSRC (3BV-15.25).
       "Keep a Good Grip on de Hoe;" 5 pp.; low, med.; solo w/piano acc.; Howard Weeden.
       New York: WMC, 1907; published separately by WMC in 1905; SCNYPL (784-B), MSRC (4BV-16.1).

42. "Since Molly Went Away;" low in C, high in E flat; solo w/piano acc; Frank L. Stanton; R.
     New York: WMC, 1907; MSRC (2BV-14.24).

43. "Somewhere;" for soprano in D; solo w/piano acc.; James Whedon.
     New York: WMC: 1907.

44. S. "You Ask Me If I Love You;" Andante con espressione; 5 pp., 2:30; low in D flat, med. in F, high in A flat; solo w/piano acc.; Lillian Bennett Thompson.
     New York: WMC, 1907; MSRC (2BV-14.39).

45. "Savior Divine;" low, high; sacred song w/piano/organ acc.; R. Palmer.
     New York: WMC, 1907.

1908

46. "The Last Goodbye;" mixed voices w/piano acc.; Harry T. Burleigh.
     New York: WMC, 1907; Philadelphia: TP, n.d.

47. "Pilgrim;" sacred song w/piano acc.; Lawrence Perry.
     New York: WMC, 1908.

48. "Now Sleeps the Crimson Petal;" low in B flat, high in D flat; solo w/piano acc.; Alfred Tennyson.
     New York: WMC, 1908.

49. "Two Words;" low in F, high in A flat; solo w/piano acc.; Edward Oxenford.
     New York: WMC, 1908.

1909

50. P.S. "Yours Alone;" 6 pp., 2 min.; low, med., high in A; solo w/piano acc.; Edward Oxenford.
     New York: WMC, 1909; MSRC (2BV-14.41).

51. "Carry Me Back to the Pine Woods;" 3 pp.; low in G, med., high in B flat; solo w/piano acc.; Anonymous.
     New York: WMC, 1909; SCNYPL (784-B), MSRC (1BV-13.5).

52. "Myrra;" low in F, med., high in A flat; solo w/piano acc.; Anonymous.
New York: WMC, 1909; MSRC (2BV-14.11).

53. P.S. **Negro Minstrel Melodies* (ed. by Burleigh); 21 songs; 52 pp.,
each 1 to 2 min.; med.; solos w/piano acc.; James E. Bland,
Stephen Foster, etc.
New York: GS, 1909; NB (0976027), SCNYPL (784.7-B), CLUP,
NN, RPB, MI, PP, TNF, MKH, NBuG, PPULC.

1910

54. "It Was Nothing But a Rose;" low, high; solo w/piano acc.; Anonymous.
New York: WMC, 1910; MSRC (1BV-13.31).

1911

55. "Tarry With Me, O My Savior;" sacred song w/piano/organ acc.;
C. L. Smith.
New York: WMC, 1911.

1912

56. "Child Jesus Comes from Heav'nly Height;" sacred song
w/piano/organ acc.; Anonymous.
New York: GR, 1912.

1914

57. P.S. **"Mother O' Mine;" solo w/piano acc., TTBB; Rudyard
Kipling.
New York: GR, 1914.

58. P.S. **Two Poems*
"Bring Her Again to Me;" Andante; 2 pp., 1:30; low in F,
med.; high; solo w/piano acc.; W. E. Henley.
New York: GR, 1914; New York: GM, 1932 under the title
"Bring Her Again, O Western Wind;" MSRC (2BV-14.33).

"The Spring, My Dear, Is No Longer Spring;" Andante sostenuto; 3 pp., 3 min; low A flat, med., high; solo w/piano acc.; W. E. Henley.
New York: GR, 1914; MSRC (2BV-14.33).

59.   P.S. "Elysium;" Andante cantabile; 4 pp., 2 min.; low in C, high in E flat; solo w/piano acc.; James Weldon Johnson.
New York: GR, 1914; MSRC (1BV-13.11), SCNYPL (784-B), JCY (V2J632E196).

60.   P.S. **"The Hour Glass;" Andante moderato; 4 pp., 2 min; low, med. in B flat, high in D flat; solo w/piano acc.; Alexander Groves.
New York: GR, 1914; SCNYPL (784-B), MSRC (1BV-13.24).

61.   P.S. **"O Southland;" 7 pp.; in C; 4-part male chorus and mixed voices, a cappella; James Weldon Johnson.
New York: GR, 1914; TTBB, 1915, 1919; SATB, 1919, 1929; JCY (V2J63202 and V2J63202b), SCNYPL (784.6-B), NB (0976005), CLUP, NN.

62.   "His Word is Love;" low in F, high in A; solo w/piano acc.; Fred G. Bowles.
New York: GR, 1914; MSRC (1BV-13.23).

63.   P.S. **Saracen Songs (a cycle)
"Almona;" Andante con moto; 3 pp., 1 min.; low, med., high in A; solo w/piano acc.; Fred G. Bowles.
"O Night of Dream and Wonder;" Molto tranquillo e ben sostenuto; 2 pp., 1:30; low, med., high in B flat min.; solo w/piano acc.; Fred G. Bowles.
"His Helmet's Blaze;" Allegro agitato; 2 pp., 30 sec.; low, med., high in A min.; solo w/piano acc.; Fred G. Bowles.
"I Hear His Footsteps, Music Sweet;" Allegretto ben ritmato; 3 pp., 2 min.; low, med., high in E min.; solo w/piano acc.; Fred G. Bowles.
"Thou Art Weary;" Andante cantabile; 2 pp., 1 min.; low, med., high in G flat; solo w/piano acc.; Fred G. Bowles.

"This Is Nirvana;" Allegretto; 3 pp., 1:30; low, med.,high in E
flat; solo w/piano acc.; Fred G. Bowles.

"Ahmed's Song of Farewell;" Andante doloroso; 4 pp., 2:30;
low, med., high in B min.-B maj.; solo w/piano acc.;
Fred G. Bowles.

New York: GR, 1914; MSRC (2BV-14.23), NB (0976043), SCNYPL
(784-B), ECPL, MB, IU, NN, RPB, CLUP.

1915

64.   P.S. **Passionale (a cycle)

"Her Eyes, Twin Pools;" Andante con moto; 3 pp., 2 min., low,
high in G; solo w/piano acc.; James Weldon Johnson.

"Your Lips Are Wine;" Maestoso; 4 pp, 2:30; low, high in
G min.; solo w/piano acc.; James Weldon Johnson.

"Your Eyes So Deep;" Andante sostenuto; 5 pp., 2:30; low,
high in G min.; solo w/piano acc.; James Weldon
Johnson.

"The Glory of the Day Was in Her Face;" Andante cantabile; 4 pp., 2:30; low, high in E flat; solo w/piano acc.;
James Weldon Johnson.

New York: GR, 1915; NB (0976039), MSRC (2BV-14.19), SCNYPL
(784-B), JCY (V2J632P26, V2J632P26b), NN, IU, ECPL, RPB.

65.   P.S. **"The Young Warrior;" Moderato, quarter=88; 6 pp., 3 min.;
low in F, high in A flat; solo w/piano acc., solo w/orch.; James
Weldon Johnson.

New York: GR, 1915; Feb., 1916, Biltmore Hotel benefit concert,
Pasquale Amato; MSRC (2BV-14.40), JCY (V2J632Y88,
V2J632Y88b, V2J632Y88i).

66.   P.S. **"The Prayer;" Andante sostenuto; 3 pp., 2:30; low in E flat,
med. in F, high in A flat; solo w/piano acc.; Arthur Symons.

New York: GR, 1915; MSRC (2BV-14.20).

67.   P.S. ***Five Songs on Poems by Laurence Hope* (a cycle)

"Worth While;" Andante cantabile; 3 pp., 2 min.; med., high
in D; solo w/piano acc., solo w/orch.; Laurence
Hope.

"The Jungle Flower;" Larghetto, quarter=80; 4 pp., 2 min.; med., high in F min.; solo w/piano acc.; Laurence Hope.

"Kashmiri;" Mesto quasi andantino; 4 pp., 3 min.; med., high in B min.; solo w/piano acc., solo w/orch.; Laurence Hope.

"Among the Fuchsias;" Andante teneramente; 4 pp., 3 min.; med., high in F min.; solo w/piano acc., solo w/orch.; Laurence Hope.

"Till I Wake;" Larghetto, quarter=92; 5 pp., 3 min.; med., high in D min.; solo w/piano acc., solo w/orch.; Laurence Hope.

New York: GR, 1915; March 19, 1915, Carnegie Hall, John McCormack; MSRC (1BV-13.14), SCNYPL (784-B), NB (0976014), NBuG, NN, OCl, PPULC, ECPL.

68. P.S. **"Just You;" Andante cantabile; 3 pp., 1 min.; low in F, med., high in A flat; solo w/piano acc., TTBB, SSAA; Madge Marie Miller; R.

New York: GR, 1915, TTBB 1921, SSAA 1927, 1941; TTBB May 7, 1921, Washington, DC, Howard University Glee Club; MSRC (1BV-13.35), SCNYPL (784-B), NB (0976005), ECHS, NN.

69. P. **"Ethiopia Saluting the Colors;" Tempo di marcia, quarter=116; 8 pp., 5 min.; low in C min., high in D min.; solo w/piano acc., solo w/orch.; Walt Whitman.

New York: GR, 1915; November 23, 1915, Carnegie Hall, Herbert Witherspoon; MSRC (1BV-13.12), ACUP (Box 191), RPB.

70. P. **"The Grey Wolf;" Moderato; 10 pp., 5 min.; low in G min., med. in B flat min., high; solo w/piano acc., solo w/orch.; Arthur Symons.

New York: GR, 1915; MSRC (1BV-13.17), SCNYPL (784-B), ACUP (Box 191), CLUP.

71. "Memory;" med.; solo w/piano acc.; Arthur Symons.
New York: GR, 1915; MSRC (2BV-14.10).

72. "He Sent Me You;" low in F, med. in A flat; solo w/piano acc.; Frederick H. Martens.

New York: GR, 1915; MSRC (1BV-13.22).

73.   "Hearts;" med. in B flat, high in D; solo w/piano acc.; C. M.
      Wilmerding.
      New York: GR, 1915; MSRC (1BV-13.19).

1916

74.   P. **"By the Pool at the Third Rosses;" Andante cantabile; 4 pp.,
      3 min.; high in D flat; solo w/piano acc., TTBB, SSA; Arthur
      Symons.
      New York: GR, 1916; January 16, 1916, Carnegie Hall, John
      McCormack; MSRC (1BV-13.4), NB (0976008), ACUP (Box 191),
      MB.

75.   P. *"The Soldier;" Moderato; 7 pp., 3:30; low in C min., med. in
      E flat min., high in G min.; solo w/piano acc.; Rupert Brooke.
      New York: GR, 1916; MSRC (2BV-14.25).

76.   P. **"Three Shadows," Andante cantabile; 6 pp., 3 min.; low in A
      flat, med. in C, high in E flat; solo w/piano acc.; Dante G.
      Rossetti.
      New York: GR, 1916; January 7, 1917, Hippodrome, John McCor-
      mack; MSRC (2BV-14.29).

77.   P. *"One Year 1914-1915;" Lento; 3 pp., 2:30; med. in A flat, high
      in C; solo w/piano acc.; Margaret M. Harlan.
      New York: GR, 1916; April 9, 1916, Carnegie Hall, John McCor-
      mack; MSRC (2BV-14.15).

78.   P.S. **"In the Wood of Finvara;" Andante sostenuto; 4 pp., 2:30;
      low in D flat, high in F; solo w/piano acc.; Arthur Symons.
      New York: GR, 1917; December, 1916, Newark, NJ, Mary Jordan;
      MSRC (1BV-13.28, SCNYPL (784-B).

79.   S. *"On Inishmaan: Isles of Aran;" Andante sostenuto; 4 pp. 2:30;
      low in E flat, high in A flat; solo w/piano acc.; Arthur Symons.
      New York: GR, 1917; October 1916, Ziegfeld Theater, Chicago,
      Christine Miller; MSRC (2BV-14.16), NB (0976038), WaU.

1917

80.   P.S. **"Little Mother of Mine;" Andante cantabile; 5 pp., 2 min.; med. in D flat, high; solo w/piano acc., SATB, TTBB, SSA, SA; Walter H. Brown; R.
New York: GR, 1917; MSRC (1BV-13.37), NB (0976005,0976008-9), SCNYPL (784-B), ECHS, CLUP, NN.

81.   "The Man in White;" low, med.; solo w/piano acc., TB, SA; Anonymous.
New York: GR, 1917; MSRC (2BV-14.9).

82.   P.S. **"The Dove and the Lily;" Poco adagio, quarter=44; 5 pp., 2 min.; med. in E flat, high in G; solo w/piano acc.; Swedish folksong.
New York: GR, 1917; May 16, 1917, St. John the Divine Cathedral, NY, Oscar Seagle; MSRC (1BV-13.8).

83.   "Dreams Tell Me Truly;" high; solo w/piano acc.; Fred G. Bowles.
New York: GR, 1917; MSRC (1BV-13.10).

84.   "In Summer;" low in E min., high in G min.; solo w/piano acc.; Josephine Nicholls.
New York: GR, 1917; MSRC (1BV-13.26).

85.   "Promis' Lan';" med., high; solo w/piano acc., TTBB, SATB; Mrs. N. J. Corey.
New York: GR, 1917, TTBB 1929; MSRC (4BV-16.14), NB (0976005), NN.

86.   P.S. **"The Sailor's Wife;" Andante sostenuto; 6 pp., 3 min.; med. in A flat, high in C; solo w/piano acc.; Mary Stewart Cutting.
New York: GR, 1917; ACUP (Box 191), MSRC (2BV-14.22).

1918

87.   P. *"Under a Blazing Star;" low, med.; solo w/piano acc.; Mildred Seitz.
New York: GR, 1918; MSRC (2BV-14.34).

1919

88. P.S. **"Down By the Sea;" Andante sostenuto, quarter=60; 4 pp.,
2 min.; low in C min., high in F min.; solo w/piano acc.;
George O'Connell.
New York: GR, 1919; MSRC (1BV-13.7), SCNYPL (784-B), ACUP
(Box 191).

89. P.S. **"Fragments;" Andante cantabile; 2 pp., 1 min.; low, med. in
E flat, high; solo w/piano acc.; Jessie Fauset.
New York: GR, 1919; MSRC (1BV-13.16), SCNYPL (784-B).

90. P. *"I Remember All;" low, med.; solo w/piano acc.; Arthur
Symons.
New York: GR, 1919; n.d., NY, Sophie Braslau; MSRC (1BV-
13.19).

91. "I Want To Die While You Love Me;" 6 pp.; low, med., high; solo
w/piano acc.; Georgia Douglas Johnson.
New York: GR, 1919; MSRC (1BV-13.30), SCNYPL (784-B).

92. "A Love Song;" 2 pp.; med.; solo w/piano acc.; John E. Bruce.
Not published; SCNYPL (ms, 784-B).

93. P.S. *"A Song of Rest;" Andante cantabile; 2 pp., 2 min.; high in
A flat; solo w/piano acc.; Fred G. Bowles.
Not published; 1919, Charles Harrison; ECHS (ms).

94. "In the Great Somewhere;" low in E flat, med. in F, high in A flat;
solo w/piano acc.; Harold Robé.
New York: GR, 1919, MSRC (1BV-13.27).

95. "Oh, My Love;" 6 pp.; high; solo w/piano acc.; Harriett Gaylord.
New York: GR, 1919; MSRC (2BV-14.12), SCNYPL (784-B).

96. P.S. **"The Victor;" high; solo w/piano acc.; George O'Connell.
New York: GR, 1919; MSRC (2BV-14.35).

97. P.S. **"Were I a Star;" Moderato, quarter=60; 3 pp., 2 min.; low-
med. in F; solo w/piano acc.; A. Musgrove Robarts.
New York: GR, 1919; December 15, 1919, Hippodrome, John
McCormack; MSRC (2BV-14.38), ACUP (Box 191).

1920

98. "Love Watches;" high; solo w/piano acc.; George O'Connell.
New York: GR, 1920; MSRC (2BV-14.6).

99. "Tell Me Once More;" med.; solo w/piano acc.; Fred G. Bowles.
New York: GR, 1920; MSRC (2BV-14.27).

100. "Listen to Yo' Guardian Angel;" med.; solo w/piano acc.; Robert
Underwood Johnson.
New York: GR, 1920.

101. "A Corn Song;" 11 pp.; low in E flat, high in G flat; solo w/piano
acc.; Paul Laurence Dunbar.
New York: GR, 1920; SCNYPL (784-B).

102. "Have You Been to Lons?" 7 pp.; low, high; solo w/piano acc.;
Gordon Johnstone.
New York: GR, 1920; MSRC (1BV-13.18), SCNYPL (784-B).

103. S. **"Southern Lullaby;" 8 pp.; high; SATB w/sop. solo, a cappella;
George V. Hobart.
New York: GR, 1920; CLUP.

1921

104. "Come With Me;" high in F; solo w/piano acc.; Lura Kelsey
Clendening.
New York: GR, 1921; MSRC (1BV-13.6).

105. "Before Meeting;" low in E flat, high in G flat; solo w/piano acc.;
Arthur Symons.
New York: GR, 1921; MSRC (1BV-13.3).

106. S. *"Ethiopia's Paean of Exultation;" 15 pp.; med.; SATB w/piano
acc.; Anna J. Cooper.
New York: GR, 1921; CLUP.

107. "Adoration;" low in D flat, high in F; solo w/piano acc.; Dora L.
Houston.
New York: GR, 1921; MSRC (1BV-13.1).

108.   "The Prayer I Make For You;" med.-high; solo w/piano acc.;
        Harold Robé.
        New York: GR, 1921; MSRC (2BV-14.21).

109.   "De Ha'nt;" med.; solo w/piano acc.; James W. Pryor.
        New York: GR, 1921; NB (0976026), NN.

110.   "The Lord's Prayer;" solo w/piano/organ acc., SATB; Matthew 6:9-
        13.
        New York: GR, 1921.

111.   P.S. **"He Met Her in the Meadow;" Andante con molto senti-
        mento; 4 pp., 2 min.; low in D flat, med., high in A flat; solo
        w/piano acc., SATB, SSA, TTBB; Harry T. Burleigh.
        New York: GR, 1921, choral arr. 1922; MSRC (1BV-13.21), NB
        (0976005, 0976009), NN, CLUP.

1922

112.   P.S. **"Exile;" Molto sostenuto; 4 pp., 1:30; low in A, med.; solo
        w/piano acc.; Inez Maree Richardson.
        New York: GR, 1922; MSRC (1BV-13.13).

113.   "The Little House of Dreams;" solo w/piano acc.; Arthur W.
        Peach.
        New York: GR, 1922; MSRC (1BV-13.36).

114.   "Love Found the Way;" low, high; solo w/piano acc.; Jesse Winne.
        New York: GR, 1922; MSRC (2BV-14.3a and 2BV-14.3b).

1923

115.   "The Dream of Love;" solo w/piano acc.; Alexander Groves.
        New York: GR, 1923.

116.   P.S. **"The Trees Have Grown So;" Lento; 4 pp., 2 min.; low, high
        in F; solo w/piano acc.; John Hanlon.
        New York: GR, 1923; MSRC (2BV-14.32).

1924

117.   "I Hope My Mother Will Be There;" 5 pp.; med.; SATB, a
       cappella; The Mayo Boys Song, a Vesper Hymn.
       New York: GR, 1924; March 31, 1924, NY, St. George's Choir.

118.   "O Brothers, Lift Your Voices;" SATB w/piano/organ acc.;
       Edward H. Bickersteth.
       New York: GR, 1924.

119.   P.S. **"The Reiland Amen;" mixed choir w/piano/organ acc.; Karl
       Reiland.
       New York: SG, 1924; St. George's, 1924.

1926

120.   "Eleven O'Clock (To Our Absent Brothers);" solo w/piano acc.;
       James F. Egan.
       New York: GR, 1926.

121.   P.S. **_Six Responses_; SATB w/piano/organ, acc.; Holy Scriptures.
       New York: GR, 1926; St. George's, 1926.

1927

122.   "Love's Likeness;" high; solo w/piano acc.; Madge M. Miller.
       New York: GR, 1927; MSRC (2BV-14.4).

123.   S. **"Fair Talladega;" 2 pp., 3 verses, 3 min.; med. in A flat; SATB
       w/piano acc.; William Pickens.
       Talladega, AL: TC, 1927; TC.

1928

124.   P.S. **"A Fatuous Tragedy;" 6 pp.; range of E flat to A flat; TTBB,
       a cappella; Homer Brewer.
       New York: GR, 1928.

125.   "Are You Smiling?" solo w/piano acc.; Hector MacCarthy.
       New York: GR, 1928.

126.   "Passing By;" solo w/piano acc., TTBB; Anonymous.
       New York: GR, 1928.

127.   P.S. **Responses for Vesper Services*; SATB w/piano/organ acc.;
       Biblical texts.
       New York: SG, 1928; St. George's, 1928.

1929

128.   P.S. **"Christ Be With Me;" SATB w/piano/organ acc.; Words
       from the poem "St. Patrick's Breast Plate."
       New York: GR, 1929.

129.   S. "The Promised Land;" 8 pp.; med.; TTBB, SATB w/mezzo
       soloist and w/piano acc.; Samuel Stennett.
       New York: GR, 1929.

130.   S. "Bethlehem;" Più lento; A min.; SATB; Ednah Proctor Clarke.
       New York: GR, 1929.

1930

131.   S. "Ho, Ro! My Nut-Brown Maiden;" 10 pp.; high; TTBB, a
       cappella; Old Highland melody.
       New York: GR, 1930.

1932

132.   "Mattinata ('Tis the Day);" SATB w/piano acc.; Edward
       Teschemacher.
       New York: GR, 1932.

133.   S. "Savior, Happy Would I Be;" SATB; Rev. Edwin H. Nevin.
       New York: GR, 1932.

1934

134.   S. "Some Rival Has Stolen My True Love Away;" TTBB; Tradi-
       tional Surrey song.
       New York: GR, 1934.

135.   "Hymn to St. Matthew."
       Unpublished.

136.   P.S. **"Lovely Dark and Lonely One;" Andante; 2 pp., 2 min.;
        med-high in C; solo w/piano acc.; Langston Hughes.
        New York: GR, 1935; May 10, 1934, Juilliard, NY, Ruby Elzy;
        MSRC (1BV-13.38), SCNYPL (784-B), JCY (V2H874L94).

1935

137.   P.S. **"May the Words;" SATB, response for Jewish Sabbath
        Service.
        New York: EE, 1935; May 10, 1935, NY, Emanu-El Choir; EE.

1936

138.   S. *"Greeting."
        Unpublished; February 29, 1936, New Rochelle, NY, Burleigh Glee
        Club.

1939

139.   S. *"Dear Ol' NCC;" SATB; Annie Day Shepard, revised by Alston
        Burleigh.
        Durham, NC: NCC, 1939; NCC.

1940

140.   "In Christ There is No East or West;" SATB; John Oxenham.
        New York: E, 1940.

141.   "I Wonder;" solo w/piano acc.; Beatrice Fenner.
        New York: GR, 1940.

Spirituals and Negro Folk Songs

1901

142.   "When de Angels Call;" 2 pp.; solo w/piano acc.; Howard Weeden.
        New York: *Everybody's Magazine*, 1901.

1913

143.   S. *"Deep River;" 3 pp.; SATB, a cappella.
       New York: GS, 1913, 1914; JCY (V3B92N32).

1914

144.   S. **"Deep River;" TTBB, SSA.
       New York: GR, 1914; NB (0976006-7), NN.

145.   S. "Dig My Grave;" with "Deep River," 7 pp.; SATB, a cappella.
       New York: GS, 1914, 1921; JCY (V3B92N32).

146.   S. *Afro-American Folk Songs* (Henry Edward Krehbiel)
           "Oh Rock Me Julie;" 1 p.; in G min.; unison chorus.
           "I'm Gwine to Alabamy;" Moderato; 1 p.; in A; unison chorus.
           "Acadian Boatmen's Song;" Con moto; 1 p; in D min.; unison
               chorus.
           "Nobody Knows the Trouble I've Seen;" Religioso; 1 p.; in G;
               unison chorus.
           "You May Bury Me in de Eas';" Lento; 1 p.; in C min.; unison
               chorus.
           "Father Abraham;" Andante; 1 p.; in G min.; unison chorus.
           "Dig My Grave;" Largo; 1 p.; in A flat; unison chorus.
           "I Look O'er Yander;" Adagio; 1 p.; in C; unison chorus.
           "O Graveyard;" Andante; 1 p.; in F min.; unison chorus.
           "Pov' piti Lolotte;" Andante cantabile; 2 pp.; in F min,; unison
               chorus.
           "Neve' a Man Speak Like This Man;" 1 p.; in B flat; unison
               chorus.
           "Jesus Heal' de Sick;" 2 pp.; in D; unison chorus.
           "Opon de Rock;" 2 pp.; in E flat; unison chorus.
       New York: GS, 1914; Krehbiel's volume is easily accessible.

1916

147.   S. "Father Abraham;" solo w/piano acc., SATB.
       New York: GS, 1916; March 25, 1917, Brooklyn Academy of Music,
       Oscar Seagle.

148.   S. "So Sad;" SATB.

New York: GS, 1916.

149.   P.S. **"Didn't My Lord Deliver Daniel?" Andante; 5 pp., 3 min.; in G min.; solo w/piano acc., SATB a cappella.
New York: GS, 1916; New York: GR, 1921; SCNYPL (784.7-B), CLUP.

1917

150.   P.S. **"Deep River;" Lento; 3 pp., 2:30; low in C, med. in D flat, high in F; solo w/piano acc.; R.
New York: GR, 1917; MSRC (3BV-15.8), SCNYPL (784-B and 784.7-B), JCY (V3B92D33), NB (0976011 and 0976030), CLSU, CLUP; copies of 1926 ms at Pierpont Morgan Library, ECHS, IaU.

151.   P.S. **"By an' By;" Andante; 3 pp., 2 min.; low in F, high; solo w/piano acc., TTBB, SSA; R.
New York: GS, 1917; New York: GR, 1917, TTBB; MSRC (3BV-15.4), SCNYPL (784.7-B), JCY (V3B92N31), NB (0976002-3), WaU, OO, IU, CLUP, MB, IaU, PPULC.

152.   P.S. **"Go Down Moses;" Lento; 4 pp., 3 min.; low in G min., med., high; solo w/piano acc., SATB, TTBB, SA or TB; R.
New York: GR, 1917; MSRC (3BV-15.15), SCNYPL (784.7-B), ACUP (Box 180), NB (0976017, 0976030, and 0976053), BM, CLUP, WaU, OO, MB, NN, ECHS.

153.   P.S. **"Swing Low, Sweet Chariot;" Slowly; 4 pp., 2 min., low in F, med., high; solo w/piano acc., SATB, TTBB, SSA, SA or TB; R.
New York: GR, 1917; June 15, 1917, Baltimore, Burleigh; MSRC (4BV-16.22), SCNYPL (784.7-B), ACUP (Box 183b), NB (0976030-1, 0976028, 0976048), NB, IU, MB, NN, ECHS, IaU.

154.   P.S. **"Nobody Knows de Trouble I've Seen;" Poco adagio; 4 pp., 2:30; low in F, med. in G, high; solo w/piano acc., TTBB, SATB a cappella, SSA; R.
New York: GR, 1917; SATB, 1924; solo, 1930; New York: CF, n.d., SATB; December 10, 1917, Chattanooga, Oscar Seagle; MSRC (4BV-16.7), SCNYPL (784.7-B), NB (0976033-4, 0976009, 0976031), CLUP, IU, MB.

155. P.S. **"I Don't Feel Noways Tired;" Moderato; 4 pp., 2 min.; low in C; solo w/piano acc., SSA; R.
New York: GR, 1917; March 25, 1917, Brooklyn Academy of Music, Oscar Seagle; MSRC (3BV-15.22), SCNYPL (784.7-B), ACUP (Box 181), NB (0976033, 0976028, 0976009), MB, NN.

156. P.S. **"I Want to Be Ready;" Andante; 3 pp., 1:30; low-med. in E flat; solo w/piano acc., SSA; R.
New York: GR, 1917; March 25, 1917, Brooklyn Academy of Music, Oscar Seagle; MSRC (3BV-15.28), ACUP (Box 181), SCNYPL (784.7-B), NB (0976033, 0976030-1, 0976028, 0976009), MB, NN, IaU.

157. P.S. **"John's Gone Down on de Island;" 4 pp., 2 min.; low in A flat-F min., high; solo w/piano acc.
New York: GR, 1917; MSRC (3BV-15.29), SCNYPL (784.7-B), NB (0976022, 0976031), NN, WaU, TNF, OO.

158. P.S. **"My Way's Cloudy;" Lento; 4 pp., 2 min.; low in D flat, med.; solo w/piano acc., SSA.
New York: GR, 1917; MSRC (4BV-16.6), ACUP (Box 182), SCNYPL (784.7-B), NB (0976028, 0976031, 0976033), MB, NN.

159. P.S. **"Sinner Please Doan Let Dis Harves' Pass;" Andante; 3 pp., 1:30; low in E min.; solo w/piano acc., SSA, SATB; R.
New York: GR, 1917; June 15, 1917, Baltimore, Burleigh; MSRC (4BV-16.18), ACUP (Box 183b), SCNYPL (784.7-B), NB (0976033, 0976045), MB, NN, ECHS.

160. P.S. **"Weepin' Mary;" Andante; 2 pp., 1 min.; low-med. in D min., high; solo w/piano acc., SSA; R.
New York: GR, 1917; MSRC (4BV-16.25), JCY (V3B92N31), SCNYPL (784.7-B), NB (0976028, 0976033), CLUP, NN, MB.

161. P.S. **"You May Bury Me in de Eas';" Lento; 4 pp., 2 min., low in F min., med.; solo w/piano acc.
New York: GR, 1917; MSRC (4BV-16.19), SCNYPL (784.7-B), JCY (V3B92N31), NB (0976028, 0976030, 0976053), MB, NN, IaU.

1918

162.   P.S. **"Oh Peter Go Ring-a Dem Bells;" Andante con moto; 3 pp.,
       1 min.; low-med. in F, high; solo w/piano acc., unison voices,
       SSA, TTBB; R.
       New York: GR, 1918; MSRC (4BV-16.9), ACUP (Box 183), JCY
       (V3B92Oh15), NB (0976031, 0976040), SCNYPL (784.7-B), MB,
       IU, TNF.

163.   P.S. **"'Tis Me, O Lord;" Moderato; 3 pp., 1 min.; low in A flat;
       solo w/piano acc., unison, TTBB a cappella, SSA, SA or TB.
       New York GR, 1918, choral arr. 1924; MSRC (4BV-16.23),
       SCNYPL (784.7-B), NB (0976031, 0976033, 0976050), MB, NN.

164.   P.S. **"I Stood on de Ribber ob Jerdon;" Andante cantabile; 4 pp.,
       2 min.; low in F, high; solo w/piano acc.; R.
       New York: GR, 1918; MSRC (3BV-15.26), SCNYPL (784.7-B),
       ACUP (Box 181), NB (0976030, 0976031, 0976033), IaU, MB, NN,
       CLUP.

165.   P.S. **"My Lord, What a Mornin';" Adagio non tanto; 4 pp., 2
       min.; low in D flat, high in E flat; solo w/piano acc., SATB
       and SSA a cappella; R.
       New York: GR, 1918, 1924; New York: CF, n.d., SATB and SSA;
       MSRC (4BV-16.5), SCNYPL (784.7-B), ACUP (Box 182), NB
       (0976025, 0976031, 0976033), MB, NN, CLUP, ECHS.

166.   P.S. **"Sometimes I Feel Like a Motherless Child;" Lamentoso; 4
       pp., 2 min.; low in D min., high; solo w/piano acc., SSA,
       SATB, SAB, unison voices; R.
       New York: GR, 1918; SSA 1919, 1949; New York: CF, n.d., SATB
       and SAB; MSRC (4BV-16.19), SCNYPL (784.7-B), ACUP (Box
       183b) NB (0976031, 0976046), CLUP, MB, TNF.

1919

167.   P.S. **"Hard Trials;" Moderato; 5 pp., 2 min.; low in E flat, med.;
       solo w/piano acc., unison voices, SSA, TTBB; R.
       New York: GR, 1919; MSRC (3BV-15.18), SCNYPL (784.7-B),
       ACUP (Box 180), NB (0976019, 0976031-2), MB, NN, ECHS.

168.   P.S. **"Oh, Didn't It Rain?" Moderato; 4 pp., 1:30; low in G, med.,
       high; solo w/piano acc., SSA, TTBB; R.
       New York: GR, 1919; January 1919, Aeolian Hall, Roland Hayes;
       MSRC (4BV-16.8), ACUP (Box 183), JCY (V3B92N31), SCNYPL
       (784.7-B), NB (0976031, 0976033, 0976035), CLUP, NN, IU, TNF,
       MB.

169.   P.S. **"Let Us Cheer the Weary Traveler;" Adagio; 4 pp., 2:30; low
       in D flat, med., high; solo w/piano acc., SATB.
       New York: GR, 1919; New York: SG, 1924; MSRC (4BV-16.2),
       SCNYPL (784.7-B), NB (0976023, 0976031, 0976033), MB, NN.

170.   P.S. **"Balm in Gilead;" Andante; 4 pp., 2 min.; low in G, med.;
       solo w/piano acc., SSA, TTBB, unison voices; R.
       New York: GR, 1919; MSRC (3BV-15.2), SCNYPL (784.7-B), NB
       (0976031), CLUP, MB, ECHS.

171.   P.S. **"Don't You Weep When I'm Gone;" Andante; 4 pp., low in
       G flat, med.-high; solo w/piano acc.
       New York: GR, 1919; MSRC (3BV-15.11), SCNYPL (784.7-B),
       ACUP (Box 179), NB (0976013, 0976033), MB.

172.   P.S. **"He's Jus' de Same Today;" Moderato; 5 pp., 2 min.; low in
       G, med.-high; solo w/piano acc.
       New York: GR, 1919; MSRC (3BV-15.21), SCNYPL (784.7-B), NB
       (0976030, 0976033), IaU.

1921

173.   P.S. **"Little David, Play on Your Harp;" Andante cantabile; 4 pp.,
       2 min.; low in F, med.-high; solo w/piano acc.
       New York: GR, 1921; MSRC (4BV-16.3), SCNYPL (784.7-B),
       ACUP (Box 182), NB (0976024, 0976033), JCY (V3B92L5), IU,
       MB, NN, ECHS.

174.   P.S. **"Oh! Rock Me, Julie;" 3 pp.; med in A min.; solo w/piano
       acc.
       New York: GR, 1921; MSRC (4BV-16.10), SCNYPL (784.7-B), NB
       (0976026, 0976036), NIC.

175.   P.S. **"Scandalize My Name;" 3 pp.; med.-high; solo w/piano acc.,
       TTBB a cappella; R.
       New York: GR, 1921, TTBB 1922; MSRC (ms 4BV-16.17),
       SCNYPL (784.7-B), ACUP (Box 183b), JCY (V1+1), NB
       (0976026), NN.

176.   "Don't You Dream of Turnin' Back;" med.; solo w/piano acc.
       New York: GR, 1921; MSRC (3BV-15.10), NB (0976012, 0976026,
       0976036), NIC.

177.   P.S. **"De Gospel Train," Moderato; 4 pp., 2 min.; low in A flat,
       high; solo w/piano acc., TTBB, SATB, SSA, SA or TB; R.
       New York: GR, 1921, SATB 1927; MSRC (3 BV-15.16), SCNYPL
       (784.7-B), ACUP (Box 180), NB (0976002, 0976033), ECHS
       (inscribed by Burleigh to Norman T. Sobel), MB, NN, IU, IaU,
       PPULC, CLUP.

178.   P.S. **"Heav'n, Heav'n;" Joyfully but not fast; 4 pp., 1:30; low in
       A flat, med.; solo w/piano acc., SSA, TTBB, SATB, SA or TB;
       R.
       New York: GR, 1921, 1922; MSRC (3BV-15.20), SCNYPL (784.7-
       B), ACUP (Box 180), NB (0976009, 0976030, 0976033), NN, IaU,
       ECHS.

179.   P.S. **"Steal Away;" Adagio e molto espressivo; 4 pp., 2:30; low in
       F, med.; solo w/piano acc., SATB.
       New York: GR, 1921, 1922; SATB 1924; MSRC (4BV-16.21),
       SCNYPL (784.7-B), ACUP (Box 183b), NB (0976033), NN, MB,
       ECHS.

1922

180.   "De Creation;" 2 pp.; TTBB a cappella.
       New York: GR, 1922.

181.   P.S. **"Couldn't Hear Nobody Pray;" Andante sostenuto; 4 pp., 2
       min.; low in D flat, high in F; solo w/piano acc, SATB w/ten.
       or sop. solo.
       New York: GR, 1922; MSRC (3BV-15.6), SCNYPL (784.7-B), JCY
       (V3B92N31), CLUP.

182.   P.S. **"Ain't Goin' to Study War No More;" Lento; 6 pp., 3 min.;
       low in A flat, high; solo w/piano acc.
       New York: GR, 1922; MSRC (3BV-15.1), SCNYPL (784.7-B), NB
       (0976031, 0976033), MB, NN, ECHS (copy of ms).

183.   P.S. **"O Rocks, Don't Fall on Me;" Moderato; 5 pp., 3 min.; low
       in D, high; solo w/piano acc.
       New York: GR, 1922; MSRC (4BV-16.12), SCNYPL (784.7-B), NB
       (0976033), MB, NN, ECHS (copy inscribed by Burleigh to Norman
       T. Sobel).

1923

184.   P.S. **_Deep River_ (with Agide Jacchia); Lento; 4 pp., 2:30; E flat;
       full orchestra w/organ.
       Unpublished; ACUP (ms Box 179), MB (ms).

1924

185.   P.S. **"Were You There?" Largo; 4 pp. 2 min.; low in E flat, med.
       in F, high; solo w/piano acc., SATB a cappella, TTBB,
       SSATTBB, SA or TB; R.
       New York: GR, 1924; SATB, SSA 1927; MSRC (4BV-16.26),
       SCNYPL (784.7-B), JCY (V3B92W4), ACUP (Box 183b), NB
       (0976033, 0976052), CLUP, MB, NN, NcU.

186.   "I'm A-Rollin';" solo w/piano acc., SATB.
       New York: GR, 1924.

187.   P.S. **"Oh, Wasn't Dat a Wide Ribber?" Larghetto; 6 pp., 3 min.;
       low in E flat; solo w/piano acc.; R.
       New York: GR, 1924; MSRC (4BV-16.11), SCNYPL (784.7-B),
       ACUP (Box 183), NB (0976029, 0976033), MB, NN.

1925

188.   P.S. **"Ev'ry Time I Feel de Spirit;" Slowly, with breadth and
       reverence; 5 pp., 3 min.; low in D, high; solo w/piano acc.,
       SATB a cappella w/alto or bar. solo; R.

New York: GR, 1925; MSRC (3BV-15.13), SCNYPL (784.7-B), JCY (V3B92E8, V3B92N31), NB (0976029, 0976033), CLUP, MB, NN.

189.   P.S. **"I Know de Lord's Laid His Hands on Me;" Moderato; 5 pp., 3 min.; low in E flat, high; solo w/piano acc., SATB.
New York: GR, 1925; MSRC (3BV-15.24), SCNYPL (784.7-B).

190.   P.S. **"Wade in de Water;" Andante; 5 pp., 3 min.; low in D min., high; solo w/piano acc., SATB a cappella.
New York: GR, 1925; MSRC (4BV-16.24), SCNYPL (784.7-B), NB (0976073), MB, NN, CLUP.

1926

191.   P.S. **"I Got a Home in A-Dat Rock;" Moderato e ben sostenuto; 4 pp., 2 min.; low in E flat, high; solo w/piano acc.
New York: GR, 1926; MSRC (3BV-15.23), SCNYPL (784.7-B), NB (0976033), MB, NN.

192.   P.S. **"Give Me Jesus;" Andante; 3 pp., 1:30; low in C, med.; solo w/piano acc.
New York: GR, 1926; MSRC (3BV-15.14), NB (0976033), MB, NN, ECHS.

193.   P.S. **"Go Down in the Lonesome Valley;" Poco adagio; 3 pp., 2 min.; low in C min., med., high; solo w/piano acc.
New York: GR, 1926; MSRC (4BV-16.4).

194.   P.S. **"Stan' Still, Jordan;" Lento; 5 pp., 3:30; low in C min., med., high; solo w/piano acc., SATB; R.
New York: GR, 1926; SATB 1929; MSRC (4BV-16.20), SCNYPL (784.7-B), NB (0976033), MB, NN, CLUP.

195.   P.S. **"Dar's a Meeting Here Tonight;" In moderate time and with devotional feeling; 4 pp., 1:30; med.-high in E flat; solo w/piano acc.
Boston: OD, 1926; MSRC (3BV-15.7), CLUP.

196.   P.S. **"Run to Jesus;" Not fast; 2 pp., 1:30; low in D min.; solo w/piano acc.
Boston: OD, 1926; MSRC (4BV-16.16), CLUP.

1927

197. P.S. **"I've Been in de Storm So Long;" Moderato; 5 pp., 2 min.; low in G min., solo w/piano acc., SATB a cappella.
New York: GR, 1927; SATB 1944; May 22, 1927, St. George's Church, Burleigh; MSRC (3BV-15.27), SCNYPL (784.7-B), NB (0976033), MB, NN, ECHS.

198. P.S. **"Hear de Lambs A-Cryin';" Andante; 5 pp., 3 min.; low in A min.; solo w/piano acc., SATB a cappella with alto or bar. solo.
New York: GR, 1927; SATB 1927; MSRC (3BV-15.19), SCNYPL (784.7-B), NB (0976033), MB, NN, ECHS.

199. P.S. **"Go Tell It on the Mountains;" Slowly; 5 pp., 2:30; low in G; solo w/piano acc., SATB w/organ acc.
New York: GR, 1927; SATB 1929; MSRC (3BV-15.17), ACUP (Box 180), NB (0976033), NN, MB, ECHS.

200. P.S. **"Ezekiel Saw de Wheel;" SATB 13 pp.; SATB two keys; solo w/piano acc., SSA a cappella, SATB a cappella, TTBB a cappella.
New York: GR, 1927; SATB 1928; 1927, Academy High School, Erie, PA; SCNYPL (784.7-B).

1928

201. P.S. **"De Blin' Man Stood on de Road and Cried;" Lento; 4 pp., 2:30; low in D flat, high; solo w/piano acc., SSA.
New York: GR, 1928; SSA 1935, 1938; MSRC (3BV-15.3), SCNYPL (784.7-B), NB (0976033), NN, MB, CLUP.

202. P.S. **"Behold That Star;" Andante moderato; 5 pp., 3 min.; low in D, high; solo w/piano acc., SATB w/organ acc., SSA; R.
New York: GR, 1928; SATB 1943; SSA 1944; ACUP (Box 179).

203. P.S. **"Don't Be Weary Traveler;" Andante teneramente; 3 pp., 1:30; low in B min., high; solo w/piano acc., SATB.
New York: GR, 1928; 1928 Old Central High School, Erie, PA; MSRC (3BV-15.9), SCNYPL (784.7-B), NB (0976033), MB, NN.

1929

204.   P.S. **"Ride On, King Jesus;" Maestoso; 5 pp., 3 min.; low in D, SATB in D flat; solo w/piano acc., SATB; R.
New York: GR, 1929; SCNYPL (784.7-B), ECHS.

205.   S. **Old Songs Hymnal (listed by category below); 208 pp. total, songs 1 p. each; med.; 4-part hymns w/piano acc.; Dorothy G. Bolton.
New York: CC, 1929; SCNYPL (784.7-B), CLUP.

      Folk Songs in the Making
            "Hear Train Coming"
            "Jesus Went on Man's Bond"
            "The Gospel Train"
            "I Heard Train Coming"
            "How Long is the Train Been Gone"
      Narrative Songs
            "Adam and Eve Walking in the Garden"
            "Better Day Coming"
            "Didn't It Rain"
            "Ezekiel"
            "He Never Said a Mumbling Word"
            "Handwriting on the Wall"
            "H. for Hannah, Hallelujah!"
            "I am the Light of the World"
            "In the Land"
            "Job, All Your Children are Gone"
            "Jonah"
            "Old Ark A-moving"
            "Pharaoh's Daughter"
            "Mary Come Running on Sunday Morning"
            "Rock That Never Give 'Way"
            "Sabbaths Have No End"
            "Tell Me Who Built the Ark"
            "You'll be a Witness for the Lord"
            "Who Built the Ark" – second version
            "Redeemed! Redeemed!"

Songs of Admonition
"Almost Done"
"A Sinner Man is so Hard to Believe"
"Bear Your Burden"
"Be Ready When He Come"
"Can't Serve God and Mamman"
"Get Right and Stay Right"
"Plumb the Line"
"De Right and Holy"
"Goodby, Gambler"
"God's Got His Eyes on You"
"God is Going to Straight Them"
"If You Want to See Jesus"
"I Work on Building Too"
"Let Old Norah"
"In the Lamb Book"
"Jesus is True"
"Keep the Ark Moving"
"Keep on to Galilee"
"Let the Church Go Rolling On"
"Keep On to Heaven Anyhow"
"Downward Roads"
"Sinner Man, Hunt You a Hiding Place"
"You Must Not be Wrong"
"You Got to Reap What You Sow"
"The Fault in You"
"You Better Mind"
"Weepin' Mary"
"You Got Jesus" (Suggestive of the game Hide the Thimble)
"You Can Go On"
Songs of Striving, Weariness and Aspiration
"Hold Out to the End"
"Climbing Up Zion's Hill"
"Please Don't Drive Me Away"
"Don't God's Children Have a Hard Time"
"I Been in the Storm So Long"
"I Want to Be There"

"Do, Lord, Remember Me"
"Don't Let It be Said Too Late"
"Don't Leave Me in the Hand of Wicked Man"
"Jesus, Come This Way"
"Little More Faith in Jesus"
"Long As I Can Feel the Spirit"
"Lord, Help the Poor and Needy"
"Lord, Don't Leave Me"
"Lord, I Cannot Stay Here by Myself"
"Lord, I Wisht I Had Wings"
"Go Chain the Lion Down"
"Lordy, Won't You Come by Here"
"My Trouble is Hard"
"Prayer is the Key"
"Somebody Knocking at Your Door"
"Sometimes I Feel Like a Motherless Child"
"Standing in the Need of Prayer"
"The Lord Will Provide"
"In the Promised Land"
"There's a Little Wheel A-turnin' "
"Got Good Religion"
"Wagging Up Zion's Hill"
"I Couldn't Hear Nobody Pray"
"I Want Jesus to Talk with Me"
"Jesus Lock the Lion Jaw"
"Shepherd, Your Lamb Gone Astray"
"Walk Jerusalem Just Like John"

Songs of Conversion

"Blood Done Sign My Name"
"Brother, Ain't You Glad"
"Go Down in Jordan"
"Hunting for My Jesus"
"Humble, You Say the Bells Done Rung"
"I Got a Key"
"I Have a Right to the Tree of Life"
"I Heard an Angel Singing"
"I'm in a Strange Land"
"Jesus Know My Heart"

"Jesus Listening"
"Leaning on the Lord"
"Been Blind But Now I See"
"Let Him Come"
"Preach the Word of God"
"Let Your Heart Catch on Fire"
"I Hope to Join That Band"
"Life-boat"
"Rock in a Weary Land"
"Newborn Again"
"Jesus in This Band"
"Sunshine in My Soul"
"Tell Me How You Love Jesus"
"That Good Old Ship of Zion"
"Soldiers of the Cross"
"The Lord Going to Wipe Away These Tears"
"There's No Gambling in the Air"
"Trouble Don't Last Always"
"Whiter Than Snow"
"Young Lamb Must Find the Way"
"When His Blood Can Make Me Whole"
Songs of Devil and Hell
"Help Me Run, Satan"
"There is No Hiding Place Down There"
"Is My Mother on Board"
Songs of Death
"Don't Cut Him Down"
"Death Going to Shake Me"
"Don't You Grieve After Me"
"Is I Got to Linger"
"Never Come Back Anymore"
"It May Be the Last Time, I Don't Know"
"Goodbye, I'm Going Home"
"I Ain't No Stranger Now"
"I Wanter Die Easy When I Die"
"Just as Well to Love Me Brother"
"Learn Me the Way"
"Motherless Children Have a Hard Time"

"Swing Low, Sweet Chariot"
"Tramping, Trying to Heaven My Home"
"What You Weeping For, Mary"
"You Going to Want Somebody on Your Bond"
"Who Go'd Down in the Grave with Me"
"Every Year Must Carry Its Number"
"You Gonter Miss Me"
"Jesus is My Only Friend"
"Everybody Got to Go"
"Humble, Praise King Jesus"
"The Grave is Dark and Lonesome"
"On the Hill"

Songs of Judgment, Resurrection, Reward
"Calling Them Saint from Mount Zion Hill"
"He Rose"
"Let Me Take a Ride on the Chariot Wheel"
"Home in That Rock"
"Got to Go to Judgment"
"Hush, Little Baby, Don't You Cry"
"Judgment Day"
"Lord, Going to Look on the Book That Day"
"My Home"
"Sit Down and Rest a Little While"
"When I Get Home"
"Land on the Shore"
"Where Will You Be"
"When the Saints March In"
"I'll Be There in That Morning"
"Don't Let This Harvest Pass"
"That Great Day"
"Mary and Martha, Peter and James"
"Won't It be a Time"
"Lord, Lord"
"I Have a Mother Over Yonder"
"And Don't You Want to Go"
"Amen"
"Blow, Gable"
"Remember Me"

"Want God's Bosom to be Your Pillow"
"I Hate to Tell You So"
"Shoes"
"Come on, Mary, and Ring the Bell"
"Wake Up the Dead"
"Going to Tell God How I Suffered"
"If You Don't Meet Jesus"
"Coming Down Jerusalem Street"
"When I Laid My Burden Down"
"City of Refuge"
"Watching and Waiting for Me"
"Wonder How Long"
"Hammer Ring"
"You better Run"
"Little David, Play on Your Harp"
"A Home in Glory"
"In My Father's House"

1930-31

206. "Who is Dat Yondah?" (with Eva Jessye); Adagio; med. in F min.;
        solo w/piano/organ acc.
      New York: GM, 1930-31; MSRC (ms dated 1930, 4BV-16.27).

207. P.S. **"Dry Bones;" med., solo w/piano acc.
      New York: GM, 1930-31; MSRC (3BV-15.12).

1932

208. "Little Child of Mary" (from "De New-born Baby"); low in G, high
        in B flat; solo w/piano acc., SATB a cappella.
      New York: GR, 1932; SATB 1938.

1934

209. P.S. **"Mister Banjo;" SATB 9 pp., SATB a cappella w/sop. solo.
      New York: GR, 1934.

1935

210.   P.S. **"Joshua Fit de Battl' ob Jericho;" Not too fast; 3 pp., 1:30; low in E min.; solo w/piano acc.
New York: GR, 1935.

211.   "O Lord, Have Mercy Upon Me;" SATB 5 pp.; SATB a cappella; R.
*New York: GR, 1935.

1938

212.   "Hold On (Keep Your Hand on the Plow);" quarter=80; SATB 13 pp.; in E min.; SATB a cappella.
New York: GR, 1938.

213.   "Walk Together Children;" SSA or TBB 5 pp.; med.; SSA or TTB a cappella.
New York: GR, 1938.

214.   "You Goin' to Reap Jus' What You Sow;" 9 pp.; SSA and SATB a cappella.
New York: GR, 1938, 1943.

Instrumental Works

1901

215.   *Six Plantation Melodies for Violin and Piano.*
Unpublished.

1910

216.   S. **From the Southland* (for piano)
"Through Moanin' Pines;" Andante semplice, quarter=66; 2 pp., 1 min.; in F sharp min.
"The Frolic;" Risoluto, quarter=176; Meno mosso, quarter=120; Andante tristezza, quarter=88; A tempo; Meno mosso; 5 pp., 2:30; in F min.-F maj.; also orchestrated.

"In de Col' Moonlight;" Andante doloramente, quarter=60;
2 pp., 1:30; in F min.

"A Jubilee;" Allegretto, ma non troppo, quarter=60; 4 pp.,
2:30; in F.

"On Bended Knees;" Andante con gran espressione, quar-
ter=40; Religioso, half note=dotted quarter; Larga-
mente; 3 pp., 2 min., in G min.

"A New Hidin'-Place;" Andante Maestoso; Quasi religioso,
quarter=56; Allargando e maestoso; 3 pp., 2 min.; in
D.

New York: WMC, 1910; Philadelphia: TP, 1914; NB (0976015), CSt,
NN, NBuG, CLUP.

1916

217.   S. **Southland Sketches* (for violin and piano)
Andante; 2:30; in A.
Adagio ma non troppo; 2:30; in D.
Allegretto grazioso; 2 min.; in F.
Allegro; Allegro, Meno mosso, Tempo I; 2:30; in G min.
New York: GR, 1916; MSRC (2BV-14.26), OCl.

Discography

Harry T. Burleigh's own voice was never recorded. Dr. Harry T. Burleigh II said: "By the time recording equipment had gotten good, Harry's voice had begun to show the ravages of time."

"Balm in Gilead" (1919). New York: Odyssey, 1945, reissued 1968 32-16-0268, Paul Robeson; New York: Vanguard, VSD 57/58, Paul Robeson; New York: Classics Record Library, 1976 30-5647, Paul Robeson; New York: Vanguard, 1958, reissued 1965, 2035, Paul Robeson, Alan Booth, pf.; New York: Columbia (CBS) C-17467D in CM-610, Paul Robeson.

"Behold That Star" (1928). New York: RCA, 1962 LM/LSC-2592, Marian Anderson, Franz Rupp, pf.

"By an' By" (1917). New York: Columbia (CBS), 1925, 91012, Roland Hayes; London: Vocalion, c. 1925, 21002 (listed by Philip Miller as A 21005, 78A), Roland Hayes, Lawrence Brown, pf.; Camden, NJ: Victor, 19743, 78E, Paul Robeson, Lawrence Brown, pf.; New York: Classics Record Library, 1976, 30-5647, Paul Robeson, Lawrence Brown pf.; New York: RCA, 1925, reissued 1972, LM-3292, Paul Robeson, Lawrence Brown, pf.; New York: Odyssey, 1945, reissued 1968, 32-16-0268, Paul Robeson, Lawrence Brown, pf.; New York: Gramophone, G-B4480.

"Deep River" (1917). Camden, NJ: Victor LRM 7006, Marian Anderson; Victor Black Seal 19227, Marian Anderson; Victor 22015, 78E, Marian Anderson; Victor 2032, 78E, Marian Anderson, Kosti Vehanen, pf.; Victor, 1927, 20783, 78E; New York: New World Records, 1927, reissued 1976, NW-247, Paul Robeson, Lawrence Brown, pf.; New York: RCA, 1927, reissued 1972, LM-3292, Paul

Robeson, Lawrence Brown, pf.; Richmond, VA: Richmond Sound Stages, RSS WO-626, Virginia Union University Choir, Odell Hobbs, conductor; New York: Musical Heritage Society, 1972, MHS-1515 SLC-70, Inia te Wiata, Maurice Till, pf.; London: Vocalion, c. 1925, R 6133, 78A, Roland Hayes, Lawrence Brown, pf.

"Ev'ry Time I Feel de Spirit" (1925). Camden, NJ: Victor LRM 7006, Marian Anderson.

"Go Down Moses" (1917). Camden, NJ: Victor LRM 7006, Marian Anderson; Victor Black Seal 19370, Marian Anderson; Victor 1799A, 78E, Marian Anderson, Kosti Vehanen, pf.; New York: RCA, 1952, reissued 1976, AVMI-1735, Marian Anderson, Franz Rupp, pf.; New York: Odyssey, 1945, reissued 1968, 32-16-0268, Paul Robeson; New York: Classics Record Library, 1976, 30-5647, Paul Robeson; New York: Vanguard, 1958, VRS-9193, Paul Robeson; London: Vocalion, 1922, A 21005, 78A and B-3032, Roland Hayes, Lawrence Brown, pf.; New York: New World Records, 1922, reissued 1976, NW-247, Roland Hayes.

"De Gospel Train" (1921). New York: RCA, 1947, reissued 1976, AVMI-1735, Marian Anderson, Franz Rupp, pf.; New York: RCA Victor Red Seal, 1956, LM-2032, Marian Anderson; New York: Period (Vocalion/ Decca) 1954, SLP-580, Inez Matthews, Jonathan Brice, pf.

"Hard Trials" (1919). New York: RCA Victor, 1962, LM/LSC-2592, Marian Anderson, Franz Rupp, pf.; Chicago: JM (American Record Club), 1977, JM 1702, Leroy O. Dorsey, Clyde Parker, pf.

"Heav'n, Heav'n" (1921). Camden, NJ: Victor Black Seal 19370, Marian Anderson; Victor, 1936, 8958B, 78E, Marian Anderson, Kosti Vehanen, pf.; New York: New World Records, reissued 1976, NW-247, Marian Anderson, Kosti Vehanen, pf.; New York: RCA, 1962, LM/LSC-2592, Marian Anderson, Franz Rupp, pf.; New York: Musical Heritage Society, 1972, MHS-1515, SLC-70, Inia te Wiata, Maurice Till, pf.

"I Don't Feel Noways Tired" (1917). New York: Gramophone, G-DA 1676, Marian Anderson, Kosti Vehanen.

"I Stood on de Ribber of Jerdon" (1918). New York: London, 1950, LPS 182, Ella Belle Davis, w/orch., Victor Olof, conductor; New York: RCA, 1962, LM/LSC-2592, Marian Anderson, Franz Rupp, pf.; New York: Gramophone G-B3381, Paul Robeson.

"I Want to be Ready" (1917). Camden, NJ: His Master's Voice, B2897, Paul Robeson; New York: RCA, 1929, reissued 1972, LM-3292, Paul Robeson.

"Jean" (1903). Camden, NJ: Victor, 64280, 78A, Evan Williams w/orch.; Germany: Odeon Records 57666, cat. no. D131, Ivor Foster.

"Just You" (1915). Camden, NJ: Victor Red Seal, 1912-17, 87261, 78A, Frieda Hempel w/orch.; Victor Red Seal, 1912-18, 64535, double face series 872, Herbert Witherspoon; New York: Columbia (CBS), A 1957 (46210), Maggie Teyte w/orch.

"Little Mother of Mine" (1917). Camden, NJ: Victor Red Seal, 1916-19, 64778, double face series 755, John McCormack; Star-Tone Records, 1943, ST-216, John Charles Thomas with unidentified orch.

"My Lord, What a Mornin'" (1918). Camden, NJ: Victor Black Seal 19560, Marian Anderson; Camden, NJ: His Master's Voice, B 2897, Paul Robeson; Washington, DC: National Office for Black Catholics 11152/11153, Chorus w/McHenry Genwright, conductor.

"Nobody Knows the Trouble I've Seen" (1917). New York: London, 1950, LPS 182, Ella Belle Davis, Hubert Greenslade, pf.; Camden, NJ: Victor Black Seal 19560, Marian Anderson; New York: RCA Red Seal, 1925-29, reissued 1972, LM 3292, Paul Robeson.

"O Lord, Have Mercy on Me" (1935). Los Angeles: PRC (Producers Releasers Company) CC-8, Illinois Wesleyan Collegiate Choir, David Nott, conductor.

"Oh, Didn't It Rain?" New York: Musical Heritage Society, 1972, MHS-1515, SLC-70, Inia te Wiata, Maurice Till, pf.; New York: RCA, 1962, LM/LSC-2592, Marian Anderson, Franz Rupp, pf.; Baltimore: Oglesby Records, 1983, SRL-1707, Isador Oglesby, John Miller, pf.

"Oh Peter Go Ring-a Dem Bells" (1918). New York: RCA, 1972, LM/LSC-2592, Marian Anderson, Franz Rupp, pf.; New York: Gramophone G-B3381, Paul Robeson.

"Oh, Wasn't Dat a Wide Ribber?" (1924). New York: RCA, 1962, LM/LSC-2592, Marian Anderson, Franz Rupp, pf.

"Ride On, King Jesus" (1929). New York: RCA, 1947, reissued 1976, AVMI-1735, Marian Anderson, Franz Rupp, pf.; New York: RCA Victor, 1956, LM-2032, Marian Anderson; Chicago: JM (American Record Club) 1977, JM-1702, Leroy O. Dorsey, Clyde Parker, pf.

"Scandalize My Name" (1922). New York: RCA, 1962, LM/LSC-2592, Marian Anderson, Franz Rupp, pf.; New York: Vanguard, 1958, VRS-9193, Paul Robeson.

"Since Molly Went Away" (1907). Camden, NJ: Victor 64624, Emilio de Gogorza w/orch.

"Sinner Please Doan Let dis Harves' Pass" (1917). New York: RCA, 1947, reissued in 1976, AVMI-1735, Marian Anderson, Franz Rupp, pf.; New York: RCA Victor Red Seal, 1956, LM-2032, Marian Anderson.

"Sometimes I Feel Like a Motherless Child" (1918). Camden, NJ: Victor LRM 7006, Marian Anderson; NY: BRC Productions (Brunswick Record Corp.), 1980, Veronica Tyler, Charles Lloyd, pf.; New York: Odyssey, 1945, 32-16-0268, Paul Robeson.

"Stan' Still Jordan" (1926). Baltimore: Praise, 1979, 658, Isador Oglesby, John Miller, pf.; Chicago: JM (American Record Club), 1977, JM-1702, Daisy Jackson, Buckner Gamby, pf.

"Swing Low, Sweet Chariot" (1917). Camden, NJ: Victor Red Seal, 1921-24, 64969, double face series 640, Mabel Garrison; London: Vocalion, c. 1925, R6133, 78A, Roland Hayes, Lawrence Brown, pf.; Baltimore: Praise, 1979, 658, Isador Oglesby, John Miller, pf.; New York: Musical Heritage Society, 1972, MHS-1515 SLC-70, Inia te Wiata, Maurice Till, pf.; New York: The London Recordings, 1904-26, EMI-RLS 719.

"Weepin' Mary" (1917). Camden, NJ: His Master's Voice, B2894, Paul Robeson.

"Were You There?" (1924). New York: London LPS 182, Ella Belle Davis, Victor Olof, conductor; Camden, NJ: Victor, 1925, 19742, 78E; New York: RCA ARL 1-1403, Sherrill Milnes, Jon Spong, pf; Los Angeles: PRC (Producers Releasers Company), CC-4, Illinois Wesleyan University Choir, Lewis E. Wikehart, conductor; New York: RCA, 1947, reissued 1976, AVMI-1735, Marian Anderson, Franz Rupp, pf.; New York: RCA Victor, 1972, LM-3292, Paul Robeson; New York: BRC Productions (Brunswick Record Corp.), 1980, Veronica Tyler, Ernest Ragogini, pf.; Los Angeles: Starline (Capitol), SRS-5192, Paul Robeson, Rutland Clapham, pf.; New York: RCA, 1972, LM-3292, Paul Robeson; New York: Gramophone G-B4480.

Dominique René de Lerma, in his *Black Music in Our Culture* (Kent, OH: Kent State University Press, 1970), n.p., lists Burleigh's *Spirituals* (not under individual titles) as recorded by Victor under these numbers: 8959, 2032, 4371, 20793, 1799, 1966, 101114, C-27, and M-554. The location of Star-Tone Records has not been ascertained.

Bibliography

Books

Abdul, Raoul. *Blacks in Classical Music*. New York: Dodd, Mead and Company, 1977.

Adams, Russell L. *Great Negroes Past and Present*. Chicago: Afro-American Publishing Co., 1963.

Albus, Harry J. *The Deep River Girl: The Life of Marian Anderson in Story Form*. Grand Rapids, MI: William B. Eerdmans Publishing Company, 1949.

Allen, Frederick Lewis. *The Great Pierpont Morgan*. New York: Harper and Brothers Publishers, 1949.

Allen, William Francis; Ward, Charles Picard; and Garrison, Lucy McKim. *Slave Songs of the United States*. New York: Peter Smith, 1929. Reprinted from the 1867 edition, New York: A. Simpson and Co.

Anderson, Marian. *My Lord, What a Morning*. New York: The Viking Press, 1956.

Aptheker, Herbert, ed. *The Correspondence of W. E. B. DuBois*. Vol. II. Amherst: University of Massachusetts Press, 1976.

Arnold, Byron. *Folksongs of Alabama*. University: University of Alabama Press, 1950.

Arvey, Verna. *In One Lifetime*. Fayetteville: University of Arkansas Press, 1984.

ASCAP Biographical Dictionary. New York and London: Jacques Cattell Press, R. R. Bowker Co., 1980.

Benoist, Andre. *The Accompanist, an Autobiography of Andre Benoist*. Neptune, NJ: Paganiniana Publications, Inc., 1978.

Berry, Lemuel. *Biographical Dictionary of Black Musicians and Music Educators*. Guthrie, OK: Educational Book Publishers, Midwest Publishing Co., 1978.

Brawley, Benjamin. *Paul Laurence Dunbar*. Port Washington, NY: Kennikat Press, Inc., 1936.

_____.*The Negro Genius*. New York: Dodd, Mead and Company, 1942.

Brooks, Tilford. *America's Black Musical Heritage*. Englewood Cliffs, NJ: Prentice-Hall, Inc., 1984.

Brown, Frank C. *North Carolina Folklore, The Music of the Folk Songs*. Vol. 5. Durham, NC: Duke University Press, 1962.

Brown, Rae Linda. *Music Printed and Manuscripts in the James Weldon Johnson Memorial Collection of Negro Arts and Letters*. New York and London: Garland Publishing, Inc., 1982.

Bullock, Ralph W. *In Spite of Handicaps*. New York: Association Press, 1927.

Burleigh, H. T., ed. *Negro Minstrel Melodies*. New York: G. Schirmer, Inc., 1909.

_____. *The Spirituals of Harry T. Burleigh*. Melville, NY: Belwin-Mills Publishing Corp., 1984.

_____, and Bolton, Dorothy G. *Old Songs Hymnal*. New York: The Century Company, 1929.

Carney, John G. *Tales of Old Erie*. Erie, PA: John G. Carney Publisher, 1958.

Chapman, John, and Sherwood, Garrison P., eds. *The Best Plays of 1894-1899*. New York: Dodd, Mead and Company, 1955.

Charters, Ann. *Nobody: The Story of Bert Williams*. London: The Macmillan Company, 1970.

Chase, Gilbert. *America's Music*. New York: McGraw-Hill Book Company, 1955.

Clapham, John. *Antonin Dvorak, Musician and Craftsman*. New York: St. Martin's Press, 1966.

_____. *Dvorak*. New York: W. W. Norton and Company, Inc., 1979.

Clough, Francis F., and Cuming, G. J. *The World's Encyclopaedia of Recorded Music*. London: Sidgwick & Jackson Limited, 1952.

Courlander, Harold. *Negro Folk Music, USA*. New York: Columbia University Press, 1963.

Crump, R. W. *Christina Rossetti: A Reference Guide*. Boston: G. K. Hall & Company, 1976.

Cullen, Countee, ed. *Caroling Dusk*. New York and London: Harper and Brothers Publishers, 1927.

Cuney-Hare, Maud. *Negro Musicians and Their Music*. New York: Da Capo Press, 1974.

Darrell, R. D. *The Gramophone Shop Encyclopedia of Recorded Music*. New York: The Gramophone Shop, Inc., 1936.

De Lerma, Dominique René. *Black Music in Our Culture*. Kent, OH: Kent State University Press, 1970.

_____. *Concert Music and Spirituals: A Selective Discography*. Nashville, TN: Fisk University, Institute for Research in Black American Music, 1981.

_____. *Reflections on Afro-American Music*. Kent, OH: Kent University Press, 1973.

DuBois, W. E. B., and Johnson, Guy. *Encyclopedia of the Negro*. New York: The Phelps-Stokes Fund, Inc., 1945.

Edwards, Charles Lincoln. *Bahama Songs and Stories: A Contribution to Folklore*. Vol. 3. Reprinted from the 1895 ed. New York: G. E. Stechert, 1942.

Fauset, Arthur Huff. *For Freedom: A Biographical Story of the American Negro*. Philadelphia: Franklin Publishing and Supply Co., 1927.

Field, Eugene. *Poems of Childhood*. New York: C. Scribner's Sons, 1904.

Finck, Henry T. *My Adventures in the Golden Age of Music*. New York and London: Funk and Wagnalls Company, 1926.

Fisher, William Arms, ed. *Seventy Negro Spirituals*. Boston: Oliver Ditson, 1926.

Foner, Philip S. *Paul Robeson Speaks*. New York: Brunner/Mazel Publishers, 1978.

Friedberg, Ruth C. *American Art Song and American Poetry*. Metuchen, NJ: Scarecrow Press, Inc., 1984.

Garland, Phyl. *The Sound of Soul*. Chicago: Henry Regnery Company, 1969.

Gilliam, Dorothy Butler. *Paul Robeson All-American*. Washington, DC: The New Republic Book Company, Inc., 1976.

Gilman, Lawrence. *Edward MacDowell*. New York: Dodd, Mead and Company, 1938.

The Gramophone Shop Encyclopedia of Recorded Music. New York: Crown Publishers, 1948.

Greene, Frank. *Composers on Record*. Metuchen, NJ: Scarecrow Press, Inc., 1985.

Haas, Robert B., ed. *William Grant Still and the Fusion of Cultures in American Music*. Los Angeles: Black Sparrow Press, 1972.

Hall, David, and Levin, Abner. *The Disc Book*. New York: Long Player Publications, Inc., 1955.

Hallowell, Emily. *Calhoun Plantation Songs*. Boston: C. W. Thompson & Co., 1907.

Hamlin, Anna M. *Father Was a Tenor*. Hicksville, NY: Exposition Press, 1978.

Hammond, L. H. *In the Vanguard of a Race*. New York: Council of Women for Home Missions and Missionary Movement of the U.S. and Canada, 1922.

Handy, W. C. *Father of the Blues, An Autobiography*. New York: The Macmillan Company, 1941.

Harlan, Louis R., and Smock, Raymond W., eds. *The Booker T. Washington Papers*. Vols. 6, 7, and 10. Urbana: University of Illinois Press, 1981.

Hayes, Roland. *My Songs*. Boston: Little, Brown and Company, 1948.

Helm, MacKinley. *Angel Mo' and Her Son Roland Hayes*. Boston: Little, Brown and Company, 1944.

Hitchcock, H. Wiley, and Sadie, Stanley, eds. *The New Grove Dictionary of American Music*. Vols. 1-4. London: Macmillan Press, Limited, 1986.

Horn, David. *The Literature of American Music in Books and Folk Music Collections*. Metuchen, NJ: Scarecrow Press, Inc., 1977.

Howard, John Tasker. *Our American Music: Three Hundred Years Of It*. New York: Thomas Y. Crowell Co. Publishers, 1931.

Jackson, George Pullen. *Down-East Spirituals and Others*. Locust Valley, NY: J. J. Augustin Publisher, n.d.

Johnson, James Weldon. *Along This Way*. New York: The Viking Press, 1933.

_____. *Black Manhattan*. New York: Atheneum, 1968; reprint ed., 1975.

_____. *Fifty Years & Other Poems*. Boston: The Cornhill Company, 1917.

_____, and Johnson, J. Rosamond. *The Book of American Negro Spirituals*. New York: The Viking Press, 1925.

Key, Pierre V. R. *John McCormack: His Own Life Story*. Boston: Small, Maynard and Company, 1918.

Kinscella, Hazel Gertrude. *Music on the Air*. New York: The Viking Press, 1934.

Klein, Herman. *The Golden Age of Opera*. London: George Routledge and Sons, Ltd., 1933.

Kolodin, Irving. *The New Guide to Recorded Music*. Garden City, NY: Doubleday & Company, Inc., 1950.

Krehbiel, Henry Edward. *Afro-American Folk Songs*. New York: G. Schirmer, Inc., 1914.

Kunitz, Stanley J., and Haycraft, Howard, eds. *Twentieth Century Authors*. New York: The H. W. Wilson Co., 1942.

Kutsch, K. J., and Riemens, Leo, eds. *A Concise Biographical Dictionary of Singers*. Philadelphia: Chilton Book Company, 1969.

Ledbetter, Gordon T. *The Great Irish Tenor*. New York: Charles Scribner's Sons, 1977.

Levy, Eugene. *James Weldon Johnson: Black Leader, Black Voice*. Chicago: University of Chicago Press, 1973.

Locke, Alain. *The Negro and His Music*. Washington, DC: The Associates in Negro Folk Education, 1936.

_____. *The Negro and His Music – Negro Art Past and Present*. New York: Arno Press and *New York Times*, 1969.

Logan, Rayford W., and Winston, Michael R., eds. *Dictionary of American Negro Biography*. New York: W. W. Norton and Company, 1982.

Lovell, John. *The Forge and the Flame*. New York: The Macmillan Company, 1972.

Lovingood, Penman. *Famous Modern Negro Musicians*. Brooklyn, NY: Press Forum Company, 1921.

Lowens, Irving. *Music and Musicians in Early America*. New York: W. W. Norton and Company, Inc., 1964.

Ludwig, Coy. *Maxfield Parrish*. New York: Watson-Guptill Publications, 1973.

Lyman, Susan Elizabeth. *The Story of New York: An Informal History of the City*. New York: Crown Publishers, Inc., 1964.

The Lynn Farnol Group, Inc., eds. *The ASCAP Biographical Dictionary of Composers, Authors and Publishers*. New York: The Lynn Farnol Group, Inc., 1966.

Mapp, Edward. *Directory of Blacks in the Performing Arts*. Metuchen, NJ: Scarecrow Press, Inc., 1978.

Martin, Jay, and Hudson, Gossie H., eds. *The Paul Laurence Dunbar Reader*. New York: Dodd, Mead and Company, 1975.

McBrier, Vivian Flagg. *R. Nathaniel Dett: His Life and Works*. Washington, DC: Associated Publishers, Inc., c. 1977.

McIlhenny, E. A. *Befo' de War Spirituals*. Boston: The Christopher Publishing House, 1933.

Miller, Philip C. *Vocal Music*. New York: Alfred A. Knopf, 1955.

Moses, Julian Morton. *Collectors' Guide to American Recordings 1895-1925*. New York: American Collectors' Exchange, 1949.

Moulton, Elizabeth. *St. George's Church, New York*. New York: St. George's Church, 1964.

Nathan, Hans. *Dan Emmett and the Rise of Early Minstrelsy*. Norman: University of Oklahoma Press, 1962.

The National Cyclopedia of American Biography. Vol. XXX. New York: James T. White and Company, 1943.

Nelson's Biographical Dictionary and Historical Reference Book. Erie, PA: The Erie Company, 1896.

Oja, Carol J. *American Music Recordings: A Discography of 20th Century U.S. Composers*. New York: Koussevitsky Music Foundation, Inc., 1982.

Overmeyer, Grace. *Famous American Composers*. New York: Thomas Y. Crowell, 1944.

Parkhurst, William, and de Bekker, L. J. *The Encyclopedia of Music and Musicians*. New York: Crown Publishers, 1937.

Parrish, Lydia. *Slave Songs of the Georgia Sea Islands*. New York: Creative Age Press, Inc., 1942.

Patterson, Lindsay, ed. *The International Library of Negro Life and History*. New York: Publishers Company, Inc. for the Association for the Study of Negro Life and History, 1967.

Patterson, Willis C. *Anthology of Art Songs by Black American Composers*. New York: Edward B. Marks Music Company, 1977.

Rasponi, Lanfranco. *The Last Prima Donnas*. New York: Alfred A Knopf, 1984.

Roach, Hildred. *Black American Music Past and Present*. Boston: Crescendo Publishing Co., 1973.

Robeson, Susan. *The Whole World in His Hands*. Secaucus, NJ: Citadel Press, 1981.

Robinson, Wilhelmena S. *International Library of Negro Life and History: Historical Negro Biographies*. New York: Publishers Company, Inc., 1967.

Rohrer, Gertrude Martin. *Music and Musicians of Pennsylvania*. Philadelphia: Theodore Presser Co., 1940.

Rossetti, Christina. *Goblin Market and Other Poems*. London: Oxford University Press, 1862.

Rublowsky, John. *Music in America*. New York: Crowell-Collier Press, 1967.

Rush, Theressa Gunnels; Meyers, Carol Fairbanks; and Arata, Esther Spring. *Black American Writers*. Vol. I. Metuchen, NJ: Scarecrow Press, Inc., 1975.

Rust, Brian. *The American Record Label Book*. New Rochelle, NY: Arlington House Publishers, 1978.

Sadie, Stanley, ed. *The New Grove Dictionary of Music and Musicians*. New York: The Macmillan Company, 1980.

Sampson, Henry T. *Blacks in Blackface, A Source Book on Early Black Musical Shows*. Metuchen, NJ: Scarecrow Press, Inc., 1980.

Sayers, W. C. Berwick. *Samuel Coleridge-Taylor, Musician: His Life and Letters*. London: Augener Ltd., 1927.

Schonzeler, H. H. *Dvorak*. London and New York: Marion Boyars, 1984.

Seton, Marie. *Paul Robeson*. London: Dennis Dobson, 1958.

Simond, Ike. *Old Slack's Reminiscence and Pocket History*. Bowling Green, OH: Bowling Green University Popular Press, 1974.

Skeeters, Paul W. *Maxfield Parrish: The Early Years 1893-1930*. Los Angeles: Nash, 1973.

Skvorecky, Josef. *Dvorak in Love*. Translated by Paul Wilson. Toronto: Lester & Orpen Dennys Limited, 1986.

Slonimsky, Nicolas, ed. *Baker's Biographical Dictionary of Musicians*. New York: Schirmer Books, 1984.

Sousa, John Philip. *Marching Along*. Boston: Hale, Cushman and Flint, 1941.

Southern, Eileen. *Biographical Dictionary of Afro-American and African Musicians*. Westport, CT: Greenwood Press, 1982.

_____. *The Music of Black Americans: A History*. New York: W. W. Norton and Company, Inc., 1971.

_____. *Readings in Black American Music*. New York: W. W. Norton and Company, Inc., 1971.

Stefan, Paul. *Anton Dvorak*. New York: The Greystone Press, Inc., 1941.

Symons, Arthur. *Collected Works of Arthur Symons*. Vols. I and II. New York: AMS Press, 1973.

Talley, Thomas. *Negro Folk Rhymes, Wise and Otherwise*. New York: The Macmillan Company, 1922.

Thompson, Oscar. *International Cyclopedia of Music and Musicians*. Edited by Nicolas Slonimsky. New York: Dodd, Mead and Company, 1952.

Tortolano, William. *Samuel Coleridge-Taylor: Anglo-Black Composer*. Metuchen, NJ: Scarecrow Press, Inc., 1977.

Townsend, Charles. *Negro Minstrels*. Upper Saddle River, NJ: Literature House/Gregg Press, 1969.

Trott, Josephine. *George Hamlin: American Singer*. Denver, CO: Nelson, 1925.

Turner, Patricia. *Afro-American Singers*. Minneapolis, MN: Challenge Productions, Inc., 1977.

Upton, William Treat. *Art-Song in America*. Boston: Oliver Ditson Company, 1930.

Van Staaten, Jan. *Slavonic Rhapsody: The Life of Antonin Dvorak*. New York: Allen, Towne and Heath, Inc., 1948.

Vehanen, Kosti. *Marian Anderson: A Portrait*. New York: Whittlesey House, 1941.

Vinson, James, ed. *Great Writers of the English Language: Poets*. New York: St. Martin's Press, 1979.

Ward, A. C., ed. *Longman Companion to Twentieth Century Literature*. Burnt Mill, Harlow, Essex: Longman Group, Ltd., 1970.

Westlake, Neda M., and Albrecht, Otto E., eds. *Marian Anderson: A Catalog of the Collection at the University of Pennsylvania Library*. Philadelphia: University of Pennsylvania Press, 1981.

White, Evelyn Davidson. *Choral Music by Afro-American Composers*. Metuchen, NJ: Scarecrow Press, Inc., 1981.

White, Evelyn Davidson. *Choral Music by Afro-American Composers*. Metuchen, NJ: Scarecrow Press, Inc., 1981.

White, Newman I. *American Negro Folk-Songs*. Hatboro, PA: Folklore Associates, Inc., 1965.

Whitman, Walt. *The Selected Poems of Walt Whitman*. New York: Walter J. Black, Inc., 1942.

Who Was Who in Literature. Detroit: Gale Research Co., 1979.

Wier, Albert E., ed. *The Macmillan Encyclopedia of Music and Musicians*. New York: The Macmillan Company, 1938.

Work, John W. *American Negro Songs and Spirituals*. New York: Bonanza Books, 1940.

_____. *Folk Song of the American Negro*. New York: Negro University Press, 1969.

Periodicals

Black Silhouette, November 10, 1971, n.p.

Borroff, Edith. "Black Musicians in the United States." *The American Music Teacher*, XX/2 (November 1972), p. 31.

Carter, Marva Griffin. "In Retrospect: Roland Hayes." *The Black Perspective in Music*, V/2 (Fall 1977), p. 189.

The Cheyney Record, III/1 (December 1922), p. 1.

The Cheyney Record, IX/1 (December 1928), pp. 1-2.

"Church Pays Tribute to Burleigh." *Musical America*, April 12, 1924, pp. 21, 27.

The Craftsman, XXIX/8 (October 1915), n.p.

Crawford, Richard. "Musical Learning in Nineteenth Century America." *American Music*, I/1 (Spring 1983), pp. 1-11.

Crisis, XII/5 (September 1916), n.p.

Crisis, July 1917, n.p.

Crisis, August 19, 1917, n.p.

Crisis, May 1920, n.p.

Crisis, May 1924, pp. 7-12.

Crisis, March 30, 1929, n.p.

Cromwell, Adelaide M. "The History of Oak Bluffs as a Popular Resort for Blacks." *The Dukes County Intelligencer*, XXVI/1 (August 1984), pp. 15-17.

Crutchfield, Will. "Brahms, by Those Who Knew Him." *Opus*, II/5 (August 1986), p. 21.

Current, Gloster B. "Paul Robeson." *The Black Perspective in Music*, IV/3 (Fall 1976), pp. 303, ff.

Curtis-Burlin, Natalie. "Black Singers and Players." *Musical Quarterly*, V/4 (April 1919), pp. 499-504.

Darrell, R. D. "Recitals and Miscellany." *High Fidelity*, XXII/10 (October 1972), pp. 116-7.

The Diapason. Obituary of Harry Thacker Burleigh. October 1949, p. 2.

The Diapason. Obituary of Melville Charlton. January 1974, p. 16.

Dvorak, Anton. "Music in America." *Harper's New Monthly Magazine*, XC/537 (February 1895), pp. 428-34.

Epstein, Dena J. "A White Origin for the Black Spiritual? An Invalid Theory and How It Grew." *American Music*, I/2 (Summer 1983), p. 58.

The Etude, LVII (May 1939), pp. 293-4.

The Etude, LVIII (August 1940), p. 511.

The Etude. Obituary of Harry Thacker Burleigh. November 1949, p. 56.

Fisher, William Arms. "Swing Low, Sweet Chariot: The Romance of a Famous Spiritual." *The Etude*, L/8 (August 1932), p. 536.

Garcia, William Burres. "Church Music by Black Composers: A Bibliography of Choral Music." *The Black Perspective in Music*, II/2 (Fall 1974), p. 148.

Garst, John F. "Mutual Reinforcement and the Origins of Spirituals." *American Music*, IV/4 (Winter 1986), pp. 390-406.

Gilchrist, Paul, and Green, Jeffrey P. "Some Recent Findings on Samuel Coleridge-Taylor." *The Black Perspective in Music*, XIII/2 (Fall 1985), pp. 163, ff.

Green, Jeffrey P. "Roland Hayes in London, 1921." *The Black Perspective in Music*, X/1 (Spring 1982), pp. 29-41.

Hampton School Journal, April 1, 1900, n.p.

Hampton School Journal, April 1, 1909, n.p.

The Hampton Student, IV/4 (May 1, 1914), p. 5.

Jackson, George Pullen. "The Genesis of the Negro Spiritual." *American Mercury*, XXVI/1 (June 1932), pp. 43-8.

James, Milton M. "Laura Wheeler Waring." *The Negro History Bulletin*, XIX/6 (March 1956), pp. 126-8.

Janifer, Ellsworth. "H. T. Burleigh Ten Years Later." *Phylon*, Summer 1960, pp. 144-54.

Johnson, James Weldon. "The Negro of Today in Music." *Charities*, October 7, 1905, n.p.

Journal of Negro History. Obituary of Laura Wheeler Waring. July 1948, pp. 385-6.

The Journal of Negro History. Obituary of Harry Thacker Burleigh, January 1950, pp. 104-5.

Kendall, John Smith. "New Orleans' Negro Minstrels." *The Louisiana Historical Quarterly*, XXX/1 (January 1947), pp. 9-14.

Kramer, A. Walter, "An American Negro Whose Music Stirs the Warring Blood of Italy." *Current Opinion*, LXI/2 (August 1916), pp. 100-1.

_____. "H. T. Burleigh: Composer by Divine Right and the American Coleridge-Taylor." *Musical America*, April 29, 1916, p. 25.

Lee, Henry. "Swing Low, Sweet Chariot." *The Black Perspective in Music*, II/1 (Spring 1974), p. 84. (Reprint of an article in *Coronet*, July 1947.)

Levy, Alan Howard. "The Search for Identity in American Music 1890-1920." *American Music*, II/2 (Summer 1984), pp. 75-6.

M., H. K. "Deep River Popularizes a Composer." *The Black Perspective in Music*, II/1 (Spring 1974), pp. 77-8. (Reprint of an article in the *Boston Evening Transcript*, March 10, 1917.)

Marsh, John L. "Harry Thacker Burleigh: Hard Knocks and Triumphant Days." *The Journal of Erie Studies*, IX/2 (Fall 1980), p. 28.

McGinty, Doris E. "The Washington Conservatory of Music." *The Black Perspective in Music*, VII/1 (Spring 1979), p. 65.

Murray, Charlotte. "The Story of Harry T. Burleigh." *The Hymn*, XVII/4 (October 1966), p. 104-11.

"Music." *The New Yorker*, January 16, 1926, pp. 20-1.

"Music." *The New Yorker*, March 20, 1937, p. 26.

"Music." *Time*, February 14, 1944, p. 48.

Musical America, April 29, 1916, p. 25.

Musical America, January 20, 1917, p. 34.

Musical America, February 10, 1917, p. 31.

Musical America, April 14, 1917, n.p.

Musical America, October 27, 1917, p. 36.

Musical America. Obituary of Harry Thacker Burleigh. October 1949, p. 26.

Musical Courier, LXVI-LXXIX, LXXXV, 1913-1919, 1922.

The Musical Forecast, August 1934, n.p.

The Musical Forecast, April 1939, n.p.

Musical Opinion, XXV/6 (August 1925), n.p.

The New Yorker, May 1986, p. 4.

Pacific Coast Musician, XXIX/2 (January 20, 1940), p. 7.

Savannah State College Bulletin, December 1962, pp. 68-73.

Southall, Geneva. "Black Composers and Religious Music." *The Black Perspective in Music*, II/1 (Spring 1974), pp. 47-8.

The Southern Workman, XLIII/7 (July 1914), p. 420.

The Southern Workman, LIII/4, (April 1924), pp. 196-7.

The Southern Workman, LIX/3 (March 30, 1930), pp. 113-20.

Southwestern Christian Advocate, March 15, 1917, pp. 9, 12.

Still, William Grant. "The Negro Musician in America." *Music Educators Journal*, LVI/5 (January 1970), pp. 100-1, 157-61.

Terry, William E. "The Negro Music Journal: An Appraisal." *The Black Perspective in Music*, V/2 (Fall 1977), pp. 146-60.

Walton, Lester A. "Harry T. Burleigh Honored Today." *The Black Perspective in Music*, II/I (Spring 1974), pp. 80-84.

Unpublished Dissertations

Allison, Roland Lewis. *Classification of the Vocal Works of Harry T. Burleigh (1866-1949) and Some Suggestions for Their Use in Teaching Diction in Singing*. Bloomington, Ind.: 1966. (Ph. D. Dissertation, University of Indiana)

Phillips, Theodore DeWitt. *The Life and Musical Compositions of S. Coleridge-Taylor*. Oberlin, Ohio: 1935. (Master of Arts Thesis, Oberlin Conservatory)

Seay, Elizabeth Irene. *A History of the North Carolina College for Negroes*. Durham, NC: 1941. (Master of Arts Thesis, Duke University)

Taylor, John E. *The Sociological and Psychological Implications of the Text of the Antebellum Negro Spirituals*. Greeley, Colo.: 1971. (Ph. D. Dissertation, University of Northern Colorado)

Liner Notes

When I Have Sung My Songs-The American Art Song 1900-1940. New World Records, 247, 1976. Notes by Philip L. Miller.

Newspapers

Advocate (Claremont, N. H.)

Amsterdam News (New York)

Baltimore Afro-American

Boston Evening Transcript

Chicago Defender

Chief-Union (Upper Sandusky, Ohio)

Cincinnati Union

Colorado Statesman (Denver)

Commercial (Bangor, Maine)

Courant (Hartford, Conn.)

Edgartown Gazette (Edgartown, Martha's Vineyard, Mass.)

Erie Daily Herald (Erie, Pa.)

Erie Dispatch (Erie, Pa.)

Erie Morning Gazette (Erie, Pa.)

Erie Morning News (Erie, Pa.)

Erie News (Erie, Pa.)

Erie Times (Erie, Pa.)

Grand Rapids Press (Grand Rapids, Mich.)

Graphic (Brownsville, Tenn.)

New York Age

New York Evening World

New York Herald

New York Herald Tribune

New York Sun

New York Sunday News

New York Times

New York Tribune

New York World

Norfolk Journal and Guide (Norfolk, Va.)

Philadelphia Tribune

Pittsburgh Courier

Pittsburgh Sun-Telegraph

St. Louis Argus

Saratoga Sun

Standard Times (New Bedford, Mass.)

Sunday Times (New Brunswick, N.J.)

Times (Boonsboro, Md.)

Vineyard Gazette (Edgartown, Martha's Vineyard, Mass.)

Virginian-Pilot (Norfolk, Va.)

Washington Bee

Washington Evening Star
Washington Post
Washington Sentinel
Washington Times
Washington Tribune
Weekly Independent (Hamburg, N. Y.)
Weekly News (Munsing, Mich.)

Chapter Notes

CHAPTER I

1. Letter to Norman Sobel from State of Maryland's Department of General Services, June 27, 1980, in Erie County Historical Society Library, Erie, Pa.

2. Roland Lewis Allison, *Classification of the Vocal Works of Harry T. Burleigh (1866-1949) and Some Suggestions for Their Use in Teaching Diction in Singing* (Indiana University, Ph.D. Dissertation, 1966), p. 102. Dr. Allison authored the Burleigh entry in *The New Grove Dictionary of Music and Musicians*. Lester A. Walton, "Harry T. Burleigh Honored Today," *The Black Perspective in Music*, Spring 1974, Vol. 2, No. 1, pp. 80-84.

3. Walton, *op. cit.*, p. 81.

4. Walton, *op. cit.*, pp. 83, 81.

5. A. Walter Kramer, "An American Negro Whose Music Stirs the Warring Blood of Italy," *Current Opinion*, August 1916, Vol. 61, No. 2, pp. 100-101.

6. John Clapham, *Antonin Dvorak, Musician and Craftsman* (New York: St. Martin's Press, 1966), p. 90.

7. *New York Herald*, April 15, 1935. Biancolli's story was published in *Negro Digest*, June 1948, pp. 26-28.

8. Maud Cuney-Hare, *Negro Musicians and Their Music* (New York: Da Capo Press, 1974), p. 59.

9. Nora Holt, *Amsterdam News*, November 30, 1946.

10. Alan Howard Levy, "The Search for Identity in American Music 1890-1920," *American Music*, Summer 1984, Vol. 2, No. 2, pp. 75-76; Eileen Southern, *The Music of Black Americans* (New York: W. W. Norton and Company, Inc., 1983), p. 266.

11.   Dominique René de Lerma, *Reflections on Afro-American Music* (Kent, OH: Kent University Press, 1973), p. 15.

12.   Alan Howard Levy, "The Search for Identity in American Music 1890-1920," *American Music*, Summer 1984, Vol. 2, No. 2, pp. 75-76; Eileen Southern, *The Music of Black Americans* (New York: W. W. Norton and Company, Inc., 1983), p. 266.

13.   John Clapham, *Dvorak* (New York: W. W. Norton, 1978), p. 133.

14.   Eileen Southern, *Readings in Black American History* (New York: W. W. Norton and Company, Inc., 1971), p. 218.

15.   Walton, *op. cit.*, pp. 82-83.

16.   James Weldon Johnson, *Black Manhattan* (New York: Atheneum, 1975), pp. 116-117.

17.   William S. Rainsford, *The Story of a Varied Life; An Autobiography* (Garden City, NY: Doubleday, Page and Company, 1922), cited in Johnson, *op. cit.*, p. 117.

18.   Elizabeth Boulton, *St. George's Church, New York* (New York: St. George's Church, 1964), pp. 177, 88; Henry Lee, "Swing Low, Sweet Chariot," *Black Perspective in Music*, Spring 1974, Vol. 2, No. 1, p. 85; Grace Overmeyer, *Famous American Composers* (New York: Thomas Y. Crowell, 1944), p. 134.

19.   The Albany incident is mentioned in the Hampton *School Journal*, April 1, 1909, and also in a letter from Sarah Ball of Hartford, Connecticut, to W. J. Henderson of the New York Public Library, dated August 12, 1956, a copy of which is in the Burleigh Collection at the Erie County Historical Society Library, hereafter cited as ECHS Library.

20.   Information from Mrs. Josephine Love, daughter of the late Dr. Kemper Harreld, now residing in Detroit, Michigan. Mrs. Love first met Burleigh in 1933 when she was a piano student at Juilliard.

21.   Frederick Lewis Allen, *The Great Pierpont Morgan* (New York: Harper and Brothers Publishers, 1949), p. 195.

22.   There is no information on the outcome of this project. Copies of this letter and all following correspondence between Burleigh and Mrs. Thurber and Mrs. Marshall were sent to the author by Dr. William C. Loring.

23.   Southern, *Readings in Black American Music*, p. 220.

24. Henry T. Sampson, *Blacks in Blackface: A Source Book on Early Black Musical Shows* (Metuchen, NJ: Scarecrow Press, 1980), p. 247.

25. *Time*, February 14, 1944, p. 48; *New York Post*, April 24, 1944. Personal information on the Burleigh family came through interviews and correspondence in 1985-1986 with Burleigh's daughter-in-law, Mrs. Erma Burleigh of Washington, DC; his grandson, Dr. Harry T. Burleigh II of Clarksburg, West Virginia; and Mrs. Josephine H. Love of Detroit.

26. James Weldon Johnson, *Along This Way* (New York: Viking Press, 1933), pp. 171-175; Benjamin Brawley, *Paul Laurence Dunbar* (Port Washington, NY: Kennikat Press, Inc., 1936), preface. Burleigh assisted Brawley with this book by collecting Dunbar's poems which composers had set to music. John G. Carney, *Tales of Old Erie* (Erie, PA: John G. Carney Publisher, 1958), p. 246; Cuney-Hare, *op. cit.*, p. 329.

27. Ann Charters, *Nobody: The Story of Bert Williams* (London: Macmillan & Company, 1970), p. 35.

28. Conversation with Dr. Eileen Southern, April 1986. Mrs. Josephine H. Love interpreted Burleigh's aloofness as the desire for a "difference in realm."

29. Allison, *op. cit.*, p. 272; Edward Mapp, *Directory of Blacks in the Performing Arts* (Metuchen, NJ: Scarecrow Press, 1978), p. 50. Further discussion of Burleigh's compositions, collaborators, texts, musical style, and dedications of various works follows in Chapters IV and V.

30. William E. Terry, "The Negro Music Journal: An Appraisal," *The Black Perspective in Music*, Vol. V, No. 2, Fall 1977, pp. 146-160.

31. *The Booker T. Washington Papers*, ed. By Louis R. Harlan and Raymond W. Smock (Urbana: University of Illinois Press, 1977), Vol. 6, pp. 67-68.

32. *Washington Papers*, Vol 7, p. 231, gives this account from *The Boston Globe*.

33. William Tortolano, *Samuel Coleridge-Taylor, Anglo-Black Composer, 1875-1912* (Metuchen, NJ: Scarecrow Press, 1977), p. 32; Cuney-Hare, *op. cit.*, pp. 244 ff.; Paul Gilchrist and Jeffrey P. Green, "Some Recent Findings on Samuel Coleridge-Taylor," *Black Perspective in Music*, Fall, 1985, Vol. 13, No. 2, pp. 163 ff.; W. C. Berwick Sayers, *Samuel Coleridge-Taylor, Musician: His Life and Letters* (London: Augener Ltd., 1927), pp. 1, 8, 168.

34. *Washington Papers*, Vol. 7, pp. 527-529, letter dated June 10, 1904.

35. Sayers, *op. cit.*, pp. 168-169, 184.

36. Information from a news or journal clipping, no name, no date, Hampton University Archives. Of the plantation songs mentioned none has been published under Burleigh's name except "Joshua Fit de Battle of Jericho."

37. James Weldon Johnson, "The Negro of Today in Music," *Charities*, October 7, 1905, pp. 58-59.

38. *The New York Age*, November 16, 1905, hereafter cited as *Age*.

39. *Age*, June 7 and July 12, 1906.

40. Sayers, *op. cit.*, p. 197. The program may be found in Tortolano, *op. cit.*, pp. 117-118.

41. *Age*, December 20, 1906; Southern, *The Music of Black Americans*, p. 308; Sayers, *op. cit.*, p. 197.

42. *Age*, March 19, 1908.

43. Conversation with Mrs. Josephine H. Love, August 1986.

44. Overmeyer, *op. cit.*, p. 138.

45. *Southwestern Christian Advocate*, March 15, 1917, pp. 9 and 12; Allison, *op. cit.*, p. 110; clipping from Hampton *School Journal*, April, 1909, n.p.

46. Gilchrist and Green, *op. cit.*, pp. 168-169. Photos in possession of Mrs. Josephine H. Love.

47. *Age*, July 19, 1908.

48. Charters, *op. cit.*, pp. 34-95. Williams and Walker have not been forgotten. In early May of 1986 a new show titled *Williams and Walker* opened at the American Place Theater in New York. It received rave reviews from *The New Yorker* and the *Amsterdam News*, whose critic spoke of the team as "giants of the earth." The show by Vincent D. Smith starred Ben Harney and Vondie Curtis-Hall.

49. As the former Harriet Gibbs, Mrs. Marshall (1896-1941) was the first black American to complete the piano course at Oberlin Conservatory in 1899. As a concert performer, teacher, and collector of folk music she worked as an educator in the Washington, DC, public schools and at the Conservatory, which she opened in 1903. Mrs. Marshall was fortunate to have on her faculty Clarence Cameron White, Azalia Hackley, and J. Hilary Taylor, editor of *The*

Negro Music Journal. She was a pioneer in bringing black concert artists to Washington from all over the United States.

50. Supporting this information are materials in the Burleigh Collections at the ECHS and Erie County Public Libraries; conversations and correspondence (1985-1986) with Mrs. Helen R. Andrews (ECHS librarian), Miss Ada Lawrence (retired Erie teacher), Dr. David Cantrell (Ft. Collins, Colorado), and Mrs. Virginia Moorhead and Mrs. Fannie Moorhead, both of Erie; and an article by Mili Roberts in the *Erie Morning News*, October 19, 1970.

51. The program was obtained through courtesy of the Erie County Public Library.

52. Published by Schirmer, the date on the frontispiece of *Negro Minstrel Melodies* is 1909, though Allison, *op. cit.*, p. 276, lists the date as 1910. Henderson was a writer and critic for both the *New York Times* and the *New York Sun*.

53. *Age*, October 27, 1910, and January 5, 1911; *Musical Courier*, January 5, 1911, Vol. LXII, No. 1, p. 24.

54. *Age*, March 16, 1911.

55. Doris E. McGinty, "The Washington Conservatory of Music," *The Black Perspective in Music*, Vol. 7, No. 1, Spring 1979, p. 65.

56. Charlotte Murray, "The Story of Harry T. Burleigh," *The Hymn*, October 1966, Vol. 17, No. 4, p. 110; Cuney-Hare, *op. cit.*, p. 328.

57. Conversations and correspondence with these persons have been invaluable for this book's purpose.

58. Overview gathered from various items appearing in the *Age* from February through October of 1913.

59. Cuney-Hare, *op. cit.*, pp. 312-313. Richardson often programmed Burleigh's works in his own solo recitals.

60. *New York Times*, April 19, 1913; *Age*, April 19, 1913; Lee, *op. cit.*, p. 85.

61. *Age*, November 4, 1913.

CHAPTER II

1. W. C. Handy, *Father of the Blues* (New York: The Macmillan Company, 1941), p. 264; James Weldon Johnson, *Black Manhattan* (New York: Atheneum, 1975), p. 116.

2. Vivian Flagg McBrier, *R. Nathaniel Dett: His Life and Works 1882-1943* (Washington, DC: Associated Publishers, Inc., c. 1977), p. 28; *The Hampton Student*, May 1, 1914, Vol. 4, No. 4, p. 5; *The Southern Workman*, July 1914, Vol. 43, No. 7, p. 420.

3. Letter to author August 16, 1986, from Dr. John Seagle, who has carried on the colony's work since Seagle's death in 1945.

4. Anna M. Hamlin, *Father Was a Tenor* (Hicksville, NY: Exposition Press, 1978), pp. 42, 59.

5. *Courier*, February 18, Vol. 68, No. 7, p. 43. Odes to Miss Miller from admirers were frequently published in the *Courier* during 1915-1916.

6. "Mother O' Mine," a setting of Rudyard Kipling's poem, was also arranged for chorus and performed the following September by the Apollo Club in Erie. Burleigh's "Little Mother of Mine" (1917) was also to be a McCormack favorite.

7. *Courier*, July 14, 1915, Vol. 71, No. 2, p. 34, and November 11, 1915, Vol. 71, No. 19, p. 39.

8. Ralph W. Bullock, *In Spite of Handicaps* (New York: Association Press, 1927), p. 41; Cuney-Hare, *op. cit.*, p. 276. Zandonai supported the Italian army with his own patriotic compositions. Also to his credit are symphonic works and operas, most notably *Francesca da Rimini*. Though he was not finally selected to finish Puccini's score of *Turandot*, he was the choice of Puccini's heirs for the task.

9. Bangor, Maine, *Commercial*, October 2, 1916.

10. *Age*, May 18, 1916.

11. *Courier*, March 23, 1916, Vol. 72, No. 12, p. 59.

12. Review of concert in Scranton, Pennsylvania, May 9, 1916, in *Courier*, May 25, 1916, Vol. 72, No. 21, p. 41.

13. Lanfranco Rasponi, *The Last Prima Donnas* (New York: Alfred A. Knopf, 1984), pp. 433-446.

14. Overview of people and events of the time was gained through 1915 issues of *Courier* and *Age*.

15. Dorothy West, "Fond Memories of a Black Childhood," *Vineyard Gazette*, June 25, 1971. West was a friend of poet Countee Cullen in the 1930s.

16. Letter to author, dated October 14, 1986, from Ms. White, successful cinema director and producer.

17. *Vineyard Gazette*, September 16, 1949; Adelaide M. Cromwell, "The History of Oak Bluffs as a Popular Resort for Blacks," *The Dukes County Intelligencer*, August, 1984, Vol. 26, No. 1, pp. 15-17.

18. *Courier*, January 20, 1916, Vol. 72, No. 3, p. 62; *Chicago Defender*, January 29, 1916.

19. A. Walter Kramer, "H. T. Burleigh: Composer by Divine Right and the American Coleridge-Taylor," *Musical America*, April 29, 1916, p. 25. Kramer, a violinist and composer himself, enjoyed several performances of his own art songs during this period.

20. *New York Times*, January 6, 1946.

21. Copy of letter, courtesy of Moorland-Spingarn Research Center.

22. *New York Times*, September 18, 1916.

23. *Age*, September 14 and October 12, 1916.

24. *Courier*, November 30, 1916, Vol. 73, No. 22, p. 10; December 14, 1916, Vol. 73, No. 24, p. 23.

25. *Courier*, October 12, 1916, Vol. 73, No. 15, p. 24; and November 9, 1916, Vol. 73, No. 19, p. 19. This Ziegfeld Theater, not to be confused with the one founded in New York in 1927, may have been a part of the Chicago Musical College begun there by Florenz Ziegfeld.

26. *Courier*, November 9, 1916, Vol. 73, No. 19, p. 19; November 23, 1916, Vol. 73, No. 20, p. 43; December 21, Vol. 73, No. 24, p. 52; *New York Times*, November 24, 1916.

27. *Washington Evening Star* and *Washington Post*, January 18, 1917. The composer of "A Corn Song" was not specified, though both Coleridge-Taylor and Burleigh had set the poem.

28. Bullock, *op. cit.*, p. 41; L. H. Hammond, *In the Vanguard of a Race* (New York: Council for Women for Home Missions and Missionary Movement of the U.S. And Canada, 1922), p. 129.

29. John Lovell, *The Forge and the Flame*, (New York: The Macmillan Company, 1972), p. 442. Seagle's performances of and comments on Burleigh's spirituals will be discussed more fully in Chapter III.

30. Letter reprinted in *Courier*, July 19, 1917, Vol. 75, No. 3, p. 16.

31. *Courier*, May 17, 1917, Vol. 74, No. 20, p. 16.

32. Allison, *op. cit.*, p. 121.

33.   *Cincinnati Union*, May 19, 1917. Included in the article were comments on specific songs and a rather lengthy biography.

34.   *New York Times*, December 2, 1971; brochure from Moorland-Spingarn Research Center.

35.   *Baltimore Afro-American*, June 16, 1917. Remarks by Burleigh prefacing his performance of a last group of spirituals will be in Chapter V.

36.   *Courier*, November 29, 1917, Vol. 75, No. 22, p. 23.

37.   *Courier*, November 22, 1917, Vol. 75, No. 21, p. 32.

38.   Program courtesy of Yale University Library.

39.   Information on the December, 1917, concerts taken from *Courier* and *Age* for that month.

40.   Southern, *The Music of Black Americans*, p. 366.

41.   *Courier*, February 14, 1918, Vol. 76, No. 7, p. 17.

42.   These two reviews were from the *San Francisco Call and Post* and the *Fresno Morning Republican*, March 4, 1918.

43.   *Courier*, May 30, 1918, Vol. 76, No.22, p. 17. The Optimists, founded by female composer Mana-Zucca, was organized for the advancement of American music and musicians.

44.   *Courier*, July 4, 1918, Vol. 77, No. 1, pp. 30-32.

45.   *New York Times*, January 31, 1919; *Courier*, February 27, 1919, Vol. 78, No. 8, p. 29; *Age*, February 8, 1919. Lawrence Brown accompanied the other segments of Hayes' recital.

46.   The Roberts, Torpadie, and McCormack reviews were in the *New York Times*, January 8, March 25, and December 16, 1919.

47.   *The Musical Forecast*, Pittsburgh, Pennsylvania, August, 1934; *Pittsburgh Courier*, September 3 and 8, 1934.

48.   Jeffrey P. Green, "Roland Hayes in London, 1921," *The Black Perspective in Music*, Vol. 10, No. 1, p. 35. "Ahmed's Farewell" is one of the *Saracen Songs*.

49.   Copy of commencement program June 11, 1920, courtesy of Moorland-Spingarn Research Center. John Hope, at that time president of Morehouse College, was awarded an honorary LL.D. Degree at the same ceremony. *Age*, June 26, 1920, gave no further details of the occasion.

50. Program of the Howard Glee Club concert courtesy of Moorland-Spingarn Research Center. Overview from *Age*, 1920-1921. The Wigmore Hall performance was mentioned in *Age*, August 26, 1921.

51. *The Cheyney Record*, December, 1922, Vol. III, No. 1, p. 1.

52. Eileen Southern, *Biographical Dictionary of Afro-American and African Musicians* (Westport, CT: Greenwood Press, 1982), p. 169.

53. *Age*, June 21, 1924.

54. Cuney-Hare, *op. cit.*, p. 327.

55. Walton, *op. cit.*, pp. 82-83.

56. Burleigh's honor was acknowledged also in *Crisis*, May, 1924, pp. 7-12; *Musical America*, April 12, 1924, p. 27, describing his music as having both "naïveté and supreme sophistication;" and *The Southern Workman*, April 1924, Vol. LIII, No. 4, pp. 196-197.

57. Dorothy Butler Gilliam, *Paul Robeson: All-American* (Washington, DC: The New Republic Book Co., Inc., 1976), pp. 42 ff. Van Vechten later became a prolific writer, critic and photographer. Both Robeson and Burleigh were among the famous people whom he photographed.

58. Cuney-Hare, *op. cit.*, p. 327; *Age*, May 16, 1925. The copy of a letter of appreciation to Burleigh, dated April 3, 1925, from the Congregation officials was obtained through the Beinecke Rare Books and Manuscripts Library at Yale University. It was signed by Louis Marshall, president, and William I. Spiegelberg, secretary.

59. News item from files of *Vineyard Gazette*, dated only "1925" in pen.

60. Overview from *Age*, 1925.

61. Letter to author from Dr. Jessye dated July 30, 1986; interview with Dr. Jessye in Detroit, Michigan, August 28, 1986.

62. Activities of 1926 from the *Age* for that year, specifically May 1, June 19, and December 18.

63. This reference to MacDowell, oddly enough, has been the only one of its kind, except a similar mention in a *New York Times* editorial of February 6, 1944, that MacDowell encouraged Burleigh "to arrange the songs of his own people." Norman Sobel, whose copious research on Burleigh is in the Erie County Historical Society Library in Erie, Pennsylvania, seemed unconvinced that Edward Mac-Dowell was actively interested in Burleigh's progress. It is possible that MacDowell's pursuance of his own career in the 1890s and pro-

gressive illness before his death in 1908 may have generated some resentment towards Burleigh, of whom Mrs. Frances MacDowell was so supportive and who probably urged their friendship. Moreover, MacDowell's heavy duties at Columbia would have allowed little time or energy for outside professional counselling or socializing, according to biographer Lawrence Gilman. Burleigh is not mentioned in Gilman's biography, *Edward MacDowell* (New York: Dodd, Mead and Company, 1938).

64. Events of 1927 reported by the *Age*, January 1, May 14 and 28, June 4 and 18, September 17, November 12, and December 3.

65. Copy of program courtesy of ECHS Library.

66. *The Cheyney Record*, December, 1928, Vol. IX, No. 1, pp. 1-2. In the twenties Murray had toured the United States as a recitalist and in 1926 had the leading female role in *Deep River*, an opera by Frank Harling and Lawrence Stallings, premiered in Philadelphia. The work, neither jazz nor Afro-American in character, was not based on Burleigh's spiritual.

67. Letter dated October 2, 1986, from Maude M. Jones, Director of Library Services at Cheyney University, renamed in 1983. Information on "Cheyney Day" and letters from Burleigh and Hill, courtesy of Dr. James Hall, Jr.

68. *Age*, April 20, 1929.

69. Lemuel Berry, *Biographical Dictionary of Black Musicians and Music Educators*, Vol. I (Guthrie, OK: Midwest Publishing Company, 1978), p. 31; *Crisis*, December, 1929, Vol. XXVI, No. 12, p. 414.

70. Information found in Norman Sobel's notes in the Erie County Historical Library, hereafter cited as Sobel's notes, ECHS Library.

71. *The Southern Workman*, March 30, 1930, Vol. LIX, No. 3, pp. 113-120; *New York Times*, February 10, 1930; *Age*, February 15, 1930.

72. *Age*, March 8, 1930.

73. *Age*, May 31, 1930.

74. Undated, unnamed news item, courtesy of the Hampton Institute Archives.

75. Letter courtesy of Marian Anderson Collection, Van Pelt Library, University of Pennsylvania.

76. Marian Anderson, *My Lord, What a Morning* (New York: Viking Press, 1956), pp. 112 ff.

77. Kosti Vehanen, *Marian Anderson, A Portrait* (Westport, CT: Greenwood Press, 1941) contains several references to Burleigh.

78. *New York Herald Tribune*, hereafter cited as *Herald Tribune*, n.d., 1941.

79. News item courtesy of Hampton Institute Archives, date and name of paper omitted. The *New York Times* did not report the event, but the *Age* carried a full article with photo, March 31, 1934.

80. Sources for 1935 activities in order are *Herald Tribune*, April 15 and May 2, 1935; Sobel's notes in ECHS Library; Allison, *op. cit.*, p. 106; and *Age*, June 11, 1935.

81. *Age*, January 25, 1936.

82. Anderson, *op. cit.*, p. 278.

83. *Age*, June 6, 1936.

84. *Age*, November 28 and December 19, 1936.

85. Norman Sobel's letter, obtained from ECHS Library, to Belwin-Mills, July 11, 1977.

86. Letter dated November 11, 1936, courtesy of Mrs. Josephine Harreld Love; interview with Mrs. Love, August, 1986. The diary, if not lost by Santini and Sons, a New York moving and storage company, may be in the possession of Dr. Harry T. Burleigh II. Dr. James Hall, Burleigh's godson, did not recall ever having seen it.

87. "Famous Baritone Soloist Creates Great Music in Vineyard Church," New Bedford, Massachusetts, *Standard Times*, August 20, 1938.

88. Some of the papers were the *Weekly Independent* of Hamburg, New York, August 4, 1938; the Brownsville, Tennessee, Graphic, August 5, 1938; the Boonsboro, Maryland, *Times*; the Claremont, New Hampshire, *Advocate*, August 11, 1938; and the Munsing, Michigan, *Weekly News*, September 2, 1938. Earlier another photo with less data had appeared in the *Pittsburgh Courier*, April 24, 1938, under the caption "Along the Classic Line." Items courtesy of Hampton University Archives.

89. *Vineyard Gazette*, January 1, 1939.

90. Copy of address from the Azalia Hackley Collection in the Detroit Public Library.

91. *Age*, August 5, 1939; *Boston Evening Transcript*, August 21, 1939.

92. *The Etude*, May, 1939, Vol. 57., pp. 293-294, and August, 1940, Vol. 58, p. 511.

93. Handy, *op. cit.*, pp. 274-276; Southern, *Readings in Black American History*, pp. 215-216; *New York Times*, October 2-4, 7 and 9, 1939.

94. Letters of March 20 and April 4, 1940, in *The Correspondence of W. E. B. DuBois*, ed. by Herbert Aptheker (Amherst: University of Massachusetts Press, 1973), pp. 22-23.

95. *Vineyard Gazette*, March 20, 1940; *Herald Tribune*, n.d., 1940, carried an in-action photo of Burleigh at the service.

96. *Herald Tribune*, April 7, 1941.

97. *Norfolk Journal and Guide*, August 16, 1941; *Herald Tribune*, August 8, 1941. An item on Burleigh's selection, appearing in the *Age*, August 16, 1941, commented: "He is meticulous in his manuscript writing, and his copy prepared for printers looks almost like copper plate."

98. *New York Times*, December 14, 1941.

99. Information concerning exhibit and Safranek material from translations from Czech sent to the author by Dr. Josef Skvorecky of Toronto.

100. Copy of letter courtesy of Yale University Library.

101. New Brunswick, New Jersey, *Sunday Times*, April 11, 1943. Miss Thomas, a teacher of piano, organ, and theory, had previously been assistant organist and choir director at Grace Episcopal Church in the Bronx.

102. News item marked "N. Y. May 22, 1944" from vertical files, Erie County Public Library.

103. New York *Amsterdam News*, February 5, 1944. The *New York Times*, February 6, 1944, also carried a fine tribute to Burleigh.

104. *Vineyard Gazette*, April 3, 1944.

105. *Erie Daily Herald*, June 9, 1944.

106. Erie newspaper, no name, June 12, 1944, in Erie County Public Library vertical file.

107. Henry Beckett, "A Mighty Voice at 77," *New York Post*, April 24, 1944.

108. Program courtesy of Hampton University Archives; letter dated November 17, 1986, from Roland M. Carter, Chairman of the Department of Music at Hampton University; phone conversations with Mrs. Davis, conductor of the Harry Burleigh Chorale, and Mrs. Wallace Campbell.

109. Philip S. Foner, *Paul Robeson Speaks* (New York: Brunner/Mazel Publishers, 1978), pp. 163 and 526.

110. *Herald Tribune*, April 15, 1946; *New York Times*, April 15, 1946; *Erie Dispatch*, April 21, 1946.

111. Lee, *op. cit.*, p. 85.

112. New York *Amsterdam News*, December 21, 1947.

113. An account by Nora Holt in *Amsterdam News*, April 3, 1948.

114. Copy of death certificate courtesy of Dr. Eileen Southern; letter to writer from Dr. Harry T. Burleigh II, August, 1986. An obituary in the *Erie Dispatch*, September 13, 1949, erroneously stated that Burleigh's body would be returned to Erie.

115. News clipping, no name, September 16, 1949, courtesy of Yale University Library.

116. Rayford W. Logan and Michael R. Winston, *Dictionary of American Negro Biography* (New York: W. W. Norton & Company, 1982), p. 80.

117. *Afro-American*, October 1, 1949; *New York Times*, April 7, 1950. A letter from Dr. Harry T. Burleigh II in August of 1986 confirmed the final settlement. James Hall, Jr., Mrs. Hall's heir and Burleigh's godson, was seventeen at the time of Burleigh's death. Dr. Hall is currently Dean of Adult and Continuing Education at York College of the City of New York in Jamaica.

CHAPTER III

1. Lee, *op. cit.*, p. 84.

2. A copy of pre-concert information sent to members by the Society's secretary, Harold Jackman, was found in the Detroit Public Library. No date for the Society's founding is given by either Southern or Grove. The *New York Times*' first mention of a concert by its members was April 30, 1956.

3. *Erie Times*, September 20, 1949.

4. Information on the Harry T. Burleigh Memorial Day and Scholarship Fund was obtained from the Norman Sobel file at the ECHS Library and from news items, not always dated, in the vertical files of the Erie County Library.

5. *Erie Morning News*, February 16, 1979; *Erie News*, August 20, 1984.

6. Copy of program obtained from Yale University Library. This particular service of spirituals was likely among the last, if not the very last, of its kind.

7. Henderson's letter, dated May 22, 1986, was shared by Mrs. Benedict with the author. Archivist Golden was of great support to Burleigh scholars Drs. David Cantrell and Roland Lewis Allison in the late 1960s. Correspondence with Mrs. Leslie Mims, St. George's co-Minister of Music with her husband George Mims, confirms the missing Burleigh records, some of which were destroyed by fire. In St. George's archives, however, are the following choral arrangements by Burleigh with copyright dates and inscriptions: "Child Jesus Comes from Heav'nly Height" (1912); "Dig My Grave" and "Deep River" (1913, "To the Chorus of the Schola Cantorum, New York, Kurt Schindler, Conductor," from the Krehbiel Collection, both *a cappella*); "Ezekiel Saw de Wheel" (1928, *a cappella*); "Heav'n, Heav'n" (1921); "Let Us Cheer the Weary Traveler" (n.d., but probably c. 1924, "Specially arranged for the musical service celebrating my thirtieth year as baritone soloist in St. George's Church, N.Y."); "My Lord, What a Mornin' " (1924, *a cappella*); "Nobody Knows de Trouble I've Seen" (1924, *a cappella*, "To the Choir of St. George's Church, N.Y., Mr. George W. Kemmer, Organist and Choirmaster"); "Ride on King Jesus" (n.d.); "Steal Away" (1924, *a cappella*); "Wade in de Water" (1925, *a cappella*); "Were You there?" (1927, *a cappella*); and Alston Burleigh's "Great Day de Righteous Marchin' " (n.d., arrangements in two keys with two different time signatures). Copies of these arrangements were sent to the author by Mrs. Mims in October 1987.

8. Yellen's pamphlet, titled "ASCAP Hails Negroes: Song Writers in Top Ranks as Creators of our Music," was published by ASCAP. Yellen became a member of ASCAP's Board of Directors in 1951. His most famous songs are the familiar "Happy Days Are Here Again," "I Wonder What's Become of Sally," "Ain't She Sweet," and "Hard Hearted Hannah."

9. Dominique René de Lerma, *Black Music in Our Culture* (Kent, OH: Kent State University Press, 1970), p. 69.

10. *Ibid.*, p. 143.

11. *Vineyard Gazette*, October 17, 1986. Another factual article by Anne Simpson was included in the same issue.

12. This review, printed in the *Vineyard Gazette*, November 6, 1986, prompts one to pity the misinformed audience.

13. Randall Pease, "Program Celebrates the Life and Music of H. T. Burleigh," *Vineyard Gazette*, November 7, 1987.

14. A copy of Snyder's paper was sent to the author.

15. Gertrude Rohrer, *Music and Musicians* (Philadelphia: Theodore Presser Co., 1940), p. 99. Gaul (1881-1945) was especially interested in choral music.

16. Marie Seton, *Paul Robeson* (London: Dennis Dobson, 1958), p. 201.

17. The tribute was signed "E. O. M." The bulletin was sent to the writer by Dr. James C. Hall, Jr.

18. Verna Arvey, *In One Lifetime* (Fayetteville: The University of Arkansas Press, 1984), pp. 59-60. Still's *Old California* for orchestra was published in 1941, but Arvey gives no specific date of this performance conducted by Monteux.

19. Robert B. Haas, ed., *William Grant Still and the Fusion of Cultures in American Music* (Los Angeles: Black Sparrow Press, 1972), p. 129.

20. William Grant Still, "The Negro Musician in America," *Music Educators Journal*, January 1970, Vol. 56, No. 5, pp. 100-101; 157-161.

21. Telephone conversation between author and John Seagle, April 1, 1986.

22. Conversation between author and Hairston, October 27, 1985, in Lafayette, Louisiana.

23. Letter to author from Snyder, January 13, 1987.

24. Bullock, *op. cit.*, p. 42.

25. Cuney-Hare, *op. cit.*, pp. 329.

26. Fragment, undated, courtesy of the Arthur B. Spingarn Collection, Howard University.

27. Norman Sobel wrote the entry on his father, Isador, for the *National Cyclopedia of American Biography*, Vol. XXX (New York: James T. White and Company, 1943), pp. 500-501. Other biographi-

cal data is found in *Nelson's Biographical Dictionary and Historical Reference Book* (Erie, PA: The Erie Company, 1896), p. 638.

28.   Norman Sobel's notes in the Burleigh Collection at the ECHS Library. In a letter dated August 8, 1986, to the author Mrs. Helen Andrews, ECHS librarian, stated that "Norman told me it was his father who helped with funds to send Burleigh to New York."

29.   Letters dated July 22 and August 2, 1985, from Mrs. Andrews to the author.

30.   Letter dated July 11, 1977, in ECHS Library.

31.   Letter from Sobel to Copyright Office, Library of Congress, March 7, 1979, in ECHS Library.

32.   Letter from Sobel to Mrs. Andrews, November 11, 1980, in ECHS Library.

33.   Letter from Library of Congress to Sobel, November 5, 1980, in ECHS Library. The excessive number, 800, may have been a typing error on Sobel's part.

34.   Letter from John Claridge to author, dated July 29, 1986.

35.   Parrish (1870-1966), who was well known for his murals, posters, and covers on several leading magazines, also illustrated numerous books. "The Dinkey Bird," which contrasts the ecstatic youth with wiry, wild hair against the background of a castle, clouds, and dark trees, was originally a fanciful illustration for Eugene Field's *Poems of Childhood*.

36.   Josef Skvorecky, *Dvorak in Love*, trans. from Czech by Paul Wilson (Toronto: Lester and Orpen Dennys Limited, 1986), p. 85. A professor of English at Erindale College, University of Toronto, Dr. Skvorecky is also the author of *The Jazz Saxophone*, *The Cowards*, *Miss Silver's Past*, and *The Engineer of Human Souls*.

37.   *Ibid.*, p.86.

38.   Letter from Dr. James Hall to author, February 26, 1987.

39.   Correspondence during August, 1986, between the author and Dr. Burleigh.

40.   Sampson, *op. cit.*, p. 347. Sampson said: "From his mother, who in her youth toured with Williams and Walker, he inherited his talent for the stage," p. 347.

41.   *New York Sunday News*, August 23, 1941.

42.   Letter to author from Dr. Burleigh, August 1986.

CHAPTER IV

1.   A. Walter Kramer, "An American Negro Whose Music Stirs the Blood of Warring Italy," *Current Opinion*, August 1916, Vol. 61, No. 2, p. 101.

2.   *Musical America*, April 12, 1924, pp. 21 and 27.

3.   Cuney-Hare, *op. cit.*, p. 326.

4.   John L. Marsh, "Harry Thacker Burleigh: Hard Knocks and Triumphant Days," *The Journal of Erie Studies*, Fall, 1980, Vol. 9, No. 2, p. 28.

5.   Ellsworth Janifer, "H. T. Burleigh Ten Years Later," *Phylon*, Summer, 1960, pp. 144-154.

6.   Murray, *op. cit.*, p. 107.

7.   *Ibid.*

8.   *New York Times*, August 11, 1890.

9.   R. W. Crump, *Christina Rossetti: A Reference Guide* (Boston: G. K. Hall & Company, 1976), pp. vii, viii, 127-128; Christina Rossetti, *Goblin Market and Other Poems* (London: Oxford University Press, 1862), p. 35.

10. *ASCAP Biographical Dictionary*, 4th ed. (New York: R. R. Bowker Company, 1980), p. 481.

11. *New York Times*, July 23, 1905.

12. Copies of piano-vocal scores discussed in this chapter were received through the courtesy of the ECHS Library, Erie County Public Library, Moorland-Spingarn Research Center, and the Schomberg Center for Black Research, and from the Marian Anderson Collection at the Van Pelt Library, University of Pennsylvania.

13. Various items in the *Age* from 1905-1914.

14. *New York Times* obituaries on Stoddard and Sears, December 21, 1961, and July 31, 1942.

15. Curiously, Sousa did not mention Pollock in his *Marching Along* (Boston: Hale, Cushman and Flint, 1941), when speaking of *Bride*, pp. 163, 180. *Bride* was called a "musical comedy" in *The Best Plays of 1894-1899*, ed. by John Chapman and Garrison P. Sherwood (New York: Dodd, Mead and Company, 1955), p. 227.

16. Eugene Levy, *James Weldon Johnson: Black Leader, Black Voice* (Chicago: Chicago University Press, 1973), p. 163.

17. The complete poem of "O Southland!" is found in James Weldon Johnson's *Fifty Years and Other Poems* (Boston: The Cornhill Company, 1917), pp. 8-9.

18. Information on Bowles was taken from *Who Was Who in Literature 1906-1934*, Vol. I (Detroit: Gale Research Co., 1979), p. 140; *The National Union Catalog*; and a letter to the writer from Foreign Relations Representative, Agnes Beard, of the Performing Right Society Limited in London, May 29, 1986. For three years preceding his death Bowles was a member of P.R.S.L. Ms. Beard sent an obituary on Bowles from *Musical Opinion*, August 1925, in which Le Gallienne was quoted.

19. Eileen Southern, *The Music of Black Americans: A History* (New York: W. W. Norton and Company, Inc., 1971), p. 285.

20. Lindsay Patterson, ed., *The International Library of Negro Life and History* (New York: Publishers Company, Inc., for the Association for the Study of Negro Life and History, 1967), p. 191.

21. This partial extract and the following one were printed for an advertising flyer by Ricordi. A copy was sent to the writer by Yale University Library. On the flyer Ricordi said: "Mr. H. T. Burleigh's *Saracen Songs* mark a new and higher standard of vocal music to English text."

22. Prefatory note by Krehbiel in the piano-vocal score of the *Hope* cycle. Brüggemann (b. 1873) was a German composer whose works include songs and instrumental, operatic, and chamber music. He also translated some of Puccini's operas.

23. Stanley J. Kunitz and Howard Haycraft, eds., *Twentieth Century Authors* (New York: The H. W. Wilson Co., 1942), p. 664.

24. H. K. M., "Deep River Popularizes a Composer" (reprinted from *Boston Evening Transcript*, March 10, 1917), *The Black Perspective in Music*, Spring 1974, Vol. 2, No. 1, pp. 77-78.

25. *Ibid.*, p. 76. McCormack's first performance of the *Hope* cycle was noted in Chapter II.

26. A McCormack performance of "Her Eyes Twin Pools" in Newark, New Jersey, in late November of 1915 was mentioned in the *Courier*, December 2, 1915, Vol. 70, No. 22, p. 52.

27. *Courier*, May 30, 1918, Vol. 76, No. 22, p. 34; obituary, *New York Times*, May 25, 1918.

28. *New York Times*, March 30, 1943; Will Crutchfield, "Brahms, by Those Who Knew Him," *Opus*, August, 1986, Vol. 2, No. 5, p. 21. Crutchfield did not specify the date of Davies' recording of Brahms.

29. *Courier*, August 15, 1918, Vol. 77, No. 7, p. 14. Garrison spoke of Burleigh as "the most notable" among a number of talented Negro composers.

30. H. K. M., *op. cit.*, p. 77.

31. *Courier*, August 29, 1918, Vol. 77, No. 9, p. 9; Kunitz and Haycraft, *op. cit.*, pp. 1377-1378. "On Inishmaan," "The Grey Wolf," "The Prayer," "By the Pool," and "Finvara" are all a part of "In Ireland" from Symons' *Images of Good and Evil*, Vol. II of *Collected Works of Arthur Symons* (New York: AMS, 1973). "Memory," "Remembrance," which Burleigh titled "I Remember All," and "Before Meeting" are included in "Days and Nights," Vol. I of the *Collected Works*. All eight poems, dated by Symons, were written between 1894 and 1900.

32. H. K. M., *op. cit.*, p. 100.

33. *Courier*, February 24, 1916, Vol. 72, No. 8, p. 50.

34. *New York Times*, May 16, 1961; Oscar Thompson, *International Cyclopedia of Music and Musicians* (New York: Dodd Mead and Company, 1952), pp. 912-913; *Courier*, May 3, 1917, Vol. 74, No. 18, pp. 40-41, and September 13, 1917, Vol. 75, No. 11, p. 32.

35. *The Selected Poems of Walt Whitman* (New York: Walter J. Black, Inc., 1942), pp. xiii-xxii.

36. *Courier*, December 2, 1915, Vol. 70, No. 22, p. 55. Other Symons songs will be discussed with 1916, 1917, and 1919 publications.

37. H. K. M., *op. cit.*, p. 78.

38. *New York Times*, December 19, 1932.

39. Janifer, *op. cit.*, pp. 144-154. H. K. M. Called "Just You" a "wholly delightful bit of melody which well deserves its popularity," *op. cit.*, p. 79.

40. Flyer courtesy of Beinecke Library at Yale University.

41. The word "rosses" is not mentioned in the poem. To the English "ross" means "scrapings from oak bark, such as moss or lichen, or

the scaly outer-portion of the oak tree bark." The title of this intimate song is rather misleading.

42. Preface to vocal score of "The Soldier" (New York: Ricordi and Company, 1916).

43. H. K. M., *op. cit.*, p. 77.

44. *Musical America*, October 27, 1917, p. 36; also see reference in Chapter II to McCormack's Hippodrome performance of "Little Mother of Mine" this year.

45. *Courier*, June 7, 1917, Vol. 74, No. 23, p.45; *New York Times*, November 27, 1917. According to a review in the *Courier*, January 10, 1918, Vol. 76, No. 2, p. 32, "The Dove and the Lily" was successfully programmed on Seagle's joint recital in Chattanooga with Augusta Bates, December 20, 1917.

46. *New York Times*, August 11, 1924. William Treat Upton mentions "The Sailor's Wife" as a "representative song" in the scant one line devoted to Burleigh in his *Art Song in America* (Boston: Oliver Ditson Co., 1930), pp. 139-140, while devoting at least a paragraph, plus generous musical examples, to approximately 150 other American composers.

47. *Courier*, November 9, 1916, Vol. 73, No. 19, p. 19.

48. *Courier*, May 3, 1917, Vol. 74, No. 18, p. 41.

49. *Musical America*, March 17, 1917, p. 36.

50. H. M. K., *op. cit.*, p. 78.

51. *Courier*, February 13, 1919, Vol. 78, No. 7, p. 37.

52. *New York Times*, August 6, 1924.

53. References to two George O'Connells were found in *New York Times* obituaries. One was a medical doctor in Lewiston, Maine, who died in 1941; the other, who died in 1934, had a large printing company in New York and was prominent in financial and political circles.

54. *New York Times*, May 3, 1961; *Age*, April 18, 1925; *Caroling Dusk*, ed. by Countee Cullen (New York: Harper and Brothers Publishers, 1927), pp. 70-71.

55. Hazel Gertrude Kinscella, *Music on the Air* (New York: The Viking Press, 1934), p. 287.

56. Both Fauset's and Johnson's poems are from Cullen, *op. cit.*, pp. 70-71 and 78.

57. *Age*, March 21, 1925.

58. *ASCAP Biographical Dictionary of Composers, Authors, and Publishers*, ed. by the Farnol Group, Inc. (New York: ASCAP, 1966), p. 606.

59. *New York Times*, December 12, 1947.

60. *New York Times*, April 23, 1926; *ASCAP Dictionary* (1980), p. 253.

61. *New York Times*, October 15, 1937; title page and preface of Johnson's *Poems of Fifty Years*, 1937.

62. Theressa Gunnels Rush, Carol Fairbanks Meyers, and Esther Spring Arata, *Black American Writers Past and Present: A Bibliographical Dictionary* (Metuchen, NJ: Scarecrow Press, Inc., 1975), p. 173.

63. *New York Times*, April 11, 1924.

64. *ASCAP Dictionary* (1980), p. 796.

65. *Musical Forecast*, September, 1923, p. 8.

66. Letter to author from Dr. Braithwaite, January 16, 1987.

67. *Age*, February 7, 1920; *New York Times*, April 7, 1954.

68. *ASCAP Biographical Dictionary*, 1980, p. 315. MacCarthy was still living in 1980, according to this publication, at age ninety-two.

69. Janifer, *op. cit.*, pp. 144-154.

70. Kunitz and Haycraft, *op. cit.*, p. 684; *Great Writers of the English Language: POETS*, ed. by James Vinson (New York: St. Martin's Press, 1979), p. 512.

71. Letter to the author from Galen Lurwick, Joplin, Missouri, January 25, 1987. Lurwick said that he knew Burleigh only through his spirituals. Supposedly "retired," Lurwick is a Professor of Music at Missouri Southern State College. He was a professional accompanist and pianist for 20th Century Fox Studios and for several touring Metropolitan Opera stars. His keen musical ear and sight reading prowess have served him well.

72. *Pacific Coast Musician*, January 20, 1940, Vol. XXIX, No. 2, p. 7, courtesy of Mrs. Barbara Stoner.

73. Willis C. Patterson, *Anthology of Art Songs by Black American Composers* (New York: Edward B. Marks Music Company, 1977), p. vii. Dr. Patterson is Associate Dean in the School of Music, University of Michigan at Ann Arbor.

74. Richard Crawford, "Musical Learning in Nineteenth Century America," *American Music*, Spring 1983, Vol. 1, No. 1., pp. 1-11.

75. Dominique René De Lerma, *Reflections on Afro-American Music* (Kent, OH: Kent University Press, 1973), p. 15.

76. Geneva Southall, "Black Composers and Religious Music," *The Black Perspective in Music*, Vol. 2, No. 1, Spring 1974, p. 48.

77. H. K. M., *op. cit.*, p. 79.

78. De Lerma, *op. cit.*, p. 254.

79. Score of No. I of *Southland Sketches* courtesy of Moorland-Spingarn Research Center, Howard University; parts II and III courtesy of Jean Snyder; and No. IV courtesy of Arizona University Library.

80. Farish's work was followed by a 1984 supplement. A telephone conversation with Vivian Baker at Stanton Music Company in Columbus, Ohio, February 27, 1987, revealed no listing of Burleigh's works in this later issue.

CHAPTER V

1. Murray, *op. cit.*, p. 108.

2. John W. Work, *American Negro Songs* (New York: Bonanza Books, 1940), p. 15.

3. Southall, *op. cit.*, pp. 44-47.

4. Lee, *op. cit.*, p. 84.

5. *Courier*, December 23, 1915, Vol. 71, No. 26, p. 47.

6. Dena J. Epstein, "A White Origin for the Black Spiritual? An Invalid Theory and How It Grew," *American Music*, Summer 1983, Vol. 1, No. 2, p. 58. Epstein, assistant music librarian at Joseph Regenstein Library, University of Chicago, is inclined to believe that the spirituals grew out of a mutual influence and exchange between blacks and whites in their social, work, and religious activities.

7. Epstein, *op. cit.*, p. 54.

8. Henry Edward Krehbiel, *Afro-American Folksongs* (New York: G. Schirmer, Inc., 1914), p. 14.

9. Epstein, *op. cit.*, pp. 57, 53-59.

10. W. J. Henderson, preface to *Negro Minstrel Melodies*, ed. by H. T. Burleigh (New York: G. Schirmer, Inc., 1909), p. iv. Higginson is

credited with organizing a "colored regiment" immediately following the Emancipation Proclamation in 1863; Cuney-Hare, *op. cit.*, p. 73.

11. George Pullen Jackson, "The Genesis of the Negro Spiritual," *American Mercury*, June 1932, Vol. 26, No. 1, pp. 43-48.

12. Krehbiel, *op. cit.*; James Weldon Johnson and J. Rosamond Johnson, *The Book of American Negro Spirituals* (New York: The Viking Press, 1925), pp. 11-50; John F. Garst, "Mutual Reinforcement and the Origins of Spirituals," *American Music*, Winter 1986, Vol. 4, No. 4, pp. 390-406.

13. Work, *op. cit.*, p. 18.

14. *Ibid.*, pp. 1-27.

15. John E. Taylor, "The Sociological and Psychological Implications of the Texts of the Antebellum Negro Spirituals," a doctoral dissertation for the School of Music at the University of Northern Colorado, 1971, p. 190.

16. *Courier*, July 7, 1915, Vol. 71, No. 26, p. 19.

17. *Courier*, June 26, 1919, Vol. 78, No. 26, p. 21.

18. Johnson, *op. cit.*, p. 48.

19. *Age*, February 25, 1928.

20. *The New Yorker*, January 16, 1926, n.p. At this time *The New Yorker* was in its third year of publication.

21. Janifer, *op. cit.*, p. 145. A. W. Kramer, in *Musical America*, October 17, 1917, p. 47, also called Burleigh's arrangements "one and all little masterpieces, settings by one of our time's most gifted song composers of melodies, which he penetrates as no other living composer."

22. Bullock, *op. cit.*, p. 40.

23. Cuney-Hare, *op. cit.*, p. 240.

24. John Tasker Howard, *Our American Music: Three Hundred Years of It* (New York: Thomas Y. Crowell Co. Publishers, 1931), p. 454.

25. *Age*, July 30, 1921.

26. Lee, *op. cit.*, pp. 84 ff.

27. Alain Locke, *The Negro and His Music* (Washington, DC: The Associates in Negro Folk Education, 1936), pp. 119-120.

28. Alain Locke, *The Negro and His Music, Negro Art: Past and Present* (New York: Arno Press and the New York Times), 1969, p. 23.

29. Handy, *op. cit.*, p. 157.

30. Harry T. Burleigh, *The Spirituals of Harry T. Burleigh* (Melville, NY: Belwin-Mills Publishing Corporation, 1984), reprinted by permission of Belwin-Mills. This preface was signed "New York, 1917, H. T. B."

31. *Baltimore Afro-American*, June 16, 1917.

32. *The Cheyney Record*, December 1922, Vol. 3, No. 1, p. 1.

33. *Courier*, November 23, 1922, Vol. 85, No. 21, p. 21.

34. "Church Pays Tribute to Burleigh," *Musical America*, April 12, 1924, pp. 21 and 27.

35. Lester A. Walton's article, "Harry T. Burleigh Honored Today at St. George's," was reprinted in *The Black Perspective in Music*, Spring 1974, Vol. 2, No. 1, p. 81.

36. Kinscella, *op. cit.*, pp. 186-189. Also included in the address were Burleigh's exact words of the preface to *The Spirituals of Harry T. Burleigh*. In Kinscella's work, pp. 7-8, results of a survey given to 500 people in the early 1930s rated Burleigh's "Deep River" fifteenth in the twenty most popular pieces out of 200.

37. Information sent to the writer by Dr. David Cantrell, a Burleigh scholar now residing in Ft. Collins, Colorado.

38. Rush, Myers, and Arata, *op. cit.*, pp. 135-136.

39. Sayers, *op. cit.*, pp. 48-49.

40. *New York Times*, April 13, 1905.

41. Charles Townsend, *Negro Minstrels* (Upper Saddle River, NJ: Literature House/Gregg Press, 1969), preface.

42. Henderson, *op. cit.*, pp. iii-vi.

43. John Smith Kendall, "New Orleans' Negro Minstrels," *The Louisiana Historical Quarterly*, January 1947, Vol. 30, No. 1, pp. 9-14.

44. Work and Hays, cited in Baker's *Biographical Dictionary of Musicians*, 7th ed., revised by Nicolas Slonimsky (New York: Schirmer Books, 1984), pp. 2529 and 981.

45. *New York Times*, May 29, 1937.

46. Ike Simond, *Old Slack's Reminiscence and Pocket History* (Bowling Green, OH: Bowling Green University Popular Press, 1974), pp. 16 and 8; Hans Nathan, *Dan Emmett and the Rise of Early Minstrelsy* (Norman: University of Oklahoma Press, 1962), pp. 227 ff.

47. There is some discrepancy on the exact year of *Jubilee Songs'* publication. Allison in his dissertation lists it as 1913; Southern gives it as 1916. *The National Union Catalog* does not list this publication. Correspondence with G. Schirmer has not clarified the circumstances of publication nor the content of the work. A letter dated April 20, 1987, to the writer from Susan P. Havas of G. Schirmer Publications stated:

> Hal Leonard Publishing Corporation is the new exclusive distributor of G. Schirmer Publications. Unfortunately, we find no listing for *Jubilee Songs of the USA*. Apparently it is out of print, and as a result we cannot supply you with any of the information you requested. We do not have an archive copy available at this time.

48. Krehbiel, *op. cit.*, p. 53.

49. *Ibid.*, pp. 87 and 91.

50. *Erie Daily Herald*, June 9, 1944.

51. Krehbiel, *op. cit.*, p. 103.

52. *Ibid.*

53. *Ibid.*, p. 142.

54. Burleigh's twelve arrangements for Krehbiel's *Afro-American Folksongs* are found on pp. 52-54, 75, 86, 90, 104-105, 110, 136-137, 159, and 160-161.

55. Newman I. White, *American Negro Folk Songs* (Hatboro, PA: Folklore Associates, Inc., 1965), p. 470.

56. Taylor, *op. cit.*, p. 134.

57. Handy, *op. cit.*, p. 194.

58. *Courier*, September 13, 1917, Vol. 75, No. 11, p. 32.

59. *Courier*, January 18, 1917, Vol. 74, No. 3, p. 24.

60. *Baltimore Afro-American*, June 16, 1917. The headlines read: "Big Crowd Hears Burleigh Sing – Premier Baritone of the Race Gives Brilliant Performance at Bethel Church."

61. H. K. M., *op. cit.*, p. 77.

62. Edith Borroff, "Black Musicians in the United States," *The American Music Teacher*, November 1972, Vol. 22, No. 2, p. 31.

63. Murray, *op. cit.*, p. 104.

64. *Musical America*, January 20, 1917, p. 34, and February 10, 1917, p. 31.

65. This information was given to the writer in a letter of April 22, 1987, and in a catalog introduction from J. Rigbie Turner, Curator of the Mary Flagler Cary Collection at the Pierpont Morgan Library. A copy of the manuscript is in the ECHS Library. Norman Sobel, who is largely responsible for the Burleigh material in this library, referred to this 1926 manuscript in D flat as "the original." A comparison of the 1917 and 1926 scores reveals no alterations or additions. The key of D flat in the 1926 ms. is the medium key (low in C, high in F).

66. Murray, *op. cit.*, p. 109; *Crisis* magazine, August 19, 1917; *Age*, March 30, 1929; *Courier*, November 1, 1917, Vol. 75, No. 18, p. 28 ("Seldom has a folksong met with such unqualified success as has 'Deep River.' ") Coleridge-Taylor had earlier arranged "Deep River" for piano solo, and William Arms Fisher also made various arrangements of it for solo and ensemble.

67. A copy of the orchestral manuscript found in the Library of Congress (M 1060.B 96/D3), the only manuscript of Burleigh's cataloged there, was sent to the writer by Dr. William C. Loring.

68. *Age*, July 8, 1922.

69. *Musical America*, October 27, 1917, p. 36.

70. Murray, *op. cit.*, p. 104.

71. Cuney-Hare, *op. cit.*, p. 70. According to Cuney-Hare, Nathaniel Dett relates it to music of the Hungarian Magyars.

72. Frank C. Brown, *North Carolina Folklore, The Music of the Folksongs*, Vol. 5 (Durham, NC: Duke University Press, 1962).

73. Taylor, *op. cit.*, p. 149. Harriet Tubman (1821-1913), a fugitive slave from Maryland, was in her colorful career writer, abolitionist, nurse, spy, reformer, and one of the first black women to receive recognition for her efforts.

74. William Arms Fisher, "Swing Low, Sweet Chariot: The Romance of a Famous Spiritual," *The Etude*, August 1932, Vol. 50, No. 8,

p. 536. Lydia Parrish claims "Swing Low" as within the purview of her *Georgia Sea Island Slave Songs*.

75. Cuney-Hare, *op. cit.*, p. 416; John W. Work categorizes this song as one of the "Sorrow Songs with Note of Joy," *op. cit.*, p. 44.

76. Cuney-Hare, *op. cit.*, p. 416.

77. *Courier*, July 4, 1918, Vol. 77, No. 1, p. 30.

78. A spiritual titled "John's on de Island on His Knees" is included in *Befo' de War Spirituals* collected by E. A. McIlhenny of Avery Island, Louisiana (Boston: The Christopher Publishing House, 1933), pp. 154-155, but neither words nor music resemble Burleigh's version. McIlhenny's guitar-like accompaniment has only two chord changes, E minor and G major.

79. Cuney-Hare, *op. cit.*, pp. 70 and 414.

80. *Ibid.*, p. 417.

81. Preface, Emily Hallowell, *Calhoun Plantation Songs*, 2nd ed. (Boston: C. W. Thompson and Company, 1907). Calhoun School was organized by two former Hampton teachers who fought valiantly for academic standards and the upgrading of Afro-Americans' welfare and education at the school.

82. Cuney-Hare, *op. cit.*, p. 417.

83. Work includes "Don't You Let Anybody Turn You Roun' " in his *American Negro Songs*, p. 89.

84. Cuney-Hare, *op. cit.*, p. 418.

85. *Age*, January 5, 1929.

86. White, *op. cit.*, p. 64.

87. *Courier*, October 12, 1916, Vol. 63, No. 15, p. 23.

88. *Courier*, December 26, 1918, Vol. 77, No. 26, p. 6; *Cleveland Plain Dealer*, December 12, 1918; *The Macmillan Encyclopedia of Music and Musicians*, ed. by Albert E. Wier (New York: The Macmillan Company, 1938), p. 410. The latter calls Dadmun "contemporary," giving no birth or death dates for him.

89. *Age*, October 3, 1936.

90. Roland Hayes, *My Songs* (Boston: Little, Brown and Company, 1948), p. 48.

91. Taylor, *op. cit.*, p. 123.

92. Photocopy courtesy of Dr. David Cantrell, Ft. Collins, Colorado; *New York Times*, January 10, 1968.

93. Work, *op. cit.*, p. 72.

94. *New York Times*, October 2, 1951.

95. *Saratoga Sun*, November 24, 1915, cited in *Courier*, December 2, 1915, Vol. 71, No. 22, p. 13. Biographical information on House taken from obituary in the *New York Times*, January 7, 1945.

96. *Age*, October 2, 1920.

97. Information from notes of Dr. David Cantrell, Ft. Collins, Colorado, who at one time planned a biography of Burleigh.

98. William Arms Fisher, ed. *Seventy Negro Spirituals* (Boston: Oliver Ditson Company, 1926), p. 142. Former harmony professor at the National Conservatory and editor for Ditson since 1898, Fisher (1861-1948) included in his collection the arrangements of ten composers, three of whom were black (J. Rosamond Johnson, Edward H. Boatner, and Harry T. Burleigh), with a photo and biographical sketch of each.

99. MacKinley Helm, *Angel Mo' and Her Son Roland Hayes* (Boston: Little, Brown and Company, 1944), p. 265.

100. *Courier*, June 12, 1919, Vol. 78, No. 24, p. 47.

101. Helm, *op. cit.*, p. 251.

102. Cuney-Hare, *op. cit.*, p. 417.

103. Byron Arnold's "Ride on King Jesus," included in his *Folksongs of Alabama* (University: University of Alabama Press, 1950), p. 184, has entirely different words and tune.

104. Letter to the writer from Garst, January 7, 1987. No further information on Bolton has been found by Garst despite his interest in hymnody and his access to Georgia libraries and to the material of hymn societies, nor through the writer's many queries to state archives and churches. Garst is the co-author with Daniel W. Patterson of a recent reprint edition of *The Social Harp* (1855).

105. Dorothy G. Bolton and Harry T. Burleigh, *Old Songs Hymnal* (New York: The Century Company, 1929), Foreword.

106. Hayes, *op. cit.*, p. 33.

107. Cuney-Hare, *op. cit.*, p. 75.

108. Allison, *op. cit.*, p. 288.

109. *New York Times*, January 25, 1941.

110. Southern, *Biographical Dictionary of Afro-American and African Musicians*, p. 208.

111. Miller's jacket notes for *Recorded Anthology of American Music – When I Have Sung My Songs – The American Art Song 1900-1940* (New World Records, 1976).

112. Murray, *op. cit.*, p. 105.

113. *Courier*, November 29, 1917, Vol. 75, No. 22, p. 7.

114. Vehanen, *op. cit.*, pp. 259-261.

115. Lovell, *op. cit.*, p. 442. Gloster B. Current, "Paul Robeson," *The Black Perspective in Music*, Fall 1976, Vol. 4, No. 3, pp. 303 ff.

116. Locke, *The Negro and His Music, Negro Art: Past and Present*, p. 23.

117. Foner, *op. cit.*, p. 300. Foner speaks of Burleigh as having "helped place Negro artists before white and mixed audiences," p. 506.

118. J. W. Johnson, *The Book of American Negro Spirituals* (New York: The Viking Press, 1925), p. 48.

119. *Courier*, June 28, 1917, Vol. 74, No. 26, p. 37.

120. *Courier*, March 22, 1917, Vol. 74, No. 21, p. 27.

121. *Courier*, March 29, 1917, Vol. 74, No. 22, p. 31.

122. *Courier*, April 19, 1917, Vol. 74, No. 25, p. 13.

123. *Courier*, May 3, 1917, Vol. 74, No. 18, p. 18.

124. *Ibid.*, p. 23.

125. *Courier*, May 17, 1917, Vol. 74, No. 20, p. 54.

126. *New York Times*, November 27, 1917.

127. *Courier*, May 24, 1917, Vol. 74, No. 21, p. 27.

128. *Ibid.*, p. 36.

129. *Courier*, November 29, 1917, Vol. 75, No. 22, p. 25.

130. *Courier*, January 10, 1918, Vol. 76, No. 2, p. 32.

131. Hayes, *op. cit.*, p. 24.

132. Letter from Lurwick to writer, January 25, 1987.

Index

Index of Works and Discography